The Biblical Companion

Index of Subjects, Themes, and Images

A DREAMSTAIRWAY BOOK

The Biblical Companion

Index of Subjects, Themes and Images

Edited by Dominic Breeze

British Library Cataloguing in Publication Data
A catalogue record for this book is available from the British Library

ISBN 978-1-907091-03-2

First published in the UK by Dreamstairway
copyright © 2009 dreamstairway

www.dreamstairway.co.uk

Introduction

The Biblical Companion : Index of Subjects, Themes and Images covers both the Old and New Testaments in more than one translation, and is intended chiefly for the interested lay-person, and also perhaps for the writer and speech-maker looking for a useful quotation. It is neither a commentary nor a criticism of the Bible itself, which is certainly the most important set of ancient books ever assembled.

To be fully understood, the Bible should be treated as one book with many styles and read as a whole like any other book, progressing smoothly from the Creation to the Apocalypse, and we would not wish to compromise its wholeness by analysing, let alone fragmenting its spiritual message. But reading the entire Bible in this way may seem a formidable (not to say boring) task, and it is our hope that this approach, by way of subjects and themes, may offer the reader an easy "way in" via some special interest or intriguing reference.

Many of the references will be found to refer to imagery rather than hard fact. Over-literal interpretation in the past has frequently caused misunderstandings when devotion shades into credulity. No-one would claim, for instance, to be descended from the "Good Samaritan" whom everybody knows to be a fictitious character in one of the parables related by Jesus; but in the books of the Old Testament ancient parables have become entangled with historical record, and occasionally folk tales with a moral have become incorporated and thereby gained a measure of divine authority. The gruesome story of a gang of little boys mauled by bears for teasing Elisha (in the Second Book of Kings) could have come straight out of some 800BC precursor of Grimm's Household Tales.

At the risk of over-stating the obvious, it may be pointed out that the Bible is well packed with ancient history interspersed with parables and moral stories, and rich in symbols, allegories, analogies, metaphors and similes. This is inevitable, for it represents mankind's relationship with the divine, and spirituality, being non-material, cannot be expressed in material terms. For example, no-one would suppose the Bible to be a farming textbook, and yet our "Farming" section is substantial. Even prophets such as Isaiah, Jeremiah and Ezekiel were close enough to the land for farming metaphors to come readily to their lips. Such references are all included here, and as such they form a valid picture of the rural scene and everyday concerns of those ancient people.

The case is similar with the category "Buildings", in which Ezekiel's purely visionary but extraordinarily detailed description of the temple of the New Jerusalem is given equal status to the historically real temple of Solomon. But this is how the Bible as a whole works: because its individual descriptions originate some from outward and others from inward perception, the general structure can be seen as a fine balance of inner and outer. Inspired writing and all religious inspiration use the outward, material imagery to portray that which is inward and non-material. Kings of the earth may always have ruled the land and the physical body, but the kingdom of heaven is within.

D.B.

Categories: Special Interests

Numbers refer to sections

Accessories 1
Affliction 2
Age 18
Altars 3
Angelic visitations 27
Armies 45
Animals 4
Atonement 32
Battles 45
Behaviour 21
Birds 4
Birth 7
Blessings 5
Buildings 6
Burial 10
Ceremonies 9
Childhood 7
Cloth, Clothes 8
Coins 48
Compensation 29
Covenants 24
Crystals 25
Culture 9
Curses 5
Customs 9
Death 10
Divination 11
Divinity 12
Dreams 13
Drink 16
Exile 26
Exports 41
Farming 14
Festivals 15
Fishing 22
Food 16
Geographical features 17
Gods 23
Grooming 1

Harness 42
Health 18
Heavens 19
Hell 19
Herbs 16
Holy places 3
Hope 32
Household 20
Human characteristics 21
Hunting 22
Idols, images 23
Imports 41
Industry 40
Infancy 7
Insects 4
Jewels 25
Judges 34
Killing 44
Kings 34
Laws 24
Lawgivers 34
Longevity 18
Marriage 37
Malice 43
Massacres 44
Measures 48
Metals 25
Migrations 26
Miracles 27
Monuments 3
Mourning 10
Music 28
Numbers, significant 38
Oaths 24
Parables 12
Passions 21
Paths 33
Penaltie 29
Plants 30

Categories (continued)

Pledges 24
Precious stones 25
Priests, prophets 31
Professions 40
Punishments 29
Repentance 32
Retribution 29
Rivers 46
Roads 33
Rulers, 34
Sacrifice 35
Servitude 36
Sex 37
Shelters 6
Shipwreck 42
Society 21
Spices 16
Suffering 2

Tools 39
Trades 40
Trading 41
Transport 42
Treasure 25
Tribute 36
Trickery 43
Vehicles, vessels 42
Violence 44
Visions 13
Wars 45
Water 46
Ways 33
Weapons 39
Weather 47
Weights 48
Wells 46
Witchcraft 11

Appendix A *Personal Names* page 486

Appendix B *Place Names* page 541

Appendix C *Races and Tribes* page 574

Line of Descent from Adam to Jesus page 580

Abbreviations: Old Testament

Am	Amos
CF	First Book of Chronicles
CS	Second Book of Chronicles
D	Daniel
De	Deuteronomy
E	Ezekiel
Ec	Ecclesiastes
Est	Esther
Ex	Exodus
Ez	Ezra
Gen	Genesis
H	Habakkuk
Hg	Haggai
Ho	Hosea
Is	Isaiah
Je	Jeremiah
Job	Job
Joe	Joel
Jon	Jonah
Jos	Joshua
Ju	Judges
KF	First Book of Kings
KS	Second Book of Kings
La	Lamentations
Le	Leviticus
Le	Leviticus
Ma	Malachi
Mi	Micah
Na	Nahum
Ne	Nehemiah
Nu	Numbers
Ob	Obadiah
Pro	Proverbs
Ps	Psalms
Ru	Ruth
SF	First Book of Samuel
So	Song of Solomon
SS	Second Book of Samuel
Z	Zechariah
Zp	Zephaniah

Abbreviations: New Testament

A	Acts of the Apostles
J	Gospel According to John
L	Gospel According to Luke
LH	Letter to the Hebrews
LJ	Letter of James
LJF	First Letter of John
LJS	Second Letter of John
LJT	Third Letter of John
LJu	Letter of Jude
LPF	First Letter of Peter
LPS	Second Letter of Peter
Mk	Gospel According to Mark
Mw	Gospel According to Matthew
PCF	First Letter of Paul to the Corinthians
PCo	Letter of Paul to the Colossians
PCS	Second Letter of Paul to the Corinthians
PE	Letter of Paul to the Ephesians
PG	Letter of Paul to the Galatians
Ph	Letter of Paul to Philemon
PPs	Letter of Paul to the Philippians
PR	Letter of Paul to the Romans
PTF	First Letter of Paul to Timothy
PTS	Second Letter of Paul to Timothy
Rev	Revelation of John
ThF	First Letter of Paul to the Thessalonians
ThS	Second Letter of Paul to the Thessalonians
Tt	Letter of Paul to Titus

1 *Accessories and grooming*

OLD TESTAMENT

aloes   Pro7; So4
  powder of   Ps45
amulet, phylactery   Ex13; De6, 11
anklet   Is3
antimony, make your eyes big with   Je4
armlet   Nu31; SS1;Is3
  gold   Nu31
canopy, wedding   Ps19
cassia   Pro7; E27
cauls, ornamental   Is3
chain, ornamental   Ex28ff; KF6; Pro1; Is3, 40; D5; E16
  gold   Ex28ff; D5
  of honour   Pro1
  silver   Is40
charm, hung about your neck   Pro3
  ornamental   Is3
  phylactery   Ex13; De6, 11
cinnamon   Pro7
coronet   Is3
cosmetics for virgins   Est2
balm   Je8, 51; E27
balsam   E27
bandage   Is1; E30. 34
bangle   Is3
beads, gold   E28
bell, golden, sown to clothes   Ex28ff
belt   SF18
  of honour   SS21
bracelet   Gen24; Nu37; SS1; Is3; E16, 23
  gold   Gen24; Nu37
braided plaits   So1
buckle   SF25
buckler   KF10; CS29, 23; Ps35; So4; Je46; E23, 26, 38ff
  gold   CS9; Ec9

1 ACCESSORIES AND GROOMING

crescent, ornamental   Ju8; Is3
crisping pin, curling iron   Is3
decked in finery   E23
discs, ornamental   I
dressed her hair, Jezebel   KS9
dressing, wound   E30
earrings   Gen35; Ex32; Nu31; Ju8; Pro25; Is3; E16; Ho2
  gold   Ex32; Nu31; Ju8; Job24; Pro25
  Ishmaelite   Ju8
finger-ring   Nu31; Est3ff, 7; Pro7, 11; So5; Is3; Je22
fragrant oil   KS20
frankincense   Is60
garland   Pro1, 4; Is28, 61
  on their heads   E23
glass, ornaments of   Is3
golden ornaments   Ju8
gum resin   Ex30ff
hair, elegantly coiled   Is3
  grew like eagle's feathers   D4
  long as goat's hair   D4
henna   So4, 7
jewels, collar of   Ps73
  decked herself with   Ho2
  nose   Is3
  wear them proudly as   Is49
jingles, adorn yourself with   Je31
liniment   Pro3
locket   Is3
lye, cleansing   Job9
medicine   Pro3, 17
  the leaf of the trees shall be for   E47
mirror   Job37
myrrh   Ps45; Pro7
  oil of   Est2
nails grew long like eagle's talons   E4
necklace   Pro25; Is3; Ho2
  jewelled chain   So1
  of jewels   So4
nose-ring   Gen24; Is3; E16
oil, anointing   Ps23, 45, 89, 92, 104, 133, 141; E16, 23
  drenched your tresses in   Is57

1 ACCESSORIES AND GROOMING

oil, fragrant   Is39
  of gladness   Is61
  skin care   Est2
ointment   Pro27; Ec9ff; So1, 4; E24
  precious   KS20
ornaments, can a maid forget her   Je2
  deck yourself out with golden   Je4
  gold   Nu31
  gold and silver   E16
  leg   Is3
  stripped of   Ex33
painting the eyes   KS9; E23
  Jezebel   KS9
pendant   Is3
  ear   E16
  gold   Nu31
  of Midianite kings   Ju8
perfume   KF10; Est2; Pro27; So1, 4ff; Is3, 28; Ho2
  blended with oil   Is57
piping, ornamental   E28
phylactery   Ex13; De6, 11
  on the forehead   De6, 11
plaited tresses   So1
pouch   SF17
privy, toilet   De23; KS10
purple, nurtured in   La4
purse   Hg1
ring   Pro7; Is3
  ear   Gen35; Ex32; Nu31; Ju8; Pro25; Is3; E16; Ho2
  finger   Nu31; Est3ff, 7; Pro7, 11; So5; Is3; Je22
  gold   Ex32; Nu31; Ju8; Pro11, 25; So5
  nose   Is37; E16
  signet   Est3ff, 7; Is3; Je22
roller bandage   E30
rosette, gold   Ex28ff; Le8
scarlet, brought up in   La4
shell, aromatic   Ex39ff
shepherd's bag   SF17
signet ring   Est3ff, 7; Is3; Je22
soap   Job9; Je2; Ma3
  do not stint the   Je2

1 ACCESSORIES AND GROOMING

soda, washing   Je2
spangles made for you at birth   E28
spices, fragrant, cosmetic   Je6
tablet, ornamental   Is3
tabret, ornamental   Je31; E28
target between shoulders   SF17
tassel at each corner of cloak   De22
   made like flowers   Nu15
toilet   De23; KS10
   trowel   De23
vanity, all is   Ec1
vermilion, painted with   Je22
wardrobe   Je38
wax   Ps22, 68, 97; Mi1
wormwood   Pro5

NEW TESTAMENT

adornment, outer   LPF3
aloes, myrrh and   J19
anoint with oil   Mk6; L10; LH1; LJ5
anointed his feet with ointment   L7
   with the oil of gladness   LH1
apron   A19
aromatic oils   Mk16
bandage   L10
beauty, inner   LPF3
   should reside not in outward adornment   LPF3
bedizened, the woman   Rev17
belt   Mw3; Mk1, 6; L12, 17; J21; A12, 21; PE6
   fasten your   L17
   leather   Mw3; Mk1
   money   Mk6
braiding hair   PTF2; LPF3
covering, head   PCF11
decked out in gold and pearls   PTF2
eyes, ointment for   Rev3
fragrant oil   Mw26; Mk16
frankincense, cargoes of   Rev18

1 ACCESSORIES AND GROOMING

garland of glory   LPF5
  of righteousness   PTS4
garlands to Jupiter   A14
girdle, golden   Rev1, 15
  leather   Mw3; Mk1
girdle, Paul's   A21
  skin   Mk1
glass darkly, we see through a   PCF13
  looking   PCS3; LJ1
hair, braiding   PTF2; LPF3
  if a man have long   PCF11
  styles, elaborate   PTF2
  woman's glory   PCF11
handkerchief   L19; A14
incense, great quantity of   Rev8
  perfumes and frankincense   Rev18
jewellery   LPF3
latchet, shoe   J1
leather belt   Mw3; Mk1
looking glass   PCF13; PCS3; LJ1
mirror   PCF13; PCS3; LJ1
money-belt   Mk6
myrrh and aloes   J19
  anointed his feet with   L7
napkin   L19; J11, 20
nard, oil of   Mk14
oil, anoint with   LJ5
  anointed sick people with   Mk6
  aromatic   Mk16
  bathed his wounds with   L10
  of exultation   LH1
  fragrant   Mw26
  of myrrh   L7
  of nard   Mk14; J12
ointment, alabaster box of   L7
  for your eyes   Rev3
  of spikenard   Mk14; J12
  very precious   Mw26
  who anointed the Lord with   J11
ointments, odours and   Rev18
  prepared   L23

1 ACCESSORIES AND GROOMING

pack for the road   Mw10
   purse or   L10, 22
   take neither stick nor   L9
   take no   Mk6
patch of unshrunk cloth   Mk2
perfume bottle   Mk14
   cargoes of   Rev18
   might have been sold   Mk14
   oil of nard   J12
   small bottle of   Mk14
   very costly   Mk14
purse   Mw10; L10, 12, 22; J13
ring, gold   LJ2
   on his finger, put a   L15
sandals, put on your   A12
   they might wear   Mk6
scarf   A19
scrip, purse nor   Mw10; L10, 22
   take no   Mk6
shoes   Mk1; L10, 15; J1; A7, 13; PE6
   not fit to unfasten   Mk1
   on his feet, put   L15
spices, funeral   L24
tassels on their robes   Mw23
veil   PCF11; PCS3f
vials full of odours   Rev5
woman's glory, flowing locks are a   PCF11
wrapping, linen   L24

2 *Affliction and Suffering*

OLD TESTAMENT

abominable thing that causes desolation   D11, 12
affliction, bound in   Ps107
  bread of   De16
  choice of by David   CF21
  in the furnace of   Is48
  the discipline of   Job36
  water of   CS18; Is30
ague, curse of the burning   Le26; De28
alas, my mother, that you ever gave me birth!   Je15
anguish and affliction, day of   Zp1
  my bowels writhe in   La1
ashes of repentance   Ex9; SS13; Est4; Job42; Je6, 25; E27
  sat down among the   Job2
baldness, examination of   Le13
beard plucked from my chin   Is50
beggary, reduced to   Zp2
blast, pestilence of   Ps195
blasting (blight)   KF8; CS6
blight, black or red   KF8; Am4; Hg2
  curse of   De28
blind and lame   Je31
  none shall come in   SS5
  the prophet Ahijah   KF14
blindness, curse of   De28
  strike this host with   KS6
blood, Nile turned to   Ex4, 7
  waters turned to   Ps105
blows, cower beneath   Ps88
  exhausted by thy   Ps39
boil, poulticed   KS20; Is38
boils, covered with   Job2
  malignant Egyptian curse of   De28
  plague of   Ex9
botch, curse of   De28

2 AFFLICTION AND SUFFERING

bowels, chronic disease of CS2
bread of despair, eat E24
brimstone, he shall rain Ps11
bruise his heel Gen3
  incurable Je30
bruises, nothing but Is1
burned, my bones are Ps102
cannibalism, reduced to KS6; Je19; La4
chin, sore on Le13
compress poultice Is1
consumption, curse of Le26; De28
contention, water of Nu5
corpses like offal in the streets Is10
courage fails E21
crippled, Asa's feet KF15
dead lay in heaps Na3
deaf man, as a Ps38
death, shadow of Ps23, 44
deeps close over me Ps69
desolation, cup of E23
  abomination of D11, 12
destruction and devastation, day of Zp1
  of Sodom Gen19
  place of Ps88
  upon all the earth Is10
dirges and laments Gen50; Ju20, 21; SF11; SS1, 3, 13; CS35;
      Job30; Ps30, 56; Je4, 7ff;
      E2, 24, 26; Am5, 8; Mi1f
disease, a loathsome Ps38
  in all my bones Ps31
  of Miriam, leprous Nu12
  from head to toe Is10
  skin, rules for De24
  sufferers from, expelled Nu5
  wasting De28; Le26; Is17
dragons, a den of Je9
  a dwelling place for Je49, 51
drought Je14; E29
  land of great Ho13
  summer Ps32
dumb man, as a Ps38

2 AFFLICTION AND SUFFERING

dung, reduced to eating their own   KS18; Is36
dust, wouldst thou turn me into   Job10
dysentery, curse of   De28
earth swallowed them   Nu16
earthquake   Ps18, 46, 60, 68, 77, 104; Is29
end is coming   E7
eruptions, curse of   De28
evils, choose one of three   SS24
eyes failing   Ps88
  grow dim   Ps69
  person with blemished   Le21
famine   Gen12, 26; Ps33, 105; Is51; Je5, 16, 18, 21, 24,
      27, 29, 32, 34, 38, 42, 44, 52; La2; E5ff, 12, 14;
      Am8
  at Gilgal   Ks4
  decreed seven years   KS8
  I will increase   E5
  in David's reign   SS21, 24
  in Judah   Ru1
  in Samaria   KF18
  make an end of them with   Je14
  on all your settlements   Am4
  ruin and havoc   Is51
  severe during siege   Ks25
  their sons and daughters shall die by   Je11
  three years   CF21
  under siege   KS7
fasting,   Ps35, 69, 109
  for the sick   Ps35
  knees weak with   Ps109
feet crippled by disease   KF15
fever   Is10; Je51
  like fire shall burn   Is10
  loins burn with   Ps38
  my mind wandered in   Ps37
  recurrent   Le26; De28
fig-plaster poultice   KS20; Is38
fire and brimstone, pour down   E38
  struck the shepherds   Job1
fit, man falls in a   Is10
flight, whole country in   Je4

2 AFFLICTION AND SUFFERING

flood Gen2, 6ff; Ps29, 69, 88, 104; Is28, 54
  the great Gen6ff; Ps104
fracture for fracture Le24
fungus infection Le14
gall, judgement turned to Am4
  to drink Je8ff
  wormwood and La3
gangrene of the foot CS16
gloom with no dawn Am5
grief, eyes dim with Job17
  full of drunkenness and E23
  head bowed in Ps35
  mine eye is consumed with Ps31
haemorrhoids SF5ff
  curse of De28
harried by enemies CF21
head, sore on Le13
  strike at Gen3
heel, strike at Gen3
helplessness, curse of De28
homelessness Ps52
horror written on their faces E27
hungry Ps107
ill, Elisha fell KS13
illness of Hezekiah Is38
ill-omened country Je2
infection, fungal Le14
inflammation, curse of De28
  of the skin Le13
issue, one that hath an SS3
itch, curse of the De28
Job's comforters Job2ff
lame debarred from altar Le21
  in both feet SS4
lament, hear my loud Ps88
  lies open before thee, my Ps38
  mark the foreheads of those who E9
lamentation is heard in Ramah Je31
leper SS3; KS5; CS26
lepers at the city gate KS7
leprosy, dull white Le13

2 AFFLICTION AND SUFFERING

leprosy, Gahazi caught   KS5
  the king struck with   KS15
leprous, Miriam became   Nu12
  Moses's hand   Ex4
massacre by invaders   Nu21, 31; De2, 3; Jos6, 8, 10f; Ju9, 11, 18, 20f;
    SF7, 15, 22; CS14
medicine, in vain shalt thou use   Je46
  thou hast no   Je30
mildew   KF8; CS6
  curse of   De28
miscarriage, country troubled with   KS2
mortified with fasting   Ps35
mould, rotting   Le13
mourning   Gen23, 37f, 50; Le21; SS13, 18; KF13; Ez10; Job30;
    Ps35, 42; Ec3; Je9, 16, 34; La5;
    E7, 24; D10; Am8; Mi1; Z12
  every head shorn in   Je48
  muzzle on my mouth   Ps39
  natural order upset   Je5
oblivion, land of   Ps88
oil for soothing wounds   Is1
ointment, wounds mollified with   Is1
pain, day of incurable   Is17
  pierces my very bones   Job30
panic shall fall on them   Z14
paralysed, Jeroboam's hand   KF13
pestilence   Ps91; Je24, 27, 29, 32, 34, 38, 42, 44; E5ff, 12, 14;
    Am4
  70,000 people died in one day of   SS24; CF21
  and famine   Je14; E5
  beasts killed by   Ex9; Ps78
  curse of   De28
  for three days   SS24; CF21
  in dens and caves they shall die by   E33
  in Egypt   Ex9
  judgement with   E38
  make an end of them with   Je14
  men and cattle shall die of a great   Je21
  of fish   Ps105
  the noisome   Ps91
  threat of   Le26
piss, they shall drink their own   KS18; Is36

2 AFFLICTION AND SUFFERING

plague   Ps78, 91
  brake in upon them   Ps106
  curse of   De28
  for the offence of Korah   Nu16
  killed 70,000 in one day   SS24; CF21
  makes orphans   La1
  of a house   Le14
  of caterpillars   KF8; CS6; Je51; Joe1ff
  of Egypt   Ps78; Am4
  of flies   Ex8; Ps105
  of frogs   Ex8; Ps78, 105
  of grasshoppers   Job39
  of grubs   Ps78; Joe2
  of hoppers   Je51; Joe1ff
  of Israelites ceased   Nu25
  of Kibroth-Hattaavah   Nu11
  of locusts   Ex8, 10; De28; KF8; CS6; Job39; Ps78, 105; Joe1ff
  of maggots   Ps105
  of moths   Job14; Ho5
  of worms, canker   Joe1ff
  tests for   Le13
  threat of   Le26
plagues upon you, all my   Ex9
poison in my food   Ps69
polluted, the water is   KS2
prison, set me free from my   Ps142
prolapse of the bowels   CS21
racked with sickness   La1
raw wounds, nothing but   Is1
rending clothes   SF4; SS1, 3, 13; KF21; KS2, 5, 19, 22; Est4; Job1; Is37
rot, her thigh shall   Nu5
rotten to the core   Ps53
ruin, a cup of   E23
  as never before   E21
  famine and havoc   Is51
ruins, Damascus a heap of   Is17
  homesteads lie in   Je25
running sores   Job2
sackcloth and ashes   Gen37; SS3, 21; KF20ff; KS6, 19;
        CF21; Ne9; Est4; Job16; Ps30. 35. 69,

2 AFFLICTION AND SUFFERING

sackcloth and ashes (cont) Is3, 15, 20, 22, 32, 37, 50;Je4, 6, 49; La2; E7, 27; D9; Joe1; Am8; Jon3
  beat your breast and put on   Je49
  every waist girded with   Je48
salt land where no man can live   Je17
scab on the head   Is3
scabs, curse of   De28
scorpions, chastise you with   KF12
scourge   Ps129
scurf in skin disease   Le13ff
seizure, Nabal had a   SF25
shadow of death   Job16; Ps23, 107; Je2
shame, end my days in   Je20
shaved every head   Je16, 48
sick-bed   Ps41
sickness, curse of   De28
  racked with   La1
sign upon hand and forehead   Ex13
skin disease, examination of   Le13
  of Miriam   Nu12
  sufferers from, expelled   Nu5
soot to cause festering boils   Ex9
sores of the head   Is1
sorrow, come forth to know only   Je20
  of heart   Le26
  their daily bread   Ps80
snuffed out like a wick   Is43
stink, the River Nile will   Ex7
stone for a pillow   Gen28
streams turned to blood   Ps78
stricken in age, Joshua   Jos23
sweating, I lay   Ps77
sword makes orphans   La1
tears, the bread of   Ps80
  water my couch with   Ps6
teeth idle with famine   Am4
terror and rapine, abandon them to   E23
terrors, the king of   Job18
thirst, infant's   La4
thirsty   Ps107
throat is sore   Ps69

2 AFFLICTION AND SUFFERING

trouble and sorrow, I found   Ps116
  man is born to   Job5
tumours, curse of   De28
   plagued with   SF5ff
ulcerated bowels   CS21
ulcers, curse of   De28
  struck down by deadly   Je16
unburied bones as dung   Je16
unclean, away!   La4
urine, constrained to drink their own   KS18; Is36
wandering in a pathless wilderness   Job12
waste away, the fat on his limbs shall   Is17
wasting disease in the day of incurable pain   Is17
  sickness   Ps196
weals, nothing but   Is1
weep, a time to   Ec3
weeping and wailing   SS15; Est4
  cheeks flushed with   Job16
  in the public squares   Is15
  is heard in Ramah   Je31
  mingled my drink with   Ps102
  Rachel for her sons   Je31
weeps in the night, she   La1
wept all night   Nu14
  I sat down and   Ne1
whirlwind, reap the   Ho8
wormwood and gall   La3
wound, grievous   Je30
wounds fester   Ps38
wrath, day of   Zp1

NEW TESTAMENT

abomination of desolation   Mw24; Mk13
affliction of hardship cannot separate us   PR8
agitation of spirit, Jesus in deep   J13
agony, men gnawed their tongues in   Rev16
beasts at Ephesus, I fought wild   PCF15
beating their breasts, they went home   L23
bed of pain, throw her on to a   Rev2

2 AFFLICTION AND SUFFERING

beggar, a blind   Mk10
bent double, she was   L13
blind and dumb   Mw12
  for a time, you shall be   A13
  from birth   J9
  man sat at the roadside   L18
  men, at the roadside sat two   Mw20
  men, Jesus followed by two   Mw9
  why was he born   J9
blood, an issue of   L8
bloody flux   A28
bodies burnt outside the camp   LH13
branded, marks of Jesus   PG6
broken-hearted, sent to heal the   L4
burden, every man shall bear his own   PG6
burn men, the sun allowed to   Rev16
calamity is upon them   ThF5
calumny for my sake, when you suffer   Mw5
cankered, gold and silver is   LJ5
convulsions, threw the boy into   Mk9
  throws him into   L9
cripple, better to enter life a   Mk9
  from birth, at the gate of the temple   A3
crippled for eighteen years   L13
  man, lame from birth   A14
cross, a stumbling-block   PCF1
  carrying his own   J19
  come down from the   Mw27
  discarded cosmic powers on the   PCo2
  endured the   LH12
  fastened him to the   Mk15
  in weakness, died on the   PCS13
  must take up the   Mk8
  obedient unto death of the   PPs2
  of Christ, enemies of the   PPs3
  on his back, put the   L23
  on which he killed the enmity   PE2
  openly displayed upon his   PG3
  peace through the shedding of blood on the   PCo1
  pressed him to carry the   Mk15
  take up his   Mw16

2 AFFLICTION AND SUFFERING

cross, the fact of Christ on his   PCF1
   took him down from the   Mk15
crowd of sick people, blind, lame and paralysed   J5
crown of thorns   Mw27; Mk15; J19
crucified through weakness   PCS13
crucifying again with their own hands   LH6
cut himself with stones   Mk5
deaf and dumb spirit   Mk9
devil, my daughter is tormented by a   Mw15
   possessed by a   Mw9
devils, sufferers possessed by   Mw4, 8
die, every day I   PCF15
disciplined by suffering   PCS6
diseases and torments, people with divers   Mw4
distress, hardships and dire straits   PCS6
drugged wine, he was offered   Mk15
dumb, a man who was   Mw9; Mk7; L11
   spirit   Mk7
epilepsy   Mw4
evil, use good to conquer   PR12
famine in that land, there arose a mighty   L15
   lay hard over the whole country   L4
   predict a severe and world-wide   A11
   the right to kill by   Rev6
famines and plagues in many places   L21
feeble-minded, comfort the   ThF5
fever, Simon's mother-in-law in the grip of   L4
foaming at the mouth   L9
foams at the mouth and grinds his teeth   Mk9
fortitude in suffering   LPF2
furnace, throw her into a   Rev2
gall of bitterness   A8
   wine mixed with   Mw27
gangrene, spread like   PTS2
gnawed their tongues in agony   Rev16
grief and torment to match her voluptuous pomp   Rev18
   and unceasing sorrow in my heart   PR9
   my heart is ready to break with   Mk14
   they were filled with   Mw17
griefs, many thorny   PTF6

2 AFFLICTION AND SUFFERING

grinds his teeth and goes rigid   Mk9
haemorrhages, suffered from   Mw9; Mk5; L8
hardship in service of the gospel   PTS2
   like a good soldier   PTS2
hardships, stand firm under   ThF3
   we must pass through many   A14
hated of all men   Mk13
humiliation, sown in, raised in glory   PCF15
hungry and thirsty and in rags   PCF4
impediment of speech   Mk7
imprisonment in Christ's cause   PPs1
infirmities, I glory in my   PCS12
issue of blood   L8
Jesus wept   L19; J11
lament in remorse, all the people shall   Rev1
leper approached him   Mw8; Mk1
lepers, cleanse   Mw10
   in Israel, many   L4
   ten men that were   L17
leprosy, a man covered with   L5
Lot's wife, remember   L17
lunatic, sore vexed   Mw17
   those which were   Mw4
mad, he hath a devil and is   J10
madman possessed by the legion of devils   Mk5
millstone hung round his neck   Mw18; Mk9; L17
mist and darkness came over him   A13
moth-eaten, your fine clothes are   LJ5
myrrh, wine mingled with   Mk15
numbness of spirit, brought upon them a   PR11
ordeal to fall on the world   Rev3
   who have passed through the great   Rev7
orphans and widows, go to the help of   LJ1
overworked, sleepless, starving   PCS6, 11
pain and grief, those who marry will have   PCF7
   racked with   Mw4
palsy, one sick of the   Mk2
   those which had the   Mw4
paralysed   Mw4, 8f; Mk2; L5
persecution for my sake, when you suffer   Mw5
   for the cause of right   Mw5

2 AFFLICTION AND SUFFERING

persecution, they fall away when there is   Mk4
   will come to Christians   PTS3
persecutions and sufferings, fortitude under   PTS3
   your faith remains steadfast under   ThS1
persecutors, pray for your   Mw5
pestilence, bereavement, famine and burning   Rev18
   fearful sights of   L21
   the right to kill by   Rev6
pitiful wretch, poor, blind and naked   Rev3
pity on us, Son of David, have   Mw9
plague, power to strike the earth with   Rev11
plagues, many sufferers from   Mk3; L7
 seven bowls full of   Rev21
   there shall be   L21
   three, in John's vision   Rev9
poison, if they drink any deadly   Mk16
poor, crippled, lame or blind, give a party for   L14
   ourselves, we bring wealth to many   PCS6
   you have among you always   J12
possessed, they brought him a man who was   Mw12
poverty, open-handed from the depths of their   PCS8
prayers and petitions, with loud cries and tears   LH5
prison, ready to go with you to   L22
rejected, the Son of Man   Mk8
ruin, lure the unstable to their   LPS2
scourge you in their synagogues, they will   Mw10
shame, they glory in their   PPs3
shipwrecked   PCS11
sick nigh unto death   PPs2
   were carried out into the streets   A5
snake hanging on to his hand   A28
Sodom, more bearable for   L10
sores and pains, only cursed God for their   Rev16
   foul malignant   Rev16
   Lazarus covered with   L16
sorrowful, yet always rejoicing   PCS6
sorrows, all these are the beginnings of   Mw24
sown in humiliation, it is raised in glory   PCF15
speech impediment   Mk7
   you will lose your power of   L1
speechless, possessed by a spirit which makes him   Mk9

2 AFFLICTION AND SUFFERING

spiked themselves on many thorny griefs   PTF6
struck down, we are not left to die   PCS4
suffer and rise from the dead, the Messiah had to
   cruelly for ten days, you will   Rev2
   for you, my happiness to   PCo1
   Messiah must   A26
suffering, Christ's cup of   PCS1
   endure the pain of undeserved   LPF2
   learned obedience in the school of   LH5
   passed through the test of   LH2
   plunge her lovers into terrible   Rev2
   take your share of   PTS1
   to come, do not fear   Rev2
   train us to endure   PR5
sufferings, a share in Christ's   LPF4
   Son of Man has to undergo great   Mk8f; L9
suicide, the jailer intended   A16
terrified, he did not know what to say, they were so   Mk9
thorn in the flesh, given me a   PCS12
torment, Hades a place of   L16
   like a scorpion's sting   Rev9
trial, stood firmly by me in my time of   L22
troubles are slight and short-lived, our   PCS4
wailing and grinding of teeth, place of   Mw8, 13
weep for yourselves and your children   L23
   no more   L7
   with them that weep   PR12
weeping and gnashing of teeth   Mw8, 24
   and lamenting for the child   L8
wept, Jesus   L19; J11
widow alone in the world   PTF5
   parable of the persistent   L18
widows, I say to   PCF7
   men who eat up the property of   L20
withered arm, man with a   Mk3; L6
wormwood, name of the star is   Rev8
wrath, God has not appointed us to   ThF5

3 *Altars, Monuments and Holy Places*

OLD TESTAMENT

altar, acacia wood   Ex27ff
  acceptable offerings on my   Is60
  at Beersheba   Gen26
  at Bethel   Gen35
  at El-bethel   Gen35
  bread on the   SF21; KF7; CF9. 23ff, 28; CS4ff, 13, 29; Ne10
  bowl   KF7
  bronze   KF7; KS16; CS1, 4; E9
  build of the proper pattern   Ju6
  built at Bethel   Ju21; De27
  buy the threshing floor to build an   SS24
  by the River Jordan   Jos22
  cedar   KF6
  censers   KF7; E8
  chest beside the   KS12
  cup, golden   CF28
  dishes, gold and silver   CF28
  drenched like the corners of the   Z9
  El-Elohy-Israel   Gen33
  Ezekiel's vision of the temple   E40ff
  facing the land of Canaan   Jos22
  fire from the Lord   KF18
  firepans   Ex27ff; Le10; KF7
  flame went towards heaven   CS7
  flowers, golden   KF7
  forks, golden   Ex27ff; CF28
  frankincense   CF9; Ne13
  gate, Jerusalem   E8
  golden   KF7; CS4
  great, at Geliloth   Jos22
  horns of the   KF1ff; Ps118; E43; Am3
  in the house of the Lord   Z14
  incense   Ex30ff; Le10, 16; KF13, 22; CF6, 9, 28; CS2, 13, 26;
  lamp-stands   KF7
  light falls in vain on my   Ma1
  Lord spurned his own   La2

3 ALTARS, MONUMENTS AND HOLY PLACES

altar, Lord's house   E8
   men lie down beside every   Am2
   mount the steps of my   SF2
   named "Witness"   Jos22
   of Abram   Gen12
   of Ahaz   KS16
   of David   SS24
   of El-Elohey-Israel   Gen33
   of Gideon   Ju6
   of God, come to the   Ps43
   of Isaac   Gen26
   of Jacob   Gen33
   of Jehovah-Nissi   Ex17
   of Jehovah-shalom   Ju6
   of Jeroboam   KF12
   of Moses at Sinai   Ex24ff
   of Noah   Gen8
   of Samuel   SF7
   of Saul   SF14
   of Solomon   KF7
   ointment   CF9
   miraculous fire on the   CS7
   on Mount Ebal   Jos8
   pattern for building the   Ju6, 21
   plan and design of the   KS16
   pot   KF7
   procession round the   Ps26
   rebuilding of the   Ez3
   rent in pieces   KF13
   saucer, golden   KF7
   saw the Lord standing by the   Am9
   set up on the threshing floor   SS24
   shovel   KF7
   snuffers, golden   KF7
   Solomon's golden   KF7
   spice   CF9
   spoons, golden   KF7
   sword swung over their blood-spattered   Ho11
   table, golden   KF7
   thorns and thistles shall grow over their   Ho10
   threshing floor   CF21; CS23

3 ALTARS, MONUMENTS AND HOLY PLACES

altar to the Lord in the heart of Egypt   Is19
  tongs, golden   KF7
  tossing bowl   KF7
  trolley   KF7; KS16, 25
  undressed stone   De27
  unhewn stone   Ex20; Jos8
  utensils   CS4, 13, 24, 35; Ez1, 8
  wafers   CF9, 23
  weeping between the porch and the   Joe2
  ye offer polluted bread on my   Mal
altars, blood-spattered   E6; Ho11
  common as heaps of stones beside a ploughed field   Ho12
  Ephraim in his sin has multiplied   Ho8
  have become his sin   Ho8
  made desolate   E6
  of Bethel   Am3
  pull down their   De7, 12
  rears her brood beside thy   Ps84
  seven, of Balaam   Nu23
  thorns grow over their   Ho10
arcades of the temple in Ezekiel's vision   E41ff
arches of the temple in Ezekiel's vision   E40
Ark of God   SS6; CF13ff; CS1ff
    send it back   SF6
    taken by Philistines   SF4ff
  of the Covenant   Ex25ff; Le16; Nu10; SF4; SS15; KF2ff, 6ff; CF6, 22, 28; CS5, 35; Je3
  of the Lord   KF2ff, 6ff
  of the Tokens   Nu4ff
  of thy power   Ps132
Baal-berith, temple of   Ju9
Bohan, stone of   Jos18
cairn of Gal-ed   Gen31
  of Jegar-sahadutka   Gen31
  of Mizpah   Gen31
censer, King Uzziah's   CS26
censers in Ezekiel's vision   E8
  in Solomon's house of the Lord   KF7
  in the tent of the Presence   Nu4
  make beaten plates of the   Nu16

3 ALTARS, MONUMENTS AND HOLY PLACES

cherubim of gold, enthroned on   Ex25ff; SF4; SS6; KF6; KS19; CF13
corridors of the temple in Ezekiel's vision   E42
court, inner   E8, 10
door-keepers, temple   Ne7, 10, 13
doors of the temple broken up   KS18
El-berith, temple of   Ju9
gallery in Ezekiel's vision of the temple   E43
Gibeon, great stone in   SS21
hill-shrine in Gibeon   KF3; CF16
  of the Hill of God   SF10
  of the Tabernacle   CF21
  what is this   E20
hill-shrines allowed to remain   KF22
  for Kemosh and Moloch   KF11ff
  I will destroy your   E6
  of Isaac   Am7
  sacrifice at the   KF3
holy of holies   Ex26ff
  offerings   CS35
  place   Ex26ff; CS35; Ec8
house of God   Ne6; Ec5; Di
  officer in charge of the   CF9
  repairs to the   CS34
  security of the   CF
  Solomon's   KF5ff; CF6
  of prayer   Is56
  of the Lord   KS16, 18, 22; CS23; Je20, 36, 38, 41
  burnt down   Je39, 52
  in Babylon   Je27
  purified   CS29
  repairs to the   Ks22
  sacred contents of the   Je51
  Solomon's   KF5ff; CF6
  time for rebuilding the   Hg1ff
  treasury in the   Z11
  vessels and trolleys in the   Je27
Jerusalem, thy holy hill   D9
memorial in the temple of the Lord   Z6
mercy seat, the Lord's   Ex26
monument of Absalom   SS18

3 ALTARS, MONUMENTS AND HOLY PLACES

monument of Eben-ezer   SF7
  of Hadadezer   SS8
  of victory   SS8; CF18
  Samuel set up a   SF7
most holy place   KF6ff; CS2ff; D9
mount of Jerusalem   Is27
mountain of God   Ex3, 19
    no man may touch the   Ex19
palaces of Zion   Ps48
pillar at Bethel   Gen35
  at Bethlehem   Gen35
  at Rachel's grave   Gen35
  in the king's vale   SS18
  of Jacob   Gen28, 31
  of salt   Gen19
  of the Lord's house   Je27
  of the temple   Je52
pillars, sacred   KF14
    break their   De7, 12
    twelve   Ex24
ramparts of Zion   Ps48
rocks called Bozez and Seneh   SF14
sacred pillars   KF14
  vessels   KF15
sanctuary, Gentiles entering her   La1
  her priests profaned the   Zp3
  horns of the altar   KF2
  in the midst of them, set my   E37
  Judah was his   Ps114
  land set aside for   E45, 48
  measurements of the   E45
  my holy   Is60
  of Moab   Is16
  of Shechem   Gen12
  of the tabernacle   Ex25ff
  of the Lord   Je24; E8
  princes profaned my   Is43
  shall be profaned, their   E7
  temple   KF6
    in Ezekiel's vision   E41ff
  thou hast defiled my   E5

3 ALTARS, MONUMENTS AND HOLY PLACES

sanctuary, vessels of the   D5
  within the veil of the tabernacle   Le16
sanctuaries of the Lord's house   Je51
sarcophagus of Og   De3
sea, molten   Je27
  of bronze   CF18; Je52
    broken up   KS25
  of cast metal   CS4
shrine at Shiloh   Je7
  inner   KF6; CS4
  Micah had a   Ju17ff
  of expiation   CF28
  Solomon's inner   CS4
  thy holy   Ps28, 74
stone at Shechem, set up a great   Jos24
  blocks of, copy of the law of Moses   Jos8
  great, at Beth-shemesh   SF6
  Joshua set up a great   Jos24
  of Bohan   Jos15, 18
  of Ezel   SF20
  of Help   SF7
  of Zoheleth   KF1
  roll a great   SF14
  Samuel set up a   SF7
  set up a great   De26
stones at Gilgal, carved   Ju3
  great pile of, at Achor   Jos7
    at Ai   Jos8
  over Absalom's body, a huge pile of   SS18
  piled against the cave at Makkedah   Jos10
  twelve, set up   Jos4
tabernacle at Gibeon   CF16
  at the hill-shrine   CF21
  bring me to thy   Ps43
  brought to Solomon   KF8
  design for the   Ex26ff
  dwelling place of the   CF6
  from one to another   CF17
  guards   CF9
  Jerusalem   Is33
  Levites placed in charge of the   Nu14

3 ALTARS, MONUMENTS AND HOLY PLACES

tabernacle Moses made in the wilderness   CF21
  of David   Is16
  of Ham   Ps78
  of the Covenant   Ex26ff
  of the Lord   Jos22; CF16; CS1
  place of refuge   Is4
  porter at the door of the   CF9
  spoiled   Je10
  violently taken away his   La2
  who shall abide in thy   Ps15
  Zadoc took a horn of oil out of the   KF1
table of the Lord   Ma1
tables, altar   CF28
temple, all cry "Glory" in his   Ps29
  avenging of his   Je51
  bitter enemies of thy   Ps69
  bow down towards thy holy   Ps138
  bow low in thy holy   Ps5
  bring sacrifices into thy   Ps66
  courts of the Lord's   Ps84
  defiled thy holy   Ps79
  fittings   Je52
  foundation may be laid   Is44
  gallery, in Ezekiel's vision   E43
  glory added to glory in my   Is60
  great hall of the   Ju9
  he heard me from his   Ps18
  holiness is the beauty of thy   Ps93
  implements removed   Je52
  in Ezekiel's vision   E8, 40ff
  Lord is in his holy   Ps11
  of Ashtoreth   SF31
  of Baal-berith   Ju9
  of the Lord   CS25ff; Z6
  prostitute   De2
  servitors   CF9; Ne3, 7, 10ff
  Samuel slept in the   SF3
  seek him in his   Ps27
  Solomon's   KF6ff
  terrace, those who dance on the   Zp1
  that uproar in the   Is66

3 ALTARS, MONUMENTS AND HOLY PLACES

temple, the Lord's   Is6
  thy holy   Ps65
  time to rebuild the   Hg1ff
  trolleys   KF7; CS4; Je27, 52
  vault of the   Ju9
  vengeance of his   Je50
  vessels   Ne13
temples, carried off my treasures into your   Joe3
  drank wine in their   Ju9
tent, David's   Is16
  for the Ark of God   CF9
  of the Covenant   Ex26ff
  of the Lord   KF1ff, 6ff
  of the Presence   Ex26, 29ff, 33ff; Le1ff; Nu1ff, 6ff, 18; De31; Jos18; SF2; KF8; CF6, 9, 23; CS1ff
  of the Tokens   Nu18; CS24
  pitched for the Ark of God   SS6
threshing floor redesigned as an altar   CS3
tomb of Abner at Hebron   SS4
  of Abraham, cave of the   Gen23
  of Rachel   SF10
  of Sarah, cave of the   Gen25
tossing-bowls, gold   CF28
  silver   Ne7
towers of Zion   Ps48
treasury, Lord's house   Ma3
vessels of the house of God   D1
  of the sanctuary   Ne10
  of the temple   D5
  sacred   KF15

NEW TESTAMENT

altar and sanctuary, between   L11
  cry, I heard the   Rev16
  fire   Rev8
  golden   LH9; Rev8f
  horns of the   Rev9
  in Athens   A17
  leave thy gift before the   Mw5
  life poured out on the   PTS4

3 ALTARS, MONUMENTS AND HOLY PLACES

altar, measure the Rev11
  of incense L1
  our, from which priests have no right to eat LH13
  shares in the PCF10
  swears by the Mw23
  to an unknown god A17
  tribe which had nothing to do with the LH7
  underneath the Rev6
altars, they have torn down thine PR11
ark of his covenant in heaven Rev11
censer, golden altar LH9; Rev8
church at Ephesus Rev2
  at Laodicea Rev3
  at Pergamum Rev2
  at Philadelphia Rev3
  at Sardis Rev3
  at Smyrna Rev2
  at Thyatira Rev2
  his body which is the PCo1
  in Jerusalem, persecution for the A8
  of God, tried to destroy the PG1
  on this rock will I build my Mw16
  supreme head to the PE1
  was left in peace to build up its strength A9
churches, seven Rev1
court of Areopagus A17
  of Mars Hill A17
Diana, temple of A19
God's temple, where the spirit of God dwells PCF3
heavenly temple, angel came out of the Rev14
holy city, entered the Mw27
   new Jerusalm Rev21
   the devil took him to the Mw4
   the Gentiles will trample underfoot Rev11
  place, called the LH9
   Paul has profaned this A21
house of God Mw12; PTF3
  of prayer for all the nations Mk11
incense altar L1; LH9; Rev8
living God, city of the LH12

3 ALTARS, MONUMENTS AND HOLY PLACES

mercy seat   LH9
monuments of the saints   Mw23
most holy place, called the   LH9
parapet of the temple, set him on a   L4
pinnacle of the temple   Mw4
sacred mountain, with him on the   LPS1
sanctuary, a material   LH9
  between altar and   L11
  curtain of the   LH9f
  gold in the   Mw23
  minister of the   LH8
  of the heavenly tent   Rev15
  this fellow is attacking our   A21
  veil of the   LH9
seats in the synagogue   Mk12
shrine of Moloch   A7
shrines, god does not live in   A17
  of Diana, silver   A19
Sion   Mw21; PR9, 11; LH12; LPF2; Rev14
Solomon's portico   J10
synagogue at Thessalonica   A17
  banned from the   J9
  began to teach in the   Mk6
  chief ruler of the   A18
  for fear of being banned from the   J12
  he taught in their   L4
  he was teaching in the   A18
  healing in the   Mw12; Mk2f
  held office in the   A18
  I have always taught in the   J18
  Jesus taught in the   Mw13
  of freedmen   A6
  of the Libertines   A6
  officials of the   A13
  prayers standing up in the   Mw6
  president of the   Mw9; Mk5; L8
  punished them in every   A26
  ruler of the   Mk5
  Sabbath they went to the   A13
  seats of honour in the   L11
  spoken in the   J6
  teach in the   Mk1

3 ALTARS, MONUMENTS AND HOLY PLACES

synagogue, they will ban you from the   J16
  they will flog you in the   Mw10
synagogues, chief seats in the   Mw23; Mk12; L20
  Saul proclaiming Jesus in the   A9
  teaching in the   Mw4
tabernacle a worldly sanctuary   LH9
  called the holiest   LH9
  of David   A15
  of the testimony   Rev15
  of witness   A7
  put off   LPS1
  true, which the Lord pitched   LH8
tabernacles, let us make here three   Mw17
temple, a spiritual   LPF2
  accused of profaning the   A24
  Anna never left the   L2
  appeared again in the   J8
  at Jerusalem   Mk11
  between the altar and the   L11
  brought Greeks into the   A21
  buildings   Mw24
  captain of the   L22; A4f
  controller of the   A4f
  court   Mk11
  curtain of the   Mw27; Mk15; L23
  daily attendance at the   A2
  dealers in the   Mw21; Mk11; L19; J2
  forsaken by God   Mw23; L13
  forty six years to build the   J2
  found him sitting in the   L2
  fund   Mw27
  gate called Beautiful   A3
  go and take your place in the   A5
  grows into a holy   PE2
  he came again into the   J8
  he came by the Spirit into the   L2
  he taught in the   Mk12
  I have always taught in the   Mw26
  I sat teaching in the   Mw26
  I was praying in the   A22
  I will pull down the   Mk14

3 ALTARS, MONUMENTS AND HOLY PLACES

   temple in heaven was laid open, God's   Rev11
     Jesus drove out all who were trading in the   Mw21
     made a robbers' cave of the   Mk11
     of Diana   A19
     of God   PCS6
       even takes his seat in the   ThS2
       is holy   PCF3
       measures the   Rev11
     of Jupiter   A14
     of our living God   PCS6
     officers   L22
     parapet of the   Mw4; L4
     people flocked to listen to him in the   L21
     pinnacle of the   L4
     police   L22; J7
     praising and blessing God in the   L24
     Romans will sweep away our   J11
     seized me in the   A26
     seized Paul and dragged him out of the   A21
     service, those who perform the   PCF9
     something greater than the   Mw12
     stones of the   Mk13
     swear by the   Mw23
     tax, collectors of   Mw17
     teaching in the   Mw26; Mk12; L20f
     traders in the   Mw21; Mk11; L19; J2
     treasury   Mk12; L21
     to pray, two men went to the   L18
     veil of the   Mk15; L23
     was filled with smoke from the glory of God   Rev15
     worship, theirs the   PR9
     you know that you are in God's   PCF3
   temples, God dwelleth not in   A17
   tent of testimony   A7; Rev15
     pitched by the Lord   LH8
     priests of the sacred   LH13
     sacred   LH13
     sanctuary   LH9
   unknown God, altar to the   A17
   Zion   Mw21; PR9, 11; LH12; LPF2; Rev14
     I lay in, a corner-stone   LPF2
     you stand before Mount   LH12

4 *Animals, Birds and Insects*

OLD TESTAMENT

adder   Ps91; Pro23
animals given as food   Gen9
  to be eaten   De14
ant   Pro6, 30
antelope   Is51
  long-horned   De14
ape   KF10; CS9
asp   De32; Job20; ps58, 91; Is11
ass   Ju10, 12; SF9, 16, 25, 27; SS16ff; KF2, 13; KS4, 7; CF5, 12;
      CS28; Ez2; Ne7; Job1, 24, 42; Pro26;
        Is1, 21, 30; E23; Z9, 14
  Balaam's   Nu22
  gelded   Gen49
  levied   Nu31
  made to speak   Nu22
  of Achsah   Jos15
  tethered to the vine   Gen49
  wild   Job6, 11, 24, 39, 41; Ps58, 104; Is32; Je2, 14; D5;   Ho8
    snuffing the wind   Je14
asses, laden   Ju19
  of Jericho slaughtered   Jos9
  straw and provender for   Ju19
baboon   SS3
badger   E16
  skin   Ex25ff; Nu4
bat   Le11; De14; Is2
bear   SF17; SS17; KS2; Pro17, 28; Is11, 59; La3; D7; Ho13; Am5
beasts of burden   Is46
bees   Ps118
  from Assyria   Is7
  swarming   Ju14
behemoth   Job40
beetle   Le11
bird   Ps8, 11
  on those hills, I know every   Ps50

4 ANIMALS, BIRDS AND INSECTS

bird, speckled   Je12
birds, caught in a snare   Ec9
  dietary laws of Moses concerning   Le11
  made to settle all over the camp   Ps78
  migration of   Je8
  of prey   Gen15; Is18; Je12, 15
  sacrifice of small   Le14
bird's nest, take only the young   De22
bison   Is34
bittern   Is14, 34; Zp2
boar, wild   Ps80
buck   De12, 14
buffalo   SS6; KF1; Is1, 34; E39; Am5
bull   Nu7; SF1; CS29; Ez6ff; Job21, 42; Ps50ff, 69, 106; Is1, 34;
       Je50; E39, 43, 45
  image   Ps106
  offering of a   Le1ff
  without blemish   Nu28ff
  yearling   Ju6
bull-calf, image of   De9
bullock   Ju6; SF14; KF18; Ez6ff; Job42; Is1, 5, 10, 34, 65; Je31, 46,
       50; E39, 43
bulls, herd of   Ps22
  sacrifice of   Ex29ff
bustard   Is14, 34; Zp2
  ruffed   Zp2
calf   SF6, 14, 28; Ps29, 68; Is11, 27; Je31, 46; E1; Am6; Mi6
  bull   Ps68
  image   De9
  Passover victim   De16
camel   Gen24, 31; Ex9; Le11; De14; Ju8ff; SF27, 30; KF4, 10;
       KS8; CF5, 12; CS9; Ez2; Ne7; Est8; Job1, 42;
       Is21, 30, 60; Je2, 49; E25; Z14
  caravan   Gen37
  neck crescents for   Ju8
camels, pestilence of   Ex9
  without number   Ju9
cankerworm   Joe1ff; Na3
caterpillar   KF8; CS6; Ps78, 105; Is33; Je51; Joe1ff
cattle   Ex9; Le3ff; SF14; CF5; Ez1; Is5, 11, 22, 46, 63;
       E14, 32, 34, 38; Ho5, 14; Joe1ff; Jon4; H3; Hg1; Z2, 13

4 ANIMALS, BIRDS AND INSECTS

cattle, offering of   Le3ff
  pestilence of   Ex9
chameleon   Le11
cheetah   H1
cobra   Ps91; Pro23; Is11
cobweb   Is59
cock   Pro30
cockatrice   Is11, 14, 59; Je8
  eggs of a   Is59
colt   Z9
coney   Le11; De14; Ps104; Pro30
cormorant   Le11; De14; Is34; Zp2
cow   Nu14; SF6; Job21; Is7, 11; Am4
  milch, harnessed to a wagon   SF6
  red, without blemish   Nu19
crane   Je8
creatures, all living   Gen1
  of the sea   Ps98
crocodile   Job40
crow   Le11; De14
cuckoo   Le11; De14
cud-chewing animals   Le11
dangerous beasts, rid your land of   Le26
deer,   Job39; Is35; La1
  white-rumped   De14
doe   Pro5
  wild   Job39
dog   SF17, 24; KS9; Ps68; Pro26; Ec9; Is56, 66; Je15
dogs, run wild like   Ps59
dove   So1ff, 5; Is38, 59, 60; Je8, 48; E7; Ho7, 11; Na2
  image of   Ps68
  oh that I had the wings of a   Ps55
  released from the ark   Gen8
dragon   Job30; Ps91; Is13, 34ff, 43, 51; Je9, 14, 49, 51; E29; Mi1; Ma1
  return from the   Ps68
dromedary   KF4; Est8; Is60, 66; Je2
dung-beetle   Is2
eagle   Le11; De14; Job9, 39; Ps103; Pro30; La4; E1, 10, 17; D4, 7; Ho8; Ob1; Is40; Je4, 48ff; Mi1; H1
  gier   De14

4 ANIMALS, BIRDS AND INSECTS

ewe   Ps78; Is7, 40, 53
  without blemish   Le4; Nu6
falcon   Le11; De14; Job28
fallow deer   KF4
fatling   SS6; KF1; Is11; E39;
fawn   Job39; So4, 7
ferret   Le11
fins and scales, creatures with   De14
flat paws, creatures with   Le11
fish   Ps8, 105; Ec9; Is19
  a great   Jon1
  dietary laws concerning   Le11
  for the asking in Egypt   Nu11
  in shoals   E47
  pestilence of   Ps105
  taken in a net   Ec9
flea   SF24, 26
flies   Ps78, 105; Ec10
  from Egypt   Is7
  plague of   Ex8; Ps105
  swarms of   Ps78
foal   Z9
food, animals given for   Le11
fox   Ne4; So2; La5; E13
frogs, plague of   Ex8; Ps78, 105
fruit bat   So2
gadfly   Je46
gazelle   De12, 14; SS2; Pro6; So2, 4, 7ff; Is13
gecko   Le11
gier   Le11; De14
glede   De14
goat   Gen27, 30ff; Le16; Nu7; De14; SF25; CS17, 29; Ez6ff;
        Ps50, 66; Pro27, 30; So4, 6; Is1, 13, 34; Je50ff;
        E27, 34, 39, 43; D4
  as scapegoat   Le16
  as sin-offering   Nu28ff
  brindled   Gen30ff
  driven into the wilderness   Le16
  mountain   Job39; Ps104
  offering of   Le3
  rock   De14

4 ANIMALS, BIRDS AND INSECTS

goat, wild   De14; So2, 8
goats, gift of 7,700   CS17
grasshopper   Le11; Job39; Ec12; Is40; Je46; Am7; Na3
  great   Na3
greyhound   Pro30
grouse, sand   Je48
grub   Ps78; Is51; Joe2
grubs, plague of   Ps78
hare   Le11; De14
hart   KF4; So2; La1
hawk   Le11; De14; Job39
heifer   Nu17; De21; Ju14; SF16; Je46, 48, 50; Ho4, 10
  broken neck in the ravine   De21
  ploughed with   Ju14
  red, without spot   Nu17
  roped   Is5
heron   Le11; De14
hoopoe   Le11; De14
hoppers   Ps105; Je51; Joe1ff; Na3
hornet   Jos24
horse   Ex9; Jos11; SS15; KF4, 9ff, 20; KS5ff; Ez2; Ne2; Est6, 8;
      Job39; Ps20, 32ff, 76, 147; Pro21, 26;
      Is2, 5, 21, 30ff, 43, 63, 66; Je4, 6, 8, 11ff, 17, 22, 46, 50ff;
      E23, 26ff, 38ff; Ho1,14; Joe2; Am6; Mi5; Na2ff; H1, 3; Hg2;
      Z1, 6, 9, 12, 14
horses, pestilence of   Ex9
hunting leopard   H1
hyena   Je12
insects, swarming   Ps80
jackal   Ju15; Ps63; So2; Is13, 34; Je50; La5; E13
jerboa   Le11; Is66
kid   Ex12; De16; Ju6, 13; SF10, 16; Ps29; So1; Is5, 11; E43
  Passover victim   De16
  without blemish   Ex12
kite   Le11; De14; Is34
lamb   Gen30; Ex12; Nu28ff; De16; SF7; KS3; CF29; CS29;
      Ez6ff; Ps144; Pro27; So4, 6; Is1, 11, 16, 34, 40, 65; Je11, 51;
      E27, 39, 45; Ho4; Am6
  black   Gen30
  Passover victim   De16
  without blemish   Ex12; Nu28ff

4 ANIMALS, BIRDS AND INSECTS

lammergeier Le11; De14
lapwing Le11; De14
leopard So4; Is11; Je5, 13; D7; Ho13; Hi
  hunting H1
leviathan Job3; Ps74, 104
lion, lioness Nu24; Ju14; SF17; SS23; KF13, 20; KS17; CS9;
      Job4, 10, 28, 38; Ps7, 10, 17, 22, 57, 91,104; So4;
      Pro19ff, 22, 26, 28; Ec9; Is5, 11, 15, 21, 30ff, 35, 38, 65;
      Je2, 4ff, 12, 25, 49ff; La3; E1, 10, 19, 22, 32; D6ff;
      Ho5, 11, 13; Joe1; Am3, 5; Mi5; Na2; Zp3; Z11
  cub De33; Job28; Ho9; Na2
lizard Pro30
  chameleon Le11
  gecko Le11
  great Le11
  sand-gecko Le11
  thorn-tailed Le11
  wall-gecko Le11
locust Ex10; Le11; KF8; CS6; Job39; Ps78, 105, 109; Pro30;
      Ec12; Is33, 40; Je46, 51; Joe1ff; Am4, 7; Na3
  desert Le11
  bald Le11
  great Le11
  green Le11
  long-headed Le11
locusts, plague of Ex10; Ps78, 105
louse, lice Ex8; So1; Is22, 41;
  plague of Ex8
maggots Ex8; Ps105; Is41, 51
  plague of Ex8; Ps105
magpie Pro30
marmot Is13, 34; Je50
mare E27
mole Le11; Is2
mole-rat Le11
monkey KF10; CS9
moth Job14; Is50ff; Ho5
mouse, mice Le11; SF5, 6; Is66
mule SS13, 18; KF1, 10; CF12; Ez2; Ne7; Est8; Ps32; Is66;
      E27; Z14
night hawk Le11; De14

47

4 ANIMALS, BIRDS AND INSECTS

nightjar   Is34
osprey   Le11; De14
ossifrage   Le11; De14
ostrich   Job39; Is43; La4
owl   Job30; Is34, 43
  desert   Le11; De14; Ps102; Is13, 34; Je50; Mi1
  fisher   Le11; De14
  great   Le11; De14
  horned   Le11; De14; Is34; Zp2
  little   Le11; De14
  long-eared   Le11; De14
  screech   Le11; De14
  short-eared   Le11; De14
  tawny   Le11; De14; Zp2
ox   Nu7; De14; SF11, 14; SS6, 24; KF1, 4, 8, 19; KS5; CF12; Ne4; Job1, 24; Ps8, 49, 66, 144;Je11; E1; D4ff; Am6
  wild   Nu23ff; Job39; Ps22, 29, 92; Is34
    with horns to gore nations   De33
pack animals   Ks3
palmer worm   Joe1ff; Am4
panther   Ho5, 13
partridge   SF26; Je17
  sand   Is34
peacock   KF10; CS9; Job39
pelican   Le11; De14; Ps102
pig   Le11; De14; Pro11; Is66
  prohibited as food   Le11
pigeon   Ho7, 11
  young, sacrifice of   Le1ff
porcupine   Is13
porpoise hide   Nu4
quail   Ex16; Nu11; Ps105
ram   Gen30; Ex25ff, 29ff; Le3; Nu5ff, 28ff; KS3; CS17, 29; Ez6ff, 10; Job42; Is1, 5, 34, 60; Je49ff; E27, 34, 39, 43, 45; D8; Mi6
  of the Atonement   Nu5
  offering of   Le3
  sacrifice of   Ex29ff
  skins   Ex25ff
  without blemish   Nu6, 28ff

4 ANIMALS, BIRDS AND INSECTS

ram, wool of   Ks3
rams, black   Gen30
  gift of 7,700   CS17
  of Nabaioth   Is60
rat   SF5, 6; Is66
raven   Le11; De14; KF17; Job38; Ps147; Pro30; So5; Is34
  released from the ark   Gen8
reptiles, carvings of   E8
rock badger   Le11; De14; Ps104; Pro30
  goat   De14
  rabbit   De14
roe, roebuck   De14; SS2; KF4; Pro5ff; So2, 3, 4; Is13
sand grouse   Je48
  partridge   Is34
  viper   Is30
scapegoat   Le16
scorpion   De18; KF12; CS10; E2
sea monster   Ps74
  serpent   Ps44, 74; Job7; Am9
serpent   Gen3; Ex4, 7; Ps58, 91, 140; Pro23, 30; Ec10;
       Is14, 65; Je8, 46; Am5, 9; Mi7
  Aaron's rod became a   Ex4, 7
  fiery flying   Is14, 30
  flying   Is14
  more crafty than other beasts   Gen3
  of bronze   Nu21
  venom of   Ps58
  venomous flying   Is30
shark   Ps74
sheep   Gen37ff; Ex9, 12; Le4; Nu31; De14; SF14, 16, 25; KF1, 4, 8;
       KS5; CF5, 12; Job1, 42; Ps44, 49, 65, Ps77ff, 80, 107, 144;
       So1; Is1, 5, 7, 11, 13, 22, 43, 53, 66; Je12, 23, 50;
       E25, 34, 36, 39, 45ff; Ho5, 12; Joe1; Am1; Mi2, 5; Z9
  levied   Nu31
  offering of   Le4
  pestilence of   Ex9
  slaughter for the Passover   Ex12
snail   Le11; Ps58
snake   Gen3, 49; Ex4, 7; Nu21; De8; Ps58, 59, 140; Pro23, 30;
       Ec10; Is14, 59, 65; Je8, 46; Am5, 9; Mi7

4 ANIMALS, BIRDS AND INSECTS

snake bite, Moses's remedy for   Nu21
  eggs   Is59
  horned, on the path   Gen49
  poisonous   Nu21; De8
  staff became a   Ex4, 7
song-birds   Ec12
sparrow   Ps84, 102; Pro26; Ec12
spider   Ps140; Pro30; Is59
stag   KF4
stallion   Je8, 50
stork   Le11; De14; Ps104; J8; Z5
swallow   Ps84; Pro26; Is38; Je8
swan   Le11; De14
swift   Je8
swine   De14; Is66
tortoise   Le11
turtle-dove   Ps74; So2; Je8
  sacrifice of   Le1ff
unclean, animals classified as   Le11
unicorn   Nu23ff; De33; Job39; Ps29, 92; Is34
viper   Gen49; Job20; Is11, 14, 30, 59; Je8
  on the road   Gen49
  sand   Is30
vulture   Job9, 15, 28, 39; Pro30; Is34; Je49; La4; Ho8; Ob1;
        Mi1; H1
  bearded   Le11; De14
  black   Le11; De14
  gier   Le11
  griffon   Le11; De14
water creatures, dietary laws concerning   Le11
weasel   Le11
whale   Job41; La4; E32
wild beasts, I will rid your land of   Le26
wolf   Gen49; Job30; Is11, 13, 34ff, 43, 65; Je5, 9ff, 14, 49, 51;
        E22; Mi1; H1; Zp3
  ravening   Gen49
worms   De28; Ps22; Is14, 41, 51, 66; Es2; Jon4; Mi7
  canker   Joe1ff; Na3
  curse of   De28
  palmer   Joe1ff; Am4
wryneck   Je8

4 ANIMALS, BIRDS AND INSECTS

NEW TESTAMENT

adder   PR3
ass   Mw21; L13f; J12; LPS2
beast   Rev13ff
birds came and ate the seeds   Mw13; Mk4; L8
  came to roost among its branches   L13
  can settle in its shade   Mk4
  gathered to eat the flesh   Rev19
  haunt for vile and loathsome   Rev18
  have their nests   Mw8
  have their roosts   L9
  lodge in the branches   Mw13
  of the air do not sow   Mw6
  unclean and hateful   Rev18
  you are worth more than the   Mw6
bear, feet like a   Rev13
bull   LH9f
  calf idol   A7
bullocks   Mw22
calf   L15; LH9
  beast like a   Rev4
  bring the fatted   L15
camel   Mw23; Mk1, 10; L18
cattle   L17; J2; LJ5
cock   Mw26; Mk13f; L22; J13, 18
colt, ass's   Mw21; J12
  which no one has yet ridden   Mk11; L19
creatures lowered in a sheet   A10f
dog returns to its own vomit   LPS2
dogs, beware of those   PPs3
  came and licked his sores   L16
  eat the scraps   Mw15
  outside are   Rev22
  throw children's bread to the   Mk7
  under the table   Mk7
  what is holy, do not give   Mw7
donkey   Mw21; L13f; J12
dove   Mw3, 10; Mk11; L3; J1f
  descending like a   Mw3
  spirit like a   Mk1

4 ANIMALS, BIRDS AND INSECTS

dragon in John's vision   Rev12f
  out of the mouth of the   Rev16
  spoke like a   Rev13
  that serpent of old,   Rev20
eagle   Mw24; L17; Rev4, 8
fish   Mw7, 13ff, 17; Mk6, 8; L5, 9, 11; J6, 21
  with a silver coin in its mouth   Mw17
foal, ass's   Mw21
fowls of the air, behold the   Mw6
    came and devoured the seed   Mw13; Mk4; L8
    may lodge under the shadow of it   Mk4
  were filled with their flesh   Rev19
fox, foxes   Mw8; L9, 13
  have their holes   L9
frogs, unclean spirits like   Rev16
gazelle   A9
gnat   Mw23
goat   Mw25; LH9ff
heifer   LH9
hen chicken   Mw23
    gathers her brood   L13
horse, black   Rev6
  red   Rev6
  sickly pale   Rev6
  white   Rev6, 19
horses and chariots, cargoes of   Rev18
  bridle, the height of a   Rev14
  in John's vision   Rev6, 9
  locusts like   Rev9
  mouth, put a bit in a   LJ3
kid, never gave me so much as a   L15
lamb among wolves   L10
  before the shearer   A8
  of God   Rev19ff
  Passover   Mk14
  with the marks of slaughter   Rev5
  without blemish   LPF1
lambs, feed my   J21
leopard, beast like a   Rev13
lion   PTS4; LH11; LPF5; Rev4f, 9f, 13
locusts   Mw3; Mk1

4 ANIMALS, BIRDS AND INSECTS

locusts in John's vision   Rev9
midge   Mw23
moth   Mw6; L12; LJ5
ox   M22; L13f; J2; A14; PCF9; PTF5 Rev4
pig   Mw7f; Mk5; L8, 15
pigeon, pigeons, offering of   L2
  dealers in   Mw21; Mk11; J2
raven   L12
scorpion   L10f; Rev9
sea-monster   Mw12
serpent, serpents   Mw7, 10, 23; Mk16; L10f; J3; PCF10; PCS11; LJ3; Rev20
  of old, the dragon   Rev20
  they shall take up   Mk16
sheep   Mw7, 9f, 12, 15, 18, 25f; Mk6, 14; L15, 17; J2, 5, 10, 21; A8; PR8; LH11, 13; LPF21; Rev18
  feed my   J2, 5, 10, 21
  for slaughter   PR8
  suppose a man has a hundred   Mw18
  will be scattered   Mk14
  without a shepherd   Mk6
  wolves dressed as   Mw7
snake, snakes   Mw7, 23; Mk16; L10f; A28; Rev9
  in John's vision   Rev9
  Paul shook off the   A28
  if they handle   Mk16
sow rolls in the mud   LPS2
sparrow   Mw10, L12
swine, a great herd of   Mw8; Mk5; L8
  casting pearls before   Mw7
  did eat, husks   L15
turtle dove   L2
viper   Mw3, 12, 23; L3; A28
vulture   Mw24; L17
whale, in the belly of the   Mw12
wild beasts   Mk1; Rev6
wolf   Mw7, 10; L10; A20
  dressed as a sheep   Mw7
  hireling sees the   J10
worm, worms, devouring   Mk9
  eaten up with   A12

5   *Blessings and Curses*

OLD TESTAMENT

accursed serpent   Gen3
  thing, take from you   Jos7
bless the Lord   Job1; Ps34, 72, 103, 115, 134
blessed, all nations shall call him   Ps72
  be they that bless you   Nu24
  the people, David   CF16
blessing be on the fruit of your body   De28
  be on you in the city   De28
  be on you in the country   De28
  be on your basket and kneading trough   De28
  be on your basket and store   De28
  be on your coming in and going out   De28
  be on your fruit and cattle   De28
  be on your granaries and labours   De28
  be on your lands and herds   De28
  for considering the poor   Ps41
  for fearing the Lord   Ps111, 128
  of Ezra   Ne8
  of Naomi   Ru2
  of Solomon   KF8
  of the Levites   Ne9
  of the people   De27
  on the man who took notice   Ru2
  recited word by word   Jos8
blindness, strike this host with   KS6
children cursed in the name of the Lord   KS2
curse against the house of Joab   SS3
  Balaam sent to lay a   Jos24
  be on he who carves an idol   De27
  be on he who fulfils not the law   De27
  be on he who lies with an animal   De27
  be on he who lies with his father's wife   De27
  be on he who lies with his mother in law   De27
  be on he who lies with his sister   De27
  be on he who lies with his wife's mother   De27

5 BLESSINGS AND CURSES

curse be on he who makes a graven image   De27
  be on he who makes a molten image   De27
  be on he who misdirects the blind   De27
  be on he who removes landmarks   De27
  be on he who sacrifices a damaged victim   Ma1
  be on he who slights his parents   De27
  be on he who smiteth his neighbour secretly   De27
  be on he who strikes a man in secret   De27
  be on he who takes reward for killing   De27
  be on he who withholds justice   De27
  be on the cheat   Ma1
  be on the fruit of your body   De28
  be on you as you come out and go in   De28
  be on you in the city   De28
  be on you in the country   De28
  be on your basket and kneading trough   De28
  be on your land and flocks   De28
  David, let him   SS16
  for defrauding tithes   Ma3
  for non-observance of the covenant   Je11
  for rebuilding Jericho   Jos6
  for trusting in man   Je17
  for withholding contributions   Ma3
  in Zechariah's vision   Z5
  lay on Jacob   Nu23
  lay on the Israelites   Nu22
  of Cain   Gen4
  of children's death   Jos6
  of darkness   Job3; Ps35, 69
  of disease   SS3; Ps69
  of early death   SF2
  of fire   Ps140
  of flight with the enemy at your heels   SS24
  of Joshua on Jericho   Jos6
  of Jotham   Ju9
  of the people   De27
  of thistles   Job31
  of weeds   Job31
  on the thief   Ju17
  on the worthless shepherd   Z11
  Lord laid upon his sanctuary a   La2

5 BLESSINGS AND CURSES

curse recited word by word   Jos8
  sevenfold   Ps79
  the day   Job3; Je20
  the proud   Ps119
  them, hired Balaam to   Ne13
  turn your blessings into a   Ma2
  you to your face, he will   Job1
cursed be Canaan   Gen9
  be they that curse you   Nu24
  by Elisha, little boys mauled by bears   KS2
  in the name of the Lord   KS2
  to crawl on your belly   Gen3
curses, he loved   Ps109
  oath of   Nu5
  set out in the law of Moses   D9
distaff, sons fit only to ply the   SS3
evil eye, man with the   Pro28
old age, no man in your house shall come to   SF2
plague on nations who warred against Jerusalem   Z14
serpent accursed   Gen3
unblessed, be it for ever   Je20

NEW TESTAMENT

accursed thing, Christ became for our sake an   PG3
beatitudes   Mw5
bless, and curse not   PR12
  the cup of blessing   PCF10
  them which persecute you   PR12
  those who persecute you   Mw5; 16
blessed, all generations shall call me   L1
  and brake the loaves   Mw14
  are they that have not seen and yet believed   J20
  are they whose iniquities are forgiven   PR4
  are ye that hunger   L6
  are ye that weep   L6
  are ye, when men shall hate you   L6
  are you, how   L6
  art thou among women   L1
  be ye poor   L6

5 BLESSINGS AND CURSES

blessed is the man to whom the Lord will not impute sin   PR4
  them, he lifted his hands and   L24
blessing and cursing out of the same mouth   LJ3
  earth receiving its share of   LH6
  he looked up to heaven and said the   Mw14
  of Abraham   PG3
  on the fruit of your womb   L1
  over the food, said   L9
  retaliate with   LPF3
  said the   Mk6
  that ye should inherit a   LPF3
  the cup of   PCF10
blessings not curses, call down   OR12
  on him who comes in the name of the Lord   L13, 19
  on your persecutors, call down   PR12
cleverness of the clever, bring to nothing   PCF1
consecrate them by the truth   J17
cured, all of them were   A5
curse, bound themselves under a great   A23
  God's, hangs over the earth   LH6
  is on everyone who is hanged from a gibbet   PG3
  is on them, God's   LPS2
  is on this rabble   J7
  of the law   PG3
  on Jesus, no one who says   PCF12
  those who rely on the law are under a   PG3
  you, bless those who   L6
cursed God for the plague of hail   Rev16
  is everyone that hangeth on a tree   PG3
  the fig tree   Mk11
curses, Peter broke into   Mk14
  their mouth is full of bitter   PR3
cursing and angry shouting, have done with   PE4
  and bitterness, whose mouth is full of   PR3
  lay aside all   PCo3
damned who believe not the truth   ThS2
delusion, God puts them under a   ThS2
God bless the king of Israel!   J12
good to those who hate you, do   Mw5
gospel to proclaim, an eternal   Rev14
grace abounding   PCS4

5 BLESSINGS AND CURSES

  grace, called me through his   PG1
    mercy and peace shall be with us   LJS1
    of God dawned upon the world   Tt2
    the gift of   LPF1
hosanna, blessings on him who comes in the name of the   Lord   J12
    in the heavens   Mk1
    in the highest   Mk11
hungry, blest are you who now go   L6
kindness and generosity dawned in the world   Tt3
law, curse of the   PG3
Lord God of Israel, blessed be the   L1
love banishes fear, perfect   LJF4
    of Christ, what can separate us from the   PR8
mercy, peace and love be yours   LJu1
money go with your damnation, your   A8
peace of God beyond our understanding   PPS4
praises and curses, out of the same mouth came   LJ3
prayers of the saints   Rev5, 8
rejoice in the Lord alway: and again I say, Rejoice   PPS4
sin no more, lest a worse thing befall thee   J5
spirit, the grace of our Lord Jesus Christ be with your   PPS4
vital fragrance that brings life   PCS2
wealth to many we bring   PCS6
weep, blest are you who   L6
wisdom of the wise, I will destroy the   PCF1
woe unto you that are rich! for ye have received your consolation   L6

6   *Buildings and Shelters*

OLD TESTAMENT

altar gate, Jerusalem   E8
  pattern for building   Ju6, 21
  rebuilding of the   Ez3
arbours, construct and live in   Le23
arcades, in Ezekiel's vision of the temple   E41ff
  in Solomon's house   KF6
arches of the temple in Ezekiel's vision   E40
apartments, royal   Est1
  winter   Je36
armoury   Ne3
banqueting hall, Belshazzar's   D5
  house   So2
barracks   Ne3
barn   Job39; Ps144; Hg2
  storage   CS32
bars, gate   Ps147, Na3
basket, builder's   Ps81
battlement   Ps84
beams   CS34; Ps104; H2
  bearer   KF6
  cedar   KF7; So1
  citadel gate   Ne2ff
  house   So1
    Solomon's   KF6
bearer beams   KF6
bedchamber   KS6, 11
bolt, knobs of   So5
bolted and barred, Jericho   Jos6
bolts and bars   Ne3
booths to live in during the pilgrim-feast   Le23; Ne8
boundary stone   Is54
braces, cedar   KF6
breach, repair of the   Is58
brick kiln   SS12; Na3
brickwork, repair the   Na3
build for the community, each fetch a log to   KS6

6 BUILDINGS AND SHELTERS

build houses, but not live in them   Zp1
builder   E27
building, decaying through sloth   Ec10
  of houses, none yet awhile   E11
cabin   Je37
canopy, wedding   Ps19
capital   Am9; Zp2
  bronze   Je52
  copper   KF7
  pillar   KS25; CS4
castle, I will pull down your   Ju8
  of Shechem   Ju9
  of Thebez   Ju9
causeway   KS18; CF26
cedar, beams of   KF7; So1
  boards, lining of   KF6
  panelling   Je22
  wood, a house of   SS5, 7
    building   CS2
  work, ruined   Zp2
ceiling, wooden   So1
cement, stones set in   Je43
cell, measurement of   E40ff
chamber, house   SS13
  temple   KF6
chapiter, pillar   KS25; CS4; Je52
  brass   KF7
cistern, rock-hewn   Ne9
citadel   KF20; Ne2; Is32
cities in the east, Moses set apart three   De4
city, Samson pulled out the gateposts of the   Ju16
  great towering   De9
  of Jerusalem pulled down   KS25
  of refuge   De19
  wall   KS6
    damaged   CS25
  which you had never built   Jos24
  without walls, Jerusalem to be a   Z2
clamps, iron   CF22
closet in Eglon's palace   Ju3
coffering in Solomon's house   KF6

6 BUILDINGS AND SHELTERS

colonnade   KS23; CF26
  in Solomon's house   KF7
columns, cedar   KF7
conduits, city to be rebuilt with   D9
coping   KF7
cord, tent   Is54
corner-stone   Ps118; Je51; Z10
  a block of granite   Is28
cornice, Solomon's house   KF7
  wooden   E41
corridors of the temple in Ezekiel's vision   E42
cottage   Is1, 24; Zp2
  shall be matchwood   Am6
court   KF7
  garden   Est1
  inner   CF28; Est4
    of stone and cedar   KF6
  of the guard, Jerusalem   Ne3
  temple, inner   E10
    in Ezekiel's vision   E40ff
  upper   Je36
courts of the house of the Lord   KS23
crib, farm   Is1
cushion, bronze pillar   KF7
elevation and plan of the temple   E43
embrasures, furnished with   KF6
dais   KS11, 22
dam   E31
demolish the house   Z5
dining-hall   SF9
door   CS3; Ps24, 107; Pro26; Is57
  bronze   Ps107
  double   KF6; E41
  frames broken up   KS18
  golden altar   KF7
  great   Ma1
  pinewood   KF6
  post   Is57
    pentagonal   KF6
    write commandments on the   De6, 11
  wild olive wood   KF6

6 BUILDINGS AND SHELTERS

doors of the temple broken up   KS18
dovecote   Is60
draught house   De23; Ju3; KS10
drawing of Jerusalem, Ezekiel's   E4
dungeon   La3; Z9
dwelling house, sale and redemption   Le25
fence   Is5
fillets, hammered bronze   KF7
   pillar   Je52
floor boards, pine   KF6
forecourt   Ez10
fortified city   KS18; Ne9; Je1, 34; D11
fortresses built   CS17
forts and towers on the wooded hills   CS27
foundations   KF5, 7; Ps11, 87; Is54; Je51
   blocks of hewn stone   KF5
   laid bare   E13; Mi1
   of the new temple   Ez3; Hg2
   of the old temple   Z8
   stones, size of   KF7
   uncovered to the bare rock   H3
   Zerubbabel laid bare the   Z14
foundry   CS4
frames, gold-covered   CS3
furnace, furnaces   Ps21, 37; D3
   tower of the   Ne12
gallery, temple in Ezekiel's vision   E43
garden court, Persian   Est1
   house, fled by way of   KS9
gate   Ps24, 87; E26
   altar   E8
   bars   Na3
   Benjamin   Je17, 37; Z14
     upper   Je20
   between the two walls   KS25; Je39, 52
   corner   KS14; CS25ff; Je31; Z14
   dung   Ne2ff, 12
   east   CS31; Ne3; Je19
   eastern, Lord's house   E10ff
   Ephraim   KS14; CS25; Ne8, 12
   fish   CS33; Ne3, 12; Zp1

6 BUILDINGS AND SHELTERS

gate, foundation   CS23
  fountain   Ne2ff, 12
  guards   KS11
  hope   Ho2
  horse   CS23; Ne3; Je31
  inner   E8
  Jeshanah   Ne3, 12
  king's   CF9
  Lord's house   E8
  middle   Je39
  Miphkad   Ne3
  mustering   Ne3
  of Asher   E48
  of Benjamin   E48
  of Dan   E48
  of Gad   E48
  of Issachar   E48
  of Joseph   E48
  of Judah   E48
  of Levi   E48
  of Naphtali   E48
  of Reuben   E48
  of Samaria   KF22
  of Simeon   E48
  of the guardhouse   Ne12
  of the Lord's house   Je7
  of the potsherds   Je19
  of Zebulun   E48
  outrunners   KS11
  Shallecheth   CF26
  sheep   Ne3, 12
  Sur   KS11
  threshold   CS23
  upper, house of the Lord   KS15; CS23
  valley   CS26; Ne2ff
  water   Ne3, 8, 12
gates, city   Ps9, 122; E48
    broken bars of   Je51
  of bronze   Is45
  of Jerusalem   KS11, 14, 25; CS23, 25ff, 31, 33; Ne2ff, 8, 12;
       Is60; Je1, 13, 17, 19ff, 31, 39, 52; Zp1; Z14

6 BUILDINGS AND SHELTERS

gates of the temple in Ezekiel's vision   E40ff
   measurements of   E40ff
   threshold of   E40ff
   vestibule of   E40ff
  old city   Ne3, 12
  new, Lord's house   Je26, 36
  set on fire   Je51
  town   Ps69
  two-leaved   Is45
  upper northern   E9
  write commandments on the   De6, 11
  gatehouse   Ne12
  gate-keeper   Ne3, 7, 11ff
  Gedaliah, mansion of   KS25
  granary   Je50
  great hall of the temple   Ju9
  guard-house   Je32f, 37, 39
  guard-tower   Je51
  hamlet, farm   Ne11
    near Gaza   De2
  hewn stone, build in   Is9
    for repairs   KS22
  hinge, door   Pro26
  homestead   Ps79; Je25
  house, building of Solomon's   KF5ff; CS2
   new, not dedicated   De20
   of Azariah   Ne3
   of cedar, David's   CF17
   of God, building the   CF22
   of hewn stone   Am5
   of ivory   KF22; Am3
   of Pharaoh's daughter   KF7
   of Solomon   KF7
   of the forest   Is22
   of Lebanon   KF7, 10; CS9
   of the heroes   Ne3
   of the high priest   Ne3
   of the Lord, rebuilding the   Ez1; Hg1ff
   parapet, necessity for   De22
   shatter from the roof down   H3
   uninhabited, a fine large   Is5

6 BUILDINGS AND SHELTERS

house, unless the Lord builds the   Ps127
houses bought and sold   Je32
   build, but not to live in   Zp1
     on their native soil   E28
   build while in exile   Je29
   I builded   Ec2
   laid waste   Zp1
   mortgaged   Ne5
hut   So1; Zp2
inner court, royal   Est4
keeper of the royal palace   KF16
kerb, measurements of   E40ff
king's house   Ne3
latch-hole   So5
lattice   Pro7; So2
lavatory, sign for a   De23
ledges of the temple in Ezekiel's vision   E40ff
lime   Am2
lintel   Am9; Zp2
lining, cedar board   KF6
lock, handles of the   So5
lodge   Is1
loft   Kf17
loopholes, cell and pilaster   E40ff
mansion   KS25
   never to be rebuilt   Is25
   of Gedaliah burnt   Je52
   towering   La2
marble   CF29
   red, blue, white and black, pavement   Est1
   pillars of   Est1
measurements, inner shrine,   KF6
   Solomon's temple   KF6
measuring line   Am7
mill   Ec12
Millo, Solomon's tower   KF6, 9, 11; KS12; CF11; CS32
mortar   Is54; E13; Na3
mosaic pavement   Est1
oil-store   CF27
overlay, gold   KF6
painting, house   Je22

6 BUILDINGS AND SHELTERS

palace adjoining Jerusalem city wall   Ne2
  Babylonian royal   D4
  in Ashdod   Am3
  in Egypt   Am3
  ivory   Ps45
  of Ben-hadad   Am1
  of Bozrah   Am1
  of Gaza   Am1
  of Jerusalem   Ne2; Am2
  of Kerioth   Am2
  of Solomon   CS2
  of Tyre   Am1
panels, cedar   KF7; Je22
parapet, new houses to include a   D22
  silver   So8
parlour   SF9
partitions, cedar board   KF6
passageway of the temple in Ezekiel's vision   E42
pavement   E40ff
  mosaic   Est1
  stone   KS16
pavilion   Ps104
  of Ben-hadad   KF20
  royal   Est1, 7; Je43; D11
peg, tent   Is54
  wall   Is22
pilaster   E40ff
  pentagonal   KF6
pillars   CS3ff
  alabaster   Est1
  bronze   KF7; CF18
  finials for   CS4
  iron   Je1
  measurements of the temple   E40ff
  marble   Est1
  pommels for   CS4
  Samson pulled down the   Ju16
  temple, in Ezekiel's vision   E40ff
pine floor boards   KF6
pitch   Is34
plan and elevation of the temple   E43

6 BUILDINGS AND SHELTERS

plan of Jerusalem, Ezekiel's   E4
  of the porch   CF28
plaster of the palace wall   D5
platform bronze   CS6
  wooden   Ne8
plumb-line, plummet   KS21; Is28; Am7
pommels, pillar   CS4
porch   Joe2; Am9; Zp2
  gate   E40
  Lord's house   E8
  plan of a   CF28
  Solomon's house   KF7
privy   De23; Ju3; KS10
property, redemption and sale of   Le25
quarries at Gilgal   Ju3
rafters   CS3, 34
  collapsed through neglect   Ec10
rampart   Ps91
  Tyre has built a   Z9
rebuild our ruined homes   Ma1
rebuilding and fabric fund   Ne7
  the temple   Ez2ff
  the walls of Jerusalem   Ne2ff
rebuilt, Gezer   KF9
  Jericho   KF16
  on its mound of ruins   Je30
  palaces shall be   E36
  Shechem   KF12
  the city shall be   Je31
  time for the house of the Lord to be   Hg1ff
recess, house   SS13
redemption of property   Le25
repairs to the house of God   CS34
  to the house of the Lord   KS12; CS24
residence at Jerusalem, the   Je39
  of the Philistine governor   SF10
roof, bed spread on the   SF9
  cedar   KF6, 7
  each to make arbours on their own   Ne8
  grass growing on the   Ps129
roof-chamber   KF17; KS4; CF28; Je22; D6; Ne3

6 BUILDINGS AND SHELTERS

roof-chamber of the summer palace   Ju3
rope, tent   Is33, 54
ruins, restore Israel's   Am9
  the temple lies in   Hg1
sale of property   Le25
sea-fortress of Sidon   Is23
settle, temple, in Ezekiel's vision   E43
shed   Is1
shelter, Jonah made himself a   Jon4
sketch for design of an altar   KS16
Solomon's building complex   CS8
square, town   Ne8
stables   KF4, 10; E25
  royal   Est7
stairs, winding   KF6
stairway of Ahaz   KS20
  spiral   KF6
stake, tent   Is54
stalls, animal   KF4; CS32; Is1; Am6; H3
steps assigned to the Levites   Ne9
  of the temple in Ezekiel's vision   E40
stone, built houses of hewn   Am5
  corner   Ps118
  foundation blocks   KF5
  granite corner   Is28
  hewn blocks for building   KF7; CF22; CS34; La3
    for repairs   KS12
    tablets of   E40ff
  set in mortar   Is54
  undressed, for Solomon's house   KF6
store-chamber   Ps33
store-cities   CS8, 11, 16ff
  Pharaoh's   Ex1
  Solomon's   KF9
storehouses   CS4; Je50
  Solomon's   KF7
store-rooms   CF27ff; Ne10, 13
  tithe   CS31
stronghold of Zion   SS5
strong-room   CF28
struts, cedar   KF6

6 BUILDINGS AND SHELTERS

suburbs of Jerusalem   KS23
summer-house   Am3
summer palace of the Moab kings   Ju3
temple, instructions for building a   Ju6, 21
  building of Solomon's   KF5ff
    time taken to build   KF9
  of Baal converted to a public toilet   KS10
  rebuild, time is ripe to   Hg1ff
  rebuilt, in Ezekiel's vision   E40ff
tent   SS7, 16; KF12; KS7f, 13; Ps19, 27, 61, 68ff, 104; So1;
       Is33, 40, 54; Je4, 6, 14, 35, 37, 49ff; La2; H3; Z12
  on the roof   SS16
  under the pomegranate tree   SF14
tent-ropes   Je10
tents of Ham   Ps78
tent villages of Basham   De3
  of Jair   Ju10; KF4
terrace, Solomon's house   KF6
  temple,   E9ff, 46; Zp1
threshold   Ps84
  measurement of   E40ff
tie-beam   Ne3
tile   E4
timber, building   KS12; Je10; Hg1
  for repairs   KS22; CS34
  for rebuilding   Ne2ff
  pine, fashioned of   E27
treasury   CS32; Ne13
  royal Persian and Median   Est3
tower   Ps9, 18, 120; E27
  of Babel   Gen11
  of David   So4
  of Hananel   Ne3, 12; Je31; Z14
  of Meah   Ne3
  of Solomon, the Millo   KF6, 9, 11; KS12; CF11; CS32
  of the furnaces   Ne3, 12
  of the hundred   Ne3, 12
  of the ovens   Ne3, 12
  round, Pharaoh's   Gen39
towers built at Jerusalem   CS26
  of Jerusalem, they will pull down the   E26

6 BUILDINGS AND SHELTERS

undersetters, base KF7
upper chamber of Ahaz KS23
    of Solomon's temple CS3
  tower of the court of the guard Ne3
vault Is45
  of the temple Ju9
vaulted pit Je37
vestibule KF6ff; CS3
  of the gate E40ff
wall Ps18, 62, 89; Ho2
  bowing Ps62
  breached Ps89
  break a hole in the E12
  broad, of Jerusalem Ne3, 12
  bronze Je1, 15
  building a E13
  dig into the E8
  farm Pro24; Is5
  found a hole in the E8
  plumbed Am7
  repair, gone up into the breach to E13
  stone Pro24
  stones will cry out from the H2
walled cities, sixty large KF4
  city Mi5
    of Tyre SS24; E26ff; Am1
walls, breaches in the Am4
  cracked and bulging Is30
  day has come for rebuilding the Mi7
  of Gaza Am1
  of Jericho fell down Jos6
  of Jerusalem destroyed Je39
    time to rebuild the Ne6
  of Rabbah Am1
  of the temple in Ezekiel's vision E43
  of Tyre, they will destroy the E26
  of Zion SS5
  repair Israel's gaping Am9
  watch tower CS20
  whitewash E13
  window Pro7; Je22; D6; Joe2; Zp2; Ma3

6 BUILDINGS AND SHELTERS

window frames   KF7
   latticed   KS1
   vestibule   E40ff
wine cellars   CF27
winter-house   Am3
women's quarters, royal   Est2

NEW TESTAMENT

architect   LH11
audience chamber   A25
barn, barns   Mw13; L12
   pull down and build greater   L12
   store in   Mw6
barracks   A21, 23
beam   L6
Beautiful Gate   A3
build with hay and straw   PCF3
builder   A4; LH11; LPF2
building a tower without calculating the cost   L14
   bonded together   PE2
   rocked, when they had ended their prayer   A4
   up, not for pulling down   PCS13
   which God has provided   PCS5
   you are God's   PCF3
buildings, you see these great   Mk13
camp, bodies burnt outside the   LH13
castle, captain's   A21f
   on guard over his   L11
city built as a square   Rev21
   gate, they kept watch on the   A9
   square, Athens   A17
closets, that ye have spoken in   L12
colonnades, a place with five   J5
corner stone   Mk12; L20; A4
     Jesus Christ the chief   PE2
     of great worth   LPF2
courtyard, governor's   Mk15
   high priest's   Mw26; Mk14; J18
courtyard, lit a fire in the   L2

6 BUILDINGS AND SHELTERS

custom house   L5
door, knocking at the   Rev3
   Peter knocked at the   A12
   prison   A5
   struggle to get through the narrow   L13
   will be opened   Mw7; L11
doors, burst open all the   A16
dungeon, Satan let loose from his   Rev20
dwelling, built into a spiritual   PE2
   places, in my father's house are many   J14
foundation, God has laid a   PE2
   laid by the apostles and prophets   PE2
   laid the   L14; PCF3
   stone   PE2
     of the holy city   Rev21
   to build on another man's   PR15
foundations of the jail were shaken   A16
   on rock   Mw7; L6
gate, beautiful   A3
   city   A16
   enter in at the strait   L13
   iron   A12
   Jesus suffered outside the   LH13
   Lazarus laid at his   LH13
   narrow   Mw7
   of the town   L7
   temple   A3
   wide   Mw7
gates of faith, thrown open the   A14
   of hell   Mw16
   twelve   Rev21
hall, Herod's judgement   A23
   of judgement   J18
headquarters, governors   J18; A23; PPs1
homestead fall desolate, let his   A1
house built on sand   Mw7
   built upon rock   Mw7; L6
   flood could not shift the   L6
   he who hath builded the   LH3
   high priest's   Mk14
   many dwelling places in my father's   J14

6 BUILDINGS AND SHELTERS

house not made by human hands   PCS5
  peace to this   L10
  Solomon built God a   A7
  to house, wandering about from   PTF5
  without foundations   L6
houses and lands sold   A4
inn   L10
jail   Mw5; A5
  foundations were shaken   A16
keystone   Mk12; L20; A4; PE2; LPF2
lecture hall   A19
main square of Philippi   A16
mansions, in my Father's house are many   J14
market place   Mw20; J2
palace, governor's   PPs1
  of the high priest   Mw26; Mk14; J18
  strong man keepeth his   L11
parapet of the temple   Mw4
pillar in the temple   Rev3
pinnacle of the temple   M4; L4
plank, great   L6
porch at the high priest's house   Mk14
  Solomon's   A3, 5
portico, Solomon's   J10; A3, 5
praetorium   Mk15
prison   Mw5, 11, 25; Mk1, 6; L21, 23; J3; A4, 12, 26; PPs1; Ph1
  doors during the night, an angel opened the   A5
  Herod had thrown John in   Mw14
  remember those in   LH13
  why I am now in   PCo4
private houses, breaking bread in   A2
    the sort that insinuate themselves into   PTS3
property and possessions, they would sell their   A2
residency, the governor's   PPs1
roof, if a man is on the   Mw24; Mk13; L17
  let him down through the   Mk2; L5
room, a large upper   Mk14
  dining   Mk14
  for the Passover supper   L22
  guest   Mk14

6 BUILDINGS AND SHELTERS

shambles PCF10
shelters, shall we make three Mw17; Mk9; L9
stairs, the castle A21
stall, ox L13
stone, building Mk12f
  rejected by the builders has become the keystone A4
streets and lanes of the city L14
tabernacle, earthly house of this PCS5
  of Moloch A7
  which is called the holiest LH9
tabernacles, let us make three Mw17; Mk9; L9
temple buildings Mw24
  parapet of the Mw4
  pillar in the Rev3
tent of the Testimony A7
  sacred LH13
  sanctuary LH9
tents, living in LH11
theatre of Ephesus A19
tiling, roof L5
timber, immense stack of LJ3
tower, building a L14
  built a watch Mk12
  fell on them at Siloam L13
upper room assembly L22; A20
wall, a high Rev21
  Damascus city PCS11
  in a basket, let him down the city A9
  whitewashed A23
walls, city L19; A9; PCS11; LH11
  of Jericho LH11
watch-tower Mw21; Mk12
whitewashed wall A23
window in the wall PCS11
   ledge A20

7 *Childhood, Birth and Infancy*

OLD TESTAMENT

babes at the breast   Joe2
  in arms of the priests killed   SF22
  newly weaned, just taken from the breast   Is28
baby, Solomon's judgement for the disputed   KF3
  substituted another for a dead   KF3
bastard offspring debarred to the tenth generation   De23
birth of Ichabod   SF4
  of Jerusalem   E16
  of Obed   Ru4
  of Samson   Ju13
  of Samuel   SF1
  of Solomon   SF1
  untimely, the curse of   Nu5
birthright of Esau   Gen25
born a time to be   Ec3
  in the wilderness   Jos5
boy, every Midianite, killed by Moses   Nu31
  every newborn Israelite, to be killed   Ex1
  every newborn, to be thrown into the Nile   Ex1
boys mauled by bears for mocking Elisha   KS2
breast, mother's   Ps8, 22
child, I will give to the Lord my   SF1
  king, Amon   KS21
    Azariah   KS15
    Joash   KS12
    Josiah   KS22
  Samuel, surely you call me   SF3
  sneezed seven times, the revived   KS4
  the living, cut in two   KF3
childbirth, Hebrew women in   Ex1
children, beheaded seventy royal   KS10
  burnt as sacrifice   Le20; KS17; CS28; Is57; E16, 23
  come back to me, apostate   Je3
  dash to the ground their   KS8; Is13; Ho13; Na3
  eaten during siege   KS6
  given in pledge   Ne5

7 CHILDHOOD, BIRTH AND INFANCY

children kept alive as possessions De20
  massacres of   Nu31; De2ff
  mauled by bears   KS2
  of her wantonness   Ho1
  of the priests' city killed   SF22
  of whoredoms   Ho1
  passed through fire   E20
  punished for their parents' misdeeds   Nu14, 31; Je29, 31;   E18; D6
  put to death   Ex1, 31; Nu21, 31; De2ff, 20ff; Jos6ff;
      Ju1, 9, 11,18, 20ff; SF7, 15, 22, 27; KF11; KS8, 10, 15,
      KS25; D6, 20; Am1
  slaughter of   Nu31; De2ff; Jos8ff; Ju21; SF15
  stoned to death   Jos7
  thrown to the lions   D6
  will eat your own, you   De28
circumcision of children   Le12; Jos5
daughter in law has proved better than sons   Ru4
father and mother, honour thy   De5
first-born, death of in Egypt   Ps78
  Israel my son   Ex4
  shall die   Ex4
  struck down   Ps105, 135ff
foster-child, Esther   Est2
girls spared alive as possessions   Nu31; De20
  spared the virgin Midianite   Nu31
high stool   E16
illegitimate children barred from membership   De23
infants at the breast   Ps8; Is49
  dashed to the ground at every street corner   Na3
leading-strings   Ho11
midwives in Egypt, Hebrew   Ex1
mother and father, honour your   De5
navel-strings not tied   E16
nurse, children's   SS4; KS11; CS22; Is49
orphan, do not oppress the   Z7
  justice for the   De10, 24; Ps10
  those who wrong the   Ma3
parents, honour your   Le20
princes of Midian beheaded   Ju7
ransom of eldest sons   Nu3

7 CHILDHOOD, BIRTH AND INFANCY

reins, children's   Ho11
sacrifice of children   Le20; KS3, 17; CS28; Is57; E16, 23
  of the Moabite king's son   KS3
salted, newborn baby   E16
shepherd boys, turn my hand against the   Z13
son, eldest, curse of Jericho   Jos6
  of a crooked and unfaithful mother   SF20
  punished for the iniquity of the father   Nu14
  youngest, curse of Jericho   Jos6
sons, disobedient, stoned to death   De21
  of Ahab beheaded   KS10
  of Saul hanged   SS21
  shall be punished to the third and fourth generation   Nu31
still-born child better than a dissatisfied man   Ec6
   may they wither like a   Ps58
suckled, Moses   Ex2
substitute Levites for eldest sons   Nu3
swaddling clothes   E16
twins of Judah   Gen38
  of Rebecca   Gen25
  of Tamar   Gen38
virgin, apparel of a   SS13
  Midianite girls spared for Israeli men   Nu31
  mourn that I must die a   Ju11
  rejoice in the dance, then shall the   Je31
  to keep King David warm   KF1
virgins be sought for your majesty, let beautiful young   Est2
  follow the king's daughters   Ps45
  for the king, commissioners appointed to bring young   Est2
weaned child   Ps131
womb, before thou camest forth from the   Je1
  formed thee from the   Is44
  he drew me from the   Ps22
  how the bones do grow in the   Ec11
  in my mother's   Ps139
  left in my mother's   Ps71
  named me from my mother's   Is49

NEW TESTAMENT

adoption, spirit of, whereby we say 'Father'   PR8
babe unskilful in the world as a   LH5

7 CHILDHOOD, BIRTH AND INFANCY

babes and sucklings, out of the mouths of   Mw21
   at breast, children and   Mw21
   be as innocent as   LPF14
   hast revealed these things unto   Mw11
babies for him to touch, they brought   L18
baby wrapped in swaddling clothes   L2
baptism, brought into the body by   PCF12
bearing children into slavery   PG4
birth, it was like an abnormal   PCF15
   of Jesus   L2
   of John the Baptist   L1
   of the child, woman shall be saved through the   PTF2
   pangs of the new age   Mw24; Mk13
   story of the Messiah's   Mw1
   to the son, she gave   L2
born again   J3
   of a woman, God sent his own son   PG4
   this day, unto you is   L2
boys in the temple shouting   Mw21
breasts that suckled you, happy the   L11
bride-chamber, children of the   Mk2
child, accept the kingdom of God like a   Mk10; L18
   also for women who are with   Mk13; L21
   birth, the universe groans as if in the pangs of   PR8
   by the Holy Ghost   Mw1
   every man who does right is his   LJF2
   grew and waxed strong in spirit   L2
   he called a   Mw18
   he took by the hand   L9
   Herod is going to search for the   Mw2
   in my name, who receives this   Mw18
   Jesus, thy holy   A4
   make careful inquiry for the   Mw2
   of God   LJF3ff
   of the devil   LJF3
   receive the kingdom of God like a little   L18
   rise up, take the   Mw2
   saved through the birth of the   PTF2
   when I was a   PCF13
   who was born, where is the   Mw2
   whoever receives this   L9

7 CHILDHOOD, BIRTH AND INFANCY

child with Mary his mother, saw the young   Mw2
  woe unto them that are with   Mk13
  woman saved through the birth of the   PTF2
childish things, I put away   PCF13
children and babes at breast sang aloud thy praise   Mw21
  are with me in bed   L11
  at the breast, alas for those who have   Mw24; Mk13; L21
  dead, I will strike her   Rev2
  fathers must not goad their   PE6
  for Abraham out of these stones   Mw3
  he laid his hands on the   Mw19
  if she have brought up   PTF5
  into slavery, bearing   PG4
  leader wins obedience from his   PTF3
  massacred by Herod   Mw2
  nurse caring fondly for her   ThF2
  obey your parents   PE6; PCo3
  of a family share the same flesh and blood   LH2
  of light, children of day   ThF5
  of light, walk as   PE5
  of the bride-chamber   Mk2
  of the highest, ye shall be the   L6
  of the kingdom, the good seed stands for the   Mw13
  of the wicked one   Mw13
  of your heavenly Father   Mw5
  parents should make provision for their   PCS12
  provoke not your   PE6
  Rachel weeping for her   Mw2
  receive in my name   Mk9
  should repay what they owe to their parents   PTF5
  sitting in the market place, they are like   L7
  suffer little   Mw9; Mk10; L18
  unless you become like little   Mw18
  we are called God's   LJF3
  we are no longer to be   Pe4
  who are not our of control   TF1
  you are my dear   PCF4
  bread of the   MW15
circumcise him, the time came to   L2
  the child, on the eighth day   L1
circumcised on my eighth day   PPS3

7 CHILDHOOD, BIRTH AND INFANCY

circumcising their children, telling them to give up   A21
circumcision makes no difference at all   PG5
   mutilation, those who insist on   PPs3
   of Jesus Christ   L2
   of John the Baptist   L1
daughter of Herodias danced   Mk6
father and mother, honour thy   Mw15, 19; PE6
   in the secret place   Mw6
fathers, do not exasperate your children   PCo3
   must not goad their children to resentment   PE6
first-born from the dead   Rev1
   male belongs to the Lord   L2
   presents to the world   LH1
honour your father and mother   Mw15, 19; PE6
infants in Christ, deal with you as   PCF3
   they brought him   L18
little children, keep yourselves from idols   LJF5
   yet a while I am with you   J13
   ones have their guardian angels in heaven   Mw18
   who shall offend one of these   Mk9
manger, laid him in a manger   L2
massacre of all children in Bethlehem   Mw2
mother, who is my   Mk3
naughtiness, lay apart all   LJ1
new-born infants crave for pure milk   LPF2
nurse, children's   THf2
parents, children should repay their   PTF5
   honour your   L18
   they show no loyalty to their   PR1
purification after birth   L2
scion and offspring of David   Rev22
son disciplined by his father   LH12
   my beloved   Mk1; L3
   of a Christian mother and a Gentile father   A16
   of David, can this be the   Mw12
   only begotten   LJF4
   working under his father, like a   PPs2
sons of God, that we should be called the   LJF3
suck, them that give   Mk13
suckled you, happy the breasts that   L11
sucklings, babes and   Mw21

7 CHILDHOOD, BIRTH AND INFANCY

suffer little children to come unto me   Mw9; Mk10; L18
swaddling clothes, wrapped him in   L2
tolerant and gentle when discipline is needed   PTS2
twin, Thomas the   J20f
womb, a cripple from his mother's   A14
  a second time, enter his mother's   J3
  his blessing is on the fruit of your   L1
  that carried you, happy the   L11
  the baby stirred in her   L1
young, let no one slight you because you are   PTF4
youth, let no man despise thy   PTF4
  turn from the wayward impulse of   PTS2

8   *Cloth and Clothes*

OLD TESTAMENT

apparel of blue and white   Est8
apron, fig leaf   Gen3
   leather   KS1
armour   SF14, 17, 31; KF10, 22; CS18; Ps45; E38
awning, violet and purple   E27
badger skin, shod with   E16
belt,   KF2; Ps109; Is5; E23, 44
   gold   D10
blue and gold is their clothing   Je10
   officers dressed in   E23
bonnet   Is3; E44
   linen   E44
breastplate   KF22; CS18; Is59
breeches, linen   Ex28ff; E44
brocade   E27
   dress of   E16
   robes of   E16, 26
broidered work   E6, 26ff
     purple   E27
buckler   KF10; CS23; Ps35; So4; Je46; E23, 26, 38ff
canvas, patterned   E27
   sail   E27
cloak   SF2, 15, 18, 21, 24; SS20; KS2; Job29; Ps102, 109; Pro31; So5; Is3, 61; E26; Mi2
   Ahijah's new   KF11
   Elijah's   KF19
   fold of Moses'   Ex4
   of fine linen and purple   Est7
   purple, of the Midian kings   Ju8
cloth, blue   Nu4
   chariot lining   E27
   cobwebs will never make   Is59
   round your waist   Is32
   scarlet   Nu4
   violet   Nu4; E27

8 CLOTH AND CLOTHES

cloth-of-gold Ps45
clothed but never warm Hg1
  in scarlet D5
clothes Ps109
  blue E23
  cast lots for Ps22
  David took from his victims SF27
  Joshua was wearing filthy Z3
  large stores of Jos22
  Saul stripped off his SF19
  symbolizing guilt Z3
  tattered cast-off Je38
  ten changes of Ju15
  the elders rent their Jos7
  thirty changes of Ju15
  torn Le13
clouts, old cast off Je38
coat So5
  long-sleeved Gen37
  of many colours Gen37
  of mail CS26; Ne4; Is59; Je46, 51
collar Ps133; Is52
  of jewels Ps73
cord Na1
  let us wind round our heads KF20
  linen E27, 40
  scarlet Jos2
  silver Ec12
  white and purple Est1
coverlet Is14
cross-dressing, prohibition of De22
crown. SS1, 12; KS11
  golden Est7; Ps21
  jewelled Z9
  Queen Vashti's Est1
  royal Est6
curtain So1; Is40
  rings, silver Est1
  tabernacle Ex26
  tent Je4, 10, 49; H3
  white, green and blue Est1

8 CLOTH AND CLOTHES

drawers, linen Ex28ff; E44
diadem Job29
dress So1, 5
  brocade E16
  fine Is3
  for men and women De22
  linen, lawn E16
dyed attire upon their heads E23
embroidered, richly Ps45
embroidery Ex28ff
  Egyptian E27
  rich and scarlet SS1
ephod surplice E25, 28ff
fabric, coloured and rolled E27
fig leaves, aprons of Gen3
flax Pro31; Is42
  and wool together De22
  line of E40
fuller KS18
garment, Babylonish Jos7
  broidered E26
  of divers colours SS13
  of splendour Is61
  put on thy beautiful Is52
  rough Z13
  seized in pledge Am2
  shared out Ps22
  stained Le13
  wear out like a Is50
  wears into tatters Is51
gauze Is3
girdle KF2; Pro31; Is3, 11, 22
  linen Je13; E16, 23
  leather KS1
goat's hair Ex25ff; SF19
greaves, Goliath wore in his legs SF17
habergeon Ne4; Job41
hangings for the grove, the women wove KS23
  tent Je49
  white, green and blue or violet Est1
hat D3

8 CLOTH AND CLOTHES

head-band   Is3
helmet   SF17; CS26; Ps60, 108; Is3, 59; Je46; E23, 27, 38
kerchief   E13
  linen   Is3
latchet, shoe   Is5
lawn dress material   E16
leather apron   KS1
  cords of   Ho11
  lining, palanquin   So3
linen   Ex25ff; Pro7, 31
  bonnet   E44
  breeches   E44
  clothed in   D10, 12
  cord   E40
  drawers   E44
  dress   E16
  dressed in   E9ff, 44
  Egyptian   E27
  embroidered   E27
  ephod   SF2, 22; SS6; CF15
  fine   CS2; Est1; Is3; E16,27
    of Egypt   Pro7
    she maketh   Pro31
  girdle   Je13; E16
  kerchief   Is3
  patterned   E27
  robes of fine   CF15
  thirty lengths of   Ju14
  thread   E40
  turban   E44
  workers, guild of   CF4
  yarn   KF10
lining, chariot   E27
  palanquin   So3
livery, attendants' and cup-bearers'   KF10; CS9
loin-cloth   E26
  sacking   Is3
mail, coat of   SF17
mantle   SF15, 28; KS2; Ez9; Is3; Mi2
  from Shinar   Jos7
  priestly   Ex28ff; Le8

8 CLOTH AND CLOTHES

mend, a time to tear and a time to   Ec3
mitre   Z3
muffler   Is3
needlework of divers colours   Ju5
net   E12
plate-armour   SF15
porpoise-hide   Ex25ff
purple and fine linen   Pro31
  stuff, seat of   So3
rags, old rotten   Je38
robe, a fold of his   Hg2
  brocade   E16, 26
  Esther's royal   Est5
  for the ministers of Baal   Ks10
  fragrant   Ps45
  he tucked up, and ran   KF18
  invest him with your   Is22
  Joseph's   Gen37
  long-sleeved   Gen37; SS13
  of coarse hair   Z13
  of Job's judgement   Job29
  of violet and white   Est7
  priestly   Ne7
  pull off the   Mi2
  rent my   Ez9
  royal   KF22; CS18; Est6
  shook out a fold of my   Ne5
  tie it in a fold of your   E5
robed in purple   D5
sackcloth   Ps30, 35, 69; Is15, 20, 22, 32, 37, 50; Je6, 49; La2; E7, 27; D9; Joe1; Am8; Jon3
  David wore   CF21
  for Jacob   Gen37
  gird themselves with   Is15
  gird up your loins with   Is32
  is my clothing   Ps69
  let us wear   KF20
  put on   SS3
  stitched together   Job16
  worn for fasting   Ne9
  worn for mourning   Est4

8 CLOTH AND CLOTHES

sacking, loin cloth of   Is3
saddle cloth   Ju5
  woollen   E27
sandals   KF2; So7; Is5, 20; E16, 24
  as symbol of property exchange   Ru4
  of stout hide   E16
sash   Pro31; Is22
  priestly   Ex28ff
scarf of gauze   Is3
scarlet and rich embroideries   SS1
  clothed in   Pro31
  dress yourself in   Je4
sew, a time to rend and a time to   Ec3
shirt   D3
shoes   KF2; Ps108; So7; Is5; E16, 24; Am2, 8
  badger-skin   E16
silk   E16
  and purple clothing   Pro31
skins, tunics of   Gen3
skirt   Is47; Je13; La1; Na2
  flounced   Is3
stomacher   Is
stuff, gorgeous   E27
surplice, ephod   Ex25, 28ff
swaddling clothes   E16
tapestry   Pro7, 31
tent covering   Je4
  curtain   So1; Is54; H3
thong, sandal   Is5
thread   Job7
  linen   E40
  scarlet   Le14; Nu19
  violet, for tassels   Nu15
tire (headdress)   E24
tow   Is1
trousers   D3
tunic   SS20
  chequered   Ex28ff
  priestly   Le8
  skin   Gen3
turban   Job29; Is3; E23; Z3

87

8 CLOTH AND CLOTHES

turban, linen   E44
   priestly   Ex28ff; Le8
uniform, officer's blue   E23
veil   Ps119; So4ff; Is3, 25; E13
   flowing   Is3
   hold it out   Ru3
   of Moses   Ex34ff
   of Solomon's temple   KF6
   of Tamar   Gen38
   of the tabernacle   Ex26ff; Le16
   sacred   Le4
   to cover the Ark   Nu4
vestments, fine   Z3
   priestly   Ex28ff; Le8ff
   wove in honour of Asherah   KS23
   violet and purple, draped in   Je10
   officers dressed in   E23
wardrobe   Je38
   keeper of   Ks22
widow's weeds worn by Tamar   Gen38
wimple   Is3
wool   KS3; Pro31; Is1, 51; E27, 34, 44; D7; Ho2
   and flax together   De22
   coarse   E27
   saddle-cloth   E27
wrist band   E13
yarn, blue   CS2
   clothes made with two kinds of   De22
   crimson, purple and violet   CS2
   violet, purple and scarlet   Ex25ff

NEW TESTAMENT

apparel, I have coveted no man's   A20
apron   A19
belt, leather   Mw3
camel hair coat   Mw3
cloak, bring my   PTS4
   fold them up like a   LH1
   him that taketh away thy   L6

8 CLOTH AND CLOTHES

cloak, hole in a new   L5
   let him have your   Mw5
   purple   J19
   sell to buy a sword   L22
   shook out the skirts of his   A18
   threw off his   Mk10
   touched the hem of his cloak   Mw9; Mk5f
   wrap around you   A12
cloaks, carpeted the road with their   M21; L19
   spread their   Mk11
   threw on the colt   L19
   yelling and waving their   A22
coat, he must not turn back for his   M24; Mk13
   let him have your   Mw5
   not to take a second   Mw10; Mk6; L7
   of camel's hair   Mw3; Mk1
   of mail   PE6
   patch an old   Mw9
   when a man takes your   L6
   without seam   J19
   wrapped about him   J21
coats that Dorcas used to make   A9
cloth, funeral   J11
   linen   Mk14
   patch of unshrunk   Mw9; Mk2
clothe you, he will not   Mw6
clothed in purple and scarlet   Rev17
clothes became dazzling white   Mw17; Mk9; L9
   decked out in expensive   PTF2
   divided by lots   Mw27; J19
   happy the man who keeps on his   Rev16
   he wore no   L8
   in the way, spread their   L19
   put away anxious thoughts about   Mw6; L12
   put on the ass   Mw21
   soldiers took possession of his   J19
   they divided among them his   Mk15; L23
   tore off the prisoners'   A16
   when they heard of it they tore their   A14
   who touched my   Mk5
clothing, cast lots for my   J19

8 CLOTH AND CLOTHES

clothing contaminated with sensuality   Lju1
  gay   LJ2
  of camel's hair   Mw3
  of John the Baptist   Mw3
  white   Rev3
cloths of purple and scarlet, cargoes of   Rev18
curtain of the temple   Mw27; Mk15; L23
  sanctuary   LH9
dress, fine linen   Rev19
  in becoming manner, women must   PTF2
dressed in purple   L16
fine clothes are moth-eaten, your   LJ5
garment drenched in blood   Rev19
  you have put on Christ as a   PG3
  young man clothed in a long white   Mk16
garments, Jesus laid aside his   J13
  moth-eaten   LJ5
  that suit God's chosen people   PCO3
  they parted his   Mk15
  two men in dazzling   L24
girdle, leathern   Mw3
  of skin   Mk1
goatskins   LH11
leather belt   Mw3
  girdle   Mw3
linen cloth   Mk14; J19f
  clothed in fine   Rev19
  dressed in the finest   L16
  dress, fine   Rev15, 19
  pure white   Rev15
  sheet   Mw27; Mk15
  silk and fine   Rev18
  wrapped his body in   L23
  wrapping   L23f
mantle, they dressed Jesus in a scarlet   Mw27
moth-eaten clothes   LJ5
    treasure   Mw6
napkin   L19
purple, a rich man dressed in   L16
  and scarlet, clothed in   Rev17
  dressed him in   Mk15

8 CLOTH AND CLOTHES

purple fabric   A16
 raiment, a man clothed in soft   L7
  became shining   Mk9
  parted among them   J19
  was white and glistening, his   L9
  white as the light   Mw17
robe, fetch a   L15
  scarlet   Mw27
  sent him back to Pilate dressed in a gorgeous   L23
  the high priest tore his   Mw26; Mk14
  wearing a white   Mk16; Rev6
robed all in white   Rev3f, 7
  down to his feet   Rev1
  in fine linen   Rev15
robes, a man in shining   A10
  love to walk up and down in long   Mk12; L20
  royal   A12
  tasselled   Mw23
  washed their   Rev7
sackcloth of hair   Rev6
  witnesses dressed in   Rev11
sail-cloth, sheet of   Mw27; Mk15; A10f
satin, a man dressed in silk and   Mw11; L7
shabby clothes, a poor man in   LJ2
sheepskins   LH11
sheet, linen   Mw27; Mk15
  of sail-cloth   Mw27; Mk15; A10f
shirt, let him have your   L6
  sues you for your   Mw5
  that Dorcas used to make   A9
  the man with two   L3
shoes   Mw10
  not fit to take off his   Mw3
silk and fine linen, cargoes of   Rev18
  and satin, a man dressed in   M11; L7
skins, dressed in   LH11
tunic, seamless   J19
veil of the sanctuary   LH9
  of the temple   Mw27; Mk15; L23
wearing of gold   LPF3
well-dressed man   LJ2

8 CLOTH AND CLOTHES

women must dress in becoming manner   PTF2
wool, scarlet   LH9
  snow-white   Rev1

9   *Culture and Custom*

OLD TESTAMENT

Ahaz, sundial of   Is38
aliens to be treated as native-born   E47
allegory of a thistle sent to a cedar   KS14
   speak to the Israelites in   E17
annals of Solomon   KF11
   of the kings of Israel   KF15f, 22; KS10, 13ff
   of the kings of Judah   KF14f, 22; KS8, 12, 14ff, 20f, 23f
   of the kings of Media and Persia   Est10
Aramaic language   D2
   speak in   Is36
Ashkelon, proclaim it not in the streets of   SS1
baton of honour   Je48
belt of honour   SS21
blessing of Solomon   CS6
book, everyone who is written in the   D12
   of genealogies   Ne7
   of Jashar   Jos10; SS1
   of Jeremiah concerning Babylon   Je51
     dictated to Baruch   Je36
   of life   Ps69; Is4
   of the law of God   Jos24
   of the law of Moses   Jos23
   of the Lord   Is34
   of the upright   SS1
   of the wars of the Lord   Nu21
   of truth   D11
   roll of a   E2f
   scroll of a   Je36
   seal the   D12
   these words written in a   Je45
   write all I have said in a   Je30
borrower and lender   Is24
boundary stone   Job24
bribe, snaps his fingers at a   Is33
   your rulers love a   Is1
bribery, officials accepting   KS16; Ez4; Ne6; Am5; Mi3

9 CULTURE AND CUSTOM

bribery, prohibition of Ex23
bruised reed, Egypt KS18
calendar KF4; Z1, 7
census of David SS24; CF21
  of Israel CF9
    and Judah SS24
  of Israelites Ex30; Nu26
  of Levites not recorded Nu1
  of male first-born Nu3
  of young Israeli men Niff
chain of honour Pro1
champions there were none Ju5
chemarims, heathen priests so-called Zp1
chronicle of daily events Est6
  royal Persian Est2
college at Jerusalem KS22
commission for Joshua Nu27
confession, make your Jos7
  of Acham Jos7
  of Ezra Ex9ff
  of Nehemiah Ne1
Gentiles, bring judgement to the Is42
  eat defiled bread among the E4
  forbidden to enter La1
  glory of the Is66
  horns of, in Zechariah's vision Z1
  Israel among the Ho8
  light to the Is49
  my name shall be great among the Ma1
  proclaim among the Joe3
  remnant of Jacob shall be among the Mi5
  their seed known among the Is61
  thy seed shall inherit Is54
  word came against the Je46
  Zion among the La2
gifts to the poor, days for giving Est9
grudge of Esau Gen27
guilt for unfaithfulness Nu5
heart, harden not your De15
  prompted not by my own Nu16
heathen, all the isles of the Zp2

9 CULTURE AND CUSTOM

heathen, ambassador sent among the   Ob1
  day of the Lord is near upon all the   Ob1
  dwell among the   E31
  gathered together, the wealth of all the   Z9
  it shall be a time of the   E30
  possession of the   E36
  priests, wipe out the name of   Zp1
  realms, break the power of   Hg2
  reproach among the   Joe2
  scattered them among the   E36
  set my glory among the   E39
  should not rule over them   Joe2
  thresh in anger   H3
Hebrew, Jonah answered, I am a   Jon1
  language   Is36
history, to brood over past   Is43
ink   E9
inkhorn   E9
interest, not to charge   De23
investment of Eleazar   Nu20
Jashar, book of   Jos10; SS1
knowledge of good and evil   Gen2
lament of Jeremiah   CS35
language, Aramaic   KS18; Ez4; Is36; D2
  Hebrew   KS18; Is36
    shouted in   CS32
  of Canaan, cities of Egypt speaking the   Is19
  of the Chaldeans   D1
  of the Jews   Is36
  turn to the people a pure   Zp3
lender and borrower   Is24
letter of Artaxerxes to Ezra   Ez7
  of Jeremiah to Babylon   Je29
  to Artaxerxes   Ex4ff
  to Asaph   Ne2
levy, enforced   KF4
literature of the Chaldeans   D1
living and the dead, Aaron between the   Nu16
lot fell to Jonah   Jon1
lots cast   Est3
  by the sailors   Jon1

9 CULTURE AND CUSTOM

lots cast to decide who should live in Jerusalem   Ne11
memorial in the temple of the Lord   Z6
money-lenders strip my people bare   Is3
month, Abib   Ex13; De16
  Adar   Ez6; Est3
  Bul   KF6
  Chisleu   Ne1; Z7
  Elul   Ne6
  Ethanim   KF8
  Kislev   Ne1; Z7
  Nisan   Ne1; Est3
  Sebat, Shebat   Z1
  Sivan   Est7
  Tebeth   Est2
  Ziv   KF6
name of the Lord, misuse of the   De5
night watch   Ps59, 90
orator, eloquent   Is3
peculiar people, to be his   De26
pedigree declared   Nu1ff
pen   Is8; E9
  and ink at his waist   E9
petition, present to the Lord   Je36
pilgrims, clamour of   Ps42
plan of the temple   E43
pledge, persons held in, to be released   Ne10
  for food, sons and daughters given as   Ne5
poem about you, they shall take up a   Mi2
  of Solomon   KF8
poet, the skill of a   Ps71
pottage, birthright sold for   Gen25
prayer of David   SS7
  of Ezra   Ez9ff
  of Habbakuk   H3
  of Hannah   SF2
  of Solomon   CS6ff; KF8
presents sent to one another   Est9
procession into the sanctuary   Ps68
  round the altar   Ps26
proverb, shall become a   De28
proverbs current in Israel   E12

9 CULTURE AND CUSTOM

proverbs, Solomon uttered 3000 KF4
provinces ruled by Ahasuerus Est1
public duty, newly married exempt from De24
publish in the palaces of Ashdod Am3
purifying the women Est2
Rahab as personification of excessive pride Job9, 26
  hacked in pieces Is51
  quelled, as Egypt Is30
refuge, cities of Nu35; De19
register of first-born males Nu3
  of genealogy Ne7
registration of Israel CF9
  of the Israelites Ex30
remission of debts De15
  year of De15
restitution for wronging another Nu5
riddle, riddles, how I read the Ps49
  of Samson Ju14
  of things past Ps77
  gift of explaining D5
righteous, let me die Nu23
rod, Aaron's Ex7
  produced almonds Nu17
  for each tribe Nu17
  lift up your Ex14
  Moses' Ex4; Nu20
  of the chosen man Nu17
  struck the rock Nu20
roll of a book Je36; E2ff
  of exiled captives Ne7
  of Israel E13
  of nations Ps87
  writing Is8
rule of life De31
rules in writing Ho8
sandal, pull off his foot De25
scapegoat presented by Aaron Le16
science, understanding D1
scribe, position of Ne8, 12
scroll, an allegorical flying Z5
  I swallowed the E3

9 CULTURE AND CUSTOM

scroll, king Jehoiakim cut and burnt the   Je36
  register the country on   Jos18
  rolled up in a   Is34
  tied up in a   Ho13
  writing   Je36
  written on both sides   E2ff
seal, shaping clay with a   Job38
seamanship in vain   Ps107
seven pillars of wisdom   Pro9
shadow moved backwards   Is38
  of the hills, looking like men   Ju9
Shamgar, in the days of   Ju5
share and share alike   SF30
  the spoils with your kinsmen   Jos22
shepherd of my people   SS5
shibboleth, if he could not pronounce   Ju12
shoe loose, house of him who has his   De25
sign put up by the door   Is57
signet   Is3
  make thee as a   Hg2
  of Darius over the mouth of the lions' den   D6
signet-ring   Je22
  the royal   Est3f, 7
similitudes, I have used   Ho12
Solomon, sayings of   Pro1ff
song at the house of the Lord   KS11
  of David   SS22
songs of Solomon number 1005   KF4
speech, a time for silence and a time for   Ec3
  recover the power of   E24
  thick and difficult   E3
splintered cane, Egypt   Is36
staff, Aaron's   Rx7
  for each tribe   Nu17
  Moses'   Ex4; Nu20
  of Judah   Gen38
  of the chosen man shall sprout   Nu17
  produced ripe almonds   Nu17
  raise high   Ex14
  struck the rock   Nu20
  the stay and the   Is3

9 CULTURE AND CUSTOM

statute, Joshua drew up   Jos24
strength of Israel   SF15
stone, tablets of   Ex24, 31
sun dial of Ahaz   Is38
supplication of Ezra   Ex9ff
  of Solomon   CS6
swimmer spreads his hands to swim   Is25
Syrian language, Aramaic   Is36
tablet, folding   E37
  inscribe the vision on   H2
  of stone   Ex24, 31; De9f
  separate leaves of   E37
  wooden   E37
  writing   Is8, 30; E37
thorn in your side   Nu33
token, Ark of the   Jos3ff
  of good faith   Jos2
true, everything he says comes   SF9
truth, water of contention brings out the   Nu5
uncircumcised, die the deaths of the   E28
  in the midst of the   E31
  into the nether parts of the earth, gone down   E32
  laid with the   E32
  never enter you again   Is52
  rascals, these   SF14
understanding, display your   De4
undertaking, to bring first-born of sons and cattle   Ne10
  to bring first kneading of dough   Ne10
  to bring first-fruits   Ne10
unsandalled man, house of the   De25
upright, book of the   Jos10; SS1
usurers lord it over them   Is3
usury, not put his money to   Ps15
  taker and giver of   Is24
wage to be paid the same day   De24
watches of the night   Ps63
wheel of fortune   Pro20
wisdom and wealth promised to Solomon   CS1
  choose men of   De1
  display your   De4
  seven pillars of   Pro9

9 CULTURE AND CUSTOM

wisdom, spirit of   De34
  who gave him lessons in   Is40
wise men, Pharaoh's   Ex7
  women   SS14, 20
witness against yourselves   Jos24
  altar of   Jos22
work not to be done on the sabbath   De5

NEW TESTAMENT

alms before men, take heed that ye do not your   Mw6
apostles, the twelve   Mw10
arguments of the wise are futile   PCF3
arrogant, God sets his face against the   LPF5
assembly, dealt with by statutory   A19
astrology   Mw2
authority, speak with   Tt2
barbarian, no question here of   PCo3
birthright, Esau sold his   LH12
book in John's vision, ate the   Rev10
  in the angel's hand   Rev10
  it is written of me in the volume of the   LH10
  of Hosea   Pr9
  of life   PPs4; Rev3
  of Moses, have you never read in the   Mk12
  of psalms   L20
  of the prophecies of Isaiah   L3
  sealed   Rev4f
  what thou seest, write in a   Rev1
  worthy to read the   Rev5
books, Paul's   PTS4
  were opened   Rev20
bread alone, man cannot live on   L4
bribe from Paul, Felix had hopes of a   A24
  offered the soldiers a substantial   Nw28
brotherhood, about love for our   ThF4
cast lots for his clothes   Mw27; Mk15; L23; J19
census, at the time of the   A5
  throughout the Roman world   L2
character, a balanced   LJ1

9 CULTURE AND CUSTOM

charity, do not announce   Mw6
  sell your possessions and give in   L12
  the greatest of these is   PCF13
chatter, avoid empty   PTS2
chosen race   LPF2
Christian movement   A19, 24
  of me, to make a   A26
Christianity, discussing the rudiments of   LH6
Christians, the disciples first got the name of   A11
circumcised, let him not be   PCF7
circumcision, beware of   PPs3
  is nothing, uncircumcision is nothing   PG6
  is of the heart, true   PR2
  or uncircumcision is neither here nor there   PCF7
  true, not the external mark in the flesh   PR2
  what is the value of   PR3
cleverness, bring to nothing the   PCF1
collection in aid of God's people   PCF16
commandments of men, they teach as doctrines the   Mw15
common fund for the benefit of the poor   PR15
commonwealth of Israel   PE2
concision, beware of the   PPs3
conduct in the body, due to him for his   PCS5
conscience, called in question by another man's   PCF10
  convicted on their own   J8
  love which springs from a good   PTF1
  train myself to keep a clear   A24
conversation be gracious, let your   PCo4
convert, you travel on sea and land to make one   Mw23
conviction in his own mind, should have reached   PR14
Council, a respected member of the   Mk15
  Jewish   J3
  Joseph a member of the   L23
  of elders   A22
councillors   L23
cross, doctrine of the   PCF1
custom house   Mw9
debate, full of   PR1
debater, where is your subtle   PCF1
deceit defiles the man   Mk7
deceptions, they revel in their own   LPS2

101

9 CULTURE AND CUSTOM

deeds, not words   LJ2
disciples followed Jesus   Mw8
   gathered round   Mw5
disputing about words   PTS2
divine folly is wiser than the wisdom of men   PCF1
   weakness is stronger than man's strength   PCF1
doctrine of the Nicolaitans   Rev2
doctrines, give up erroneous   PTF1
doubter is like a heaving sea   LJ1
elder, never be harsh with an   PTF5
   ordination as an   PTF4
elders of the nation   Mw21, 26, 28; Mk8, 11, 14f; L7, 9, 20, 22;
     A4, 14f, 20, 23ff; PTF4f; Tt1; LJ5; LPF5
   appointed in each congregation   A14, 20
   I appeal to the   LPF5
   in each town, institute   Tt1
   laying on of hands of the   PTF4
   send for the   LJ5
   rejected of the   Mk8
   who commit sins   PTF5
   worthy of a double stipend   PTF5
envy, fine thing to deserve honest   PG4
Epicurean philosopher   A17
epistle, commandant to the governor   A23
   of commendation   PCS3
estate among them, divided his   L15
evangelist   PE4
experts in goodness but simpletons in evil   PR6
fables, cunningly devised   LPS1
   ears turned unto   PTS4
   give heed to   PTF1
   Jewish   TE1
   old wives'   PTF4
faith divorced from deeds is barren   LJ2
   excludes pride   PR3
figures of speech, I have been using   J16
folly defiles the man   Mk7
fool, let no one take me for a   PCS11
foolishness defiles the man   Mk7
fools, how gladly you bear with   PCS11
fortitude in suffering   LPF2

9 CULTURE AND CUSTOM

freedmen, synagogue of   A6
friend of the world, enemy of God   LJ4
friendly advice, give him   ThS3
genealogies, interminable   PTF1
  steer clear of   Tt3
Gentile origin, greetings to our brothers of   A15
    she was of   Mk7
Gentiles, a light to lighten the   L2; A13
  and Jews, he has made the two one   PE2
  deliver him to the   Mw20
  Galilee of the   Mw4
  he shall be delivered unto the   L18
  hindering us from speaking to the   ThF2
  mystery among the   PCo1
  Jerusalem shall be trodden down of the   L21
  Paul an apostle to the   PG2
  seek after all these things   Mw6
  shall deliver him to the   Mk10
  to proclaim his Son among the   PG1
  will he go to teach the   J7
gibberish to me, his words will be   PCF14
gifts we possess differ   PR12
giveth, he that, let him do it with simplicity   PR12
glory and honour, crowned with   LH2
God loves a cheerful giver   PCS9
godless world, do not set your heart on the   LJ2
gospel, Gentiles should believe the   A15
  he proclaimed the   L4
  must be proclaimed before the end   Mk13
  of God   Mk1
  of the kingdom will be proclaimed   Mw24
  set apart for the service of the   PR1
  to make known the mystery of the   PE6
  twelve whom he would send out to proclaim the   Mk3
Greek, Hebrew and Latin, inscription in   J19
  in letters of   L23
  language   A9, 21
  those who spoke   A6
greeting, do not give him a   LJS1
handwriting of ordinances, blotting out the   Pco2

9 CULTURE AND CUSTOM

heathen at heart and deaf to the truth   A7
  do as much, even the   Mw5
  do not go babbling on like the   Mw6
  Galilee   Mw4
  to run after, these things are for the   Mw6; L12
  revelation to the   L2
Hebrew born and bred   PPs3
  in letters of   L23
  language   A21
  Latin and Greek, inscription in   J19
  so am I   PCS11
  those who spoke   A6
heir under guardians and trustees   PG4
heresies, import disastrous   LPS2
heresy, they call Christianity   A24
Herodian party and partisans   Mw22; Mk3, 12
hidden truth, I may know ever   PCF13
high-minded lovers of pleasure   PTS3
history, he fixed the epochs of their   A17
hospitable without complaining, be   PG1
human invention, the gospel is no   PG1
humble, God favours the   LPF5
humility, wrap yourselves in the garment of   LPF5
ideas belonging to this world   PCo2
idle habits, hold aloof from   ThS3
ink   PCS3; LJS1; LJT1
inscription, an altar bearing the   A17
  fastened to the cross   Mw27; J19
insight, love may grow in knowledge and   PPs1
inspired wisdom, could not hold their own against the   A6
instinct like brute beasts   LJu1
institution, submit yourselves to every human   LPF2
instruct and admonish each other   PCo3
integrity as a coat of mail   Pe6
Israel my people   Mw2
Jewish converts out of control   TF1
  council   J3
  matters, an expert in all   A26
Jewry, teaching throughout all   L23
Jews, Peter an apostle to the   PG2
Judaism, former convert to   A6

9 CULTURE AND CUSTOM

key of knowledge   L11
knowledge into words, can put the deepest   PCF12
   of every kind, equipped with   PR15
   of God, rears its proud head against the   PCS10
   of the truth, incapable of reaching   PTS3
   shall vanish away   PCF13
   taken away the key of   L11
   the contradiction of so-called   PTF6
   with self control, supplement your   LPS1
language not an ambiguous blend of yes and no   PCS1
   spoken, bewildered, each heard his own   A2
Latin Greek and Hebrew, inscription in   J19
   in letters of   L23
learning, where is your man of   PCF1
leaven of the Pharisees, beware the   Mw16; L12
lecture-hall, held discussions daily in the   A19
letter from the apostles to the Gentiles   A15
   my purpose in writing this   PCS13
   to the governor from the commandant   A23
   written not with ink   PCS3
   written on the pages of the heart   PCS3
letters from the council of the elders   A22
   of authorization, Saul applied for   A9
   of introduction, do we need   PCS3
liberate Israel, we were hoping that he was the man to   L24
libertines, synagogue of the   A6
licence to speak, women have no   PCF14
light of nature, by the   PR2
like fathers, like sons   A7
living stone rejected by me   LPF2
lots cast for his clothing   Mw27; Mk15; L23; J19
   to decide a replacement for Judas   A1
love must not be a matter of words   LJF3
lower nature, behaviour that belongs to   PG5
manners, evil communications corrupt good   PCF15
meditate upon these things   PPs4
meetings, women should not address the   PCF14
   do more harm than good, your   PCF11
   not staying away from our   LH10
mercenary greed, past masters in   LPS2
Messiah, Paul's cogent proof that Jesus was the   A9

9 CULTURE AND CUSTOM

minds are plunged in darkness, their misguided   PR1
  have grown as hard as stone   PE4
  of disbelievers, nothing is pure to   Tt1
missionary to the Gentiles   PR11
modesty and respect, make your defence with, CPF3
  that comes of wisdom   LJ3
morals and self control, questions of   A24
mythology, stop their ears and turn to   PTS4
myths, have nothing to do with godless   PTF4
  interminable   PTF1
  Jewish   TF1
nation, elders of the   Mw21, 26, 28; Mk8, 11, 14f; L7, 9, 20, 22;
      A4, 14, 20, 23ff; PTF4f; Tt1; LJ5; LPF5
  you are a dedicated   LPF2
national religion, the practice of our   PG1
nature, depths of God's own   PCF2
  lower, behaviour that belongs to   PG5
Nicolaitans, doctrine of the   Rev2
notebooks, Paul's   PTS4
notions, pagans with good-for-nothing   PE4
obscure passages, Paul's letters contain   LPS3
offence, we avoid giving   PCS6
old wives tales   PTF4
ordination as an elder   PTF4
overbearing, bishop must not be   TF1
pagan, treat him as you would a   Mw18
pagans can recognize as good, even   LPF2
paper   LJS1
parchment, Paul's   PTS4
passages which referred to Jesus in the scriptures   L24
passing age, god of this   PCS4
pay, worker earns his   PTF5
pen   LJT1
peculiar people, ye are a   LPF2
   zealous of good works   Tt2
petitions, prayers and intercessions offered for all   PTF2
Pharisaic party   A15, 23
Pharisee   Mw3, 5, 9, 12, 15f, 19, 21ff, 27; Mk2, 7f, 10, 12;   L5ff, 1ff;
      J1, 3f, 7ff, 11f, 18; A5, 15, 23, 26; PPs3
philosophers, Epicurean and Stoic   A17
philosophy, vain deceit   PCo2

9 CULTURE AND CUSTOM

plain speaking, no figure of speech   J16
prayers for appearance sake   Mk12
preaching in all the towns   A8
presbytery of elders   PTF4
proclaim the message   PTS4
profane babblings, shun   PTS3
propagandist for foreign deities   A17
proselyte, ye compass sea and land to make one   Mw23
proselytes, both Jews and   A2
  followed Paul and Barnabas, many   A13
proverbs, I have spoken in   J16
public reading of the scriptures   PTF4
  speaking and teaching, to refrain from   A4
publican, Matthew the   Mw10
publicans and sinners   Mw9
pupil content to share his teacher's lot   Mw10
purification, dispute about   J3
qualification comes from God   PCS3
race, all the runners run the   PCF9
reasoning powers become atrophied   PTF6
religion, let us hold fast to the   LH4
  men who pour scorn on   LJu1
  men who scoff at   LPS3
  points of disagreement about   A25
  the enemies of   LJu1
  who preserve the outward form of   PTS3
resurrection, Sadducees deny there is any   Mk12; L20; A23
  whose wife will she be at the   Mk12
reverence and respect, to those to whom they are due   PR13
rich man will disappear like a flower   LJ1
righteousness, the garland of   PTS4
ringleader of the Nazarene sect   A24
roll of the living   PPs4; Rev3, 13, 17, 20f, 23
Roman, rescued him, having understood that he was a   A23
Sadducean party   A5
Sadducees   Mw3, 16, 22; Mk12; L20; A4f, 23
Sanhedrin, Israeli senate of   A5
searcher of men's hearts and thoughts   Rev2
seal, delivered under my own   PR15
  of God on the forehead   Rev9

9 CULTURE AND CUSTOM

seal upon us, set his   PCS1
sealed book   Rev4
seals, seven   Rev5ff
sect, no one has a good word to say about this   A28
  of our religion, the straitest   A26
  of the Nazarenes   A24
self-control with fortitude   LPS1
self-deceived, we are   LJF1
schemes, dupes of their deceitful   PE4
science falsely so called, opposition of   PTF6
schoolmaster   PG3
scraps from the rich man's table   L16
scribe   Mw2, 5, 7ff, 12f, 15ff, 20, 23, 26; Mk1f, 7ff, 14f;
    L5, 9, 11, 15, 20, 22f; J8; A4, 6, 23
scripture has its use, every inspired   PTS3
scriptures diligently, you study   J5
  he opened their minds to understand the   L24
scroll, ate the   Rev10
  in John's vision   Rev5ff, 10
  in the hand of the angel   Rev10
  of the prophet Isaiah   L4
  sealed with seven seals   Rev5ff
  write what you see on a   Rev1
  written of me in the   LH10
scrutiny, bishops, deacons, must undergo   PTF3
shook hands upon it   PG2
simpletons in evil, experts in goodness   PR16
snobbery, you must never show   LJ2
sophistries, we demolish   PCS10
speculation and controversies over the law are pointless   Tt3
  breed quarrels   PTS2
speech, use wholesome   Tt2
spirit, Sadducees deny that there is any   A23
  of error   LJF4
  of truth   L4ff; LJF4
spokesmen, Moses has never lacked   A15
stipend, elders worthy of a double   PTF5
Stoic philosophers   A17
study how best to talk to each person   PCo4
stumbling-block, not to find me a   Mw11

9 CULTURE AND CUSTOM

stumbling-block to one of these little ones   Mw18
  to the Jews   PCF1
symbolic, things that happened to them were   PCF10
tablets of stone, written in   PCS3
tales artfully spun   LPS1
teach yourself, do you fail to   PR2
teacher, bishop must be a good   PTF3
  I do not permit a woman to be a   PTF2
  should be a good servant of the Lord   PTS2
  should employ his gift in teaching   PR12
  the law was a   PG3
  tolerant and gentle in discipline   PTS1f
  you have one   Mw23
  you need no other   LJF2
teachers at Antioch, prophets and   A13
  by this time you ought to be   LH5
  false   LPS2
  God has appointed   PCF12
  his gifts, some to be   PE4
  not many of you should become   LJ3
  of moral law   PTF1
  say Elijah must come first   Mk9
  surrounded by   L2
  to tickle their fancy   PTS4
  without understanding   PTF1
teaching, behaviour flouts the wholesome   PTF1
  followed step by step   PTS3
  infection of their   PTS1
  requires patience   PTS4
  the gift of   PR12
  things they should not   Tt1
  to move his hearers with wholesome   Tt1
  until I arrive, devote your attention to   PTF4
  whirled about by every fresh gust of   PE4
  all sorts of outlandish   LH13
  traditions of man-made   PCo2
temperate in all things   Tt2
tests for elders   Tt1
think on these things   PPs4
thinking has ended in futility, all their   PR1
tongue, a small member, can make huge claims   LJ13

9 CULTURE AND CUSTOM

tongues of ecstasy   A19; PCF13f
  they will speak in strange   Mk16
traditions of my ancestors   PG1
  of my fathers, zealous in the   PG1
treat others as you would like them to treat you   L6
truth, be straightforward in your proclamation of   PTS2
  belong to the realm of   LJ3
  blind to the   PR11
  by our grasp of   PCS6
  loins girt about with   PE6
  lost their grip of the   PTF6
  recommend ourselves by declaring the   PCS6
  scripture has its use for teaching the   PTS3
  what is   J18
tutor, the law was a kind of   PG3
uncircumcised, you who are called the   PE2
uncircumcision or circumcision, neither here nor there   PCF7
  or circumcision is nothing   PG6
understand by instinct like brute beasts   LJu1
  pour abuse upon things they do not   LPS2; LJu1
understanding, wisdom and spiritual   PCo1
vanity, speak great swelling words of   LPS2
verbal questions and quibbles   PTF6
virtue with knowledge, supplement your   LPS1
vow, hair cut off because of a   A18
washing before the meal   Mk7; L11
wickedness defiles the man   Mk7
widow's mite   Mk12; L21
will that the universe might be brought into a unity   PE1
wisdom and spiritual understanding   PCo1
  and vision, spiritual powers of   PE1
  become a fool to gain true   PCF3
  demonic   LJ3
  fleshly   PCS1
  Greeks look for   PCF1
  I speak of God's hidden   PCF2
  if you fall short in   LJ1
  it has an air of   PCo2
  of this world is foolishness with God   PCF3
  they boast of their   PR1
wise by the standards of this passing age   PCF3

9 CULTURE AND CUSTOM

wise man now, where is your   PCF1
  or clever, who among you is   LJ3
  speech, gift of   PCF12
  you are, do not keep thinking how   PR12
wit's end, I am at my   PG4
words as your sword   PE6
  gone astray in a wilderness of   PTF1
  so secret that human lips may not repeat them   PCS12
world, love of the, is enmity to God   LJ4
worldly minds, futile conceit of   PCo2
  standards have ceased to count in our estimate   PCS5
worth of everything, judge the   PCF2
wrangles, quibbles which give rise to endless   PTF6
wreath, to win a fading   PCF9
writing tablet   L1
written, what I have written, I have   J19
yoke-fellow, true   PPs4
zeal for God is an ill-informed zeal   PR10
Zealot party, member of the   Mw10
  Simon the   Mw10; Mk3; L6; A1
zealous in the traditions of my fathers   PG1

10   *Death, Burial and Mourning*

OLD TESTAMENT

anointed the bodies with spices   SF31
ashes, handfuls of   Ex9
  I repent in   Job42
  Mordecai put on   Est4
  over her, Tamar threw   SS13
  sprinkle over yourself   Je6, 25
  wallow themselves in   E27
  wallow thyself in   Je6
beds of sackcloth and ashes   SS21; Est4; Is58
bier heaped with spices   CS16
  of Abner   SS3
bones of Joseph   Ex13
    buried in Shechem   Jos24
  shall lie in the wilderness   Nu4
broke his neck, Eli   SF4
burial beneath an oak   Gen35
  carry him out for   Am6
  ground   KS23; E39
  he alone shall have proper   KF14
  I will grant you   Na1
  man of God at Bethel   KF13
  of Abdon   Ju12
  of Abijah   CS13
  of Abijam   KF15
  of Ahaz   KS16; CS28
  of Ahaziah   KS9; CS22
  of Ahithophel   SS17
  of Amaziah   KS14; CS25
  of Asa   KS15; CS16
  of Asahel   SS2
  of Azariah   KS15
  of Baasha   KF16
  of bones of Joseph   Jos24
  of David   KF2

10 DEATH, BURIAL AND MOURNING

burial of Eleazar   Jos24
  of Elisha   KS13
  of Elon   Ju12
  of Gideon   Ju8
  of the head of Ishbosheth   SS4
  of Hezekiah   CS32
  of Jacob   Gen50
  of Jair   Ju10
  of Jehoahaz   KS13
  of Jehoash   KS14
  of Jehoiada   CS24
  of Jehoshaphat   KF22; CS21
  of Jehu   KS10
  of Jephthah   Ju12
  of Joab   KF2
  of Joash   KS12; CS24
  of Joram   KS8; CS21
  of Joshua   Jos24; Ju2
  of Josiah   Ks23; CS35
  of Jotham   KS15; CS27
  of Manasseh   KS21; CS33
  of Omri   KF16
  of Reheboam   KF14; CS12
  of Samson   Ju16
  of Samuel   SF25
  of Sarah   Gen23
  of Saul and his sons   SF31; SS21
  of Saul's bones   CF10
  of Solomon   KF11; CS9
  of Tola   Ju10
  of Uzziah   CS26
    place among the refuse of mankind   Is53
      of David   Ne3
      of Moses unknown   De34
buried at Topheth   Je7
carcase trodden under feet   Is14
common grave   Je26
corpse trampled underfoot   Is14
corpses lay like offal in the streets   Is10
day of wrath   Je26
dead and living, Aaron stood between   Nu16

10 DEATH, BURIAL AND MOURNING

dead, communicating with the   SF28
  past counting, their bodies lay in heaps   Na3
death, accidental   De19
  by hanging   De21
  by stoning   De13ff
  chafes no more in   Job3
  cords of   Ps116
  dust of   Ps22
  end of childish resentment   Job5
  for adultery   De22
  for dreamers   De22
  for kidnappers   De24
  for losing virginity   De22
  for miscreants   De13
  for own sin only   De24
  for prophets   De13
  for rapists   De22
  for worshipping other gods   De17
  in childbirth   SF4
  insatiable as   H2
  land of   Ps49
  of Aaron   Nu20
  of Abijah   CS13
  of Abijam   KF15
  of Abimelech   Ju9
  of Abinadab   SF31; CF10
  of Abner   SS3
  of Absalom   SS18
  of Adonijah   KF2
  of Ahab   KF22; KS3; CS18
  of Ahaz   KS16; CS28
  of Ahaziah   KS1, 9; CS22
  of Ahithophel   SS17
  of Amasa   SS20
  of Amaziah   KS14; CS25
  of Amon   CS33
  of Asa   KF15; CS16
  of Asahel   SS2
  of Athaliah   KS11
  of Azariah   KS15
  of Baasha   KF16

10 DEATH, BURIAL AND MOURNING

death of Balaam   Nu31
  of Bathsheba's son   SS12
  of Chilion   Ru1
  of David   KF2; CF29
  of Elah   KF16
  of Eleazar   Jos24
  of Eli and his sons   SF4
  of Elimelech   Ru1
  of Elisha   KS13
  of Ezekiel's wife   E24
  of Goliath   SF17; SS21
  of Hazael   KS13
  of Hezekiah   KS20; CS32
  of Ishbosheth   SS4
  of Jehoahaz   KS13, 23
  of Jehoash   KS14
  of Jehoiada   CS24
  of Jehoiakim   KS24
  of Jehoram   KS9
  of Jehoshaphat   KF22; CS21
  of Jehu   KS10
  of Jezebel   KS9
  of Joab   KF2
  of Joash   KS12; CS24
  of Job   Job42
  of Jonathan   SF31; CF10
  of Joram   KS8; CS21
  of Joshua   Jos24; Ju2
  of Josiah   KS23; CS35
  of Jotham   KS15; CS27
  of Hanamiah   Je28
  of Mahlon   Ru1
  of Malchishua   SF31; CF10
  of Manasseh   KS21; CS33
  of Menahem   KS15
  of Miriam   Nu20
  of Moses   De34
  of Nabal   SF25
  of Naboth   KF21
  of Nadab   KF15
  of Omri   KF16

10 DEATH, BURIAL AND MOURNING

death of Reheboam   KF14; CS12
   of Rezin   KS1
   of Samuel   SF25
   of Saul   SF31; SS1; CF10
   of Saul's sons   SS21
   of Sennacherib   CS32
   of Shallum   KS15
   of Sheba   SS20
   of Shimei   KF2
   of Shophach   CF19
   of Solomon   KF11; CS9
   of Tibni   KF16
   of Uriah   SS11
   of Uzza   CF13
   of Uzzah   SS6
   of Uzziah   CS26
   of Zechariah   KS15
   of Zimri   KF16
   satisfaction for   Gen9
   shadow of   Job16; Ps23, 44, 107
   sleep the sleep of   Ps13
   terrors of   Ps55
   valley of the shadow of   Ps23
die, a time to   Ec3
   on the same day, Hophni and Phinhas shall   SF2
   you shall not rise from your bed; you will   KS1
died, on the seventh day the boy   SS12
dirge, harp tuned for a   Job30
   I will chant over the desert pastures   Je9
   sing it as a   E24
   teach one another this   Je9
   they will raise over you   E26ff
   those skilled in the   Am5
dirges and laments   E2
dust on his head   SF4
   sprinkle yourselves with   Mi1
earth on their heads   Ne9
embalmer   Am6
embalming of Jacob   Gen5o
   of Joseph   Gen50
fast, proclaim a   KF21

10 DEATH, BURIAL AND MOURNING

fasted, Ahab   KF21
  and lamented   Ju20
fasted for the child, David   SS12
  three days in mourning   SF31
  till evening   SS1, 3
fasting, weeping and beating of the breast   Est4
garden-tomb   CS33
  at Uzza   KS21
gash himself in mourning   Je16
grave, cruel as the   So8
  common   Je26
  dug yourself a   Ps49
  eternal home   Ps49
  I will ransom them from the power of the   Ho13
  jealousy as cruel as the   So8
  lying in the quiet   Job3
  never satisfied   Pro30
  set in the recesses of the abyss   E32
  sleep in the   Ps88
  swallow them alive as the   Pro1
  the silent   Ps94
  their jaws are a   Je5
  there is no knowledge or wisdom in the   Ec9
  those who go down to the   Ps22
  touching, cleansing after   Nu19
  whither thou goest   Ec9
  with the wicked, assigned a   Is53
graves, bring the bones out of their   Je8
  I will open your   E37
  keeping vigil crouching among   Is65
  those long in their   Is26
  took the bones from   KS23
hair, O Jerusalem, cut off your   Je7
  tear out their   E27
hanged himself, Ahithophel   SS17
hewed him out a sepulchure   Is22
keening, skilled in   Je9
lament for Abner   SS3
  for Jacob   Gen50
  in thy book, enter my   Ps56
  of David   SS1

10 DEATH, BURIAL AND MOURNING

lament of Jeremiah   CS35
   raise upon the high bare places   Je7
lament, teach your daughters the   Je9
   thrice told   Mi2
lamentation, a place of   Mi1
   the people broke into   SF11
   the princes broke into   SS13
   there shall be   Am5
   turn your songs into   Am8
lamented and fasted till evening   Ju20
   the people at Bethel   Ju21
laments and dirges   E2
   turned into dancing   E2
mourned for Absalom, David   SS13
   for Amnon, David   SS13
   for the man of God   KF13
   three whole weeks, Daniel   D10
mourner, go like a   Ps42
   professional   Je9
mourning, a time for   Ec3
   beat their breasts in   Je34
   cover upper lips in   E24
   enter not into the house of   Je16
   feast   Je16
   for Bathshua   Gen38
   for Jacob   Gen50
   for Joseph   Gen37
   for Sarah   Gen23
   for the offence   Ez10
   harp tuned to   Job30
   I will turn your pilgrim-feasts into   Am8
   in Jerusalem, a great   Z12
   Judah had finished   Gen38
   lay prostrate in   Ps35
   like doves of the valleys   E7
   of Abraham   Gen23
   of Egyptians   Gen50
   of Jacob   Gen37
   of Joseph   Gen50
   our dances turned to   La5
   patches on our head   Le21

10 DEATH, BURIAL AND MOURNING

mourning rites   Je16
  shave your head in   Je16, 48; Mi1
perish, if I   Est4
remembrance, day of   Ex12
rent clothes and dust on his head   SF4
  her robe, Tamar   SS13
  his clothes, Ahab   KF21
    David   SS1, 13
    Hezekiah   Ks19; Is37
    Job   Job1
    Josiah   KS22
    Mordecai   Est4
    the king of Israel   KS5
  his mantle in two, Elisha   KS2
  their clothes, all the people   SS3
sackcloth   Gen37; SS3; KF20ff; CF21; Ne9; Est4; Job16;
      Ps30, 35, 69; Is3, 15, 20f, 32, 37, 50; Je6, 49; La2;
      E7, 27; D9; Joe1; Am8; Jon3
  Ahab put on   KF21
  and ashes, a bed of   Est4
    make his bed on   Is58
  as a bed   SS21
  clothed themselves in   La2
  David wore   CF21
  Israelites clothes in   Ne9
  Mordecai put on   Est4
  put on   SS3; E27; Je4
  round your waist   Am8
  sat in ashes and put on   Jon3
  stitched together   Job16
  the king wore   KS6
  they will go in   E7
  wrap yourself in   Je6
  wrapped himself in, Hezekiah   KS19; Is37
sepulchre, an open   Ps5; Je5
  hewed him out a   Is22
  of Ahaziah at Jerusalem   KS9
  on high, he that heweth a   Is22
  took the bones out of the   KS23
  of David   Ne3
shave his head in mourning   Je16, 48; Mi1

10 DEATH, BURIAL AND MOURNING

shaved heads   E7
   your heads   Am8
shaving the head and putting on sackcloth   Is22
shroud, worms their   Job27
snuffed out like a wick   Is43
spices, anointed the bodies with   SF31
   burial   CS16
unburied bones as dung on the face of the earth   Je16
wailing, those skilled in   Am5
   women   Je19
weep, a time to   Ec3
weeping and wailing   Est4
   countryside re-echoed with their   SS15
wept and went barefoot, David   SS15
   David for Absalom   SS18f
     for Saul and Jonathan   SS1
withers like a flower   Job14
wrath, day of   Zp1

NEW TESTAMENT

anointing for burial   Mk14
ashes, sackcloth and   Mw11; L10
bearers, funeral   L7
bier   L7
body of Jesus, Joseph asked Pilate for the   Mw27; Mk15;   L23; J19
burial, anointed my body for   Mk14
   custom, according to the Jewish   J19
   gaze upon their corpses and refuse them   Rev11
   of Stephen   A8
   place   Mw27
   preparing me for   Mw26
   sheet   Mw27; Mk15; L23; J19
buried the body of John the Baptist   Mw14
   with him in baptism   PCo2
bury my father first, let me go and   Mw8; L9
   their dead, leave the dead to   Mw8; L9
burying, anoint my body to the   Mk14
cave tomb   J11

10 DEATH, BURIAL AND MOURNING

cemetery for aliens   Mw27
Christian dead will rise   ThF4
cloud of death, those who live under   L1
corpse, corpses, vultures gather by the   L17
  desert was strewn with their   PCF10
corruption, that his flesh never suffered   A2
cross, took the body of Jesus down from the   Mw27; Mk15; L23; J19
dead are raised to life, how the   L7
  but sleepeth, the maid is not   Mw9
  Christ was raised from the   PCF15
  first-born from the   Rev1
  four days, Lazarus has been   J11
  God raised him from the   A3
  in Christ shall rise first   ThF4
  judged according to their   Rev20
  raised from the   Mw17
  receiving baptism on behalf of the   PCF15
  resurrection of the   PCF15
  shall be raised incorruptible   PCF15
  standing before the throne   Rev20
  until the Son of Man had risen from the   Mk9
  will rise immortal   PCF15
death and mourning, an end to   Rev21
  at his command, him who had   LH2
  broken the power of   PTS1
  crossed over from   LJF3
  has no claim, on such the second   Rev20
  hold the keys of   Rev1
  in our body, wherever we go, we carry   PCS4
  in tasting, he should stand for us all   LH2
  is gain to me   PPs1
  it is written that the Messiah shall suffer   L24
  lake of fire is the second   Rev20
  last enemy to be abolished is   PCF15
  no longer under the dominion of   PR6
  obedient unto   PPs2
  of Herod   Mw2; A12
  of Jesus   Mw27; Mk15; L23; J19
  of Stephen   A7
  on a cross, accepted even   Pps2

10 DEATH, BURIAL AND MOURNING

death, passed from, to life   J5; LHF3
  powers of, shall never conquer it   Mw16
  ready to go with you to   L22
  second   Rev2
  showed himself after   A1
  sinking towards   PE4
  stayed in Egypt until Herod's   Mw2
  the rider's name was   Rev6
  the wages of sin is   PR6
  thou wilt not abandon my soul to   A2
  unto death, the savour of   PCS2
  where is your victory?   PCF15
  will seek but not find   Rev9
death's domain, the keys of   Rev1
decay, though our outward humanity is   PCS4
depart, and be with Christ   PPs1
died and rose again, Jesus   ThF4
  as Christians, those who   ThF4
  every living thing in the sea   Rev16
  for us that we might live   ThF5
  Herod was eaten up with worms and   A12
  Jesus gave a loud cry and   Mw27; Mk15; L23; J19
  my daughter has just   Mw9
  of poisoned water, great numbers of men   Rev8
  Tabitha fell ill and   A9
  with these words he   L23
dropped dead at his feet, Sapphira   A5
    when Ananias heard these words he   A5
dust on their heads, threw   Rev18
dying we still live on   PCS6
follow me, and leave the dead to bury their dead   Mw8
foreigners, a burial place for   Mw27
funeral, met a   L7
  pall, black as a   Rev6
gave up the ghost, Jesus   Mw27; Mk15; L23; J19
grave, able to deliver him from the   LH5
  all who are in the, shall come out   J5
  rock   Mw27
  their throat is an open   PR3
grave-clothes   J11
graves opened, rocks split and   Mw27

10 DEATH, BURIAL AND MOURNING

graves shall not suffer their dead bodies to be put in   Rev11
  unmarked   L11
grief will be turned to joy   J16
  you are plunged into   J16
grieve like the rests of men, you should not   ThF4
guard at the tomb of Jesus   Mw27; Mk15; L23; J19
Lazarus has fallen asleep, but I shall go and wake him   J11
let the dead bury their dead   Mw8; L9
linen wrappings   Mw27; Mk15; L23f; J19f
mourn with the mourners   PR12
mourning, turn your laughter into   LJ4
myrrh and aloes   J19;
   oil of   L7
perfumes, prepared spices and   L23f
raised from the dead, he has been   Mw28
  to life again, the dead are   L20
raises from the dead and gives them life   J5
raising of the dead, scoffed when they heard about   A17
realm of death, who does not love is in the   LJF3
resurrection, entered the Holy City after his   Nw27
  from the dead, finally arrived at the   PPs3
  of the dead   Mw22
rise from the dead, when good people   L14
   he must   J20
   on the third day   L24
   the Son of Man to   Mk8
rising from the dead, discussed among themselves   Mk9
sackcloth and ashes   Mw11
   sitting in   L10
  dressed in   Rev6
sepulchre, found the stone rolled away from the   Mw28; Mk16; L24;
    J20
  hewn in stone   L23
  in the garden was a new   J19
  laid him in a   A13
  of David   A2
  rolled a great stone to the door of the   Mw27; Mk15
  their throat is an open   PR3
  they came to the   Mk16
  taken the Lord our of the   J20
  whitewashed   Mw23

10 DEATH, BURIAL AND MOURNING

sepulchres of the prophets, ye build the   L11
   of the righteous, garnish the   Mw2
shroud of Jesus   Mw27; Mk15; L23f; J19f
   of Lazarus   J11
sleep in death, those who   ThF4
spices, they prepared sweet   Mk16; L23f
spirit, he bowed his head and gave up his   Mw27; Mk15; L23; J19
   Lord Jesus, receive my   A7
stinketh, by this time he   J11
three days after being killed he will rise again   Mk9
tomb, already been four days in the   J11
   cut out of the rock   Mw27; Mk15; L23
   David's   A2
   found the stone rolled away from the   Mw28; Mk16; L24; J20
   laid him in a   A13
   Jesus laid in the   J19
   laid the body of John the Baptist in a   Mk6
   Mary came to the   J20
   of Jesus   Mw28
   they went into the   Mk16
tombs, came from among the   Mk5
   covered with whitewash   Mw23
   he stayed among the   L8
   of the prophets   M23; L11
   two men who came out from the   Mw8
touch me not; for I am not yet ascended   J20
vultures gather where the corpse is   L17
weep not; she is not dead, but sleepeth   L8
weeping, Mary stood at the tomb outside   J20
wormwood, water turned to   Rev8

11 *Divination and Witchcraft*

OLD TESTAMENT

astrology   Is47
  Babylonian   D2, 4ff
augur, at the fork in the highway   E21
  let none be found   De18
auguries, Babylonian   E21
  by consulting the livers of beasts   E21
augury, Balaam practised   KS17
  Israelites practised   KS17
  prophets offer them worthless   Je14
  signs of the times, men skilled at reading   CF12
Bands, Beauty, Favour and Union, staffs in Zechariah's oracle   Z11
capture of souls, magical   E13
cast lots at the fork in the road   E21
    with arrows   E21
charmer, let none be found   De18
charms, the Lord will take away   Is3
day for a year   E4
dead, calling up the   SF28
  consulting the, Saul and the witch of En-dor   SF28
demons, wantonly following   Le17
devil, a-whoring after the   Le17
divination   KS17, 21; CS33
  Balaam did not resort to   Nu24
  darkness shall bring you no   Mi3
  prohibition of   Le19
  prophets take money for their   Mi3
  theirs is a lie   E22
diviners   Is3, 44
  and seers shall blush for shame   Mi3
  Babylonian   D2, 5
  do not listen to your   Je27, 29
  let none be found   De18

125

11 DIVINATION AND WITCHCRAFT

diviners, make fools of   Is44
  see false signs   Z10
  stripped of all   Is3
enchanters   Is3
  let none be found   De18
enchantments   KS17; CS33; Ls47
  Balaam did not seek   Nu24
En-dor, witch of   SF28
evil spirits would seize Saul   SF16ff
exorcists, Babylonian   D1, 5
false prophets, I frustrate them   Is44
  visions   E13
familiar, let none consult a   De18
  spirit   KS21ff; CS33; Is8, 19, 29
    a woman who has a   SF28
fate, god of   Is65
foretell the future month by month   Is47
fortune, in honour of   Is65
gash not yourselves   De14
ghost   Is8, 29
  of Samuel   SF28
ghosts and spirits   Is19
    got rid of those who called up   KS23; SF28
    who traffic with   SF28
  dealt with   CS33
  let none traffic with   De18
  resorting to   Le19ff
  Saul had resorted to   CF10
  who dealt with   KS21
ghostly form coming up from the earth   SF28
herbal magic   Job18
lots, the king of Babylon cast   E21
magic wrist-bands   E13
  pursuit of souls   E13
magicians   Is47
  Babylonian   D1, 4ff
  Belteshazzar, chief of the   D4
  of Darius   D5
  of Pharaoh   Ex7
necromancers, let none be found   De18
observing times,   CS33

11 DIVINATION AND WITCHCRAFT

oracle, oracles, Balaam uttered   Nu23ff
  Benjamites sought   Ju20
  concerning Jerusalem, Ezekiel's   E12
oracle, oracles from God   Is14
  of Damascus   Is17
  of Dumah   Is21
  of Egypt   Is19
  of Habbakuk   H1
  of Isaiah   Is13
  of Malachi   Ma1ff
  of Moab   Is15
  of Tyre   Is23
  of the Arabs   Is21
  of the Beasts of the South   Is30
  of the valley of vision   Is22
  of the wilderness   Is21
  of Zechariah   Z9, 12
  seal the   Is8
oracle-mongers   Is19
prognosticators, monthly   Is47
Samuel's ghost   SF28
seers and diviners shall blush for shame   Mi3
soothsayers   Is2, 57
  among you, there shall be no more   Mi5
  Babylonian   D2, 4ff
  do not listen to your   Je27, 29
  let none be found   De18
  like the Philistines   Is2
  thou shalt have no more   Mi5
soothsaying   KS21; CS33
  prohibition of   Le19
sorcerers, Babylonian   D2
  do not listen to your   Je27
  I will destroy your   Mi5
  I will testify against   Ma3
  let none be found   De18
  Pharaoh's   Ex7
sorceress   Is57
  Jezebel's   KS9
sorcery   CS33
  mistress of   Na3

11 DIVINATION AND WITCHCRAFT

spells, gift of unbinding   D5
  let none cast   De18
  magic   Is47
spirits, dealt with   KS21; CS33
  familiar   SF28; CS33
  resorting to   Le19ff
  those who call up   SF28
  traffic with, let none   De18
stargazers   Is47
staves in Zechariah's oracle   Z11
times, an observer of   De18
vision is false, their   E22
  oracle of Isaiah   Is13
wise men of Darius   D5
  women, do not listen to your   Je27
witch, let none be found   De18
  of En-dor   SF28
witchcraft   CS33
  I will cut off   Mi5
  mistress of   Na3
  of Jezebel   KS9
wizards   SF28; KS21ff; CS33; Is8, 19
  let none be found   De18
year for a day   E4

NEW TESTAMENT

astrologers from the east   Mw2
bewitched, you must have been   PG3
curious arts, those who used   A19
day of the Lord is already here, alleging the   ThS2
demonic wisdom   LJ3
devil's sign, conscience branded with the   PTF4
divination, damsel possessed with a spirit of   A16
doctrines inspired by devils   PTF4
elemental spirits   PG4
exorcism   A19
exorcists, some strolling Jewish   A19
fortunes, brought a large profit by telling   A16
great power of magic   A8
lie, signs and miracles of the   ThS2

11 DIVINATION AND WITCHCRAFT

magic books publicly burnt   A19
  great power of   A8
  Samaritans were carried away by Simon's   A8
magic, those who formerly practised   A19
magical arts, Simon practised   A8
  spells   A19
magician, Simon   A8
oracles, the ABC of God's   LH5
oracular utterance   A16
powers of the air, spiritual   PE2
sign, conscience branded with the devil's   PTF4
signs and miracles of the lie   ThS2
slave-girl who was possessed   A16
soothsaying, brought her masters much gain by   A16
sorcerer, Bar-Jesus by name   A13
sorcerers, outside are   Rev22
sorceries, bewitched them with   A8
sorcery and idolatry belong to the lower nature   PG5
  deceived all nations, your   Rev18
  Simon used   A8
spirit of divination   A16
  possessed by an oracular   A16
spirits, ability to distinguish true from false   PCF12
  elemental   PG4
we observed the rising of his star   Mw2
wisdom, demonic   LJ3
wise men, three   Mw2
witchcraft, work of the flesh   PG5

12   *Divinity*

OLD TESTAMENT

Amen, God whose name is   Is65
Ancient of Days   D7
beauty of holiness   CS20
cherubim, enthroned on the   Is37
city of God   Ps46, 48, 87
  of the Lord   Is60
creator   Ps75, 78
  of the wide world   Is40
Eden, Garden of   Gen2; Joe2
  garden of God   E28, 31
    of the Lord   Is51
God, city of   Ps46, 48, 87
  house of   Ps42, 92
  know that I am   Ps46
  of gods, your god is indeed   D2
  of heaven   Jos2
  of Hosts   Je15
  of Israel   Je7f, 11ff
  of Jacob   Is2
  the mystery of   Job11
  whose name is Amen   Is65
heaven   Ps2, 11, 14, 19, 33, 36, 53, 57, 65, 76, 80, 85, 103, 113, 115,
    Ps123, 135f, 146; Pro30; Is24
  highest   Ps71, Is7
  of heavens   Ps148
  God of   Jos2
holiness, the beauty of   CS20
  the splendour of   Ps29
holy city   Is48
  dwelling   Ps46; Z2
  ground   Ex3
  habitation   Je25
  hill   Ps43, 48, 99; Is56ff
    flaunt your pride on my   Zp3
    God's   E28

12 DIVINITY

holy hill, the lofty hill of Israel   E20
   who shall dwell in thy   Os15
   worship at his   Ps99
   Zion   Joe2
  is the Lord of Hosts   Is6
  land   Z2
  mountain   Ps78; Is66; Je31; Joe2ff; Ob1; Z8
   of Jerusalem   Is27
  name   Le24
  of Holies in Ezekiel's vision   E41ff
  One   Is40ff
   of Israel   Is10f; Je51
   of Jacob   Is29
  place   Ps68, 74, 150
   in Ezekiel's vision   E41ff
   Most   KF6ff; CS2ff; D9
  Spirit from me, take not thy   Ps51
  temple, my prayer reached thee in thy   Jon2
   the Lord from his   Mi1
   the lord is in his   H2
Immanuel   Is7ff
Jehovah   Ex3ff
  my name is   Ex6
  the Lord is   Is12, 26
Jehovah, whose name is   Ps83
living God, sons of the   Ho1
Lord appeared in a burning bush   Ex3
  blessed be the   KF1
  cloud filling the house of the   KF8
  God of Abraham, Isaac and Israel   CS30
   of Hosts   Je5; Am3; Ho12; Am4ff, 9
   of Israel   KS22
  is witness   SF12
  of Hosts   SS5ff; KS3; CF17; Ps46, 48, 59, 69, 80, 84, 89; Is1f;
      Je6ff, 20, 23, 25, 29ff, 48ff; Mi4; Na3; H2; Hg1ff;
      Z1ff; Ma1ff
   city of the   Ps48
   enthroned upon the cherubim   SF4
   God of Israel   Je16, 19, 27ff, 32ff, 39, 42f, 46, 48, 50; Zp2
   holy is the   Is6

12 DIVINITY

Lord of hosts, praise the   Je33
    was with him   CF11
  seeth not as man seeth   SF16
  spirit of the   Ju3; CS15, 20, 24
  the God of heaven   Jon1
    of Israel   Je35
  the Holy One of Israel   Je50
  the mountain of the   Mi4
  worship the   Ps96
  your God consuming fire   De4
Lord's house   Joe3
  pillars of the earth are the   SF2
love which never fails   Is54
Messiah the Prince   D9
Mighty One of Jacob   Is49, 60
redeemer liveth, I know that my   Job19
refuge, the Lord is a sure   Na1
robe of light   Ps104
splendour of holiness   Ps29
still small voice   KF19
watcher, a Holy One   D4
Zion, building in bloodshed   Mi3
  city of   Ps48
  holy hill   Joe2
  nobody's friend   Je30
  palaces of   Ps48
  this is   Je30
  which abideth forever   Ps125
  which cannot be moved   Ps125

NEW TESTAMENT

Alpha and Omega, the First and the Last   Rev1f, 21f
ascended, I have not yet   J20
behold the Lamb of God   J1
Blessed One, son of the   Mk14
Christ of God, Peter answering said the   L9
  Jesus which is called   Mw27
  Son of the living God   Mw16
  they knew that he was   L4

12 DIVINITY

Christ, thou art the   Mk8
dayspring from on high hath visited us   L1
divine secret kept in silence for long ages   PR16
  Emmanuel, he shall be called   Mw1
  which being interpreted is, God with us   Mw1
eternal kingdom, full and free admission into the   LPS1
  life, harvest of   PG6
    I give them   J10
    inner spring welling up for   J4
    shall possess   J6
    the end is   PR6
    the righteous will enter   Mw25
Father, comes in the glory of his   Mk8
  heavenly   Mw5f
  in heaven, give praise to your   Mw5
    our   Mw6, 10
  into thy hands I commit my spirit   L23
  who sees what is secret   Mw6
First and Last, Alpha and Omega   Rev1f, 21f
glory as befits the Father's only son   J1
God alone is good   Mk10; L18
  descended like a dove, the Spirit of   Mw3
  has never been seen   LJF4
  is love   LJF4
  is with us   Mw1
  of Abraham, I am the   Mw22; Mk12
  of Isaac, I am the   Mw22; Mk12
  of Israel, give praise to the   Mw15
  of Jacob, I am the   Mw22; Mk12
  of love and peace will be with you   LCS13
  our Father   PCo1; ThS1
  the Father   PE1; PPs1; PTS1; ThF1; LPF1
  the Son of   Mw4
  they shall see   Mw5
  with us, Emmanuel   Mw1
Godhead, complete being of the   PCo2
God's chosen, for the sake of   Mw24
    One   J1
  Messiah   L9, 23
  secret is Christ himself   PCo2
gospel of God's grace   A20

12 DIVINITY

grace of God, hold fast to the   A13
heavenly Father gives to those who ask   Mw7
   it was revealed to you by my   Mw16
   the will of my   Mw7, 18
Holy Ghost   Mw1, 3, 8, 12, 28; Mk1; L10; J14; A2, 11; PR9,
     14f; PCF6; PCS6; PE1; LH3, 6, 10
   kingdom of God is joy in the   PR14
  his name is   L1
  holy, holy, Lord God Almighty   Rev4
  One of God   Mk1; L4; J6
   who art and wast the   Rev16
Holy Spirit   Mw1, 3, 8, 12, 28; Mk1; L10; J14; A2, 11; PR9,
     14f; PCF6; PCS6; PE1; LH3, 6, 10
   the indwelling   PCF6
   by the power of the   PR15
   he received from his Father the   A2
   he will baptize you with the   Mw3
   Jesus exulted in the   L10
I am with you always, to the end of time   Mw28
immortal, invisible, the only God   PTF1
Jesus Christ is in you   PCS13
King eternal, the only wise God   PTF1
  of kings and Lord of Lords   PTF6; Rev17, 19
Kingdom of God, accept like a child the   L18
   already come to power, before they have seen the   Mk9
   already come upon you   Mw12; L11
   belongs to such as these   Mk10
   flesh and blood can never possess the   PCF15
   is joy inspired by the Holy Spirit   PR14
   is like a mustard seed   L13
   is like this   Mk4
   is like yeast   L13
   is upon you   Mk1
   is within you   L17
  of heaven is theirs   Mw5
   is upon you   M4, 10
   keys of the   Mw16
   parables of the   Mw13
   the least in the   Mw11
   to know the secrets of the   Mw13
Lamb of God   J1

12 DIVINITY

light of the world, I am the   J9
Lord has risen, it is true   L24
  of lords and King of kings   PTF6; Rev17, 19
  your God, put to the test   Mw4
Lord's prayer   Mw6, 11
love, God-given   PCo1
many who are first will be last, and the last first   Mw19
Messiah   Mw1f, 16, 22, 27; Mk8, 14; L2, 4, 22; J1; A2, 8; PR9
  are you the   Mk14; L2
  from the patriarchs in natural descent sprang the   PR9
  Jesus called the   Mw1, 27
  proclaiming the   A8
  resurrection of the   A2
  Son of the living God   Mw16
  the Lord   L2
  they knew that he was the   L4
  we have found the   J1
  what is your opinion about the   Mw22
  you are the   Mk8
Most High God, Jesus Son of the   L8
   you will be sons of the   L6
mystery of the kingdom, given to know   Mw13; Mk4, 12; L8
One God, and one mediator between God and man   PTF2
  who sat upon the great white throne   Rev20
parable of the alert servants   L12
    bad servant   Mw24
    bags of gold   Mw25
    banquet   L14
    beam in the eye   Mw7
    beggar Lazarus   L16f
    birds   Mw6
    blind guides   Mw15, 23; L6
    bridegroom   Mw9; Mk2; L5
    bullying servant   L12
    buried treasure   Mw13
    bushel   Mw5
    camel and needle   Mw19
    candle   Mw5; L8, 11
    clean house   Mw12
    children   Mw18

12 DIVINITY

parable of the closed door   L13
  cloth patch   Mw9; L5
  clothing the naked   Mw25
  court case   M5; L12
  counting the cost   L14
  crop   Mw13
  darnel   Mw13
  debt   Mw18
  debtor   Mw5
  dinner party   L14
  dutiful servant   L17
  faithful servant   Mw25
  feeding the hungry   Mw25
  fig tree   Mw24; Mk13; L13, 21
  fishing net   Mw13
  five virgins   Mw25
  foundations on a rock   Mw7
  friend in need   L11
  fruit   Mw7, 12
  fruitful tree   L6
  fruiting vine   J15
  gnat and the camel   Mw23
  gold bags   Mw25
  good Samaritan   L10
  grain of wheat   J12
  grapes and thistles   L6
  great gulf fixed   L17
  green tree   Mw24
  harvest   Mw13
  highest room   L14
  hired labourers   Mw20
  house built on the rock   Mw7; L6
    swept clean   L11
  householder   Mw24; L12
  hungry and thirsty   Mw25
  innkeeper   L10
  king's banquet   Mw22
  lamp   Mw5, 25; Mk4; L8, 11
  leaven   Mw13
  lilies of the field   Mw6; L12
  loaves   L11

12 DIVINITY

parable of the lost sheep   Mw18; L15
   man who amasses wealth   L12
   marching to battle   L14
   midge and the camel   Mw23
   money on deposit   L19
   money-lender   L7
   mote in the eye   Mw7
   mountain   Mw17
   mustard seed   Mw13, 17; Mk4; L13
   narrow door   L13
   neighbour   L10
   new wine   Mw9; L5
   patched coat   Mw9; Mk2
   pearl of great value   Mw13
   pearls before swine   Mw7
   persistent widow   L18
   Pharisee and the tax-gatherer   L18
   place at table   L14
   prodigal son   L15
   profit   L19
   publican and the Pharisee   L18
   ravens   L12
   remitted debt   Mw18
   rich landowner   L12
     man to enter the kingdom   Mw19; L18
     man and the beggar   L16
     man's steward   L16
   salt   Mw5; L14
   seed   Mw13
   servants   L19
   servant's debt   Mw18
   sheepfold   J10
   shepherd   Mw25
   shepherd's voice   J10
   sinner who repenteth   L15
   sons in the vineyard   Mw21
   son's wedding feast   Mw22
   sower   Mw13; Mk4; L8
   sparrows   Mw10
   speck in the eye   Mw7; L6
   steward   Mw20

12 DIVINITY

parable of the stored-up treasure   Mw6
    storehouses   L12
    strong man   L11
    talents   Mw25
    tares   Mw13
    teacher and pupil   L6
    ten pounds   L19
    tenant vine-growers   L20
    town on a hill   Mw5
    trees   Mw3
    thief in the night   Mw24; L12
    tower   L14
    treasure   Mw6
    trusty servant   Mw24
    unclean spirit   Mw12
    unjust judge   L18
    unshrunk cloth   Mk2
    usury   Mw25
    vineyard and the hired labourers   Mw20
      and the murderous tenants   Mw21; Mk12; L20
      and the sons   Mw21
    virgins   Mw25
    war   L14
    weather   Mw16
    wedding feast   Mw22; L14
    whitened sepulchre   Mw23
    wicked spirits   L11
    wineskin   Mw9; Mk2; L5
    wise virgins   Mw25
    withered branch   J15
    yeast   Mw13
peace, God of   PR15
  of God which passeth all understanding   PPs4
prince of life whom God hath raised   A3
raised from the dead, his Son whom he   ThF1
resurrection from the dead   J21
  preaching about Jesus and the   A17
revelation of Jesus Christ   PG1
  of the glory of God   PCS4
Righteous One, appointed you to see the   A22
risen from the dead   PTS2

12 DIVINITY

Saviour, Jesus Christ   Mw1
  of the world, we know that he is   J4
secret, kept the divine   PR16
  of Christ, I understand the   PE3
Son made heir to the whole universe   LH1
  of God, if you are indeed the   Mw4, 27
    Jesus Christ the   Mw4; Mk1
    shouting you are the   L4
    truly you are the   Mw14
  of Man coming on a cloud   L21
    is come to save that which was lost   Mw18
    is glorified, now the   J13
    is not come to destroy, but to save   L9
    seated at the right hand of God   Mk14
    standing at the right hand of God   Mk14; A7
    to be glorified, hour has come for thee   J12
    to stand in the presence of the   L21
    who do men say is the   Mw16
    will be seated at the right hand of God   L22
  of the Most High, he will bear the title   L1
soul, shepherd and guardian of your   LPF2
Spirit, divine dispensation of the   PCS3
  of God   Mw3, 12
    knows what God is, only the   PCF2
throne for ever and ever   LH1
  of God   LH12
  of grace, let us come boldly unto the   LH4
thou art my Son, my Beloved   L3
truly this man was a Son of God   Mk15
universal giver of life   A17
wise, to God only   PR16
Word of God is divine and active   LH4
  was with God at the beginning   J1
worship, it is God you must   Rev19
you did not choose me: I chose you   J15

13   Dreams and Visions

OLD TESTAMENT

angel in Zechariah's vision   Z1ff
apparition loomed before me   Job4
augury, prophets offer them worthless   Je14
barrel in Zechariah's vision, a great   Z5
beacon in the darkness   Ps112
beast with ten horns in Daniel's vision   D7
behemoth   Job40
chariots of fire   KS2, 6
city of truth, vision of Jerusalem   Z8
cloud, a pillar of   De31
  filling the house of the Lord   KF8
cockatrice   Is11, 14, 59; Je8
comet, arise from Israel   Nu24
court for owls   Is34
  in Daniel's vision   D7
crown in Zechariah's vision   Z6
day darkened into night   Am5
demon of the night   So3
diviners, do not be deceived by   Je29
dragon   Job30; Ps6, 74, 91; Is13, 27, s4f, 43, 51; Je9, 14, 49, 51; E29; Mi1; Ma2
  that is in the sea   Ps74; Is27
dream at daybreak   Ps97
  fade as a   Is29
  I have had a   Je23
  let him tell his   Je23
  of a barley loaf   Ju7
  of a gold image, Nebuchadnezzar's   D2
  of a great tree, Nebuchadnezzar's   D4
  of bread   Gen40
  of cows   Gen41
  of Gideon's attack   Ju7
  of grapes   Gen40
  of kine   Gen41
  of sheaves   Gen37

13 DREAMS AND VISIONS

dream of stale barley cake   Ju7
  of sun and moon   Gen37
  Pharaoh's   Gen41
  Solomon's   KF3
dreamer of dreams arise among you   De13
dreams, Daniel had a gift for interpreting   D1
  diviners have told false   Z10
  gift of interpreting   D1, 5
  multitude of   Ec5
  no longer answers me by   SF28
  of Daniel   D7
  of Nebuchadnezzar   D2, 4
  of Pharaoh   Gen41
  or of prophets, whether by   SF28
  wise women whom you set to dream   Je29
epah in Zechariah's vision, woman in an   Z5
false visions   E13
feet of clay   D2
fiery flying serpent   Is14, 30
Gabriel, appearance in Daniel's vision   D8ff
ghosts and spirits,   Le19f; De18; Ju9; SF16f, 28; KS21, 23; CF10; CS33; Is8, 19, 29
goat and ram fighting in Daniel's vision   D8
gods, sons of   Gen6
habitations of dragons   Is34
heavenly being, Daniel's vision of a   D10
heavens grow murky as smoke   Is51
  turn black   Je4
holy place trodden down in Daniel's vision   D8
horns in Zechariah's vision   Z1
horses of fire   KS2, 6
image in Nebuchadnezzar's dream   D2
imagination, vision springs from their own   Je23
Jehovah-shammah, city in Ezekiel's vision   E48
Jeremiah, vision of   Je24
lamp-stand of gold in Zechariah's vision   Z4
leviathan, primeval sea-serpent   Is27
man, gleaming, in Daniel's vision   D10
Michael in Daniel's vision   D10
mirage   Is35
moon darkened, sun and   Joe2ff

13 DREAMS AND VISIONS

moon shall not give its light   E32
mountains of copper, brass or bronze   Z6
phantom, moves like a   Ps39
phantoms, pursuing empty   Je2
pillar of cloud   Ex41; De31
  of fire   Ex14
pillars of smoke   So3
prophecy of Ahijah   CS9
Possession, the stone called, in Zechariah's vision   Z4
portents in the sky   Joe2
ram and goat fighting in Daniel's vision   D8
religion thrown to the ground in Daniel's vision   D8
roll, a flying   Z5
saints, horn of the beast made war with the   D8
sea, beasts arising from in Daniel's vision   D7
  monster   Ps74
  serpent   Job7; Ps44, 74; Is27; Amp
    leviathan, that primeval   Is27
signs and portents   Ps105, 135
    thou didst work in Egypt   Je32
  in the heavens   Je10
spirit came forward, a   KF22
stargazers   Is47
starry heavens, majestic as the   So6
stars forbear to shine   Joe2f
  grow dim   Ec12
  withdraw their shining   Joe2
staves representing Favour and Union   Z11
stone called Possession in Zechariah's vision   Z4
  with seven eyes   Z4
sun and moon darkened   Joe2f
time of the end in Daniel's vision   D8
trance, Daniel fell in a   D10
unicorn   Nu23ff; De33; Job39; Ps29, 92; Is34
  like the horn of a   De33
vision, announce in a   Ps89
  ashamed of the   Z13
  false   E12
  from a prophet, men will seek   E7
  from the imagination   Je23
  from the Lord, her prophets have received no   La2

13 DREAMS AND VISIONS

vision, he feared to show Eli the   SF3
  in those days none was granted   SF3
  is false, their   E22
  of abomination, Ezekiel's   E8
  of Abram   Gen15
  of Amos   Am1ff
  of animals fighting   D8
  of beasts coming from the sea   D7
  of death to the Israelites   E9
  of Ezekiel   E40ff
  of flying roll   Z5
  of gleaming man   D10
  of Habbakuk   H1
  of Hagar   Gen16
  of temple rebuilt, Ezekiel's   E40ff
  of Iddo the seer   CS9
  of Isaiah   CS32; Is1ff
  of man on a bay horse   Z1
  of Micah   Mi1ff
  of Nahum   Na1f
  of ram and goat fighting   D8
  of religion cast down   D8
  of stone called Possession   Z4
  of vessel of God, Ezekiel's   E1, 10
  night shall bring you no   Mi3
  springs from their own imagination   Je23
  write down the   H2
visions, Daniel had a gift for interpreting   D1
  false and painted shams   La2
  fraudulent delusions   La2
  of Daniel   D7
  of Jeremiah   Je24
  of Zechariah   Z1ff, 6
  prophets offer them false   Je14
woman with wings in Zechariah's vision   Z5

NEW TESTAMENT

alive for evermore, now I am   Rev1
angel appeared to Joseph in a dream   Mw1f

13 DREAMS AND VISIONS

angel of God, vision in which he saw an   A10
angels, seen a vision of   L24
Babylon the great, the mother of whores   Rev17
beast, all on earth will worship the   Rev13
  from the mouth of the   Rev16
  full of eyes   Rev4
  scarlet, in John's vision   Rev17
breastplates of brimstone and jacinth   Rev9
cataclysm in John's vision   Rev8
chain in his hand, a great   Rev20
clouds, Son of Man coming on the   Mw26; Mk14; L21
creature with a human face   Rev4
crown of life   Rev2
crowns lay before the throne   Rev4
Day of Christ   PPs1f
  of God will set the heavens ablaze   LPS3
  of the Lord comes like a thief in the night   ThF5
door in heaven   Rev4
dream, angel of the Lord appeared in a   Mw1f
  warned not to go back to Herod in a   Mw2
dreams lead them to defile the body   LJu1
  your old men shall dream   A2
earth lit up with the angel's splendour   Rev18
eyes all over, inside and out   Rev4
  flamed like fire   Rev1
Faithful and True, the rider's name was   Rev19
fallen is Babylon the great   Rev18
furnace, smoke rose like a great   Rev9
garden of God   Rev2
ghost, they thought they were seeing a   L24
glass, a sea of   Rev4
God's right hand, Stephen saw Jesus standing at   A7
hair on his head was white as snow-white wool   Rev1
heaven, new Jerusalem coming down out of   Rev3
horsemen of the Apocalypse   Rev6
horses had lions' heads   Rev9
key of David   Rev3
kingdom of the beast   Rev16
Lamb of God   Rev5ff, 14, 17
lake of fire in John's vision   Rev19f
last trump   PCF15

13 DREAMS AND VISIONS

light from heaven, shined round him a   A9
   of day failed, a third of the   Rev8
living creatures covered with eyes   Rev4f
   one, the first and the last   Rev1
marriage of the Lamb   Rev19
martyrs, drunk on the blood of   Rev17
Mount Zion, vision of   Rev14
new heavens and a new earth   LPS3
   name known to none but him that receives it   Rev2
old order has passed away   Rev21
One who sits on the throne   Rev4
paradise of God, tree of life in the midst of the   Rev2
Pergamum, home of Satan   Rev2
pillar of cloud   PCF10
portent in heaven, great and astonishing   Rev15
revelation granted by the Lord   PCS12
   his secret was made known to me by a   PE3
   of John   Rev1ff
sea of glass shot with fire   Rev15
seal of the living God   Rev7
secret hidden for long ages   PCo1
serpent of old that led the world astray   Rev12
    the dragon, that   Rev20
shadows, with him there is no play of passing shadows   LJ1
sign from heaven, asked him for a   Mk8
   that heralds the Son of Man   Mw24
signs and portents, believe without seeing   J4
snakes, horses' tales like   Rev9
Son of God whose eyes flame like fire   Rev2
Spirit carried me away to a high mountain   Rev21
   I was caught up by the   Rev4
spirits, before his throne stood seven   Rev1ff
splendour of the Lord, possess for your own the   ThS2
synagogue, Satan's   Rev2f
throne in heaven   Rev4
trance, Peter fell into a   A10f
tree of life, the right to eat from the   Rev2
trump of God   ThF4
vengeance of the Lamb   Rev6
victory to our God who sits on the throne   Rev7
vision, Ananias had a   A9

13 DREAMS AND VISIONS

vision, angel's intervention he thought was just a   A12
  Cornelius had a   A10
  heavenly, I did not disobey the   A26
  of angels, seen a   L24
  in which he saw an angel of God   A10
  Lord spoke to Paul in a   A18
  of a Macedonian came to Paul   A16
  of angels, they had seen a   L24
  of the holy city   Rev21
  of the sheet full of creatures   A10f
  of the transfiguration   Mw17
  of their own, try to enter some   PCo2
  Peter puzzling over the meaning of the   A10
  realized that he had seen a   L1
  Saul had a   A9
  spiritual powers of wisdom and   PE1
visions granted by the Lord   PCS12
  your young men shall see   A2
voice, from the cloud came a   Mk9; L9
washed in the blood of the Lamb   Rev7
wedding day of the Lamb   Rev19
white stone   Rev2
wife of the Lamb   Rev21
winepress of God's wrath   Rev14
worthy is the Lamb that was slain   Rev5

14   *Farming*

OLD TESTAMENT

acres, vineyard of five   Is5
asses, Job owned five hundred   Job1
  latterly Job owned a thousand   Job42
  set in charge of   CF27
barley   Ex9; KF4; CF11; CS32; Job31; Is28; Je41; E4, 13, 45; Ho3; Joe1
  harvest   Ru1ff; SS21
  land of   De8
barn   Job39; Ps144; Pro3; Joe1; Hg2
  floor   KS6
  storage   CS32
basket for another's grapes   De23
  of first fruits   De26
beans   E4
blasting, plant disease   Ps105; Am4; Hg2
blight, black and red   Am4; Hg2
  curse of   De28
breeding, selective   Gen31
briars   Mi7; Na1
broadcast sowing   Is28
budding, vine   Is18
buffalo, domestic   E39; Am5
bull   Is10; Je50; E39, 43, 45
bullock   Is34, 65; Je50; E39, 43
  fatted   Is5; Je46
  unaccustomed to the yoke   Je31
bulls, herd of   Ps22
bushels, ten of seed shall return only a peck   Is5
calf   Is11, 27; E1; Am6; Mi6
  stall-fed   Je46
  unbroken to the yoke   Je31
calves released from a stall   Ma4
  stalled   SF6
camel pasture   E25
camels, in charge of   CF27

147

14 FARMING

camels, Job owned 3000   Job1
  latterly Job owned 6000   Job42
cartwheels to crush corn   Is28
cattle   SS17; Ps49ff, 147ff; Ec2; Is11, 22, 46, 63; Je31;
      E14, 32, 34, 38; Ho5, 14; Joe1ff; Jon4; H3; Hg1; Z2, 13
  grew fat   Is5
  herds in the plains   CS26
  I had more than any   Ec2
  levied   Nu19
  lost to plague   Ps78
  of Jericho, slaughtered   Jos6
  pen   Ju5; Ho14
  stalls   Cs32
  vast herds of   Je49
chaff   Is5, 17, 29, 33, 40ff, 47
  as flames consumeth   Is5
  before the wind   Ls17, 41
  blown from the threshing floor   Ho13
  carried off   Is40
  driven by the desert wind   Je13
  fly lie   Is29
  gone like   Is47
  swept away like   D2
  vanish like   Zp2
churn   Pro30
cleaving wood   Ec10
corn   De33; CS31, 32; Job28; Ps4, 65, 72; Pro3; Is17, 55, 62;
      Je31; La2, 5; E36; Ho2, 7f, 10, 14; Joe2; Am8ff; Hg1ff;
      Z9, 12
  and wine, a land of   De33
  beginning to sprout   Am7
  contributions of   Ne10
  every hill shall wave with   Am9
  floor   Ho9
  grinding   La5
  land of   Is36
  late   Am7
  pluck ears to rub   De23
  ruined crop of   Joe1
  sprouting   Am7
  they shall eat your   E25

14 FARMING

corn, those who bring in the   Is62
  threshing   Is21
  tithe of   CS31
cornfields   SF8
cottage in a vineyard   Is1
cow   Nu19; SF6; Job21; Is7, 11; Am4
  of Bashan   Am4
crib, ox and ass   Is1
crook, shepherd's   Ps23; Mi7
crop will be scorched   Is17
crops destroyed by eastern tribes   Ju6
  early   Ps72
  forgo the seventh year   Ne10
  make the ground yield heavy   E36
  rain falling upon   Ps72
cucumbers, field of   Is1
  plot of   Je10
cummin, beaten out with a rod   Is28
  scatter seed of   Is28
cuttings, strike   Is17
dealer, animal   Z11
dew heavy at harvest time   Is18
dresser of sycomore figs   Am7
digged, not pruned nor   Is5
dill seed sown broadcast   Is28
ditch   Is22
dovecote   Is60
drought, curse of   De28
  I have proclaimed   Hg1
  scorching   *Is25*
  summer   Ps32
dunghill   Ps113; La4; Am4
  straw trodden for a   Is25
dyke   Joe1
ear of corn   Job24, Is17
ewe   Ps78; Is7
  before the shearers   Is53
  fresh from dipping   So6
  lead to water   Is40
  shorn   So4
fallow, break up your   Ho10

14 FARMING

fallow, land in seventh year to lie   Ex23; Le25
fan, threshing   Is41
fanner, winnowing   Je51
farm   Pro24
  land from the wilderness   Je4
  of Joshua   SF6
farmer   CS26; Je14; Am1, 5
farmers, prosperous, utterly ruined   Is16
farming villages, tithes of   Ne10
farms, they made off to their   Ne13
fatling   Is11; E39
fatten the flock for slaughter   Z11
fence   Ps26
  vineyard   Is5
field   Pro24; Joe2
  all the valley and every   Je31
  edges, harvest left for the poor   Le19f
  fuller's   KS18
  of barley   SS14
  of cucumbers   Is1
  of lentils   SS23
  ruined   Joe1
  to field, you who join   Is5
fields   Ps50, 107, 144; So7; Is32
  flocks in her green   E34
  invaders shall devour their   Ho5
  mortgaged   Ne5
  of Heshbon   Is16
  parcelled out   Mi2
  ploughed   Je26; Mi3
  sale and purchase of   Je32
  sow   Ps107
  teeming life of the   Ps50
figs killed by heavy rain   Ps78
fig-tree   Mi4; Na3; H3; Z3
fig-trees, a land of   De8
first-born of flocks and herds   De12
first-fruits, sacrifice of   De26
fitch beaten out with a staff   Is28
  mixed in a bowl   E4
flax   Ex9; Is19; Ho2

14 FARMING

flax stalks laid out   Jos2
flock   Is13, 17, 40; Je5ff, 25, 49ff; E24ff, 34, 45; Joe1; Am6ff; Jon3; Mi5, 7; Z10ff
  round it up, with no man to   Is13
  where is my beautiful   Is13
flocks   Job24; Ps77, 79ff, 100, 107; Pro27; So1; Ho5; Zp2
  a couching place for   E25
  a refuge to fold   Je33
  as a shepherd watches his   Je31
  a pasture, scattered   Je10
  carry off their   Je49
  graze their   Is14
  herds and   SF8, 27, 30
  I had more than any   Ec2
  in charge of   CF27
  of Kedar   Is60
  scattered   Je23, 50
  shall couch there   Zp2
flock-master   Je14, 25; Na3
fodder, well-seasoned   Is30
fold bereft of its flock   H3
folds, goat   Ps50
  sheep   Nu32
forest of the Perizzites, clear for yourselves   Jos17
fruit of your land, bless the   De7
  they shall eat thy   E25
  trees   Ne9; Ps148
    planted all kinds   Ec2
fruitful land turned into salt waste   Ps107
furrow, plough   Ps129
  water   Ps65
furrows of the fields   Ho10
garden   So4ff; Is66
  by a river   Nu24
  close-locked   So4
  lodge in a   Is1
  of nut trees   So6
  of Uzza   KS21
  the king's   KS25
  royal   Est7
  Persian court   Est1

14 FARMING

garden, plant in exile   Je29
  plant your   Is17
  vegetable, irrigated your land like a   De11
  watered, like a   Je31
  well-watered   Is58
gardens   KS5
  laid waste   Am4
  make   Am9
  orchards and, I made   Ec2
garner   Joe1
gather stones, a time to   Ec3
glean, in the cornfields   Ru2
  leaving loose ears   Le19f
gleaners, reserve edges of harvest for poor   Le19f
gleanings   Is17; Je49; Ob1
  last of the vintage   Mi7
goat   Gen30; Ps50, 66; Pro27, 30; So4, 6; Is13; E27, 34, 39, 43
grain   Joe2
  beat out the   Is27
  land of   KS18; Is36
  making offerings of   Ex29ff
  parched   Jos5
  sift but get no   Je12
  stored   Gen41
  this year you shall eat shed   Is37
  to feed your foes   Is62
granary   Pro3; Je50; Joe1
grapes, eat another's   De23
  gleaning   Is17, 24
  leave gleanings of   De24
  treading   Je25; Joe3; Mi6
  you shall tread, but not drink the wine of   Mi6
grape-gatherers   Je6, 49; Ob1
grass   Ps37, 58, 72, 90, 102f, 147; Is51
  clothes the hills with   Ps147
  ephemeral   Ps103
  fade like   Ps90
  field, in every man's   Z10
  mower   Ps129
  new   Pro27
  spring, fresh as   Is66

14 FARMING

grass withered   Ps102
grazing flock which stampedes   Mi2
  good, in Midianite country   Nu32
  ground, flocks on   E34
  they shall find on the dunes   Is49
grinding meal   Ec12
grub, curse of the   De28
hamlets with surrounding fields   Ne11
harness, ox   SS24
harnessed two milch cows to the wagon   SF6
harrow   SS12
  the furrows   Job39
  the land   Ho10
harvest   Pro10, 12, 20, 25ff; Is16, 18, 23; Je5, 8; Ho2, 6; Joe2ff; Am4; H2
  barns for   CS32
  blasted   Hg1ff
  dew heavy at   Is18
  disappointed of their   Je12
  first fruits of   Je2
  fixed seasons of   Je5
  land shall yield its   Ps85
  leave a swathe for the gleaners   De24
  lost to drought   Joe1
    to locusts   Ps78
  offering the rites of   Le23
  rain at   Pro26
  reap a fruitful   Ps107
  snow at   Pro25
  thanksgiving   Ex23
  time   Je50ff
harvesters   Ps129; Is16f; Je48
harvesting wheat   SF6
harvestman   Je9
hay   Pro27; Is15
heath, flock that dwells on meadow and   Mi7
  rough   Je26; Mi1, 3
hedge   Ps80; Je49; E13; Na3
  of thorns   Ho2
  whoso breaketh a   Ec10
heifer   Is15; Je46, 48, 50; Ho4, 10

14 FARMING

heifer on a rope   Is5
herb garden   KF21
herbs of every field wither   Je12
   shrivel all their green   Is42
herds   Ps107; Pro27; So1; Je5, 31; Ho5; Jon3; H3
   divided   Gen32
   in charge of   CF27
   laden with great   Jos22
   vast   Je49
herdsman, herdsmen   SF21; Am1, 7
   ancestor of all   Gen4
hoed, neither pruned nor   Is5
homesteads   Ps79
honey, tithe of   CS31
hurdle   Job18
husbandman   KS25; Je32, 51ff; Joel; Am5; Z13
hut, shepherd's   So1; Zp2
irrigate a grove of growing trees   Ec2
keeper of the royal forests   Ne2
kids   So1; Is11; E43
   shall graze broad acres   Is5
kine of Bashan   Am4
lamb   Gen30; Ps144; Pro27; So4, 6; Is11, 16, 65; E27, 39, 45; Ho4; Am6
   carry in his bosom   Is40
lambs to the slaughter   Je51
land, ancestral, Naboth's vineyard   KF21
   littered with stones   KS3
   on which you had not laboured   Jos24
lentil   E4
lodge in a garden   Is1
logging raft   KF5
locusts   KF8; CS6; Job39; Ps78, 105; Je46, 51; Joe1ff
   curse of   De28
   east wind bringing   Ex10
   plague of   Ex8, 10
   swarm hatched out   Am7
   west wind dispersing   Ex10
mattock   SF13; Is2, 7; Joe3; Mi4
meadow   Ps65; Is16
   graze flocks in my   Is14

14 FARMING

meadow, lambs in a broad   Ho4
meadows of Moab   Je48
mildew   Am4; Hg2
millet   E4
millet   E4
mower, grass   Ps129
mowing   Am7
muzzle the threshing ox, do not   De25
nursery-ground   E17
nut trees, garden of   So6
oil, pressing olive   Job24
olive   Ho14; Am4
  crop   H3
  drop, the curse of   De28
  groves   De6
    mortgaged   Ne5
    which you did not plant   Jos24
  oil, pressing   Job24
  tree   Z4
    beaten and stripped   Is24
    do not strip the   De24
  yards   SF8; Ne5
olives, a land of   De8
  you shall press, but not use the oil   Mi6
orchard, orchards   H3
  pomegranate   So4
  and gardens, I have made   Ec2
  of Heshbon   Is16
ox goad   Ju3
ploughing   KF19
oxen   KF1, 4, 8, 19; Ne5; Ps8, 66; Is7, 22, 30; E1; Am6
  Job owned five hundred yoke of   Job1
palm trees, vale of   De34
pastor   Je1
pasture   Ps23, 37, 65, 83; Is32; Je49ff; La1; Ho13; Joe1ff; Am1
  broad   Is30
  cattle, in the vale of Achor   Is65
  desert   Je9
  each grazing his own strip of   Je6
  flocks at   Je10

14 FARMING

pasture by the sea   Zp2
  in the desert sands   Is49
  perennial   Je49f
  ravaged rich   Z11
  shall be in all high places   Is49
  wild, have all dried up   Je23
pastured fat bullocks   Is5
peck, ten bushels shall return only a   Is5
pen, cattle   Ho14
pests to destroy your produce   Ma3
pestilence, beasts killed by   Ps78
  of camels   Ex9
  of cattle   Ex9
  of horses   Ex9
  of sheep   Ex9
plant anew the waste land   E36
plantations   E34
  watered by the furrows   E17
plough, plow   Ju14; Pro20ff
  for the sowing   Is28
  furrows   Ps129
  with oxen   Am6
ploughed field   J26; Mi3
    heaped stones beside a   Ho12
ploughlands of Gilead   Am1
ploughman   Ps129; Is28, 61; Je14, 51; Am9
ploughing ox   KF19
ploughshare, plowshare   SF13; Is2; Joe3; Mi4
plot of cucumbers   Je10
pomegranates, a land of   De8
  orchard of   So4
press, oil   Job24
  wine   Job24; Pro3
produce lost to grubs   Ps78
provender, clean   Is30
pruned nor hoed, neither   Is5
pruning hook, pruning knife   Is2, 18; Joe3; Mi4
rain at harvest   Pro26
  falling on crops   Ps72
rains, failed   Joe1
rams   Gen30; E27, 34, 39, 43, 45; Is5; Je49f; Mi6

14 FARMING

rams of Nabaioth   Is60
reap   Ps126
   leaving the field edges   Le19f
   the early crop   Is51
reapers   KS4; Je9, 50; Am2, 9
ridges, levelling   Ps65
ring, iron tethering   D4
rye wheat   Ex9; Is28
salt waste, fruitful land turned into   Ps107
sand, the hidden wealth of   De33
scarecrow in a plot of cucumbers   Je10
scatter stones, a time to   Ec3
season, to everything there is a   Ec3
seed, a bag of   Ps126
self-sown grain   Is37
shearer   Is53
shearing   Gen38; SF6; SS13
   house   Ks10
sheaves   Ps72, 126
   bringing in the   Ne13
   carrying home the   Ps126
   of corn   Z12
   offering of   Le3f
   Ruth may glean among the   Ru2
   to the threshing floor   Mi4
sheep   SS6, 13, 17; KF1, 4, 8, 18; Ps8, 44, 49, 65, 77f, 80, 107, 144; So1;
      Is7, 11, 13, 22, 53; Ne5; E25, 34, 36, 39, 45ff; Ho5, 12; Joe1;
      Am1; Mi2, 5; Z9
   breeder   KS3
   dip   So4, 6
   farmer   Am1
   follow the tracks of   So1
   in distress for lack of a shepherd   Z10
   Jacob's   Gen37
   Job owned 7000   Job1
   latterly Job owned 14000   Job42
   led to the slaughter   Je11
   plot of land for a hundred   Jos24
   shall be scattered   Z13
   tethered   Is5
   to the slaughter   Is53

14 FARMING

sheep walk   E25
  without a shepherd, Israel is like   CS18
sheepcote   SS6
sheepfold   Ju5; SF24; CS32; Ps68, 78; Is13; Je50; Mi1; Zp2
sheepmaster   KS3
shed in a field of cucumbers   Is1
shepherd   Gen4; Job24; Ps23, 28, 49, 78ff, 95, 100; So1; Is13;
      Je2, 6, 10, 12, 25, 31, 43, 49ff; E34; Ho12; Am1, 3; Mi5, 7; Na3;
      Zp2; Z10ff
  Abel was a   Gen4
  abomination in Egypt, held to be   Gen46
  boys, turn my hand against   Z13
  foreigners shall serve as   Is61
  who lets the flock scatter   Je23
  worthless, who abandons his sheep   Z11
shepherdess, Rachel was a   Gen29
shepherd's hut   KS10; Zp2
sickle   SF13; Je50; Joe3
  for another's corn   De23
sift but get no grain   Je12
sifting wheat   SS4
slaughter, fatten stock for   Z11
sledge, threshing   Is28
slips of cedar set in soil   E17
  set   Is17
snow at harvest   Pro25
soil, Uzziah loved the   CS26
sow but not reap, you shall   Mi6
  thy seed in the morning   Ec11
sowed much but reaped little   Hg1
sower in Babylon, every   Je50
sowing seed   Am9
    broadcast   Is28
spelt   Ex9; E4
spring rain failed   Je3
stable   KF110; E25
stall, ass knows its master's   Is1
  calves'   Am6; Ma4
  cattle   CS32; Job39; H3
stall-fed calves   Je46
sterile land   KF9

14 FARMING

stone wall   Pro24; Is5
store chambers   Ps33
straw   KF4; Is11, 25
stray animals, rules concerning   De22
   let them, any that   Z11
strike root like the poplar   Ho14
stubble   Is5, 10, 33, 40, 47; Je13
   burning   Joe2
   parched and dry   Na1
summer fruit, last gathering of   Mi7
sun, precious fruits brought forth by the   De33
swathes behind the reaper   Je9
terraced hills   E38
till your lands, aliens shall   Is61
tillage   CF27
   of your fields   Is23
tilled, land now desolate shall be   E36
tiller of the soil, Cain was a   Gen4
tilling land   Pro28; Z13
thorn hedge, sharper than a   Mi7
threshed with a sledge   Is28
threshing   Je50; Am1
   corn   Is21; Ho10
   floor   SS6, 24; CF13, 21; CS3; Job39; Is21; Je51; D2;
       Ho9, 13; Joe2; Mi4
     contributions from   Nu15
     corn from   Nu18
     Philistines plundering the   SF23
     winnowing barley on the   Ru2
   instruments   SS24
     iron   Am1
     with teeth   Is41
   sledge   SS24; Job41; Is28
     iron-spiked   Am1
     sharp   Is41
   start your   Mi4
transplanted, can it flourish?   E17
treading grapes   Joe3; Am9
   winepresses   Ne13
tree fellers   CS2
trenched land   Is5

14 FARMING

vine   Gen9, 49; Ju9; Nu20; KF4; KS4, 18; Ps78, 80, 105, 128;
        Job15; So6ff; Je6, 8, 31, 48; Is1, 3, 5, 7, 16, 18, 24,
        Is27, 32, 34, 36ff, 61; La2; E15, 17, 19; Joe1f; Mi1, 4; Na2;
        H3; Hg2; Z3, 8; Ma3
   choice red   Je2
   leaf withers from the   Is34
vine-dressers   KS25; CF27; CS26; Is61; Je39, 52; Joe1
vines, aliens shall tend your   Is61
   killed by hailstones   Ps78
   land of   De8
   of Sibmah   Is16
   place for planting   Mi1
   red   Is5
   sicken   Is24
vineyard   SF8; KF4, 21; KS5, 18; CF27; Ne9; Job24; Pro24, 32;
       So1, 7ff; Is3, 5, 16, 18, 27; Ho2; Je12, 31, 35; Am5, 9; Mi1
   buying and selling a   Je32
   by the waterside   E19
   cottage in a   Is1
   five acres of   Is5
   mortgaged   Ne5
   Naboth's   KF21
   new, unused   De20
   no second crop   De22
   Noah's   Gen9
   of En-gedi   So1
   shelter in a   Is1
   wall of a   Pro24
vineyards at Timnath   Ju14
   derelict   Is5
   I planted   Ec2
   laid waste   Am4
   land of   Is36
   of red wine   Is27
   pillaged their   Na2
   plant   Ps107; Is37; E28
     but shall not drink the wine of   Zp1
   planted pleasant   Am5
   which you did not plant   De6; Jos24
vintage   Je48; Ho2; Joe1; Am9
   last gleanings of the   Mi7

14 FARMING

vintagers   Je6, 49; Ob1
walls, vineyard   Pro24; Is5
watering herds at time of drought   KF18
watermelons   Nu11
wheat   Ex9; SF12; KF5; CS2; Pro27; So7; Is28; Je12, 31, 41;
    E4, 27, 45; Joe1; Am5, 8
  harvest   SF6, 12
    time of   Ju15
  land of   De8
  men sow, and reap thistles   Je12
winepress   KS6; Job24; Is63; La1; Joe3; Z14
  hewed out of stone   Is5
  of Moab   Is16
winnowers   Je51
  barley   Ru3
  wind too strong   Je4
woodman   CS2; Ps74
wool production   KS3; Is1, 51; D7; Ho2
yield, a mere gallon from five acres of vineyard   Is5
  a mere peck from ten bushels of seed   Is5
yoke   KF19; La1, 5; Mi2; Na1
  of iron   De28
  of oxen   Je51
  ox and ass separately   De22
  ploughing   Ho10f

NEW TESTAMENT

barley   J6
  measures of   Rev6
barn, barns, collect the wheat into my   Mw13
  ravens have no   L12
  pull down and build greater   L12
brushwood   Mk11
bull   LH9f
calf   LH9
  fatted   L15
cattle, dealers in   J2
  fattening yourselves like   LJ5
  feeding   L17

14 FARMING

chaff, he will burn on a fire Mw3; L3
corn Mw12f; Mk4; L6, 12, 17; A7, 27; PTF5, 9
  ears of Mk2, 4; L6
  in Egypt A7
  ox that treadeth out the PCF9; PTF5
  storehouses for L12
  two women grinding L17
  was scorched Mk4
cornfield, cornfields Mk2; L6
  Jesus went through the Mw12
crop, farmer has first claim on the PTS2
  his land may yield precious LJ5
  I sent you to reap a J4
  is heavy, but labourers are scarce Mw9f
  send labourers to harvest his L10
crops in their seasons, he sends you A14
  land yielded heavy L12
once more the land bore LJ5
darnel sowed among the wheat Mw13
ditch Mw12, 15
  both fall in the L6
dung and dig about the fig tree L13
  heap, useless on the L14
  hill L14
ears of corn, began to pluck Mk2
    plucking L6
fan, winnowing Mw3; L3
farm Mk6; L9, 15
  elder son was out on the L15
farmer PTS2
  can only wait in patience LJ5
fat beasts Mw22
fatling Mw22
fatted calf L15
field, darnel in the Mw13
  flower of the LPF1; LJ1
  if a man is in the Mk13
  is the world Mw13
  like treasure buried in a Mw13
  lilies of the Mw6; L12
  two men shall be in the L17

14 FARMING

fields are already white, ripe for harvest   J4
  comes back from the   L17
  cut brushwood in the   Mk11
  he who is in the   L17
  sent him into his   L15
  shepherds in the   L2
  the men who mowed your   LJ5
flax   Mw12
flock, feed the   LPF5
  keeping watch over their   L2
  not sheep of my   J10
  savage wolves will not spare the   A20
  tending a   PCF9
  will be scattered   Mw26
fold, sheep not belonging to this   J10
garden across the Kedron ravine   J18
  near Golgotha   J19
  you are God's   PCF3
garner, gather his wheat into the   Mw3; L3
grafted wild olive   PR11
grain of wheat   J12
granary   Mw3; L3
grape-harvest, earth's   Rev14
grinding corn, two women   L17
harvest, bears a rich   J12
  by their perseverance yield a   L8
  first fruits of the   PCF15
  four months more and then comes   J4
  is the end of time   Mw13
  let both grow together until the   Mw13
  of corruption, he will reap   PG6
  of an honest life   LH12
  of faith, reap the   LPF1
  of righteousness   PPs1
  of the Spirit   PG5
  of their toil   J4
  multiply it and swell the   PCS9
  reaped by peacemakers   LJ3
  send forth labourers into his   L10
    labourers to   Mw9
  time has come   Mk4

14 FARMING

harvest to come, first fruits of the   PR8
hay and straw, build with   PCF3
hedge, vineyard   Mw21
hedgerows, on the highways and among the   L14
heifers   LH9
herd of pigs, a large   L8
hireling shepherd   J10
homestead shall fall desolate   A1
husbandman   Mw21; Mk12; L20; J15; PTS3; LJ5
   tenant   Mk12
husks that the swine did eat   L15
labourer worthy of his hire   PTF5
lambs among wolves   L10
land, I have bought a piece of   L14
   salt is useless on the   L14
landowners, attached himself to one of the local   L15
lopped some of the branches   PR11
manure and dig around it   L13
manager, laid him in a   L2, 13
muzzle the threshing ox, you shall not   PCF9; PTF5
mowed your fields, the men who   LJ5
oxen   Mw22; L14; J2; A14
   I have bought five yoke of   L14
pasture, go and find   J10
   leaves the flock in the open   L15
pigs, a large herd of   L8
   sent him to mind the   L15
plant or water, whether they work as a team   PCF3
plot of land, Judas bought a   A1
plough, plow   L9; PCF9
ploughing, plowing, a servant   L17
ploughman   PCF9
reap and store in barns, birds no not   Mw6
   bountifully, sow bountifully   PCS9
   stretch out your sickle and   Rev1
   the harvest of faith   LPF1
   what you did not sow   L19
reaper   Mw13; J4
reapers are angels, the   Mw13
   unpaid   LJ5
reaping, sparse sowing, sparse   PCS9

14 FARMING

seed fell along the footpath, some   Mw13; Mk4; L8
  fell on stony ground, some   Mw13; Mk4; L8
  for sowing, he who provides the   PCS9
  I planted the   PCF3
shearer   A8
sheep   Mw9, 12, 15; L17; J2, 5, 10, 21; A8; PR8; Rev18
  a servant minding   L17
  and cattle, cargoes of   Rev18
  dealers in   J2
  fold   J10
  for slaughter   PR8
  he calls by name   J10
  hears his voice   J10
  lost   Mw15
  market   J5
  of my flock   J10
  straying like   LPF2
  tend my   J21
  which fell into the ditch   Mw12
  without a shepherd   Mw9
shepherd   Mw2, 9, 25f; Mk6, 14; L2; L10; A20; LPF2, 5; LJu1
  I am the good   J10
  of my people Israel   Mw2
  of the church   A20
  of the sheep, great   LH13
  the Lamb will be their   Rev7
sickle   Mk4; Rev14
slaughter, the day for   LJ5
slaughtered, led like sheep to be   A8
sow and reap and store in barns   Mw6
  birds of the air do not   Mw6
  bountifully, reap bountifully   PCS9
  reap what you did not   L19
  seed in the field of his lower nature   PG6
sower   Mk4; J4
  parable of the   Mk4
  went out to sow   Mw13
sowing, sparse reaping, sparse   PCS9
sows, a man reaps what he   PG6
stall, ox and ass   L13
steward, farm   Mw20

14 FARMING

storehouse   L12
stubble   PCF3
swine did eat, husks that the   L15
  herd of many   Mk5; L8
  sent him to feed   L15
swineherd   Mk5
tares   Mw13
tenant vine-growers   Mw12; L20
thistles choked the corn   Mk4
thresh in the hope of getting some of the produce   PCF9
thresher   PCF9
threshing floor   Mw3; L3
  ox, you shall not muzzle the   PCF9; PTF5
vine dresser   L13
  grower   Mw21
  growers, tenant   Mk12; L20
vineyard   Mw20f; Mk12; L13, 20; PCF9
  parable of the   Mw20f; Mk12; L20
vintage season   Mw21
wall, vineyard   Mw21; Mk12
wheat, a thousand bushels of   L16
  corn of   J12
  gather into his granary   Mw3
  measure of   Rev6
  measured   L16
  or some other grain   PCF15
  sifts you like   L22
  sowed tares among the   Mw13
winnow his threshing floor   Mw3; L3
winnowing fan   Mw3
wolf harries the flock and scatters the sheep   J10
yoke   A15; PG5
  of oxen, I have bought five   L14

15 *Feasts, Fasts and Festivals*

OLD TESTAMENT

ablution ritual   Ex30ff
abstention from wine and strong drink   Nu6
abstinence, appoint a day of   Joe1f
acclamation, day of   Nu29
anointing, rites of   Ex25ff; Le8
appointed seasons, commemoration of   Ne10; La2
assemblies   Is1
assembly, citizens in   Mi6
atonement, day of   Le24
banquet, Esther's   Est5ff
  in honour of Esther   Est2
  is set out   Is21
  of Ahasuerus   Est1
  of Balshazzar   D5
  of Nabal   SF25
  royal, for the women   Est1
banqueting hall, Balshazzar's   D5
blood not to be eaten   Le3, 17
bread from heaven   Ne9
ceremonial, sacred   Am5
ceremonies   Is1
circumcise your hearts   De10, 30; Je4
circumcised, Israeli people again   Jos5
  those born in the wilderness   Jos5
circumcision for every male   Ex13
  of Moses   Ex4
  of Shechem's men   Gen34
  rite of   Le12
  sign of   Gen17
consecrated from birth   Ju13
convocation, holy   Le24
danced for Joy, David and all Israel   SS6
dancers of King Saul   SF18
day of atonement   Le24
  of acclamation   Nu29

15 FEASTS, FASTS AND FESTIVALS

drunk, David made Uriah   SS11
fast, Daniel's three-week   D10
  day, read the words of the Lord on the   Je36
  earth on their heads for the   Ne9
  people of Ninevah ordered a public   Jon3
  proclaim a solemn   Joe1f
  the Israelites assembled for a   Ne9
  why do we   Is58
fasted all day, confessing   SF7
fasting, Daniel spent the night   D6
  in sackcloth and ashes   D9
  in the fifth and seventh months   Z7
  in the fourth, seventh and tenth months   Z8
fatted calves, feasting on   Am6
feast, Absalom prepared a   SS13
  annual appointed   CS8
  at the hill shrine   SF9
  days, I despise your   Am5
    ritual of   E46
  David gave for Abner   SS3
  for seven days they kept the   Ne8
  for the Aramaean army   KS6
  instead of mourning   Is22
  live in leafy arbours during the   Ne8
  of fatlings   Is25
  of Hezekiah   CS8
  of Job's sons   Job1
  of new moons   SF20; KS4; CS2, 8; Ez3; Ne10; Ps81; Is1, 66;
      E45f; Am8
  of tabernacles   CS8
  of the Passover   Le23; Nu28; De16; Jos5; CS7, 30, 35; Ez6; E45
  of the seventh month   Ne8
  of unleavened bread   CS8, 30, 35
  of weeks   CS8
  on the fourteenth and fifteenth day of Adar   Est9
  pilgrim   Ex5, 10, 23; Le23; Nu28ff; De31; KF8, 12;
      CS5, 8, 30, 35; Ez3, 6; Ps81; Is29; E45; Ho9; Am5, 8;
      Z14; Ma2
  Zion, city of our solemn   Is33
feasts, all the set   Ez3

15 FEASTS, FASTS AND FESTIVALS

feasts, appointed   Is1, 5
  keep thy solemn   Na1
  lure them to ruin   Ps69
  rich and sumptuous   Ps63
festal assembly   La2
  day   Ho7, 9
festival, Jerusalem at the time of   E36
  new moon   SF20; CS2, 8
  of citizens of Shechem   Ju9
  of joy and gladness   Z8
  of Purim, origins of   Est9
festivals, I cannot tolerate your   Is1
  I will put a stop to her   Ho2
first fruit, day of   Nu28ff
  male, dedicated   De15
  rights   De21
forbidden fruit for three years   Le19
garland   Ps142; Is28, 61; La5
hallowed fiftieth year   Le25
harvest thanksgiving   Ex23
jubilee, year of   Le25
liquor, they drink   Am2
merry with wine, King Ahasuerus   Est1
myrtle branches   Ne8
new moon, ceremony of the   Ho2; Am8
    commemoration of the   Ne10
    feast of the   SF20; CS2, 8; Ps81; Ez3; Is1; E45ff
    month by month at the   Is66
    nor sabbath, neither   KS4
olive branches   Ne8
palm branches   Ne8
Passover, feast of the   Le23; Nu9, 28; De16; Jos5; CS7, 30, 35; Ez6; E45
  penalty for neglecting the   Nu9
pilgrim-feast   Nu28ff; De16; KF8, 12; CS5, 8, 30 35; Ps81; I s29; E45; Am5, 8; Ma2
  all must keep   Ex10
  in the wilderness   E5
  of tabernacles   De16, 31; Ez3; Z14
  of Unleavened Bread   Ex23; Le23; De16; Ez6
  Solomon's   KF8

15 FEASTS, FASTS AND FESTIVALS

pilgrim-feast, the day of the Lord's   Ho9
pilgrimage to Shiloh, annual   Ju21
  make your   Na1
  put a stop to her   Ho2
procession of choirs   Ne12
purification, ceremonies of   Le11ff; Nu19, 31
Purim, festival of   Est9
sabbath, day of joy   Is58
  do not work on the   Je17
  from one to another   Is66
  her priests have disregarded my   E22
  holy, they shall keep my   E44
  I cannot endure   Is1
  keep holy   De5
    as I commanded your forefathers   Je17
  keeps undefiled   Is56
  offerings according to the law of Moses   CS8
  opened only on the   E46
  penalties for breaking the   Nu15
  prince shall be responsible for the   E45
  profaning the   Ex31ff
  put a stop to her   Ho2
  rest on the   Ex16
  tenth day of the seventh month   Le16
  they had polluted my   E20
  thou hast profaned my   E22
  when will it be past   Am8
  whole-offerings on the   CS2
sacred seasons   Is1; E45
shaving, cleansing by   Nu6
  Levites ceremony of   Nu8
  Nazarite ritual of   Nu6
  the body   Nu8
table, delights of the   Ps141
teetotal, Rechabites   Je35
unclean animals   Le11
  ritually   Nu5
uncircumcised lips of Moses   Ex6
  their ears are   Je6
Unleavened Bread, feast of   Ex23; Le23; De16; Ez6

15 FEASTS, FASTS AND FESTIVALS

NEW TESTAMENT

anoint with oil in the name of the Lord   LJ5
banquet, Herod's   Mk6
   not one of those who were invited shall taste my   L14
baptism, accepted John's   L7
   an appeal made to God   LPF3
   as a token of repentance   A13, 19
   in the one Spirit   PCF12
   Noah's flood prefigured the water of   LPF3
   of Jesus Christ   Mw3
   of John the Baptist   Mk1; L20
     was it from God, or from man?   Mk11
     Whence was it   Mw21
   of the doctrine of   LH6
   on behalf of the dead   PCF15
   that I am baptized with   Mw20
   they all received   PCF10
   you were buried with him in   PCo2
baptize in the name of the Father   Mw28
   in water   J1
   you with the Holy Spirit and with fire   L3
baptized, bishop must not be newly   PTF3
   in the river Jordan   Mw3
   Jesus, John the Baptist   Mw3
   many Corinthians were   A18
   Saul was   A9
   the eunuch, Philip   A8
   when Jesus too had been   L3
   with water, John   A1
birthday, Herod's   Mk6
blood, abstain from   A15, 21
bread is my own flesh   J6
circumcise on the sabbath   J7
circumcised, is happiness confined to the   PR4
   they must be   A15
   those who were not   A15
   Timothy out of consideration for the Jews   A16
circumcision, Christ's way of   PCo2
   has value, provided you keep the law   PR2

15 FEASTS, FASTS AND FESTIVALS

circumcision, if you receive   PG5
  of Jesus   L2
  of John the Baptist   L1
  telling them to give up   A21
cleansing rites   LH6
debauchery or vice, no   PR13
Dedication, Festival of the   J10
drunkenness, no revelling or   PR13
  revelling, work of the flesh   PG5
Easter   A12
eat, drink and be merry   L12
eating and drinking, kingdom of God is not   PR14
fast, Pharisees were keeping a   Mk2
  twice a week, I   L18
  was already over   A27
  when you, do not look gloomy like the hypocrites   Mw6
  while they were keeping a   A13
fasted forty days and nights, Jesus   Mw4
fasting and praying day and night   L2
  approving ourselves in   PCS6
  for forty days   L4
  John's disciples are much given to   L5
  this kind goeth not out but by prayer and   Mw17
fatted calf, bring the   L15
feast for you, I have prepared this   Mw22
  in honour of the bull-calf   A7
  in the kingdom of God, happy the man who shall   L14
  Levi made him a great   L5
  of Tabernacles   J7
  to celebrate the day, let us have a   L15
  wedding   L14; J2
  with Abraham, Isaac and Jacob   Mw8
feasted in great magnificence every day   L16
feasts, love to have places of honour at   Mk12; L20
festival, observance of   PCo2
  of the Dedication   J10
  of the Passover   Mk14; J5, 12f; PCF5
  of Unleavened Bread   Mk14; L22; A12
  season, custom to release a prisoner at the   Mw27
garlands, oxen and   A14
holy day, let no man judge you in observance of an   Pco2

15 FEASTS, FASTS AND FESTIVALS

Holy Ghost, baptize with the   A1
   communion of the   PCS13
last supper   Mk14; J13
laying on of hands   A8; LH6
Lord's day   Rev1
   supper, impossible for you to eat the   PCF11
love feasts, a blot on your   LJu1
marriage supper of the Lamb   Rev19
meal, Passover   J18
Mosaic practice of circumcision   A15
myrrh, anointed his feet with   L7
new moon, observance of the   PCo2
palms in their hands   Rev7
party for lunch or supper   L14
   wedding   L12
Passover   Mw26; Mk14; L2, 22; J2, 5, 11ff; 18f; A12, 20; PCF5; LH11
   eve of the   J19
   feast of   A12
   festival   Mk14; L2; J2, 12f; PCF5
   go to Jerusalem for the   L2
   hymn   Mk14
   lambs being slaughtered   Mk14
   Moses celebrated the   LH11
   season   J18
   supper   Mk14
Pentecost   A20; PCF16
pilgrims come to the festival   J12
place of honour, do not sit in the   L14
Preparation day   Mk15
prisoner to be released at the festive season   Mw27
procession, captives in Christ's triumphal   PCS2
purification, Jewish rites of   J2
purify themselves before the Passover   J11
reception, Levi held a big   L5
rites of cleansing   LH9
   of purification   J2
rooms at feasts, the chief   L20
Sabbath came, he began to teach when   Mk6
  day before the   Mk15
  daybreak after the   Mw28; Mk16

15 FEASTS, FASTS AND FESTIVALS

Sabbath, forbidden on the   Mw12
  he began to teach on the   Mk1
  he was not only breaking the   J5
  observance of the   PCo2
  pray it may not be the   Mw24
  rest awaits the people of God   LH4
  Son of Man is sovereign over the   Mw12; L6
  was a day of great solemnity   J19
  was made for man, not man for the Sabbath   Mk2
  why are they doing what is forbidden on the   Mk2
  you are not allowed to carry your bed on the   J5
seats of honour in the synagogues   L11
shave their heads in ritual purification   A21
strangled, abstain from anything that has been   A15, 21
supper in Jesus's honour   J12
  last   Mk14; L22
  Lord's   PCF11
  Passover   Mw26; Mk14; L22
sworn not to eat or drink   A23
Tabernacles, feast of   J7
table, may eat and drink at my   L22
take this and eat, this is my body   Mw26; Mk14
this is my blood, the blood of the covenant   Mw26; Mk14
Unleavened Bread, festival of   Mw26; L22; A12, 20
wedding feast is ready   Mw22
Whitsuntide   PCF16

16   *Food, Drink and Spices*

OLD TESTAMENT

allowance of food, daily   Ne5; Je40; E4; D1
almond   Je1
apple   So2, 7ff; Joe1
apricot   So2, 7
banquet of Adonijah   KF1
  of Nabal   SF25
banqueting house   So2
barley   Ex9; SS14, 17; KF4; CF11; CS2; Job31; Ls28; Je41;
       E4, 13, 45; Ho3; Joe1
  cake   Ju7; E4
  loaf   KS4
beans   SS17; E4
bitter-apples   KS4
blood, on no account eat   De12
  they ate meat with the   SF14
bread   SF16f, 21, 28; SS6; KS4; CF16; Ne5; Job42; Ps14, 37, 53, 78,
       Ps80, 102, 104, 127,132ff; Pro4, 25, 28; Ec9; Is3ff, 55, 58;
       Je5, 37ff, 41ff, 52; La1, 4f; E4f, 12ff, 24, 44ff; D10; Ho2, 9;
       Am4, 8; Hg2; Ma1
  alone, man cannot live by   De8
  bakes on the fire   Is44
  brought by ravens   KF17
  clean and unclean   E4
  corn   Is28
  daily   Ps105
  from heaven   Ex16; Ps105
  land of   Is36
  of angels   Ps78
  of the Presence   Ex25ff, 35
  shall not lack   Is51
  unleavened   E45
broth   Gen25; Ju6; KS4; E24; Hg2
butter   SS17; Job20; Ps55; Pro30; Is7
  in a lordly dish   Ju5
butter-cake, manna tasted like   Nu11

16 FOOD, DRINK AND SPICES

cake   SS13; CF23; Ho7
  baked on hot stones   KF19
  barley   E4
  crescent   Je7, 44
  fig   CF12
  of dried figs   SF25
  of manna   Nu11
  of unleavened bread   SF28
  make a small   KF17
  Nazirite offering of   Nu6
  raisin   CF12, 16; Ho3
  unleavened   Le23; Ju6
    and bitter herbs   Nu9
cheese   SF17; SS13; Job10
corn   De33; KS4, 18; CS31ff; Job28; Ps4, 65, 72; Pro3; Ne5;
      Is17, 55, 62; Je31; La2, 5; E36; Ho2, 7f, 10, 14; Joe2; Am8ff;
      Hg1ff; Z9, 12
  ears in the husk   KS4
  they shall eat your   E25
  those who bring in the   Is62
cracknels   KF14
cream   Job20
cream-cheese   SF17
crops destroyed by eastern tribes   Ju6
cucumber   Is1; Je10
curds   SS17; Job20; Is7
dates   So7
donkeys head as siege food   KS6
dough   SS13; Ne10; E44
  kneading   Je7; Ho7
"doves' dung", locust beans   KS6
drink, strong   De14
drunk, Ben-hadad became   KF20
  king Elah became   KF16
  Nabal became   SF25
  Noah became   Gen9
  with a bitter draught   Ps60
drunkards   Ps69
fat not to be eaten   Le3
fatted calf   SF28; Am6
feast of Abimelech   Gen26

16 FOOD, DRINK AND SPICES

feast of Isaac   Gen26
  of Jacob   Gen29, 31
  of Joseph   Gen43
  of Laban   Gen29, 31
fermented, eat nothing   Ex12
figs   SF25, 30; CF12; Ne13; Ps78; So2; Is28; Je8, 24, 29; Ho9; Joe1ff; Na3; Hg2; Mi7
fish   Ne13
flour   KF4, 17; CF9, 23; E16, 46
food, daily allowance of   Ne5; Je40; E4; D1
fowl prepared for the table   KF4; Ne5
fruit   SS16; Ne9; Ps148; Ec2; Mi7
  forbidden   Gen3
  they shall eat thy   E25
gall, root from which springs   De29
  their grapes are   De32
gleaning   Is17, 24
gourds, wild   KS4; Jon4
grain, a land of   KS18
  of heaven   Ps78
grapes   Ne13; Job15, 24; So2, 7; Is5, 62f, 65; Je8, 25, 31; La1; Ho9; Joe3; Am9; Ob1; Mi7
  eat another's   De23
  gleaning   De24; Is17, 24
  red, of Sibmah   Is16
  those who gather, shall drink   Is62
  treading   Je25; Joe3; Mi6
herbs   KS4; Pro15; Is18; La3
  bitter   Nu9; La3
    and unleavened cakes   Nu9
honey   Gen43; Ju14; SS17; KF14; KS18; Job20; Ps119, 81, 118; Pro5, 24ff; Je11, 32, 41; So4ff; Is7; E3, 16, 20, 27
  a land of   De8
  what is sweeter than?   Ju14
honeycomb   SF14; Ps19; Pro5, 24, 27; So4ff
kneaded dough   SS13
kneading, contribution from the first   Nu15
leaven, rid your house of   Ex12
lentils   Gen25; SS17, 23; E4
liquor   Is5; Am2
locust beans   KS6

16 FOOD, DRINK AND SPICES

loaf   SF10, 17, 25; SS6, 16; KF14; CF16
  barley   KS4
  daily ration of one   Je37
manna ceased at Gilgal   Jos5
  like coriander seed   Nu11
  rained down   Ps78
  tasted like butter-cake   Nu11
  they called the food   Ex16
marrow, fatling   Is25
meal   SF1, 28; SS17; KF4; KS4; CF12; Is47; E27
  women grinding   Ec12
meat   SS6; Ps78, 106; Pro30; E24
  brought by ravens   KF17
  "give us to eat"   Nu11
  portion of   CF16
  roast   Is44
  rules for eating   De12
  with the blood in it   SF14
melon   Nu11
milk   Job10, 29; So4ff; Is7; Je11, 32; La4; E20, 25; Joe3
  and honey, flowing with   Ex3; Le20; Nu13; De11, 26ff
  churning of   Pro30
  goat's   Pro27
  mother's, do not boil a kid in its   De14
  sheep's   E34
  skin full of   Ju4
millet   E4
mulberry   Is40
nitre upon vinegar   Pro25
nuts   So6
oil   KF17; SF9, 10, 16; KS18; CF12; CS2, 31ff; Ez6; Ne5, 10; Job24, 29; Ps55, 109; Pro21; Is39, 57, 61; Je31, 40ff; E27, 45; Ho2, 12; Joe1ff; Am6; Mi6; Hg1f
olive   SF8; Ps128; Ho14; H3; Hg2
  oil   Ex30ff; KF5; E16
  pounded   Ex27f; Nu28
onions   Nu11
parched grain   SS17
pastry   CF23
pigs, those who eat the flesh of   Is66
poison of dragon is their vine   De32

16 FOOD, DRINK AND SPICES

pomegranate   SF4; So4, 6, 8; Je52; Joe1; Hg2
  juice   So8
pottage   Gen25; KS4; Hg2
  sold his birthright for a mess of   Gen25
provender and straw for the asses   Ju19
pulse   D1
raisins   SF30; KF14; CF12, 16; So2
  cake of   SS6; Ho3
  clusters of   SS16
  ration, daily   Ne5; Je40; E4; D1
rats, those who eat the flesh of   Is66
salt   KS2, 14; Ez4, 6ff; Job6, 32; E43, 47
  sowed the site with   Ju9
shewbread   Ex25ff; Nu4
skin full of milk   Ju4
spice   KF10; KS20; CS9, 32; Ps75; So4f, 8; Is39; Je6; E24
  choicest   E27
  golden   Is60
  powdered   So3
spices, aloe   Ps45; So4
  balm   Gen37; E27
  balsam   Gen43; Ex25ff; So6; Ez7
  calamus   Ex30; So4; E27
  camphire   So1, 4
  caper bud   Ec12
  cassia   Ex30f; Ps45; Pro7; E27
  cinnamon   Ex30f; Pro7; So2, 4
  coriander seed   Nu11
  cummin   Is28
  dill   Is28
  frankincense   So3ff
  henna   So4, 7
  myrrh   Gen37, 43;
    a bunch of   So1
  saffron   So4
  spikenard   So1, 4
spice-bearing mountains   So8
spiced wine   Ps75; Pro9; So7f; Is65
spelt   E4
starvation, curse of   De28
stew   E24

16 FOOD, DRINK AND SPICES

stewing meat   SF2
strong drink, addiction to   Is28
summer fruits   SS16; Is16; Je40; Am8; Mi7
sweet cane   So4; Is43; Je6; E27
swine's flesh, eating   Is65
syrup   KF14; Ps19; So4f; E27
thirst, curse of   De28
topers, confirmed   Is28
unleavened cakes   Le8; Jos5
  bread   Ex12; KS23
vegetables to eat, give us only   D1
venison for Isaac   Gen27
vinegar   Nu6; Ps69; Pro10, 25
  shall drink no   Nu6
water to drink, give us only   D1
watermelon   Nu11
wax   Ps68, 97
wheat   Ex9; SF12; SS17; KF5; CS2; Ez6; Pro27; So7; Is28; Je12,31, 41;
    E4, 27, 45; Joe1; Am5, 8
  flour   Ps81
wine   Gen9; Nu18; De14; Ju13; SF1, 10, 16, 25; SS6, 16; KS6, 18;
    CF9, 12, 27; CS2, 31ff; Ez6; Ne2, 5, 10, 13; Est1; Ps4, 60, 75,
    Ps78; Pro3ff, 20ff, 31; Is5, 22, 24, 27ff, 36, 49, 51, 56, 65; Ec9;
    So1, 4ff, 7; J13, 23, 25, 31, J35, 40, 48, 51; La2; E27, 44;
    D5, 10; Ho2f, 7, 9; Joe1ff; Am2, 9; Mi2; H2; Zp1; Hg1ff; Z9ff
  addicted to   Is28
  daily allowance of   D1
  drink with rejoicing   De14
  let foreigners drink the new   Is62
  mixed with water   Is1
  mulled   So8
  offering of   Le23
  on the lees, well refined   Is25
  produce of the press   Nu18
  prohibited in the tent of the Presence   Le10
  settled on its lees   Je48
  spiced   Ps75; Pro9; So7f; Is65
  wash robes in   Gen49
  well matured, strained clear   Is25
wine-cellar   CF227

16 FOOD, DRINK AND SPICES

wine-garden   So2
wine-press   Nu18; KS6; Job24; Ls63; La1; Joe3; Z14

NEW TESTAMENT

anise   Mw23
appetite, all that panders to the   LJF2
  is their god   PPs3
baking, bread of a new   PCF5
  meal   Rev6
  measure   Rev6
bread   Mw4, 6f, 12, 14ff, 26; Mk2, 6ff, 14; L4, 6f, 9, 11, 14f, 22,
    L24; J6, 13, 21; A2, 12, 20, 27; PCF5, 10f; PCS9; ThS3; LH9
  a stone when he asks for   Mw7
  alone, man cannot live by   Mw4; L4
  are we to spend twenty pounds on   Mk6
  daily   M6; L11
  dipped in the dish   J13
  during supper he took   Mk14
  enough and to spare, hired servants have   L15
  forgotten to take   Mw16; Mk8
  from heaven, he gave them   J6
  give us each day our daily   M6; L11
  he broke   L24
  he who eats   J13
  he who provides the   PCS9
  I was not speaking about   Mw16
  if a son should ask for   L11
  Jesus took   Mw26
  of a new baking   PCF5
  of life   J6
  sacred   Mk2
  take no   Mk6
  tell these stones to become   Mw4; L4
  they had forgotten to take with them   Mw6; Mk8
  they wash not their hands when they eat   Mw15
  to eat, took sacred   L6
  to take the children's   Mk7
  unleavened   L22; A12; PCF5

16 FOOD, DRINK AND SPICES

bread, where are we to buy   J6
  with unwashed hands, eat   Mk7
  work, and eat their own   ThS3
cinnamon and spice, cargoes of   Rev18
cummin   Mw23
dill   Mw23
dinner   L14
dough, consecrated   PR11
  leaven in the   PG5
  leavens all the   PCF5
drinker, a bishop must not be a   Tt1
drinking, not given to excessive   PTF3
  they have been   A2
drunkards are drunk at night   ThF5
  no grabbers or   PCF6
drunkenness, do not give way   PE5
  revelry and tippling, you lived in   LPF4
eat and drink, for tomorrow we die, let us   PCF15
  or drink, sworn not to   A23
    take you to task about what you   PCo2
  who will not work shall not   ThS3
  without raising questions of conscience   PCF10
eating food with defiled hands   Mk7
eats and drinks judgement on himself   PCF11
egg, offer a scorpion when he asks for an   L11
fig   Mw7, 21, 24; Mk11; L6, 13; LJ3; Rev6
fish, broiled   L24
  a few small   Mw15; Mk8
  five loaves and two   Mw14; Mk6; L9; J6
  offer a snake when he asks for   L11
  offered him a piece of   L24
flour   Mw13; L13; Rev6, 18
  and wheat, cargoes of   Rev18
food and drink, put away anxious thoughts about   Mw6; L12
  and good cheer in plenty, he gives you   A14
  anyone who has must share   L3
  consecrated to heathen deities   PCF8
  is for the belly and the belly for food   PCF6
  of eternal life   J6
  the Son of Man will give you   J6
  they ate the same supernatural   PCF10

16 FOOD, DRINK AND SPICES

food, they had gone a long time without   A27
   was locusts and wild honey, John's   Mw3
fruit of the vine   L22
glutton, lazy   Tt1
grape   Mw7; L6; Rev14
greed, never been a cloak for   ThF2
herbs, all manner of   L11
   another who is weak eateth   PR14
   tithes of   Mw23
honey, his food was wild   Mw3; Mk1
   sweet as   Rev10
honeycomb   L24
hyssop   LH9
leaven   Mw13; Mk8; L13; PCF5; PG5
   hid in three measures of meal   L13
   of Herod, beware the   Mk8
   of the Pharisees, be on your guard against   Mk8
leavened bread   PCF5
locusts, fed on   Mw3; Mk1
loaf   Mw14f; Mk8; L9, 11; PCF10
   they had only one, in the boat   Mk8
loaves and two fishes, five   Mw14; Mk6; L0; J6
   how many have you?
lunch   L14
manna, I will give you hidden   Rev2
   jar containing   LH9
   our ancestors had   J6
marjoram   J19; LH9
meal, leaven in   Mw13; L13
   wait on me while I have my   L17
meat, he who abstains from eating   PR14
   he who eats   PR14
   that has been offered to idols   A15
milk instead of solid food   PCF3; LH5
   tend a flock without using its   PCF9
mint   M23; L11
new wine must be put in new bottles   Mw9; Mk2
oil, olive   L16; Rev6
olives   LJ3; Rev6
rations at the proper time, issue their   L12
rue   L1

16 FOOD, DRINK AND SPICES

salt   Mw5; Mk9; L14; PCo4
sober, keep awake and   ThF5
   temperate, leader must be   PTF3
sop, he dipped the   J13
sour wine   Mw27; Mk15; L23; J19
spice and cinnamon, cargoes of   Rev18
spices   J19
strong drink, he shall never touch   L1
    slaves to   Tt2
supper, Passover   Mw26; Mk14; L14; J13
table, he took his place at   L7
unleavened bread   L22; A12; PCF5
vegetables, who eats only   PR14
vinegar, offered him a sponge full of   Mw27; Mk15; L23; J19
wheat, measure of   Rev6
wine   Mw9, 11, 26f; Mk2, 15; L1, 5, 7, 10, 23; J2, 19; A2; PR14; PE5;
     PTF3, 5; LPF4; Rev6, 14, 16, 18
  cargoes of   Rev18
  fierce   Rev16, 18
  for thy stomach's sake   PTF5
  he shall never touch   L1
  he was offered drugged   Mk15
  mingled with myrrh   Mk15
  mixed with gall   Mw27
  new   Mk2
  not given to   PTF3
  offered him their sour   L23
  sour   Mw27; Mk15; L23; J19
  sponge soaked in sour   Mw27; Mk15; L23; J19
  take a little   PTF5
  these men are full of new   A2
  to abstain from drinking   PR14
  water turned into   J2
  wherein is excess   PE5
yeast   Mw13, L13

17 *Geographical Features*

OLD TESTAMENT

bitumen used as mortar   Gen11
  pits of Siddim   Gen14
brimstone   Is30, 36
cave at Makkedah   Jos10
  at Mount Horeb   KF19
  Elijah's   KF19
  in the Rock of Etam   Ju15
  of Abraham's tomb   Gen23
  of Adullam   SF22; SS23; CF11; Mi1
  of Lot   Gen19
  of Machpelah   Gen23
  of Sarah's tomb   Gen25
  prophets hidden in the   KF18
  robbers'   Je7
  Saul went to relieve himself in the   SF24
caves, forced to find themselves   Ju6
  in the rocks   Is2
clay   Na3
  in the brick kiln   Je43
crag, towering   Ps71
earth trembled, heaven quaked   Ju5
  two mule loads of   KS5
earthquake blocking the valley   Z14
fen a waste of   Is14
flint   Is5, 50; Je5; E3
forest of Hareth   SF22
gorge of Arron   KS10
  of the Arabah   Am6
  of the Kidron   SS15; KF2, 15; KS23; CS15; 29ff; Je31
  of Shittim   Joe3
gullies   Ps104
heath   Mi1, 3
  open   Is32
hill of Bashan   Ps68
  of Gareb   Je31

17 GEOGRAPHICAL FEATURES

hill of Mizar   Ps42f
  of Samaria   Am4, 6
lime   Am2
Mount Carmel   Am1, 9
  of Esau   Ob1
  of Olives   Z14
  Paran   H3
  Zion   Ob1; Mi4
mountain   Ps2, 11, 15, 18, 24, 30, 65, 104, 144
  Abarim   De32
  Amana   So4
  Baalah   Jos15
  Baal-hermon   Ju3
  Carmel   KF18; KS2
  Ebal   De11, 26ff; Jos8
  Ephraim   Je4
  Ephron   Jos15
  Gaash   Jos24; Ju2
  Galud   Ju7
  Gerizim   De11, 27; Jos8; Ju9
  Gilboa   SF31; SS1; CF10
  Gilead   So4, 6
  Heres   Ju1
  Hermon   Jos11ff; CF5; Ps42, 89, 133; So4
  Hor   Nu20; Ps106
  Horeb   KF19; Ps106
  Jearim   Jos15
  Lebanon   Ju3
  like the lofty   Ps36
  Moriah   CS3
  my holy   Is65
  Nebo   De32, 34
  of the Lord's house   Is2
  Paran   De33
  Perazim   Is28
  Pisgah   De34
  Seir   Jos15
  Senir   So4
  Sinai   Ne9; Ps68
  Tabor   Ju4; Ps89; Ho5
  your holy   Je31

17 GEOGRAPHICAL FEATURES

mountain, Zalmon   Ju9
  Zion   Ps48, 74, 125f, 128f; Is8, 10, 18, 24, 29, 31, 37
mountains of Bether   So2
  of Israel   E33ff
  of Samaria   Am3ff
  of Seir   E35
  shudder   Is54, 64
  spice-bearing   So8
nitre   Pro25
oil, a land of   De8
  from the flinty rock   De32
ore   Je6
pass of Michmash   SF13
pitch, ark coated with   Gen6
plain full of bones   E37
  of Dura   D3
potash   Is1
ravine, break a heifer's neck in a   De21
  of Besor   SF30
  of Kerith   KF17
ravines, land of many   De10
  of Gaash   SS23; CF11
rock, dividing   SF23
  of Bozez   SF14
  of Oreb   Is10
  of the wild goats   SF24
  Seneh   SF14
  strike the   Ex17
salt, pillar of   Gen19
saltpit   Zp2
sand dunes   Is41
slime pits   Gen14
spice-bearing mountains   So8
thickets, Jordan's dense   Z11
vale of Achor   Is65
  of Aven   Am1
  of Elah   SF17, 21
  of Gibeon   Is28
  of Jezreel   Ho1
  of Jordan   SF31
  of Megiddo   CS35; Z12

17 GEOGRAPHICAL FEATURES

vale of Rephaim SS5, 23; CF11, 14; Is17
  of Trouble Ho2
valley Ps23, 65, 104
  blocked as by an earthquake Z14
  of Abarim E39
  of Achor Ho2
  of Ben-hinnom KS23; CS28, 33; Je7, 19, 32
  of Berakah CS20
  of Blessing CS20
  of Craftsmen Ne11
  of Decision Joe3
  of Gog's Horde E39
  of Hamon-gog E39
  of Hinnom Ne11
  of Jehoshaphat Joe3
  of Jordan SF31
  of Megiddon Z12
  of Rephaim SS5, 23; CF11, 14; Is17
  of Salt KS14; CF18; CS25
  of Slaughter Je7, 19
  of Succoth Ps108
  of the Dead Bodies Je31
  of the Lord's Judgement Joe3
  of Vision Is22
  of Woods Ne11
  of Zeboim SF13
  of Zephathah Cs14
valleys shall be lifted up Is40

NEW TESTAMENT

bay with a sandy beach A27
cave, robbers' Mw21; Mk11; L19
caves, hiding in LH11; Rev6
clay, potter's PR9
creek into which to thrust the ship A27
desert, time of testing in the LH3
  was strewn with their corpses PCF10
earthquake, a violent Rev6, 8, 11

17 GEOGRAPHICAL FEATURES

earthquake like none before in human history   Rev16
   suddenly there was a violent   A16
hill called Olivet   L19
   shall be brought low   L3
hills, seven, on which the woman sits   Rev17
   take to the   L21
Mount of Olives   Mw21, 24, 26; Mk11, 13f; L19, 21f; J8; A1
   sermon on the   Mw5
   Sinai   Mw5; A7; PG4; LH12
   Zion   PR9, 11; LH12; LPF2; Rev14
mountain and island moved from its place   Rev6
   blazing, hurled into the sea   Rev8
   in Galilee   Mw28
   led them up a high   Mw17; Mk9
   our fathers worshipped on this   J4
   sacred   LPS1
   Spirit carries me to a high   Rev21
   the devil took him to a very high mountain   Mw4
mountains and crags, fall on us   Rev6
   fall on us, then shall they say   L23
   seven   Rev17
hillside, went to pray up the   Mk6
quicksands   A27
Ravine of Kedron   J18
uplands of Juday   L1
valley, Jordan,
   shall be filled, every   L3
wilderness, Jesus in the   Mw4; Mk1; L1
   Judaean   Mw3

18 Health and Longevity

OLD TESTAMENT

affliction, bound in   Ps107
age of king Ahaz   KS16
   Amaziah   KS14
   Amon   KS21
   Azariah   KS14f
   Darius   D5
   David   SS5
   Hezekiah   KS18
   Ishbosheth   SS2
   Jehoahaz   KS23
   Jehoiachin   KS23
   Jehoiada   CS24
   Jehoiakin   KS24
   Jehoshaphat   KF22
   Jeroboam   KF15
   Joash   KS12
   Joram   K38
   Josiah   KS21
   Jotham   KS15
   Manasseh   KS21
   Reheboam   KF14; CS12
   Saul   SF13
   Zedekiah   KS24
of matriarch Sarah : 127 years   Gen23
of patriarch Aaron : 123 years   Ex7; Nu33
   Abraham : 175 years   Gen25
   Adam : 930 years   Gen5
   Amram : 137 years   Ex6
   Arphaxad : 438 years   Gen11
   Eber : 464 years   Gen11
   Enoch : 365 years   Gen5
   Enosh : 905 years   Gen5
   Isaac : 180 years   Gen35

18 HEALTH AND LONGEVITY

age of patriarch Ishmael : 137 years   Gen25
    Jacob : 147 years   Gen47
    Jared : 962 years   Gen5
    Job : approx 200 years   Job42
    Joseph : 110 years   Gen50
    Joshua : 110 years   Jos24; Ju2
    Kenan : 910 years   Gen5
    Kohath : 133 years   Gen5
    Lamech : 777 years   Gen5
    Levi : 137 years   Ex6
    Mahalalel : 895 years   Gen5
    Methuselah : 969 years   Gen5
    Moses : 120 years   Ex7; De31, 34
    Nahor : 138 years   Gen11
    Noah : 950 years   Gen9
    Peleg : 239 years   Gen11
    Reu : 239 years   Gen11
    Serug : 230 years   Gen11
    Seth : 912 years   Gen5
    Shelah : 433 years   Gen11
    Shem : 600 years   Gen11
aged, honour the   Le19
ague, burning   Le26; De28
baldness, infectious   Le13
bandage   Is1; E30, 34
blind, debarred   Le21
  respect the   Le19
blindness   De28; SS5; KF14; KS6; Je31
boil, poulticed   KS20; Is38
boils   Ex9; De28; KS20; Job2; Is38
bowels, anguish of   La1
  disease of   CS21
  prolapse of   CS21
breath, noisome   Job19
consumption   Le26; De28
corpse, touching an unclean   Nu6, 19; De21; Hg2
crippled feet   SS4; KF15
deaf, respect for the   Le9
deafness   Ps38
deformities   Le21
disease   Ps31, 38; Is10

18 HEALTH AND LONGEVITY

disease, leprous   Nu12
  skin   Nu5; De24
  wasting   Le26; De28; Ps106; Is17
dislocation of the hip   Gen32
dribbling down his beard   SF21
ears shall tingle   KS21
eruptions   De28
excrement, disposal of   De23
eyes, blemished   Le21
eyesight, failing   Ps69, 88
fat, folds of   Ps73
  man, Eglon   Ju3
feet, crippled   SS4; KF15
  gangrene of the   CS16
fever   Le26; De28; Ps37f; Is10; Je51
  recurrent   Le26; De28
fig poultice   KS20
fit, falls in a   Is10
gangrene   CS16
gluttony   Pro23
growth, abnormal   Le21
haemorrhoids   De28; SF5ff
hair, grey, a crown of glory   Pro16
   dignity of old men   Pro20
   respect for   Le19
   turned white   Ho7
  yellow and sparse   Le13
halting speech   Ex4, 6
head sores   Le13; Is1, 3
heal, a time to   Ec3
health to your navel   Pro3
illness of Elisha   KS13
  of Hezekiah   Is38
inflammation   Le13; De28
issue of blood   SS3
itch, persistent   De28
lame and blind   Je31
lameness   KF20
left handed   Ju3
leprosy   Ex4; Le13; Nu12; SS3; KS5, 15, 20; CS26
leprous hand   Ex4

18 HEALTH AND LONGEVITY

madness, curse of   De28
medicine   Je30, 46
miscarriage   KS2
misshapen brow   Le21
navel, health to your   Pro3
nostrils, eat till it comes out at your   Ju11
ointment, treatment by   Is1
old age, no man in your house shall come to   SF2
over-grown people   Le21
pain, incurable   Is17
  pierces my bones   Job30
paralysed hand   KF13
pestilence   Ex9; Le26; De28; SS24; CF21; Ps91; Je14, 21, 24, Je27, 29, 32, 34, 38, 42, 44; E5, 33, 38
phlegm, garments bespattered with   Job30
plague   Le13ff, 26; Nu11, 16, 25; De28; SS24; La1; Ps78, 91, 106
polluted water   KS2
poultice   KS20; Is1, 38
prolapse of the bowels   CS21
rib, Adam's   Gen2
ruddy cheeks, David had   SF16
scabs, head   De28; Is3
scurf   Le13f
seizure   SF25
sickness, racked with   La1
skin disease, cleansing   Le5ff, 13f
  infection   Le13; Nu5, 12; De28
  scorched black   Na1
sluggard   Pro6
sore throat   Ps69
sores, running   Job2
spittle fell down his beard   SF21
stones, wounded in the   De23
strength of Samson   Ju16
stricken in age, Joshua was   Jos23
stunted growth   Le21
sweating, I lay   Ps77
testicles, wounded in the   De23
tumours   De28; SF5ff
turned his face to the wall   KS20

193

18 HEALTH AND LONGEVITY

ulcerated bowels   CS21
ulcers   De28; Je16
unclean condition   Le5, 22
  cry   Le13
under-grown people   Le21
washing before the meal   L11
waste away, fat on his limbs shall   Is17
wasting disease   Le26; De28; Ps106; Is17
wounds, binds up our   Ho6
  dressed with vinegar   Pro25

NEW TESTAMENT

age of Abraham   PR4
  of Jesus Christ   L2
  of the girl raised by Jesus   Mk5
  of the widow Anna   L2
ailment and disease, curing every kind of   Mw9
ailments, take a little wine for your frequent   PTF5
anointed with oil, sick people   Mk6
bandage   L10
bed-ridden with paralysis   A9
bent double, she was   L13
blind beggar   Mk10
  for a time   A13
  from birth   J9
  man at the gate   Mw20
    at the roadside   L18
  men, Jesus was followed by two   Mw9
  people, he restored sight on many   L7
  recover their sight, tell him how they   L7
  to announce recovery of sight   L4
bloody flux   A28
clay of the spittle, made   J9
convulsions, threw the boy into   Mk9
crippled folk cured   A8
  for eighteen years   L13
  from birth   A3
  man lame from birth   A14
cure his son, begged him to   J4

18 HEALTH AND LONGEVITY

cured, saw that he had the faith to be   A14
  sufferers from every kind of illness   Mw4
  you, your faith has   L17
dangerously ill, he was   PPs2
deaf and dumb   Mk9
  brought him a man who was   Mk7
  hear, tell him how the   L7
digestion, take a little wine for your   PTF5
disabled limb will regain its former powers   LH12
disease, power to cure   L9
  suffering from one or another   L4
diseases, cured many sufferers from   L7
  divers   Mw4
  he lifted from us   Mw8
  were rid of their   A19
dropsy, a man suffering from   L14
dysentery   A28
dull of hearing   LH5
dumb man began to speak   L11
  man who was   Mw9; Mk7
epilepsy   Mw4, 17
epileptic, my son is   Mw17
faith has cured you,   Mw9; Mk5; L8, 17; A14
  to be cured, saw that he had the   A14
feeble minded, comfort the   ThF5
fever, he stood over her and rebuked the   L4
  left her and she waited upon them   Mk1
  left him at the exact time   J4
  mother in law in bed with   Mw8; Mk1
  recurrent bouts of   A28
fits, epileptic   Mw17
foams at the mouth, grinds his teeth, and goes rigid   Mk9
gangrene   PTS2
haemorrhages, suffered from   Mw9; Mk5; L8
healed him, laid his hands upon him and   A28
healers, God has appointed   PCF12
healing all manner of sickness   Mw4
  for all mankind   Tt2
  of nations, leaves of the trees for   Ev22
  the gift of   PCF12
  went about doing good and   A10

18 HEALTH AND LONGEVITY

ill, is one of you   LJ5
   they brought all who were   Mk1
illness, he took away our   Mw8
   or infirmity, curing   Mw4
   sufferers from every kind of   Mw4
impediment, speech   Mk7
infirmities, cured many of their   L7
   multitudes to be cured of their   L5
issue of blood   Mw9
lame walk, tell him how the   L7
laying on of hands   Mk8, 16; L13; A28; PTF4; PTS1
leper, approached by a   Mk1
   Simon the   Mw26; Mk14
lepers made clean   L7
leprosy   Mw8, 10, 26; Mk1, 14; L4f, 17
   left him immediately   L5
lunatic, healed those which were   Mw4
madman had been cured, told them how the   L8
palsies, many taken with   A8
palsy, healed those that had the   Mw4
   sick of the   Mw4, 8f; Mk2; L5; A8f
paralysis, healing of   Mw4, 8f; Mk2; L5; A8f
"physician, heal thyself"   L4
plagues, cured many sufferers from   Mk3; L7
recurrent bouts of fever and dysentery   A28
sick carried into the streets   A5
   healed all who were   Mw8
   laid out in the market places   Mk6
   on whom they laid their hands will recover   Mk16
   people, a crowd of   J5
     came crowding in to touch him   Mk3
     they cured many   Mk6
   that are there, heal the   L10
sight, recovery of   L4
speech impediment   Mk7
speechless   Mk9
stretcher, stretchers   Mk2, 6; J5; A5
   brought the sick on   Mk6
withered arm, man with a   Mk3; L3
wounds, bandaged his   L10

19   *Heavens and Hell*

OLD TESTAMENT

Abaddon   Job26; Pro15, 27
abyss   Ps36, 143; Pro1; Is38
    fire to devour the great   Am7
    go down to the   Ps28
    gone down to the stony   Is14
    sinking into the   Ps30
    swallow me up   Ps69
    those that go down to the   E26, 31ff
    thou hast plunged me into the lowest   Ps88
    to the depths of the   Is14
Adversary, Satan the   Z3
Aldebaran   Job9, 38
Arcturus   Job9
Amanus, the southern sky   Ps150
Azazel   Le16
Belial, a man of   SS20
    certain sons of   Ju19
    Eli's sons were sons of   SF2
    sons of, bore witness against Naboth   SF21
    this man of   SF25
brimstone   Is30, 34
Capella   Am5
chambers of the south   Job9
circle of southern stars   Job9
constellations   Is13
crescent-cakes offered to the queen of heaven   Je7, 44
day darkened into night   Am5
demon of the night   So3
dog-star   Job38
drink offerings poured to the queen of heaven   Je44
earth, arches his ceiling over the   Am9
eclipse of the sun   Am5, 8

19 HEAVENS AND HELL

heaven   Ps2, 11, 14, 19, 33, 36, 53, 57, 65, 76, 80, 85, 103,
    Ps113, 115, 123, 135f, 146; Pro30; Is24
  cover the, and make the stars go dark   E32
  every activity under   Ec3
  four quarters of   Je49
  highest   Ps71; Is7
  host of   Ps33
  of heavens   Ps148
  vault of   Ps150
heavenly host in Daniel's vision   D8
heavens   Ps8, 19, 33, 50, 57, 89, 96, 104, 108, 136, 138; Pro3; Je10
  builds his stair up to the   Am9
  creator of   Is45
  grow murky as smoke   Is51
  he roars across   Je25
  if man could measure the   Je31
  if they climb up to   Am9
  lift your eyes to the   Is40
  limits to the   Is40
  music of the   Ps19
  new   Is66
  rain righteousness   Is45
  signs in the   Je10
  the ancient   Ps68
  turn black   Je4
hell, Job11; Ps9; Pro7; Is14, 28
  casteth down to   E31
  though they dig into   Am9
horse statues in honour of the sun   KS23
host of heaven   KS17, 21, 23; Ps33; Is24; Je8
  altars for   CS33
  aspired to be as great as   D8
  bow down on the housetops to worship   Zp1
  burned incense to, priests of Baal   KS23
  incense burned to in Judah   Je19, 44
  innumerable   Je33
  lest thou lift up thine eyes unto   De4
  sacrifices to   Je19
  those who worship the   Zp1
  worships the Lord God   Ne9

19 HEAVENS AND HELL

Lucifer, morning star   Is14
Mazzaroth   Job38
moon   Ps8, 72, 74, 89, 136, 148; Ec12; Is13, 24; Je8
  and stars for a light by night   Je31
  beautiful as the   So6
  burned incense to the   KS23
  nor raise your eyes to the   De4
  precious things put forth by the   De33
  sacrifices to the   KS23
  shall grow pale   Is24
  shall not give its light   E32
  stand in the vale of Aijalon   Jos10
  to measure the year   Ps104
  turned to blood   Joe2
morning star   Is14
music of the heavens   Ps19
Navigator's Line   Job38
new moon, ceremony of the   Ho2; Am8
  commemoration of the   Ne10
  feast of the   SF20; CS2, 8; Ps81; Ez3; Is1; E45ff
  month by month at the   Is66
  sabbaths and appointed seasons   CF23
Orion   Job9; Am5
Orion's Belt   Job38
pit   Ps16, 94; Pro1, 28; Is14
  go down into the   Ps30
  of death   Ps49, 103, 107
  of destruction   Ps55
  sending you down to the   E28
  them that descend to the   E26
  then didst bring me up alive from the   Jon2
  went down alive to the   Nu16
planets, burned incense to the   KS23
Pleiades   Job9, 38; Am5
portents in the sky   Joe2
queen of heaven   Je7
    bake crescent-cakes for   Je7, 44
    burn incense to   Je44
    pour drink offering to   Je44
rising sun, prostrating themselves to the   E8
sacrifices to the host of heaven   Je19

19 HEAVENS AND HELL

sacrifices to the queen of heaven   Je44
Satan   CF1; Job1ff; Ps109
  the Adversary   Z3
seven stars   Am5
Sheol   Job7, 11, 14, 17, 21, 24, 26; Ps6, 9, 16, 18, 30f, 49, 55, 86,
      Ps88f, 116, 139, 141; Ec9; Pro1, 5, 7, 15, 27; Is5, 14, 28,
      Is38; Je7, 19; H2
  burns to the depths of   De32
  gates of   Is57
  go down to alive   Nu16
  he sends down to   SF2
  if they dig down to   Am9
  oh, for your sting!   Ho13
  out of the belly of   Jon2
  shall I redeem him from   Ho13
  the lowest   Is7
  warrior chieftains in   E32
  went down to   E31
shooting star   Is5
signs in the havens, do not be awed by   Je10
star, of your god which ye made   Am5
  shines forth out of Jacob   Nu24
stargazers   Is47
starry heavens, majestic as the   So6
stars   Ps8, 147ff; Is13
  as numerous as   De1
  forbear to shine   Joe2f
  grow dim   Ec12
  nor raise your eyes to the   De4
  the seven   Am5
  to rule by night   Ps136
  withdraw their shining   Joe2
sun   Ps19, 72, 74, 89, 104, 136, 148; Ec12; So6; Is13, 24; Je8
  burned incense to the   KS23
  for a light by day, who gave the   Je31
  from the rising to the setting   Ps50, 113
  hides its face in shame   Is24
  prostrating themselves to the rising   E8
  rises, and rises again   Ec1
  sacrificed to the   KS23
  shall be dark   Joe2

19 HEAVENS AND HELL

  sun shall be turned into darkness   Joe2
    stand still   Jos10
    toil under the   Ec1
    veil with a cloud   E32
    and moon darkened   Joe2f
  Taurus   Am5
  Teman, the south, turn your face towards   E20
  three days of darkness   Ex10
  Tophet   KS23; Is30; Je7, 19
  vault of heaven, shine like the bright   D12
  vaulted roof of the earth   Is40
  Vintager constellation   Am5
  Zaphon, northern sky   Ps89
  zodiac, can you bring out the signs of the   Job38

NEW TESTAMENT

  Abaddon, angel of the abyss   Rev9
  abyss, angel given the key of the   Rev9
    angel of the   Rev9
    beast that comes up from the   Rev11
    begged him not to banish them to the   L8
    threw him into the   Rev20
    who can go down to the   PR10
    yet to ascend out of the   Rev17
  angels in heaven will not know   Mk13
    the devil and his   Mw25
  Apollyon, angel of the abyss   Rev9
  antichrist, the arch-deceiver   LJS1
    the spirit of   LJF4
    was to come, you were told   LJF2
  beast, armies of the   Rev19
    had not worshipped the   Rev20
    scarlet   Rev17
    thrown into the lake of fire   Rev19
  Beelzebub   Mw10, 12
    he is possessed by   Mk3
    prince of devils   L11
  Belial   PCS6
  blood, fire, and drifting smoke, signs on earth   A2

19 HEAVENS AND HELL

brimstone, lake of fire and   Rev20
  rained fire and   L17
celestial bodies   PCF15
cosmic powers, our fight is against   PE6
created, everything that God   PTF4
creation under heaven, the whole   PCo1
darkness, bound beneath the   LJu1
  his kingdom was plunged in   Rev16
  is passing and the real light already shines   LJ2
  let light shine out of   PCS4
  those who live in   L1
  to light, turn them from   A26
day like a thousand years with the Lord   LPS3
demonic earth-bound sensual wisdom   LJ3
demons, a dwelling place for   Rev18
  partners with   PCF10
  sacrifice to   PCF10
  table of   PCF10
destroyer, destroyed by the   PCF10
  the angel of the abyss   Rev9
devil, a man possessed by the   L4
  anything beyond "yes" and "no" comes from the   Mw5
  came out and the dumb man began to speak   L11
  carries off the word from their hearts   L8
  child of the   LJF3
  dashed him to the ground   L9
  devices of the   PE6
  entered Judas   J13
  gone to the   PTF5
  had death at his command   LH2
  he hath a   J10
  healing all who were oppressed by the   A10
  his angels   Mw25
  in debate with Archangel Michael   LJu1
  Jesus rebuked the   Mw17
    tempted by the   Mw4
  judgement contrived by the   PTF3
  leave no loop-hole for the   PE4
  Michael in debate with the   LJu1
  now we know that thou hast a   J8
  one of you is a   J6

19 HEAVENS AND HELL

devil, possessed with the   Mk5
  seducer   Rev20
  set him on a parapet of the temple,   Mw4
  sinneth from the beginning   LJF3
  stand up to the   LJ4
  tempted by the   L4
  tempting Jesus   Mw4
  that he might destroy the works of the   LJF3
  that serpent of old   Rev20
  thou child of the   A13
  thou hast a   J7
  thrown down to earth   Rev12
  took him to a very high mountain   Mw4
  was cast out   Mw9
  wiles of the   PE6
  your adversary the   LPF5
  your father is the   J8
devils, a commission to drive out   Mk3
  a man who was possessed by   L8
  authority to overcome   L9
  Beelzebub, prince of the   L11
  by the finger of God that I drive out   L11
  by the prince of devils he drives out   Mk3
  cast out   Mw10
    in your name   M7
  drove out many   Mk1
  habitation of   Rev18
  had cast out seven   Mk16
  had come out of Mary Magdalene, seven   L8
  had taken possession of him, so many   L8
  have faith like that   LJ2
  in your name, we saw a man driving out   Mk9; L9
  possessed by   Mw4, 8
  snare   PTS2
  submit to us in your name   L10
  subversive doctrines inspired by   PTF4
  the table of   PCF10
  they drove out many   Mk6
  they sacrifice to   PCF10
  will cast out many   Mk16
  with power to work miracles   Rev16

19 HEAVENS AND HELL

domain of darkness, rescued us from the   PCF1
earth, swear not by   Mw5
   will be laid bare   LPs3
elemental spirits, slaves to the   PGF4
     teachings centred on the   PCo2
elements, spirits of the   PG4
   will disintegrate in flames   LPS3
eternal fire, thrown into the   Mw18
   life promised long ages ago   Tt1
   ruin, punishment of   ThS1
evil one, because you have mastered the   LJF2
     carries off what has been sown in his heart   Mw13
     flaming arrows of the   PE6
     godless world lies in the power of the   LJF5
     guard you from the   ThS3
     save us from the   Mw6
   spirit answered back   A19
     open men's eyes, could an   J10
   spirits came out of them   A19
     cured many sufferers from   L7
     possessed by   A19
   superhuman forces of   PE6
false prophets will arise, many   Mw24
fire from heaven may we call down   L9
fires of hell, be thrown into the   Mw18
firmament, shine like stars in the   PPs2
foul spirit, haunt of every   Rev18
   spirits like frogs   Rev16
get thee behind me, Satan   Mw4, 16; Mk8; L4
God's footstool, earth is   Mw5
   throne, heaven is   Mw5
great light flashed from the sky   A22
grinding of teeth, place of wailing and   Mw8, 13
Hades close behind death   Rev6
   gave up the dead   Rev20
   place of torment   L16
   torment in   L16
heaven, a great wonder in   Rev12
   a light from   A26
   a voice sounded from   A12
   and earth and sea, God who made   A14

19 HEAVENS AND HELL

heaven and earth, Lord of   A17
  and on earth, brought into unity, all in   PE1
  as it is in   L11
  asked him for a sign from   Mk8
  bread from   J6
  coming with the clouds of   Mk14
  demanded a sign from   L11
  door opened in   Rev4
  eternal house in   PCS5
  first-born citizens of   LH12
  from the farthest bounds of   Mk13
  glory to God in highest   L2
  great is your reward in   Mw5
  has no favourites, master in   PE6
  he was parted from them and carried up into L24
  he was to be taken up to   L9
  hope stored up for you in   PCo1
  inheritance kept for you in   LPF1
  is my throne and earth my footstool   A7
  is theirs, kingdom of   Mw5
  it was not David who went up to   A2
  Jesus looked up to   Mk6; J17
  living bread come down from J6
  Lord Jesus was taken up into Mk16
  many will come to the feast in the kingdom of   Mw8
  may we call down fire from   L9
  morning sun from   L1
  never-failing treasure in   L12
  opened and the Holy Spirit descended   L3
    at that moment   Mw3
  our Father which art in   L11
  over one sinner that repenteth, joy shall be in   L15
  rained fire from   L17
  rejoice, because your names are written in   L10
  retribution revealed from   PR1
  roar of a vast throng in   Rev19
  shall be shaken, the powers of   L21
  silence in   Rev8
  store up treasure in   Mw6
  swear not by   M5
  symbol of Diana which fell from   A19

19 HEAVENS AND HELL

heaven, the angels in   Mw22
  the kingdom of   Mw5
  the Lord himself will descend from   ThF4
  there came a voice from   L3
  third   PCS12
  this voice from   LPS1
  to swear by   Mw23
  until he was taken up to   A1
  voice from   L3; J12; Rev18
  voices heard in   Rev11
  war broke out in   Rev12
  we are citizens of   PPS3
  when your Lord is revealed from   ThS1
  who can go up to   PR10
  wide open, I saw   Rev19
    you shall see   J1
  you have a rich reward in   Mw5
    will have riches in   L18
  your Father in   Mw23
heavenly bodies, the splendour of   PCF15
  country   LH11
  host, a great company of the   L2
  realms, enthroned him in the   PE2
    every blessing in the   PE1
heavens ablaze, day of God will set the   LPS3
  forces of evil in the   PE6
  Hosanna in the   Mk11
  new, and a new earth   LPS3
  shall pass away but thou endurest   LH1
  will disappear with a great rushing sound   LPS3
hell and the unquenchable fire   Mk9
  better to lose one part, than be thrown into   Mw5
  consigned to the dark pits of   LPS2
  fire, shall be in danger of   Mw5
  fit for   Mw23
  followed by death   Rev6
  gates of   Mw16
  has authority to cast into   L12
  how can you escape being condemned to   Mw23
  should not prevail, gates of   Mw16
  the child of   Mw23

19 HEAVENS AND HELL

hell, the keys of   Rev1
  thou shalt be thrust down to   L10
    wilt not leave my soul in   A2
  thrown into the fires of   Mw18
  who sneers at his brother will answer for it in   Mw5
host of heaven, gave them up to worship the   A7
lake of fire in John's vision   Rev19ff
Legion, name is   Mk5; L8
life everlasting, believe on him to   PTF1
light, God is   LJF1
  marvellous, out of darkness   LPF2
  more brilliant than the sun   A26
  Satan masquerades as an angel of   PCS11
  shines on in the dark   J1
  the honest man comes to the   J3
  the Lord God will give them   Rev22
  walk as children of   PE5
  which no man can approach, dwelling in the   PTF6
  with darkness, what communion hath   PCS6
lights of heaven, Father of the   LJ1
moon all red as blood   Rev6
  has a splendour   PCF15
  portents will appear in the   L21
  shall be turned to blood   A2
  third part struck   Rev8
  will not give her light   Mw24; Mk13
morning star   LPS1; Rev2
natural world, elements of the   PCo2
new heaven and a new earth   Rev21
  moon, observance of   PCo2
night, there will be no   Rev21f
paradise, caught up into   PCS12
  today you shall be with me in   L23
perdition, on the way to   PCS2
pit, bottomless   Rev9, 17, 20
   key of the   Rev9
portents will appear in sun, moon and stars   L21
possessed by devils   Mw4, 8f; Mk1, 5, 16; L4, 8ff
prince of devils   Mw9; Mk3
  of the power of the air   PE2
realm above, aspire to the   Pco3

19 HEAVENS AND HELL

realm, higher   PCo3
  of light, God's people in the   PCo1
revelation, the light of   PCS4
Satan, away with you   Mw16; Mk8
  begone   Mw4
  beneath your feet, will crush   PR16
  bruise under your feet   PR16
  comes and carries off the word   Mk4
  consigned to   PTF1
  deep secrets of   Rev2
  divided against himself   Mw12; L11
  drive out Satan, how can   Mk3
  entered Judas Iscariot   L22; J13
  fell like lightning out of the sky   L10
  filled thy heart to lie to the Holy Spirit   A5
  get thee behind me   Mw4, 16; Mk8; L4
  has his throne   Rev2
  himself masquerades as an angel of light   PCS11
  if Satan casts out   Mw12
  keep prisoner by   L13
  let loose from his dungeon   L20
  messenger of   PCS12
  must not get the better of us   PCS2
  possessed your mind   A5
  sifts you like wheat   L22
  tempted by   Mk1; PCF7
  that serpent of old   Rev20
  the work of   ThS2
  this man is to be consigned to   PCF5
  thrown down to earth   Rev12
  thwarted us   ThF2
  to God, from the dominion of   A26
  turned aside after   PTF5
Satan's synagogue   Rev2f
seducing spirits   PTF4
serpent called the devil, that old   Rev12
shaft of the abyss   Rev9
sky, terror and great portents in the   L21
  vanished   Rev6
sound from heaven as of a mighty rushing wind   A2
spirit, Jesus rebuked the unclean   L9

19 HEAVENS AND HELL

spirit open men's eyes, could an evil   J10
  possessed by an unclean   Mk5, 7, 9; L4
  unclean, commanded to come out   L8
spirits begged him to let them go into the pigs   L8
  evil, cured many suffering from   L7
  of the universe, elemental   PCo2
  seducing   PTF4
  unclean, like frogs   Rev16
    would fall at his feet   Mk3
star called wormwood   Rev8
  fallen from heaven to earth   Rev9
  great, shot from the sky   Rev8
  I am the bright   Rev22
  in glory, one differeth from another   PCF15
  of dawn   Rev2
  we observed the rising of his   Mw2
  went ahead of them until it stopped above the place   Mw2
stars fell to earth   Rev6
  have a splendour   PCF15
  in a dark world, shine like   PPs2
  in his right hand he held seven   Rev1
  in the firmament   PPs2
  portents will appear in   L21
  seven   Rev2f
  third part struck   Rev8
  twelve, a crown of   Rev12
  will fall from the sky   Mw24; Mk13
  wandered from their course   LJu1
sulphur, rained fire and   L17
sun allowed to burn men with its flames   Rev16
  has a splendour of its own   PCF15
  his face shone like the   Mw17; Rev1
  light more brilliant than the   A26
  or moon, city had no need of   A26
  or stars, no sign of, for days on end   A27
  portents will appear in the   L21
  righteous will shine as brightly as the   Mw13
  rise on good and bad alike   Mw5
  shall be turned to darkness   A2
  third part will be struck   Rev8
  will be darkened   Mw24; Mk13

19 HEAVENS AND HELL

sun, woman robed in the   Rev12
sun's light failed   L23
temptation of Jesus   Mw4
tempted by the devil   Mw4
tempter approached him   Mw4
  tempted you   ThF3
thousand years like a day with the Lord   LPS3
throne of the beast   Rev16
torment, Hades place of   L16
unclean spirit, a haunt for every   Rev18
  commanded to come out of the man   L8
  Jesus rebuked the   Mk9; L9
  possessed by an   Mk1, 5, 7; L4
  wanders over the deserts   L11
 spirits came out with a loud cry   A8
  gave them authority to cast out   Mw10; Mk6
  harassed by   A5
  he gives orders to   L4
  like frogs   Rev16
  would fall at his feet   Mk3
universe created through him and for him   PCo1
wailing and grinding of teeth   Mw8, 13
wandering stars   LJu1
weeping and gnashing of teeth   Mw8, 13

20 Household

OLD TESTAMENT

awl   De15
axe   De15, 19
ball, children's   Is22
barrel   KF17
basin   SS17; CS4; Je52
  bronze   Ex30ff; KF7
  gold   Ez1
  silver   Ez1
basket   De23; KS10; Ps81; Je6, 24; Am4, 8
  rush   Ex2
  watertight   Ex2
bed   SK19; SS13; KF17; KS4; Ps6, 36, 132; Pro7, 26; So3; Is28, 57; E23; D4, 7; Ho7; Am3, 6; Mi2
  perfumed   Pro7
bedchamber   Ec10
bed-covering   Is28
bedroom   Ec10
bell   Ex28ff
bellows   Pro26
bench   E27
besom   Is14
bit   Ps32
blanket   SS11, 17; Ks8; Is28
bolts and bars   Ne3
bottle   SS16; Je13, 48; Ho7
  earthen   Je19
bowl   SS17; KS2, 16; Is22, 51, 65; Je35, 52; Am6; Z9, 14
  golden   Ex25ff; Ez1, 8; Ec12
  mixing   E4
  silver   Nu7
  table of the Presence   Nu4
  tossing   Ex27ff; Nu7
brazier   Je36; Z12
bridle   Ps32; Pro26

20 HOUSEHOLD

bucket   Is40
candle   Pro24, 29, 31; Je25; Zp1
candlestick   Nu4; KS4; Je52; D5
  gold   Rx25ff
  seven branch   Z4
canopy, wedding   Ps19
carding, weaving and spinning   Is19
cask   E27
cauldron   SF2; CS35; Job41; Is65; Je1, 52; E11, 24; Mi3
charger, gold   Ez1
  silver   Nu7; Ez1
chest   KS12; CS24; So5
  cedar wood   E27
churn   Pro30
cistern, rock-hewn   De6; Ne9
clay, potter's   Is29, 41, 45, 64
  pot   Ps2
cleanse hands with lye   Job9
coals   Ps11, 19; La4
cord   Na1
  leather   Ho11
couch   SS11; Ps6; So1; E16; Am3, 6
  of gold and silver   Est1
coverlet   Is14
crisping pins   Is3
crucible   Ps12
cruse   KF14, 17, 19; KS2
cup   Ps11, 16, 23, 75; Pro23; Is22, 28, 51; Je25, 35, 49, 52;
  gold   Est1; Je51
  silver   KS12
curtain   So1; Is40
  rings, silver   Est1
  tabernacle   Ex26
  tent   Is54; Je4, 10, 49; H3; La4; E23; Z12
curtains, green, white and blue   Est1
dish, gold   Ex25ff
  lordly   Ju5
  silver   Nu7
  table of the Presence   Nu4
distaff   SS3; Pro31

20 HOUSEHOLD

earthenware   Is45
  glazed   Pro26
  jar   Je19
  pitcher   La4
fan   Je51
fire-pan   CS4; Je52
firewood, payment for   La5
fish basket   Am4
flagon   Ex25f; SF1, 10; SS6, 16; Is22; Je52; So8; Ho3
  gold   Ex25f
  table of the Presence   Nu4
flask   SK10; KF14, 17; KS9; Ps56
flesh-hook   Nu4
footstool   CS9; Ps99, 110, 132
fuel, dung   E4
furniture   CF9; Na2
glazed earthenware   Pro26
goatskin container   Ps33
goblet   Gen44; So7
  golden   Gen44
griddle   Le6; CF23
  iron   E4
grinding meal   Ec12
gum resin   Ex30f
hand-mill   Je25
hangings, white, green and blue or violet   Est1
harness   Je46; Mi1
head-rest, palanquin   So3
hearth   Ps102; Je36; Z12
hide, reins of   Ho11
horn for oil   SF16; KF1
ink   Je36
jar   Ru2; KF17; Je51
  earthenware   Je19, 32
  go and drink from the   Ru2
  of provisions   Ju7
  storage   Je40
  wine   Je13
jug   SS17
kettle   SF2
kindling wood from discarded weapons   E39

20 HOUSEHOLD

ladder, Jacob's vision of a   Gen28
lamp   Ex25ff; KS4; CF28; Ps18, 132; Pro20, 31; Je25; E1;   D5, 10; Z4
  trim the   Ex27
lampstand   CF28; Je52; Z4
  gold   Ex25f; CS4, 13
    in Zechariah's vision   Z4
  of beaten gold   Nu8
lantern   Zp1
laver   KF7; KS16; CS4
lye, cleansing   Job9
mattress   SS17
millstone   Je25; Is47
mirror   Job37
mortar and pestle   Pro27
muzzle   Ps39
nail   Z10
net   E12
oil, lamp   Z4
ointment   So1, 4
oven   Ne12; Ps102; La5; Ma4
  bakers   Ho7
paint, vermilion   Je22
palanquin   So3
pallet   SS11; Is14; Ho7
pan   SF2; SS13; CS35
  iron   E4
pen   Ps45
  diamond-tipped   Je17
penknife   Je36
pestle and mortar   Pro27
pillow   SF19; Ps6; E13
pipes, lamp   Z4
pitcher   KF17, 19; Ec12
  earthenware   La4
pot   Ex27ff; SF2; KS4, 25; CS4, 35; Job41; Ec7; Is22, 45;   Je1, 35, 52; E24; Mi3; Z14
potsherd   Job2; Ps22; Pro26; Is30; E23
pressing vat, pressfat   Hg2
reins   Ho11
rings, silver curtain   Est1

20 HOUSEHOLD

rope   SF19; Is3, 5; Je10, 38
rug   SF19; Is21
saddle, ass   KS4
saucer   Nu4, 7; KS25; CS4, 24; Je52
   of incense   Nu7
scales   Je32
seat   KS4
shard   Job2; Ps22; Pro26; Is30; E23
shovel   Ex27f; KS25
sieve   Am4, 9
skin, wine   SF16, 25; Ne5; Job14; Ps119
snuffdish   Nu4
snuffer   KS12, 25; CS4; Je52
soap   Job9; Je2
soot   La4
spindle   Pro31
spinning   Is19
spoon   Nu7; KS25; Je52
   of incense   Nu7
stewpot   E11
stool   KF10; E16
   high   E16
sundial   Is38
table   Nu4ff; KS4; Ps23, 41, 69, 78; Is28, 65; E23, 40ff
tent covering   Je4
   curtain   So1; H3
   hangings   Je49
   peg   Z10
toilet, sign for a   De23
tongs   CS4
torch, blazing   Z12
trowel for burying excrement   De23
vat   Is63; Joe2f; Hg2
   juice from the   Nu18
   wine   Pro3; Je48
vessels, brass   E27
   bronze   KS25; Je52; E27
     or copper   CF18
   clay   Je18
   earthen   SS17; Je19
   gold   KS24

20 HOUSEHOLD

gold and silver   CF18, 28
  silver   Ez8
    and gold   CS24; KF10; D11
    gold and copper   SS8
  small bowls and pots   Is22
  storage   Je40
vial   SF6
wagon   SF6
wardrobe   Je38
wash-bowl   Ps108
water, payment for   La5
  jar   SF26
wax   Ps22, 68, 97; Mi1
weaving   Is19, 38
web and thrum, weaving   Is38
wick, smouldering   Is42
  snuffed out   Is43
wheel, potter's   Je18
whip   Na3
  horse   Pro26
wine jar   Je13
  press   Ju7; Ne13; La1; Ho9; Hg2
  skin   SF16, 25; Ne5; Job14; Ps119
  vat   Hg2; Z14
yoke   Je31; Ho11; Na1

NEW TESTAMENT

alabaster box   Mw26; Mk14; L7
baggage, packed our   A21
bandage   L10
basin   L8; J3
basket   Mw4ff; Mk6, 8; J6; A9; PCS11
bed   Mw9; Mk4, 6; L5, 8, 11, 17; J5; A5, 9, 28; LJ5
  children with me in   L11
  do you put the lamp under the   Mk4
  two men in one   L17
board and lodging   ThS3
bonfire   A28

20 HOUSEHOLD

bottle   Mw9; Mk2, 14; L5
  perfume   Mk14
  wine   L5
bowl   Mw26; Mk7; Rev15, 17
  copper   Mk7
  gold   Rev15
box, alabaster   M26; Mk14; L7
bucket   J4
candle   Mw5; Mk4; L8, 11, 15; Rev18, 22
candlestick   Mw5; Mk4; L8f, 11; Rev1f, 11
chair   Mw23
charcoal   J18
charger   Mw14; Mk6
cord   L5
couch   L5; A5
cup   Mw10, 20, 23, 26; Mk7, 9f; L11, 22; J18; PCF10f; PCS1, 7; PPs2; Rev17
cushion, asleep on a   Mk4
dish   Mw23; Mk6, 14
earthenware   PCS4; PTS2; Rev2
flask of oil   Mw25; L7
footstool   Mk12; L20; LH1, 10; LJ2
glass   Rev15, 21
  looking   PCS3; LJ1
guest chamber   Mk14; L22
homes of your own, have you no   PCF11
hospitality, practice   PR12
  remember to show   LH13
house swept clean and tidy   L11
household, Caesar's   PPs4
  manages his own   PTF3
householder   Mw20
ink   PCS3; LJS1; LJT1
jar   L22; J4, 19; LH9
jug   Mk7
key   Rev1, 9
lamp   Mw5f, 25; Mk4; L8, 11f, 15; J5; A20; LPS1; Rev1f, 4, 11, 18, 22
  stand   Mk4; L8, 11; LH9
lantern   J18
lodging, board and   A10; ThS3; PTF5

20 HOUSEHOLD

looking glass   PCS3; LJ1
market place   Mk6f; L7; A16
meal-tub   Mk4
millstone   Mw18; Mk9; L17; Rev18
mirror   PCS3; LJ1
needle   Mk10; L18
oil   Mw25; L16; Rev18
oven   L12
pail   Mw13
pen and ink   LJT1
perfume bottle   Mk14
pitcher, water   Mk14; L22
plate   L11
platter   Mw23; L11
pot   Mk7; J4; PR9; PCS4; LH9
room ready for me, have a   Ph1
shop and buy some oil, go to the   Mw25
spin nor weave, they neither   L12
sponge   Mw27; Mk15; J19
stone jar   J2
   tablet   PCS3
stove   Mw6; L12
stretcher   Nk2, 6; J5; A5
sweep out the house   L15
table   Mw21; Mk7, 11, 14; L1, 7, 12, 16, 22, 24; J2, 13; PR11; PCF20; LH9; LPS2
   scraps from the rich man's table   L16
   writing   L1
tablet, writing   L1
tablets of stone   PCS3
torch   J18
   flaming   Rev4, 8
utensils of gold and silver   PTS2
   of wood and earthenware   PTS2
vessel, brazen   Mk7
   earthen   PCS4
vial   Rev5, 15ff, 21
washing hands   Mk7
water jar   Mk14; J2, 4
   pot, stone   J2
weave, they neither spin nor   L12

20 HOUSEHOLD

wick, smouldering   Mw12
wine bottle   L5
  skin   Mw9; Mk2; L5
winepress, winefat   Mw21; Mk12; Rev14, 19
  hewed out a   Mw21
wood, utensils of   PTS2

21 *Human Passions, Social Perceptions*

OLD TESTAMENT

afraid, naked and   Gen3
ambidextrous, David's men with slings and arrows   CF12
antimony, make your eyes big with   Je4
appearances, men judge by   SF16
apple of his eye   De32; Z2
baldness   Le13
beard, Aaron's   Ps133
    dribbling down his   SF21
beauty, Absalom was greatly admired for his   SS14
    display her   Est1
    surpass all mankind in   Ps45
beggar us, did you come to   Ju14
beloved of the Lord, Solomon was   SS12
bewilderment, curse of   De28
blind debarred from the altar   Le21
    respect for the   Le19
boast of Adonijah   KF1
born to trouble, man is   Job5
bribe, do not accept a   De16
broke wind, Achsah   Jos15; Ju1
brother's keeper   Gen4
brow like adamant, harder than flint   E3
    misshapen, debarring a person   Le21
choice of life and good, or death and evil   De30
churl is his name and churlish his nature   SF25
circumcision of children   Le12; Jos5
cleansing of skin disease   Le14
    ritual   Le5ff
close-fisted, be not   De15
closet, relieving himself in the   Ju3
clothes symbolizing guilt   Z3

21 HUMAN PASSIONS, SOCIAL PERCEPTIONS

comfort to you, is your religion no   Job4
corpse, contact with a   Hg2
  found in open country   De21
  touching an unclean   Nu6, 19
courage failed us   Jos2
  flowed away   Jos1
  melted away   Jos5
covet, you shall not   De5, 7
dead body, contact with a   Nu6, 19; De21; Hg2
deaf, respect for the   Le19
deformed animals unacceptable as offerings   Le22
  people debarred from the altar   Le21
dislocated Jacob's thigh   Gen32
dribbling down his beard   SF21
drunkard   Pro23
drunken stupor goes in rags   Pro23
ear tryeth words as the mouth tasteth meat   Job34
ears shall tingle, both his   KS21
embrace, a time to   Ec3
eye for eye   De19
eyes darker than wine   Gen49
  like doves   So1
excrement, disposal of   De23
exposed his person, David   SS6
fat, folds of   Ps73
  man, Eglon was a very   Ju3
feet dipped in the Jordan   Jos3
flowing locks, leaders in Israel had   Ju5
fool is destroyed by his own angry passions   Job5
foot for foot   De19
forelock, seized me by the   E8
friend, my own dear   Ps55
giant, an Amorite   Am2
  Benaiah killed a   CF11
  Goliath   SF17, 21; SS21; CF20
  Og, king of Bashan   De3
giants, Anakim   De9
  descendants of the Anakim   De1
  Emim, great and numerous   De2
  on earth in those days   Gen5
  Rephaim   De3

21 HUMAN PASSIONS, SOCIAL PERCEPTIONS

giants, Zamzummin   De3
gift opens the door to the giver   Pro18
gird up thy loins now like a man   Job40
glutton   Pro23
gossip   Pro11ff, 18, 20, 26
grudge of Esau   Gen27
guilt, clothes symbolizing   Z3
hair cut every year   SS14
   flowing, leaders in Israel had   Ju5
   grey, respect for   Le19
   long and plaited   Nu6
   method of cutting   Le19
   of his head shall fall, not one   SF14
   polled his   SS14
   rules for Nazirites   Nu6
   yellow and sparse   Le13
hairy man, Esau was a   Gen27
hand for hand   De19
   white as snow   Ex4
handsome with ruddy cheeks, David was   SF16
happy the man whom God rebukes!   Job5
hardened their necks   KS17
haughty glances, casting   KS19
heal, a time to   Ec3
heroes of old   Gen6
hip and thigh, Samson smote them   Ju15
    strike adversary's   De33
   the angel touched Jacob's   Gen32
hope deferred makes the heart sick   Pro13
hospitality of the old man of Gibeah   Je19
house of the unsandalled man   De25
humility, Moses a man of   Nu12
idiots, he makes priests to behave like   Job12
jealousy, fit of   Nu5
   image of   E8
   joy, you will find   De12
keeper, am I my brother's   Gen4
kiss, David greeted Absalom with a   SS14
laugh, a time to   Ec3
laws of nature on earth   Job38
led astray by lavish gifts of wine   Job36

21 HUMAN PASSIONS, SOCIAL PERCEPTIONS

left-handed, Ehud son of Gera   Ju3
likeness of God   Gen5
lips moulded in grace   Ps45
love, a time to   Ec3
  your neighbour   Le19
madness, curse of   De28
man by man, come forward   Jos7
  God formed   Gen2
  in our image   Gen1
mark of Cain   Gen4
meek, Moses was very   Nu12
mortal, God is not, that he should lie   Nu23
  man is only a worm   Job25
naked and afraid   Gen3
  both were   Gen2
navel, it shall be health to your   Pro3
neighbour, love your   Le19
nostrils, eat until it comes out at your   Nu11
open-handed, be   De15
over and under grown people debarred from the altar   Le21
pisseth against the wall, every one that   KF16, 21; KS9
pompous talk is dust and ashes   Job13
poor will always be with you   De15
present, made Jerusalem a   Je40
pride fed on beautiful jewels   E7
proud, do not become   De8
renown, men of   Gen6
rib, Adam's   Gen2
ring in your nose, I will put a   KS19
sandals in holy place, take off   Jos5
scorn on princes, he heaps   Job12
shave edge of the beard   Le19f
  for ritual cleansing   Le14
  not your forelocks   De14
shaved, if my head were   Ju16
skin disease   Le13
  scorched black   Na1
sluggard   Pro6
speech, a man of halting   Ex4, 6
spit in his face   De25
spittle fall down his beard, he let   SF21

21 HUMAN PASSIONS, SOCIAL PERCEPTIONS

stones, wounded in the   De23
stubborn, not any more   De10
stunted growth, debarred people of   Le21
strength was their God, dismayed all whose   H1
   what gives Samson his   Ju16
sweating, I lay   Ps77
tattoo forbidden   Le19
teeth whiter than milk   Gen1
tooth for tooth   Le24; De19
trance, as a man in a   Nu24
   of Abraham   Gen15
try again. come on one and all   Job17
turned his face to the wall, Hezekiah   KS20
uncircumcised brutes   CF10
unclean, cry   Le13
  persons debarred   Le22
  state of being   Le5
vanity, all is   Ec1
washed their feet and ate and drank   Ju19
weak, if my head were shaved I should be   Ju16
winebibber   Pro23
wind, Achsah broke   Jos15
wisdom, die without ever finding   Job4
  let silence be your   Job13
  surpassed all men, Solomon's   KF4
wise, can a fool grow   Job11
wish come true is a staff of life   Pro13
wounds dressed with vinegar   Pro25
  he will bind up our   Ho6
wrestling, Jacob   Gen32

NEW TESTAMENT

affection, inordinate   PCo3
  warmth of mutual   PR12
anger, lay aside all   PCo3
animal body comes first, and then the spiritual   PCF15
anxious thoughts, put away   Mw6
appearance sake, they say long prayers for   L20
arrogance defiles the man   Mk7

21 HUMAN PASSIONS, SOCIAL PERCEPTIONS

athlete   PTS2
bad company is the ruin of a good character   PCF15
   language must not pass your lips   PE4
beam in thine own eye   L6
behold the man   J19
belly, whose god is their   PPs3
besides ourselves, if we are   PCS5
bewildered, we are never at our wits' end   PCS4
blind leading the blind   Mw15
boaster, the tongue is a   LJ3
boastings, you rejoice in your   LJ4
bodies are limbs and organs of Christ, your   PCF6
body, all of us form one   PR12
   animal and spiritual   PCF15
   exiles as long as we are at home in the   PCS5
   our vile   PPs3
   take no thought for your   L12
courage! the victory is mine   J16
covetousness defiles the man   Mk7
   mortify your   PCo3
crooked and warped generation   PPs2
cup of happiness   PPs2
currying favour, do you think I am   PG1
desires, foolish harmful   PTF6
   godless ways and worldly   Tt2
dishonest in little things   L16
dishonesty, renounced the hidden things of   PCS4
distress, helping others in   PR12
distribution to every man according as he had need   A4
drinker, a glutton and a   C7
drunkard, any Christian who is a   PCF5
drunkenness, do not let your minds be dulled by   L21
duty to help the weak by hard work   A20
earthly things, their minds are set on   PPs3
encourage one another   LH3
enemies, love your   L6
envy defiles the man   Mk7
evil eye defiles the man   Mk7
   thoughts come from inside   Mk7
     why do you harbour   Mw9
eye, speck of sawdust in your   Mw7; L6

21 HUMAN PASSIONS, SOCIAL PERCEPTIONS

eye, the lamp of the body   Mw6
faith as a grain of mustard seed   L17
   in him, even his brothers had no   J7
   on earth? will the son of man find   L18
   you will all fall from your   Mk14
fear, shaking with   PCF2
   they were taken with great   L8
fellow workers risked their necks   PR16
flattering words, we never used   ThF2
flesh can give birth only to flesh   J3
   is weak, spirit is willing but the   Mk14
folly, bear with me in my   PCS11
forerunner, you will be the Lord's   L1
forgive the wrongs you have done   Mk11
forgiving one another   PCo3
free, truth will set you   J8
friend of publicans and sinners   L7
gentle spirit, those of a   Mk5
gentleness, patience, humility, put on the garments of   PCo3
give, and it shall be given unto you   L6
glutton and a drinker   L7
God, those who know their need of   Mw5
good and evil, to discriminate between   LH5
   deeds, widow must produce evidence of   PTF5
   none save God is   L18
goodness, must be no limit to your   Mw15
greed which makes an idol of gain   PE5
greet one another with a kiss of peace   PR16
greetings in the markets   L11, 20
grumblers and malcontents, a set of   LJu1
hair cut off, Paul had his   A18
hairs on your head have all been counted   Mw10
happy are those who hear the word of God   L11
   is the man who does not find me a stumbling-block   L7
hates his brother, if he   LJF2
hear, if you have ears to   Mk4
heart, discerner of the thoughts and intents of the   LH4
hearts at rest, set your troubled   J14
   harden not your   LH4
helping others in distress   PR12
honest in little things   L16

21 HUMAN PASSIONS, SOCIAL PERCEPTIONS

honest man comes to the light   J3
honour and dishonour are alike our lot   PCS6
human level of your lower nature   PCF3
   lot with all its ups and downs   PPs4
    nature, lay aside that old   PE4
    pride in the presence of God, no place for   PCF1
humble, gentle and patient, be always   PE4
humility, gentleness, patience, put on   PCO3
hypocrites make a show of charity   Mw6
inner man to be strengthened by his Spirit   PE3
innocence of our behaviour   PCS6
innocent as doves   Mw10
insults for my sake, when you suffer   Mw5
irreligious and worldly, law aimed at the   PTF1
jealousy, quarrelling, quibbles which give rise to   PTF6
joyful, be joyful with the   PR12
kingdom of God is within you   L17
kiss, greet one another with a holy   PCF16
  of love, greet one another with the   LPF
  of peace, greet all our brothers with the   PCS13; ThF5
law is spiritual, but I am carnal   PR7
least among you all, he is the greatest   L9
liar, he that saith I know him is a   LJF2
lie not to one another   PCo3
life is more than food, and body than clothes   Mw6
little man, being a   L19
lodging, Peter gave them a night's   A10
loose livers, have nothing to do with   PCF5
love and peace, pursue   PTS2
  cancels innumerable sins   LPF4
  cannot wrong a neighbour   PR13
  first, put   PCF4
  for one another   PPs2
  fortitude and gentleness, pursue   PTF6
  if I have not   PCF13
  is all sincerity   PR12
  man who does not   LJF3
  more than ordinary   PCS2
  mount and overflow, let your   ThF3
  one another   J13; LJF3; LJS1
  rule of   ThF4

21 HUMAN PASSIONS, SOCIAL PERCEPTIONS

love shows itself in action   LJF3
  toward all men   ThF3
  will never come to an end   PCF13
  you have lost your early   Rev2
  your enemies and do good   L6
  your neighbour as yourself   Mk12; PG5; LJ2
    they were told   Mw5
loved, the disciple whom Jesus   J13
lower nature, living on the purely human level of your   PCF3
    the desires of your   PG5
    those who live on the level of our   PR8
malice, lay aside all   PCo3
mammon of unrighteousness   L16
men, made in the likeness of   PPs2
mercy shall be shown to them   Mw5
mind and spirit, you must be made new in   PE4
morally uncircumcised   PCo2
mortal part may be absorbed into life immortal   PCS5
naked and ashamed for all to see   Rev16
  you clothed me   Mw25
nature, desires of your lower   PG5
  has no claims on us, lower   PR8
neighbour, who is my   L10
nervous, weak and shaking with fear   PCF2
novelty, hearing about the latest   A17
out of his mind, people were saying that he was   Mk3
parents, men with no respect for   PTS3
passed by on the other side   L10
passions and desires, lower nature with its   PG5
patience and kindness, by our   PCS6
  humility, gentleness, put on the garments of   PCo3
  of Job, ye have heard of the   LJ5
  of the saints   Rev14
  under ill-treatment, a pattern of   LJ5
patient towards all men   ThF5
peace is my parting gift to you   J14
  live in   PCS13
  on earth, do you suppose I came to establish   L12
  pursue the things that make for   PR14
  such as the world cannot give   J14
  with all men, live at   PR12

21 HUMAN PASSIONS, SOCIAL PERCEPTIONS

peace with one another, be at   Mk9
peacemakers, sons of God   Mw5
pleasure in the place of God, men who put   PTS3
pompous ignoramus, I call him a   PTF6
poor with you always   Mk14; J12
possessions held in common   A4
praise and blame are alike our lot   PCS6
pretence or sincerity, Christ is set forth   PPs1
pride defiles the man   Mk7
  he rises in his   ThS2
  in outward show and not in inward worth   PCS5
  lest being lifted up with   PTF3
  never make mere man a cause for   PCF3
  what room is left for human   PR3
proud, instruct the rich not to be   PTF6
  knowing nothing   PTF6
publicans and sinners, drew near unto him all the   L15
  do not even the   Mw5
pure, to the pure all things are   TF1
  hearts, those of, shall see God   Mw5
quarrels among you, there are   PCF1
relations, make provisions for   PTF5
religion, making a show of   Mw6
reputation, they valued their   J12
respect for their parents, men with no   PTS3
riches, deceitfulness of   Mk4
riotous living, wasted his substance in   L15
salutations in the market place, who love   Mk12; L11
scorn, they laughed him to   Mw9
secret place   Mw6
  your good deed must be   Mw6
self importance, filled with   PCF4
    swollen with   PTS3
  indulgence, a widow given over to   PTF5
  mortification   PCo2
sensuality, human teaching of no use in combating   PCo2
share what you have with others   LH13
sin, exacting obedience to the body's desires   PR6
  transient pleasures of   LH11
sincere love, recommend ourselves by   PCS6
Son of Man came eating and drinking   L7

21 HUMAN PASSIONS, SOCIAL PERCEPTIONS

Son of Man has nowhere to lay his head   Mw8; L9
   who speaks a word against the   L12
sorrowful shall find consolation   Mw5
soul, tell out, my   L1
speaking things best left unspoken   PTF5
spirit is willing but the flesh is weak   Mk14
   of God, refuses what belongs to the   PCF2
spiritual gift, I want to bring you some   PR1
spite and passion, have done with   PE4
stature, add one cubit to his   L12
staying power, they have no   Mk4
strangers to the truth   LJ1
superstition, questions of their own   A25
temperance, honesty and godliness, live a life of   Tt2
temptation, lead us not into   L11
   which shall come upon all the world   Rev3
   of those who want to be rich   PTF6
tempted, he himself has suffered being   LH2
trance, fell into a   A22
true self, he will find his   Mw16
truth, believers who have inward knowledge of the   PTF4
   fasten on the belt of   PE6
   with his neighbour, speak every man   PE4
uncircumcised, morally   PCo2
unjust in the least, he that is   L16
vanity, no room for personal   PPs2
   speaking words of   LPS2
vegetarian   PR14
warmth of mutual affection   PR12
warped and crooked generation   PPs2
wasted his substance in riotous living   L15
watch and pray   Mw26; Mk14
way of peace, guide our feet unto the   L1
weak, nervous and shaking with fear   PCF2
weakness, sown in, raised to power   PCF15
weaknesses, able to sympathise with our   LH4
whitewashed wall   A23
wits are beclouded, their   PE4
word became flesh   J1

22   *Hunting and Fishing*

OLD TESTAMENT

angle for fish   H1
dead-fall trap   Job18; Pro22, 26, 28; Je48; La3
deer pursued by hunter   La1
drag-net   H1
fish, dying   Ex7
  for the asking in Egypt   Nu11
  in shoals   E47
  basket   Am4
fisherman   Is19; Je16; E26, 47
fishhook   E29; Am4; H1
fishing equipment   Job41
fowler   Ps91, 124; Pro6; Je5; Ho9
fowler's snare   Ps91
  trap   Ps124
gaff, fishing   Job41
gin trap   Is8; Am3
harpoon   Job41
hook, barbed   Nu33; Jos23; E29; Am4; H1
hunter   Job15; Ps91; Pro6, 12; Is13, 24; Je16, 48; La1; Ho12; Mi7
  Esau became a skilful   Gen25
  mighty before the Lord   Gen10
  Nimrod was a mighty   Gen10
hunting equipment   Job18
huntsman   Ps22
net   Pro1, 29; E12
  antelopes caught in the   Is51
  fishing   Ec9; Is19; E26, 32, 47; H1
  fowler's   Pro1, 29; Je5; Ho7
  hunter's   Job18; Mi7
  wild bull in a   Is51
noose, hunting   Job18; Pro7

22 HUNTING AND FISHING

partridge over the hills, as one might hunt   SF26
pit, lion caught in a   E19
  hunter's   Job18; Pro26, 28; Is24; Je48; La3
pitfall   Pro22, 26, 28
scare, hunter's   Is24; Je48; La3
snare   Ps91, 141f; Pro7, 20, 22, 29; Is8, 24
  fowler's   Ps91; Ec9; Am3
  hunter's   Job18; Je5, 48, 50
spear, fish   Job41
trap, fowler's   Ho9
  gin   Is8; Am3
  hunter's   Ps91; Is24; Je48; Am3
  metal   Job18
  toothed   Job41
trawls, fishing   H1

NEW TESTAMENT

boat, fisherman's   Mw4; Mk1
  towing a full net   J21
casting-net   Mk1
fish, a great multitude of   L5
  made a big haul of   L5
  net full of   J21
  that comes to the hook   Mw17
fishermen   Mk1; L5
  of Galilee   Mw4
fishers of men, I will make you   Mk1
fishing, I am going out   J21
  net   Mk1
hook, go to the sea and cast an   Mw17
hunted, we are never abandoned   PCS4
mending their nets   Mw4
net, fishing   Mw4; L5; J21
  let down into the sea   Mw13
  nets began to split   L5
    overhauling their   Mw4; Mk1

22 HUNTING AND FISHING

ship, fishing   Mw4; Mk1
snare   PR11; PCF7; PTF6
   caught in the devil's   PTF3
   of the devil   PTS2
   shall it come, as a   L21
trap, a snare and a   PR11
   great day closes upon you like a   L21
traps the wise in their own cunning   PCF3

23   *Idols, Gods and Images*

OLD TESTAMENT

Adonis   Is17
Adrammelech, Sepharvaim idol   KS17
allegiance to other gods   Ju2
altar, brick   Is65
  fiery   Is29
  Hezekiah suppressed   Is36
  made by their own hands   Is17
  stones, grinds their   Is27
altars for the hosts of heaven   KS21
  foreign, suppressed   CS14
  God himself will hack down their   Ho10
  horns of their   Je17
  made by Manasseh   KS23
  of Baal smashed   KS11
  pagan, broken up   CS31
  to burn sacrifices to Baal   Je11
Amon, god of No   Je46
Ammonites, god of   KS23
Anammelech, Sepharvaim idol   KS17
Apis, bull god   Je46
Asherah   KF11, 15; KS13, 21, 23; CS15
  four hundred prophets of   KF18
Ashima, idol of Hamath   KS17
Ashimah, goddess of Samaria   Am8
Ashtaroth, Canaanite gods   Ju2, 10; SF7, 12
  banished by the Israelites   SF7
Ashtoreth, Sidonian goddess   KF11, 15; KS13, 21, 23; CS15
Assyria, gods of   KS19
Avvites, idols of the   KS17
Baal, Canaanite god   Ju2, 6; KF16, 18, 22; KS3, 10ff, 17, 23; Je7, 23; Ho2, 13
  Ahab worshipped   KF16

23 IDOLS, GODS AND IMAGES

Baal, Ahaziah worshipped KF22
  all the ministers of KS10
  altars to KF16; Je11
  burnt sacrifices to Je11
  burnt their sons as whole-offerings to Je19
  four hundred and fifty prophets of KF18
  god of shame Je3
  of Peor De4; Ps106
  pleading the cause of Ju6
  prophesied in the name of Je2
  prophets of, summoned KS10
  sacred pillar of KS3
  sacrifices burnt to KS3
  shrines to Je19
  taught my people to swear by Je12
  tear down the altar of Ju6
  temple of KS10ff
    made into a privy Ks10
    pulled down CS23
  wipe out the last remnant of Zp1
  whole-offerings to Je19
  worship, they were guilty of Ho13
Baal-berith, idol of Ju8
Baal-peor, they resorted to Ho9
    worship of Nu25
Baal-zebub Ks1
Baalim, idols of Ju2, 8, 10; SF7, 12; CS17, 23f, 28, 33ff; Ho11
  I have not followed Je2
  rebuilt altars to CS33
  she burnt sacrifices to the Ho2
  the Israelites banished SF1
    worshipped Ju2
  they followed Je9
Babylonians, idols of the KS17
Bamah hill-shrine E20
Bel Is46; Je50ff
bull-calf in metal Ne9
bull-god Apis Je46
bull-gods in Gilgal, sacrifice to Ho12
burnt their sons as whole-offerings to Baal Je19

23 IDOLS, GODS AND IMAGES

burnt offerings to Baal   KS10
  their children in the fire, Sepharvites   KS17
calf gods   Ho8, 10, 13
    of Beth-aven   Ho10
  image   Ho13
  molten   Ps106
calves, images of   CS11, 13
  cast image of   KS17
  golden   Ex32; CS13
    Jehu maintained   KS10
Canaanite gods, Ashtaroth   Ju2, 10; SF7, 12
carved figures shall be scattered, her   Mi1
  images   Ps78; Je10
    shall not make   De5
    burnt offerings before   Ho11
carves an idol, a curse on he who   De27
cast image made with 200 pieces of silver   Ju17
chariots of the sun, he burnt   KS23
Chemosh, Moabite god   KF11
children, you sacrificed my   E16
Chiun and Moloch, your images   Am5
clay, feet of   D2
Cuthites, idols of the   KS17
Dagon, broken   SF5
  fallen   SF5
  Philistine god   Ju16; SF5
  temple of   CF10ff
demons, foreign   Ps106
  hill-shrines of the   KS23; CS11
  sacrificed to foreign   De32
  they consort with   Ju5
desecrated the hill-shrines   KS23
drink-offerings, idolatrous   E20
    to other gods   Je7, 32
Ekron, Baal-zebub god of   KS1
ephod, Micah made an   Ju17ff
  of Gideon, set up to be worshipped   Ju8
evil spirit sent to Abimelech   Ju9
false gods, give up   SF12
    may abandon loyalty, men who worship   Jon2
    of Noph   E30

23 IDOLS, GODS AND IMAGES

feet of clay, image in Nebuchadnezzar's dream   D2
fetish, take their orders from a   Ho4
figure carved in relief   De4
fire, children made to pass through   KS17
   made his sons pass through   KS17
   not to pass through   De18
   pass through in honour of Molech   KS23
   passed his son through   KS16, 21
   you pass your sons through   E20
garden rites   Is66
   shrines   Is1
gardens, offering sacrifices in   Is65
god, bull   Je46
   cried out for help, each to his   Jon1
   daughters of a foreign   Ma2
   fashion gold and silver into a   Is46
   foreign   Ps81; Is17
   of fate   Is65
   strange   Ps81
goddess Asherah, Ashtoreth   KF11, 15; KS13
   Ashima   Am8
   of the field   So2f
   of the Sidonians   KS23
gods   Ps29, 81ff; 106, 135
   ancestral   Jos24; SF7; D11
   as many as you have towns   Je11
   banish the foreign   Jos24; SF7
   beloved of women   D11
   burning incense to his   Je48
     offerings to their   Je48
     sacrifices to other   Je19, 44
   can give the answer, none but the   D2
   Canaanite   Ju2ff
   consigned to the fire   Is37
   declare what will happen, then we shall know   Is41
   drink-offerings to other   Je19, 32
   gold calves as   KF12
   household   Z10
   I love foreign   Je2
   led astray by false   Am2
   made out of wood and stone   De4

23   IDOLS, GODS AND IMAGES

gods, must not follow other   Jos23; Je28
  of all nations   Ps96
  of bronze and iron   D5
  of Egypt, houses of the   Je43
  of gold and silver   D5
  of metal   Le19
  of Seir, sacrificed to   CS25
  of silver and gold   Ex20
  of the earth   Zp2
  of the household, Teraphim   E21
  of wood and stone   D5
  powerless to help   Je2
  run after other, to your own ruin   Je7
  served alien   Je5
  temples of the Egyptian   Je43
  that are no gods, sworn by   Je5
  they resort to other   Ho3
  they went after other   Ju2
  trusted in false   Je13
  we will not serve your   D3
  worshipping other   De17
  you have taken my   Ju18
  you shall have no other   De5
golden calf of Aaron   Ex32
  calves, Jehu maintained the worship of   KS10
  image of Nebuchadnezzar   D3
graven images, a land of   Je50
    beaten to pieces   Mi1
    burned incense to   Ho11
    confounded by   Je10, 51
    curse on the maker of   De27
    do not make   De4
    hew down the   De12
    I will cut off your   Mi5; Na1
    molten, profitable for nothing   Is44
    of Babylon   Is21
    provoked me to anger with their   Je8
    served their   KS17
    that trust in   Is42
    what profiteth   H2
    workman melteth   Is40

23 IDOLS, GODS AND IMAGES

groves, sacred   KS11; Is17, 27; Je17
    burn their   De12
    cut down their   Ju6; CS14ff
    for Baal   KS21
    I will pluck up   Mi5
    prophets of the   KF18
    they have made their   KF14
Hamath, Ashima the idol of   KS17
Hamathites, idols of   KS17
heathen priests suppressed   KS23
hill-shrines   KF3, 11ff, 22; KS12ff, 17ff, 21, 23; CS1, 11, 14ff, 17; CS20, 28, 31, 33; Ps78; Is6, 15ff, 36
    allowed to remain   KS12
    at all their settlements   KS17
    at Gibeon   CS1
    broken up   CS31
    called Bamah   E20
    destruction of   E6
    he desecrated all   KS23
    he rebuilt   KS21
    Hezekiah suppressed   KS18
    leave in ruins   Nu33
    of Aven   Ho10
    of Jeroboam   KS23
    of Judah   Mi1
    of the demons   KS23
    of the Hill of God   SF10
    of the satyrs   KS23
    rebuilt   CS33
    sacrificing at   Je48
    suppressed   CS14, 17, 31
homage to other gods, you shall not pay   KS17
horns of their altars   Je17
household gods   Ju17ff; SF19; E21
    got rid of   KS23
    make mischievous promises   Z10
    shall live without   Ho3
human bones, filled their places with   KS23
idol   Ps16, 31, 96, 106; Is44f, 48, 57
  and image will I hew down   Na1
  carved   Nu33

23 IDOLS, GODS AND IMAGES

idol, despised broken   Je22
  every goldsmith is discredited by his   Je51
  figures of reptiles, beasts and vermin   E8
  forbidden   Le26
  gold   Is31
  king, take up the shrine of an   Am5
  set up in Dan   Ju18
  sheathed in gold   Is30
  they burn sacrifices to a mere   Je18
  to make a carved   Ju17
  what use is an   H2
  worship an   Is66
idolatry in Gilead   Ho12
idols, all who vaunt   Ps97
  Asa did away with   KF15
  banish your loathsome   Je4
  buried   Gen35
  carved round the walls   E8
  David carried off the Philistine   SS5
  defiled the land   E36
  destroy their   DE7
  erase the names of   Z13
  fashioned their silver into   Ho13
  fling down your slain before your   E6
  four kingdoms full of   Is10
  go awhoring after their   E6
  hack down their   De12
  have spoken vanity   Z10
  I will cleanse you from the taint of your   E36
  I will punish Babylon's   Je51
  Josiah got rid of   Ks23
  land filled with   Is2
  let them come forward, these   Is41
  loathsome   Je7
  make a waste heap of   Mi1
  making dumb   H2
  men of Judah worshipped   CS24
  never again be defiled with   E37
  of Egypt   Is19
  of gold   Is2
  of Israel   E18

23 IDOLS, GODS AND IMAGES

idols of Manasseh   KS21
  of Philistines burnt by David   CF14
  of silver,   Is2, 31
  provoke me to anger with   Je25
  purged   CS34
  raisin-cakes offered to their   Ho3
  set up their loathsome   Je32
  silver and gold   Ps115, 135; Ho8
  slaughtering their sons as an offering to   E23
  suppressed by Asa   CS15
  the city that makes herself   E22
  the dead lumber of their   Je16
  their eyes have gone roving wantonly after   E6
  these people have set their hearts on   E14
  they are mad upon their   Je50
  they worshipped   KS17
  turn away from your   E14
  to defy all wooden   E21
  you lift up your eyes to   E33
idol-worship, Jezebel's   KS9
image, a source of lies   H2
  and idol will I hew down   Na1
  broken down   CS34
  bull   Ps106
  calf   CS11, 13; Ps106
  carved   CS34; Ps78
  cast, Baalim   CS28
    metal   Nu33
  confounded by his graven   Je10
  gold, Nebuchadnezzar made a   D3
  graven   De4; CS34
  laid in bed   SF19
  molten   CS34
    is falsehood   Je10
  Nebuchadnezzar's dream   D2
  of a bull-calf   Ne9
  of cast metal   Ho13
  which craftsman sets up   Is40
images, all who worship   Ps97
  burnt offerings before carved   Ho11
  burnt one and all   Mi1

23 IDOLS, GODS AND IMAGES

images, carved, are a sham   Je10
  cherished, profit nobody   Is44
  I will destroy your   M5
  made jewels into vile   E7
  molten gold   Is30
  of Baal, burnt   KS10
    smashed   KS11
  of Beth-shemesh, he shall break   Je43
  of cast metal   KS17
  of gods cast in metal   D11
  of Israel shall be broken   E6
  of lust at Jerusalem   E8
  pedestals of your   Am5
  sacred   Is17
  sacrificing children to   E16
  shall live without   Ho3
  shall not stand   Is27
  silvered   Is30
  under every green tree   KF14
incense   Is43, 60
  an abomination   Is1
  burnt as a token   Is66
    for idols   E8, 23
    on brick altars   Is65
    on the mountains   I65
    to Baal   Je7, 11
    to Baalim   Ho2
    to graven images   Ho11
    to his gods   Je48
    to other gods   Je1, 19, 44
    in pagan rites   KS14ff, 22ff
    offered to Baal   Je32
    to gods   Je11
  they burn up on the hills   Ho4
incense-altars   Is17, 27
    destroyed   E6
    hacked down   CS34
    suppressed   Cs14
Kemosh, Ammonite god   Ju11
  Moabite god   KF11; KS23
magic ring   Is66

23 IDOLS, GODS AND IMAGES

Malcham, Milcom   Zp1
Manasseh, idols of   KS21
Marduk, Merodach, god of Babylon   Je50
Milcom, Ammonite god   SS12; KF11; KS23; CF20, 29; Je49
  those who swear by   Zp1
Moabite god, Chemosh   KF11
Moabites, idols of the   KS23
Molech, Ammonite god   KF11; KS23
  giving children to   Le20
  surrendering their sons and daughters to   Je32
Moloch and Chiun, your images   Am5
molten images   KS17; Is42
    curse upon him who makes   De27
    falsehood   Je10, 51
    I will cut off   Na1
    of silver   Ho13
    what profiteth   H2
monuments, who lodge in the   Is65
mountain-shrine   E18
Nebo, image carried in procession   Is46
Nehushtan, bronze serpent of Moses   KS18
Nergal, idol of Cuth   KS17
Nibhaz, idol of the Avvites   KS17
Nisroch, Assyrian idol   KS19; Is37
No, god of Amon   Je46
Noph, false gods of   E30
oaks, sacred   Is1
offerings on the hills, your men burn   Ho4
Philistine god, Dagon   Ju16; SF5
pillars, sacred   CS14, 31
    forbidden   Le26
    he will smash   Je43
    I will destroy your   Mi5
poles, sacred   CS14, 24, 31, 33
    burn their   De12
    by every spreading tree   Je17
    cut down   CS14, 31
    I will pull down your   Mi5
power, subdue the ancient   De33
priests of the high places, slew all the   KS23
  of the hill-shrines from every class   KS17

23 IDOLS, GODS AND IMAGES

processions, images carried in your   Is46
purge of idols   CS34
raisin-cake offered to idols   Ho3
Rimmon, Babylonian god of storms   KS5
   temple of   KS5
rites, your vile and abominable   E5
sacred groves   De12; Ju6; KF14, 18; KS11, 21; CS14ff; Is17; Je17;
       Mi5
   oaks   Is1
   pillars   Le26; KS3, 10, 17ff, 23; CS14, 31; Je43; Ho3, 110;
       Mi5
     broke down   KS23
     Hezekiah smashed   KS23
     I will destroy your   Mi5
     of Baal   KS3, 10
     of Beth-shemesh   Je43
     shall live without   Ho3
     smashed   CS14, 31
   poles   KF14, 16; KS10, 13, 17ff, 23; CS11, 14, 24, 31, 33;
       Is17, 27
     by every spreading tree   Je17
     cut down   Ju6; KS23
     Hezekiah destroyed   Ks18
     in hill-shrines   Is6
     I will pull down your   Mi5
     of Baal, burnt   KS10
sacrifice at every leafy tree   E20
   at hill-shrines   KS14ff
   child   Le20; Ju11; KS3, 16f, 21, 23; CS33; Ps106; Is57; Je7, 19, 32;
       E16, 20, 23; Ho13
     first-born sons, redeemed   Ex13
     offered in gardens   Is65
     on the mountain tops   Ho4
     to Baal   Je11, 19, 32
       a great   Ks10
     to Baalim   CS28
     to bull-gods   Ho12
     to other gods, they have burnt   KS22
Samaria, Ashimah goddess of   Am8
satyr   Is13, 34
   hill-shrine of the   KS23; CS11

23 IDOLS, GODS AND IMAGES

Seir, sacrificed to the gods of   CS25
Sepharvaim idol, Adrammelech   KS17
    Anammelech   KS17
Sepharvites burnt their children in the fire   KS17
serpent of brass or bronze, fiery, the standard of Moses   Nu21; KS18
seven altars of Balaam   Nu23
shrines, garden   Is1
  hill, of Canaan   Nu33
  of his own carved image   E8
  to Baal   Je19, 32
Sidonian goddess, Ashtoreth   KS23
  idols   KS23
slaughtering their own sons as an offering to idols   E23
smoke-offerings   KS12
soothing odour, idolatrous offering of   E20
spirits and goddesses of the field   So2ff
Succoth-benoth, Babylonian idol   KS17
tabernacle of Moloch and Chiun   Am5
Tammuz, women wailing for   E8
Tartak, Avvite idol   KS17
temple of Nisroch   Is37
temples, he will set fire to   Je43
  Israel hath forgotten his maker, and buildeth   Ho8
  of Baal   Ks10
  of the Egyptian gods   Je43
Teraphim idols   SF15
   Micah made   Ju77ff; E21
   abide without   Ho3
  household gods   Ju17ff; E21
tree, sacrifices under every spreading   KS16
whole-offerings to Baal   KS10
wood and stone, their gods were mere   KS19
   tribes of other lands who worship   E20

NEW TESTAMENT

angel worship   PCo2
Areopagite, follower of Mars   A17

23 IDOLS, GODS AND IMAGES

Areopagus, court of   A17
Baal   PR11
Babylon the Great, God did not forget   Rev16
bartered away the true God for a false one   PR1
beast in John's vision   Rev13
  the whole world worshipped the   Rev13
bombast and blasphemy, the beast was allowed to mouth   Rev13
bull-calf, feast in honour of the   A7
dark world, potentates of this   PE6
deities, heathen   PCF8
deity like an image   A17
  propagandist for some foreign   A17
demons, they sacrifice to   PCF10
devils, they sacrifice to   PCF10
  worship of   Rev9
Diana of the Ephesians, great is   A19
  silver shrines of   A19
  temple of   A19
divine pre-eminence, Diana brought down from her   A19
false god, bartered away the true God for a   PR1
  gods, be on watch against   LJF5
    food consecrated to   PCF8
    you abominate   PR2
feast in honour of the bull-calf   A7
god himself, claiming to be a   ThS2
  of this passing age   PCS4
  they changed their minds and said, he is a   A28
goddess Diana   A19
goddess, uttered no blasphemy against our   A19
gods, be on watch against false   LJF5
  dumb heathen   PCF12
  false   PCF8; LJF5
  have come down to us in human form   A14
  made by human hands are not gods at all   A19
  setter forth of strange   A17
  slaves of beings which are no   PG4
graven by art, gold, silver, or stone   A17
great is Diana of the Ephesians!   A19
heaven, symbol of Diana which fell from   A19
host of heaven, gave them up to worship the   A7

23 IDOLS, GODS AND IMAGES

idol, anything but an   PCF10
  bull-calf   A7
  of gain, greed which makes an   PE5
idolater, no, hath any inheritance   PE5
  no, will possess the kingdom   PCF6
idolaters, do not be   PCF10
  outside are   Rev22
  pagan   PCF5
idolatry and sorcery belong to lower nature   PG5
  greed no less than   PCo3
  city given over to   A17
  is covetousness   PCo3
  shun   PCF10
  so accustomed to   PCF8
idols, abstain from contact with   A15
    from meat offered to   A21
  Athens was full of   A17
  dumb   PCF12
  eat food sacrificed to   Rev2
  food consecrated to   PCF8
  forbidden worship of   LPF4
  little children, keep yourselves from   LJF5
  of gold, silver, bronze, stone and wood   Rev9
  of the heathen   PCS6
  what agreement hath the temple of God with   PCS6
  worship of   Rev9
  you turned from   ThF1
image in gold or silver   A17
  of Baal, not boweth the knee to the   PR11
  of the beast, to worship the   Rev13, 16
  shaped like mortal man, exchanging God for an   PR1
images like birds, beasts and creeping things   PR1
Jupiter, image which fell down from   A19
  priest of   A14
  temple of   A14
  they called Barnabbas   A14
mark of the beast   Rev14, 16
Mars, follower of   A17
  hill   A17
Mercurius   A14
Mercury, they called Paul   A14

23 IDOLS, GODS AND IMAGES

Moloch, tabernacle of   A7
  the shrine of   A7
new moon, observance of the   PCo2
obeyed the commander of the spiritual powers of the air   PE2
objects of worship   A17
pagans, give up living like   PE4
powers of the air, spiritual   PE2
Rephan, Rephem, Remphan, star of the god   A7
reverence to created things instead of to the Creator   PR1
sacrifice to idols, food   Rev2
sanctuary of Diana   A19
slaves to elemental spirits   PG4
special days, you keep   PG4
spirits of the elements   PG4
star of the god Rephan   A7
superstitious, in all things ye are too   A17
tabernacle of Moloch   A7
temple, eat in the idol's   PCF8
  warden of Diana, the Ephesus   A19
temples, God dwelleth not in   A17
vileness of their own desires, given up to the   PR1
worship created things instead of the Creator   PR1
  I was looking at the objects of your   A17

24 Laws, Oaths, Pledges and Covenants

OLD TESTAMENT

adulterers, testify against   Ma3
adultery, laws regarding   D22
advisers. king's, on misdemeanour   Est1
aid, every remaining Jew may claim   Ez1
alliance with Pharaoh, agreement of   KF15
allowance for Jehoiachin   KS25
   governor's   Ne5
Annals of Solomon   KF11
   of the kings of Israel   KF15ff, 22; KS1, 10, 13ff
   of the king of Judah   KF15, 22; KS28, 12ff, 20ff
   of the kings of Judah and Israel   CS20, 24f, 27f, 32, 35ff
arbitrators, Ezra to appoint   Ez7
archives of Babylon   Ez6
Ark of the Covenant   Ex25ff; Le16; Nu10; De10, 31; Jos3ff, 8;
     Ju2; SF4; SS15; CF6, 22, 28; CS5, 35; Je3
   custodian of the   SF7
bill of divorcement   Is50
book of Moses   Ez6; Ne13
   of the chronicles of the kings of Israel   KS1, 10
   of the chronicles of the kings of Judah   KS8
   of the covenant   KS22
   of the kings if Israel and Judah   CS20, 24f, 27f, 32, 35ff
   of the law   KS22
   of the law of the Lord   CS17, 34
   of the law of Moses   Ne8
   of the manner of the kingdom   SF10
books of the chronicles   KF15ff
boundary, men who move their neighbour's   Ho5
   stone   Pro15; Is54
bribe   Ps15; Pro15

24 LAWS, OATHS, PLEDGES AND COVENANTS

bribery makes a crooked answer   De16
   the wise man blind   De16
bribes, hands full of   Ps26
   Samuel's sons took   SF8
calumnies heaped upon me   Ps109
  of the nations   Ps89
  sanctimonious   Ps94
  they spread   Ps73
census of Solomon   CS2
champion, God shall be   Ps59
  to their cause   Is19
college at Jerusalem   KS22
commandment to bless   Nu23
commandments, find joy in his   Ps112
  fix my eyes on   Ps119
  observe his   KF2
  ten, declared by Moses   Ex20
  they did not keep his   KS17
commands, do serve my   Ps89
common lands attached to cities   CS31
   surrounding towns   Nu35
compact, Jonathan and David made a solemn   SF18
compensation for wrongdoing   Nu5
complaint against Moses and Aaron   Nu16
contributions, defrauding over   Ma3
counsel, let us seek   KF22
  of the people   Ps33
  the Lord's   Ps33
counsellor   Is40
  like those of old   Is1
  Pharaoh's   Is19
  stripped of every   Is3
council, if they have stood in my   Je23
court   Ps127
  in Daniel's vision   D7
  institution of the   Ex18
  of the tabernacle   Ex27ff
  sat, and the books were opened   D7
covenant, Ahab to Ben-hadad   KF20
  anger in his heart against the   D11
  annulment of in Zechariah's oracle   Z11

24 LAWS, OATHS, PLEDGES AND COVENANTS

Covenant, Ark of the   Ex25f; Le16; Nu10; De10, 31; Jos3f, 8;
　　Ju20; SF4; SS15; CF6, 22, 28; CS5, 35; Je3
　calf of the, divided in two   Je34
　cut out your right eyes   SF11
　faithful to his   Ps78
　faithfully keeping the   D9
　from long ago   Ps105
　have not betrayed thy   Ps44
　hold fast to my   Is56
　I have made   Ps89
　I will make a new   Je31f
　keep his   Ps25, 103
　keep in mind his   Ps111
　let us make   Ez10
　listen to the terms of this   Je11
　made with thee   Ps50
　make with your   Is55
　not kept God's   Ps78
　of Joshua with the people   Jos24
　of security of tenure   Nu25
　recalled his   Ps106
　remember thy   Je14
　remembered   Ex2
　renewed   Ne9
　sealed in blood   Z9
　tablets of the   KF8
　they have broken my   Ho6, 8
　they have violated the eternal   Is24
　to seek guidance of the Lord   CS15
　when the Lord made his   KS17
　which shall last forever   E16
　with Abram   Gen15
　with Abraham   Gen17
　with David   SS3
　with Noah   Gen9
　with the Lord, they forsook their   Je22
　with the people   Jos24
　with them, an everlasting   E37
　with wild beasts   Ho2
　you have violated the   E16
crime after crime of Gaza   Am1

24 LAWS, OATHS, PLEDGES AND COVENANTS

crime after crime of Israel   Am2
   of Tyre   Am1
custom tax   Ez4
debt, men in, gathered round David   SF22
   remission of   De15
decree, royal   Est1, 3, 9
   of forced labour   Est10
decrees, cherish thy   Ps119
deed of divorce   Is50
   of land purchase   Je32
deeds in an earthenware jar, deposit the   Je32
defraud with tithes and contributions   Ma3
distrain on his goods   Ps109
divorce, bill of   Is50
drunkenness   Pro23
dwelling house, sale and redemption of   Le25
edict regarding extermination of all Jews   Est3ff
elder, stripped of every   Is3
elders, there will be no counsel from   E7
evidences, subscribe and seal   Je33
expiation, ceremony of   CF28
   for extortion   Le6
   for Israel, to make   CF6; CS29
   for lies   Le6
   rites of   Le4ff
   shrine of   CF28
extortion, expiation for   Le6
he will take a tenth of your vintage by   SF8
   put no trust in   Ps62
false witness, bearing   Pro6
fast proclaimed by Ezra   Ez8
   for all Judah   CS20
fine imposed on Judah by Egypt   CS36
   on Judah of silver and gold   KS23
fines, unjust   Am2
fire, malicious   Le10
   restitution for causing   Ex22
foreigner, showing justice towards a   KF8
gifts to slaves relating to inheritance   E46
gossip, spreading cruel   Ps38, 52
governor's allowance   Ne5

24 LAWS, OATHS, PLEDGES AND COVENANTS

guilt of bloodshed, saved me from   SF25
  pardons all Ps103
  symbolized by clothes Z3
  wash away Ps51
  wiped out Ps78
Hall of Judgement KF7
houses, mortgaged Ne5
human valuation Le27
impartiality, necessity for De1
inheritance, allotment of Ne36
  daughters placed on same footing as sons Jos17
  Hebron for Caleb Jos14
  land taken by Joshua Jos11
  Levites to have no material De18
  of land, registry of Jos18
  of the Levites, the Lord is the Jos13
  Ruth acquired with Ru4
  passed down Nu27
  possession of Nu27
  turned to strangers La5
injustice, loose the fetters of Is58
intermarriage forbidden Jos23
inventory for the house of the Lord Ez1
  of temple treasures Ez8
judge and prophetess, Deborah Ju4
  between many people, he will be Mi4
  fairly De1
  God himself is Ps50, 75
  if only I were appointed SS15
  Lord who art a righteous Je11
  of the earth Ps94
  over Israel, Abdon Ju12
    Elon Ju12
    Ibzan Ju12
    Jair Ju10
    Jephthah Ju12
    Samson Ju15ff
    Tola Ju10
  stripped of every Is3
  swift to do right Is16
  the earth Ps82

24 LAWS, OATHS, PLEDGES AND COVENANTS

judges appointed by Jehosaphat   CS19
  Ezra to appoint   Ez7
  over them, the Lord set   Ju2
  what they once were   Is1
judgement belongs to God   De1
  breastplate of   Ex18ff
  conform to my   Ps89
  every case to bring before the king for   SS15
  Lord sits high in   Is5
  of Solomon   KF3
  rising in   Ps76
  Valley of the Lord's   Joe3
  regarding who is the mother   KF3
judgements, just, are your   Ps58
justice   Ps9ff, 67, 101
  administer true   Z7
  alone pursue   De16
  always on his lips   Ps37
  and equity   Ps99
  and judgement of their own making   H1
  comes out perverted   H1
  court of   Is28
  dawns like morning light   Ho6
  do not pervert the course of   De16
  give me   Ps26
  heavens proclaim his   Ps50
  judge mankind with   Ps75
  in the courts, enthrone   Am5
  my own   Ps72
  rule with   Is32
  shall redeem Zion   Is1
  spirit of   Is28
  they went to Deborah for   Ju4
  use as a plumb-line   Is28
  wear the belt of   Is11
  when the inhabitants of the world learn   Is26
  who taught him   Is40
justly, to love loyalty, to act   Mi6
land, common, surrounding towns   Nu35; CS31
  register of   Jos18
  tenure by slaves   E46

24 LAWS, OATHS, PLEDGES AND COVENANTS

land-mark   Pro22ff
law and justice, the branch of David will maintain   Je33
  book of God's   Jos24
    be ever on your lips   Jos1
    contrives a mischief under cover of the   Ps94
    grows effete   H1
    her priests have done violence to my   E22
    if his sons forsake my   Ps89
    of God   Ps37
    of Moses   KF2; KS23; CS23, 25; Ez3, 7; Ne8
      all foreshadowed by the   D9
      perform everything in the   Jos23
      turn not aside from the   Jos23
    swerve not from thy   Ps119
    stands firm, thy   Ps93
    the people assemble to study the   Ne8
    they that keep the   Pro28
    words of, inscribed   De27
lawgiver, Gad in the position of   De33
  the Lord is our   Is33
lawlessness and robbery, put an end to   E45
laws and statutes, she has rebelled against my   E5
    and teachings, you did not obey his   Je44
  Jerusalem rejected my   E5
  live humbly by his   Zp2
  of nature on earth   Job38
  of the Medes and Persians   Est1
  shame on you who make unjust   Is10
  they have broken the   Is24
  you have not kept my   E11
letters of King Ahasuerus   Est1
levies on merchandise   CS9
levy, general   Ez4, 7
  on all men of wealth   KS15
  Solomon raised forced   KF5
licence to obtain timber   Ez3
litigation spreads like a poisonous weed   Ho10
loan, pledges for a   De24
lost property, rules concerning   De22
lot, Benjamin was picked by   SF10
  territories were assigned by   Jos14

24 LAWS, OATHS, PLEDGES AND COVENANTS

lots cast for land   Jos18
   to apportion blame   SF14
   to decide local residence   Ne11
manumission, rules of   E46
misdemeanours, wise men versed in   Est1
money lending, rules of   Ex22
mortgage, house and farm   Ne5
Moses and tables of stone   KF8
oath and solemn vow   Ps119
  binding obligation of an   Nu30
  captains put on   KS11
  David answered with an   SS4
  for the life of Rahab   Jos2
  Jonathan had not heard his father's   SF14
  no respect for an   Ps55
  not to be broken   Ps132
  of allegiance   CS36
  of David regarding Solomon   KF1
    to Bathsheba   KF1
  of David's officers that he should never again go to war   SS21
  of Ezra   Ez10
  of Moses to Caleb   Jos14
  of Saul, that Jonathan should die   SF14
  pervert the course of justice with an   SF8
  pledged to the Gibeonites   Jos9
  trial for unfaithfulness involving an   Nu5
  laws of taking an   Nu30
oaths are imposed and broken   Ho4
  are perjury, their   Ps144
offence at Peor, remember our   Jos22
orders sent to exterminate all Jews, young and old   Est3ff
ordinance, Joshua drew up an   Jos24
  of King Darius   D6
oppression of the poor, strangers and widows, forbidden   Z7
orphan his rights, they do not give   Is1
Passover, ordered the people to keep the   KS23
patrimony, acquired Ruth with his   Ru4
  allotment of   Nu36
  daughters placed on the same footing as sons   Jos17
  of Hebron for Caleb   Jos14

24 LAWS, OATHS, PLEDGES AND COVENANTS

patrimony of land, registry of   Jos18
   taken by Joshua   Jos11
   of Levites not to include land   De18
     is the Lord God   Jos13
   passed down   Nu27
   turned over to strangers   La5
pensioner, Jehoiachin made   KS25
pensioners, Jezebel's   KF18
perjurer shall be swept away, every   Z5
perjurers, I will testify against   Ma3
persons, valuation of   Le27
pledge, children given in, for food   Ne5
  cloak, taken as   De24
  for loans   De24
  goods taken in   H2
  Joshua to the Gibeonites   Jos9
  millstone not to be taken in   De24
  people held in, to be released   Ne10
  remission of   De15
poll tax   Ez4, 7
possession of inheritance   Nu27
proclamation of Asa   KF15
property exchange, sandal as a symbol of   Ru4
  lost, rules concerning   De22
  mortgage of   Ne5
  redemption of   Le25
  sale of   Le25
  valuation and dedication of   Le27
propitiation, rites of   Le4ff
punishments outlined by Moses   Ex21ff
purchase by King David of a threshing floor   CF21
ransomed, Jonathan by the people   SF14
rebate, Solomon's house   KF6
redeem your pledged sons   KF4
redemption of property   Le25
  right of, to buy land   Je32
reforms of Nehemiah   Ne12
register of land for patrimony   Jos18
remission of debt   De15
right and wrong, King David can decide between   SS14
righteousness, the Lord is our   Je23

24 LAWS, OATHS, PLEDGES AND COVENANTS

rod of iron   Ps2
rumours, penalty for carrying false   Ex23
sabbath, buying and selling on   Ne10
  collecting produce on   Ne13
  do no work on the   Je17
  forgotten   La1ff
  keep holy as I commanded your forefathers   Je17
  laws and penalties regarding the   Ex31; Nu15
  selling merchandise on   Ne13
  treading wine on   Ne13
sale of property   Le25
scandal-mongers   Ps101
scroll regarding the nature of a king   SF10
security of tenure   Nu25
  covenant of   Nu25
seduction, penalty for   Ex22
sentence, observe justice in passing   Ps51
sexual wrongdoing, penalties for   Le20; De22
sin whispers to the wicked man   Ps36
sins of my youth   Ps25
  unwitting   Ps19
slander   Ps38, 50, 52, 73, 120
  mutter all day long   Ps38
  the tongue of   Ps120
solemn oath, made light of   E16
sons punished for their father's crime   Nu14, 31
sorcerers, testify against   Ma3
statutes, keeping thy   Ps119
  observe his   KF2
  refused to conform to the   E5
  they renounce my   Ps89
  they have disobeyed my   Is24
  you have not conformed to my   E11
stolen goods   Ps62
stone, boundary marker   Is54
  tablets of, inscribed   Ex24, 31ff
stoning as a legal requirement   De13ff
stray animals, rules concerning   De22
stumbling blocks of the wicked   Zp1
swear that you will not hand me back   SF30
sword of the Lord and of Gideon   Ju7

24 LAWS, OATHS, PLEDGES AND COVENANTS

tablets of Moses CS5
  of stone Ex24, 31; KF8; CS5
    replacements for the Ex34
    shattered Ex32
talebearer Pro18, 26
tax, annual CS24
  land Ez4, 7
  poll Ez4, 7
  mortgaging in order to pay Ne5
  priests, Levites and temple servitors exempt from Ez7
taxes paid to Pharaoh KS23
tenth, the king will take a SF8
tenure, security of Nu25
testify against wrongdoers, I will Ma3
testimony of witnesses Nu35
thief as your friend, you take a Ps50
  shall be swept away, every Z5
thummin, symbol of agreement Ex28ff
tithe, bring to the chosen place De12
  defrauding the Ma3
  of all produce CS31
  of corn, storage of the Ne13
  of farm produce Ne10
  of honey CS31
  of oil, storage facilities for Ne13
  of wine, storage facilities for Ne13
  for farming villages Ne10
  for Levites Nu18
  laws of Le27
  set aside each year De14
  storerooms CS31
toll, daily, of bread and wine Ne5
    to the value of forty shekels of silver Ne5
  tribute and custom KF10; Ez4
traitors, double-dyed are they indeed! Is24
  no mercy on Ps59, 78
treaty between Ahab and Ben-hadad KF20
tribute tax Ez4
  paid to Jotham CS27
tyrants brought low Ps107
urim, symbol of judgement Ex18ff

24 LAWS, OATHS, PLEDGES AND COVENANTS

usury, law concerning   Le25
  limitation of by Moses   Ex22
  not to give money for   Ps15
valiant for the truth   Je9
valuation of property   Le27
value of persons, legal   Le27
vengeance   Ps18
voluntary service   Ez1
vow, binding obligation of a   Nu30
  fulfil any   De23
  laws concerning a   Nu30
  Nazirite, the   Nu6
  of Hannah   SF1
  pay your   Na1
water of affliction   CS18; Is30
  of contention   Nu5
wickedness symbolized by the woman in the barrel   Z5
wisdom and prosperity, Solomon vouchsafed   KF3
wise men versed in misdemeanours   Est1
witness, bearing false   Ex23
  false, judgement of   De19
  malicious   Ps35
  summon heaven and earth as   De30
  testimony of a   Nu35
witnesses, testimony of two or three   De17
  trustworthy   Is8
writ, issued by the king   Est3f
  to recall the order of destruction   Est7

NEW TESTAMENT

accuser is Moses   J5
accusers to state their case, ordered his   A23
  where are thine   J8
adultery, do not commit   Mw19; Mk10; L18; PR13; LJ2
adversary the devil   LPF5
advocate, give you another to be your   J14
  the spirit of truth   J15
accuser is Moses   J5
  to state their case, ordered his   A23

24 LAWS, OATHS, PLEDGES AND COVENANTS

accuser, we have an   LJF2
  will not come, if I do not go   J16
ancestral law, thoroughly trained in every point of   A22
appeal to Caesar   A25
arbitrate, who set me over you to judge or   L12
Ark of the Covenant   LH9
arrest anyone, authorizing him to   A9
bill of divorcement   Mk10
blasphemy against the Holy Ghost shall not be forgiven   Mw12
  defiles the man   Mk7
  this is   Mk2
  you have heard the   Mw26; Mk14
book of the law   PG3
bound over   A17
capital charge against me, there was no   A28
case against him, I find no   J18f
circumcised is a debtor to do the whole law   PG5
circumcision, covenant of   A7
  Moses gave you the law of   J7
codicil, no one else can add a   PG3
commandment, a new, that ye love one another   J13
  is holy and just   PR7
  of God made of none effect by your tradition   Mw15
  sin found its opportunity in the   PR7
  which is the greatest   Mw22
commandments and doctrines of men   PCo2
  keep the   Mw19
  of merely human origin   Tt1
  through the Holy Ghost, given   A1
  which is the first of all the   Mk12
commands, to love God is to keep his   LJF5
constable   Mw5
council, brought Stephen before the   A6
  he was brought before their   L22
  ordered to assemble   A22
  Paul fixed his eyes on the   A23
court cautioned them not to speak   A4
  come to terms while you are both on your way to   Mw5
  Gallio had them ejected from   A18
  he must answer for it to the   Mw5

24 LAWS, OATHS, PLEDGES AND COVENANTS

court, is it not they who drag you into   LJ2
  Pilate's   A3
  set upon Paul and brought him to   A18
  to support me, no one came into   PTS4
  will hand you over to the   Mw10
covenant, a new   LH8
  abrogated the old   PCS3
  blood of the   Mw26
  cannot be invalidated by a law   PG3
  is abolished in Christ, the old   PCS3
  the law, their   PR9
  this cup is a new   PCF11
  to dispense his new   PCS3
  which decayeth and waxeth old is ready to vanish away   LH8
  which God made to your fathers   A3
covet, thou shalt not   PR7, 13
custom house   Mw9
debt, sold to meet the   Mw18
debtors, parable of the   L7
decrees of Caesar, contrary to the   A17
  of the law, cancelled the   PCo2
defence, do not worry how to conduct your   L12
  have you nothing to say in your   Mk15
  not to prepare your   L21
  Paul made his   A26
defraud, do not   Mk10
divorce, legality of   Mk10
dock, appear in the   PPs1
  for God's promise that I stand in the   A26
evidence, if I spoke amiss, state it in   J18
examined by scourging   A22
eye for eye, tooth by tooth, they were told   Mw5
  witnesses of his majesty   LPS1
faith, Christ ends the law for everyone who has   PR10
false evidence, do not give   Mk10; L18
  many came forward with   Mw26; Mk14
  witness against Stephen   A6
  do not bear   Mw19; Mk10; PR13
father and mother, honour your   L18
fidelity, gentleness and self control, no law dealing with   PG5

24 LAWS, OATHS, PLEDGES AND COVENANTS

flog a Roman citizen, can you legally   A22
forgive, and ye shall be forgiven   L6
   the offender, you must   PCS2
fraud defiles the man   Mk7
governors, you will be brought before   Mw10
guardians and trustees, heir is under   PG4
honour your father and mother   Mw19; Mk7, 10
impeached by Jews, I am   A26
instructed by the law, you know right from wrong   PR2
judge anyone, the Father does not   J5
   are equally guilty, you the   PR2
   men living and dead, who is to   PTS4
   not, and ye shall not be judged   L6
   ourselves, we should not be judged   PCF11
   the all-just   PTS4
   the quick and the dead   PTS4
   the world, God's people who are to   PCF6
   who set me over you to   L12
judged by a man of his choosing, he will have the world   A17
   in the light of Spirit, needs to be   PCF2
   judge not, and ye shall not be   L6
judgement, convince them of divine   J16
   falls under the Lord's   PCF11
   hall, Herod's   A23
   hall of   J18
   justice of God's   ThS1
   must begin in the house of God, the time has come that   LPF4
   on myself, I do not pass   PCF4
   on your brother, why do you pass   PR14
   seat of Christ, we shall all stand before the   PR14
   of Gallio   A18
   Son of Man given the right to pass   J5
   that you expose yourselves to   LJ5
   the coming   A24
   to bring all men to   LJu1
   world come before you for   PCF6
judges, appointed for them   A13
judging your fellow man you judge yourself   PR2
jurisdiction of the governor   L20

24 LAWS, OATHS, PLEDGES AND COVENANTS

justice, integrity, pursue   PTS2
  of God, anger cannot promote the   LJ1
    pursue   PTF6
kill, thou shalt not   L18; PR13; LJ2
law a temporary measure   PG3
  and the prophets, after readings from the   A13
    I believe all that is written in the   A24
    that is the   Mw7
    until John it was the   L16
  avoid contentions and strivings about the   Tt3
  bickering about your Jewish   A18
  book, Moses sprinkled with blood the   LH9
  brings only the consciousness of sin   PR3
  brought nothing to perfection   LH7
  can bring only retribution   PR4
  cancelled the bond of the   PCo2
  Christ ends the, for everyone who has faith   PR10
  contains but a shadow   LH10
  controversial matters in their   A23
  converts, staunch upholders of the   A21
  court, pagan   PCF6
  curse of the   PG3
  devout observer of the   J7
  did not Moses give you the   J7
  did you receive the Spirit by keeping the   PG3
  do not suppose that I have come to abolish the   Mw5
  doctor of   Mw5, 8, 12, 16, 20f, 23; Mk1ff, 7f, 10ff, 14l
    L2, 5, 9, 15, 20, 22; J8; A4ff, 23
  engraved upon stone dispensed death   PCS3
  flout the emperor's   A17
  he annulled the   PE2
  in the absence of, no reckoning is kept of sin   PR5
  instructed by the, you know right from wrong   PR2
  is good, if a man use it lawfully   PTF1
  is in itself holy   PR7
  is not aimed at good citizens   PTF1
  led by the Spirit, you are not under   PG5
  limitation by death of the   PR7
  no one is justified before God in terms of   PG3
  oath which supersedes the   LH7
  obligation to keep the entire   PG5

24 LAWS, OATHS, PLEDGES AND COVENANTS

law of Moses, appealing to the   A28
   everything written about me in the   L24
   is read, every time the   PCS3
   outside the pale of the   PR2
   there was no acquittal under the   A13
   they are subject to the   PCF9
   they must be told to keep the   A15
   those who have sinned under the   PR2
   without pity   LH10
   rabble which cares nothing for the   J7
   speculations and controversies over, are pointless   Tt3
   take him away and try him by your own   J18
   teachers of the   L5
   they are their own   PR2
   those within the pale of the   PR3
   through the, I died to law   PG2
   tithe   LH7
   to fail, than one tittle of the   L16
   we are discharged from the   PR7
   where there is no, there can be no breach   PR4
   with one another, going to   PCF6
   condemns to death, but the Spirit gives life   PCS3
   you are no longer under   PR6
lawless and unruly, law is aimed at the   PTF1
lawsuits, overreach his brother in   ThF4
lawyer   Mw2, 9, 15
legal offence, to make wrongdoing a   PG3
love, joy, peace, no law dealing with such things as   PG5
   the Lord your God with all your heart   Mw22
   the whole law is summed up in   PR13
   thy neighbour as thyself   Mw19, 22
magistrate   L12; A16f; Tt3
marriage law, obligations of the   PR7
mediator, there is one   PTF2
mercy triumphs over judgement   LJ2
murder, do not commit   Mw5, 19; Mk10; L18; LJ2
no case to answer, I can find   L23
note of dismissal in divorce   Mk10
oath, bound by his   Mw23
   our forefathers were told, do not break your   Mw5
   provides confirmation to end disputes   LH6

24 LAWS, OATHS, PLEDGES AND COVENANTS

oath, emperor's   A25
  of Christ, lives laid open before the   PCS5
trustees, heir under guardians and   PG4
will and testament   PG3
witness, God is my   PR1
  to the truth, my task to bear   J18
witnesses, need we call further   L22
  supported by two or three   PTF5
  three, the Spirit, the water, and the blood   LJF5

25 *Metals, Treasures and Precious Stones*

OLD TESTAMENT

adamant   E3
agate   Ex28. 39; Is54; E27
alabaster   Job28
  mosaic of   Est1
  pillars of   Est1
alloy, silver   E22
amber   E1, 8
assay, refining for   Je9; Z13
bdellium   Gen2
  as the colour of manna   Nu11
beryl   So5; E1, 10, 28; D10
brass   Nu31; De8; SF17; SS8; Job28, 40; Is60; Je6, 52; E1, 8, 22, 24, 27; D2, 4f, 8, 10; Z6
  altar   E9
  Goliath's armour of   SF17
  heaven shall be   De28
  hooves of   Mi4
  molten out of the stone   Job28
  pillars of   Je52
  temple fitments of   Je52
  vessels of   SS8; E27
  you may dig   De8
bronze   Ex26ff, 30, 35ff; Nu16, 21; De33; Ju16; SF17; SS8, 21ff; KF7, 14; KS16, 25; Job40; E40; CF15, 18, 22, CF29; CS1f, 4, 12, 24; Ps18, 107; Is43, 60; Je1, 15, 39, Je52; D2, 5, 7, 10; Z6
  altar   Ex39; KS16; CS1, 4; E9
  and iron, your bolts to be   De33
  arrowhead   Ps18
  beyond reckoning   KF7
    weighing   KS25

25 METALS, TREASURES AND PRECIOUS STONES

bronze, capital of   Je52
  cherubim   KF7
  cymbals   CF15
  door   Ps107
  fetters of   Ju16; KS25; Je39, 52
  gate-bars of   KF4
  gates   Is45
  Goliath's armour of   SF17
  great quantity of   SS8
  hooves of   Mi4
  implements   Ex30, 38
  lions   KF7
  more than can be weighed   CF22
  oxen   KF7
  pillars   Je52
    broken up   KS25
  Samson in fetters of   Ju16
  sea of   KF7ff
    broken up   KS25
    dismantled   KS16
  serpent of Moses   Nu21
  shields   KF14
  spear   SS21
  temple fitments of   Je52
  vessels of   KS25; Le52
  wall of   Je1, 15
  your shoes to be   De33
  Zedekiah in fetters of   KS25, 39; Job28; E28
carbuncle   Is54; E27ff
chrysolite   Ex28, 39; Job28; E28
copper   Ex25, 31, 35; Nu31; De8; Jos6, 22; SS8; CF18; CS2, 4, 24; Is60; Je6; E22, 24; D2; Z6
  beyond reckoning   CS4
  laden with   Jos22
  offering of   Ex25ff
  red   Ez8
  smelted from the ore   Job28
  vessels of   SS8
    at Jericho   Jos6
coral   Pro3, 8, 20; E27
  black   Job28; E27

25 METALS, TREASURES AND PRECIOUS STONES

coral, branching   La4
  red   Job28; Pro3, 8, 11
cornelian   Gen2; Ex25, 28, 35, 39; CF29; Job28
  engraved   Ex28
crucible, refining   E22
crystal   Job28
diamond   E28
display of royal treasure   Est1
dross of silver   E22
  silver is become   Is1
ebony   E27
emerald   E27ff
felspar, green   Ex28ff, 39; E28
firestone   Is54
garnet   Ex27, 28, 29; Is54
  green   Ex39
  purple   Ex27fff, 39
gold   Gen24, 41, 44; Ex3, 11ff, 20, 25f, 28, 31f, 35f, 39; Le8;
      Nu4, 7ff, 22, 24, 31; De7ff, 29; Ju8; Jos6ff, 22; SF6;
      SS1, 8, 12, 21; KF6f, 9f, 12f, 20; KS7, 14, 16, 18, 20, 25;
      CF18, 22, 28ff; CS1f, 4, 8f, 12, 15, 21, 24, 32; Ez1, 8;
      Est1, 5, 8; Job3, 28, 31; Ps19, 68, 105, 115,119;
      Pro3, 8, 16ff, 20, 22, 25, 27; Ec2; Is2, 31, 39, 60; Je10, 52;
      La4; E7, 28, 38; D2, 5, 11; Ho2, 8; Joe3; Na2; H2; Zp1;
      Hg2; Z6, 9, 14; Ma3
  100,000 talents of   CF22
  and silver couches   Est1
    gods of   Ex20; D5
    offerings of   Nu7
  altar   Ex39ff; Nu4
    implements   Ex37
  assayed   Z13
  bags of   Is46
  band   Ex30
  bar weighing 50 shekels   Jos7
  bell   Ex28, 39
  beaten   Ex25, 39; Nu8; KF10
  bowl   Ec12
  bracelet   Gen24; Nu37
  buckler   CS9; Ec9
  carvings   KF12

25 METALS, TREASURES AND PRECIOUS STONES

gold chain   Gen41; Ex28; KF6ff; D5
  common as stones   CS1
  crown of   SS12; Ps21
  crucible for   Pro27
  cup   Je51
  dust   Job28
  earrings   Ex32; Nu31; Ju8; Job42; Pro25
  fasteners   Ex26
  from Ophir   D10
  from Sheba   Ps72
  haemorrhoids modelled in   SF6
  headrest, palanquin   So3
  hooks   Ex36
  imported from Ophir   CS8ff
  laden with   Jos22
  lamp-stand   Ex37; Nu8; Z4
  nose-ring   Gen24
  Nubian   Pro25
  of Havilah   Gen2
  of Jericho   Jos6
  of Ophir   Ps45; Is13; Je10; D10
  of Uphaz   D10
  ornaments   Ex35; Nu31; Ju8; Pro25; Je4; E16
  overlay   Ex25, 30, 36
  pendant   Nu31
  plating   Ex25; Is40
  quiver   SS8; CF18
  rats modelled in   SF6
  red   KF6, 10; CS4; Job28
  rings   Ex28, 30, 32, 39; Nu31; Ju8; Pro11, 25; So5
  rosette   Ex28ff; Le8
  sceptre   Est4
  shield   SS8; KF14
  trade in   E27
  tumours modelled in   SF6
  vessels   Ex37; SS8; KS12; D5
golden image of a bull calf, Aaron's   Ex32
  wedge of Ophir   Is13
iron   Nu31; De8, 27ff, 33; Jos6, 22; Ju1, 4; SS12; CF20, 22, 29;
      CS2, 18, 24; Job40ff; Pro27; Is10, 48, 60; Je6, 15;
      E4, 22, 27; D2, 4ff

25 METALS, TREASURES AND PRECIOUS STONES

iron and bronze, your bolts shall be   De33
  bands of   Je28
  bars   Ps107
  bright   E27
  chain   Ps107
  chariots   Jos15; Ju1, 4
  collar   Ps105, 107
  earth shall be   De28
  engraving   Job19
  for altar stones, no tool of   De27
  great store of   CF22
  harrows of   SS12
  horns of   KF22; CS18; Mi4
  laden with   Jos22
  ore   De8
  pen of   Je17
  pillar of   Je1
  ring   D4
  rod   Ps2
  sarcophagus   De3
  spearhead   SF17
  spikes   Am1
  tools   De27; SS12; KF6; CF20; Je17
  vessels at Jericho   Jos60
  weapons of   Job20
  whetted edge of   Ec10
  won from the earth   Job28
  wrought   E27
ivory   KF22; CS9; So7; E27; Am3, 6
  benches of   E27
  panelled with   Ps45
  plaque of   So5
jade   Ex28ff, 39; E28
jasper   Ex28ff, 39; E28
  green   Ex28
  red   Is54; E27
jewelled chain necklace   So1
jewellery, ask for   Ex11
  silver and gold   Ex3, 11
jewels   So7; Is3, 49, 54, 61; E7; Ho2; Z9; Ma3
  collar of   Ps73

25 METALS, TREASURES AND PRECIOUS STONES

jewels, decked herself with   Ho2
  forehead   E16
  necklace of   So1
  nose   Is3
  of gold   SS1
  precious   Pro20
  wear them proudly as   Is49
lapis lazuli   Ex28, 39; Job28; So5; Is54; Je6; La4; E1, 10
lead   Nu31; Job19; E22, 27; Z5
malachite, mosaic of   Est1
marble   So5
metal, cast   Ex34; Nu33
  clay for   KF7
  image   Ex20, 32; Le10; Nu33; De9; KF12, 17; CS13, 28, 34; Ne9; Ps115, 135; Je10, 51; Is2, 30f, 40, 42, 46; D3, 5, 11; Ho8, 13
  foundry   KF7
  precious   Je52
  smelting   E1, 22
money for temple repairs   Ks12
mosaic pavement   Est1
mother-of-pearl mosaic   Est1
mould, bronze   KF7
onyx   Ex25ff; CF27; Job28; E28
orichale   Ez8
ornaments, crafted   Gen24, 35; Ex28, 32; Le8; Nu31, 37; De6, 11; Ju8; SS1; KF6; Est3f, 7; Job42; Ps73; Pro1, 3, 4, 7, 11, 25; So1, 4ff; Is3, 28, 37, 40, 49, 61; Je2, 4, 22, 31; D5; E16, 23, 28; D5; Ho2
pearls   Job28
precious metal   Je52
  stones   Ex28, 35; SS12; KF10; CF20, 29; CS3, 9, 32; Ps68; D11
    crown set with   SS12
    engraved   Ex28
    in an idol's crown   CF20
    trade in   E27
red copper   Ez8
  gold   Job28
refined as silver   Z13
refiner's fire   Ma3

25 METALS, TREASURES AND PRECIOUS STONES

ruby   Pro3, 8, 20, 31; La4
sapphire   Ex24; Job28; So5; Ls54; La4; E1, 10, 28
  pavement of   Ex24
sardin, sardius   Ex28, 39; E28
sea of cast metal   KF7
silver   Gen24, 42f, 47; Ex3, 11f, 21f, 25f, 31, 25f, 38; Le27;
      Nu3, 7, 18, 22, 24, 31; De2, 7, 14, 29; Jos6ff, 22; Ju5, 16ff; SF9;
      SS8, 18, 21, 24; KF7, 10, 15, 20ff; KS7, 12, 14, 16, 18, 20, 25;
      CF18ff, 28ff; CS1f, 15, 17, 21, CS24, 32, 34; Ez1, 8; Ne7;
      Job3, 27f; Ps12, 68, 105, 115, 119; Pro2f, 8, 16f, 22, 25ff; Ec2, 5;
      So1; Is2, 13, 31, 39, 46, 48, 60; Je10, 32, 52; E7, 27f, 38;
      D2, 5, 11; Ho2f, 8f, 13; Joe3; Am2, 8; Na2; H2; Zp1;
      Hg2; Z6, 9, 14; M3
  100 pieces for parcel of ground   Jos24
  200 shekels of   Jos7
  1,000,000 talents of   CF22
  alloyed with copper, tin, iron and lead   E22
  and gold couches   Est1
  as common as stones   KF10; CS1
  beaten   Je10
  chain   Is40
  cord   Ec12
  dross from the   Pro25
  for tithes   De14
  goblet   Gen44
  great quantity of   CS17
  laden with   Jos22
  melt down   KS22; E1, 22
  melted in crucible   E22
  melting pot for   Pro27
  mines   Job28
  of Jericho   Jos6
  ornaments   E16
  palanquin poles   So3
  pieces of   SS8, 24; So8; Is7
  quarter shekel   SF9
  ransom money of   Nu3
  reckoned of no value by Solomon   KF10
  refined as   Ps66; Z13
  rings, curtain   Est1

25 METALS, TREASURES AND PRECIOUS STONES

silver sockets   Ex26
  spurious   Je6
silver studs   Is40
  thirty pieces of   Z11
  to be paid for killing the Jews   Est3
  to purchase food   De2
  turned into base metal   Is1
  vessels   Nu7; SS8; KS12; Ne7; D5
silverlings   Is7
steel   Je15
tin   Nu31; Is1; E22, 27
topaz   Ex28, 39; Job28; So5; E1, 10, 28; D10
treasure, buried   Pro2
  display of the royal   Est1
  hidden in the sand   De33
  no end to their   Is2
treasuries, royal palace   KS18
treasury of Judah   Is39
  of the Lord's house   Jos6
  the royal Persian   Est3
turquoise   Ex28, 39
  mosaic of   Est1

NEW TESTAMENT

alabaster box   Mw26; Mk14; L7
amethyst   Rev21
bank, money paid into the   L19
belt, money   Mk6
beryl   Rev21
brass, burnished   Rev1f
  merchandise of   Rev18
  to fill your purse   Mw10
brazen vessel   Mk7
bronze   Rev9
  cargoes of   Rev18
burnished brass   Rev1f
cankered, gold and silver is   LJ5
chalcedony   Rev21
chest of the temple, treasury   Mw27; Mk12; L21

25 METALS, TREASURES AND PRECIOUS STONES

copper   Mk7
  to fill your purse   Mw10
cornelian   Rev4, 21
chrysolite   Rev21
chrysoprase, chrysoprasus   Rev21
crystal   Rev4, 21f
emerald   Rev4, 21
furnace, refined in a   Rev1
filthy lucre, given to   Tt1
    greedy of   PTF3
    not for   LPF5
gold   Mw2, 10, 23; PCF3; LPF1; Rev9
  and silver have rusted away   LJ5
    is cankered   LJ5
  bedizened with   Rev17
  cargoes of   Rev18
  city of pure   Rev21
  crowns of   Rev4
  cup   Rev17
  decked out in   PTF2
  five bags of   Mw25
  I have coveted no man's   A20
  image in   A17
  lamps, seven   Rev1f
  measuring   Rev21
  offered him   Mw2
  or silver, I have no   A3
  passes through the assayer's fire   LPF1
  plated   LH9
  refined in the fire   Rev3
  rings   LJ2
  streets of the holy city   Rev21
  utensils   PTS2
  wearing of   LPF3
golden altar   LH9; Rev8
  bowl   Rev5, 15
  candlesticks, seven   Rev1f
  censer   LH9; Rev8
  crown   Rev14
  girdle   Rev15
  jar   LH9

25 METALS, TREASURES AND PRECIOUS STONES

golden pot   LH9
  vials   Rev5, 15
iron   Rev9
  cargoes of   Rev18
  gate   A12
ivory, cargoes of   Rev18
  vessels of   Rev18
jacinth   Rev21
  breastplates of in John's vision   Rev9
jasper   Rev4, 21
jewellery   LPF3
jewels and pearls, bedizened with   Rev17
    cargoes of   Rev18
  radiance of some priceless   Rev21
lapis lazuli   Rev21
lucre, filthy   PTF3; Tt1; LPF5
mammon, ye cannot serve God and   Mw6; L16
marble, cargoes of   Rev18
money and self, men will love nothing but   PTS3
  do not live for   LH13
  go with you to damnation, your   A8
  grubbing, deacons must not be   PTF3
  love of, is the root of all evil   PTF6
  Pharisees loved   L16
  thought that the gift of God may be purchased with   A8
  you cannot serve God and   M6; L16
pearl   Mw7, 13
pearls, bedizened with   Rev17
  cargoes of   Rev18
  decked out in   PTF2
  gate of, in John's vision   Rev21
precious stones   PCF3
    and pearls, decked with   Rev17
refined brass   Rev1
rich, those who want to be   PTF6
riches have rotted, your   LJ5
  of Christ, unfathomable   PE3
rusty, where treasure grows   Mw6
sapphire   Rev21
sardine stone   Rev4
sardius   Rev21

25 METALS, TREASURES AND PRECIOUS STONES

sardonyx   Rev21
silver   Mw10; PCF3; Rev9
  and gold had rusted away   LJ5
  cargoes of   Rev18
  I have coveted no man's   A20
  image in   A17
  or gold, I have no   A3
  pieces   Mk12; A19
  shrines of Diana   A19
  thirty pieces of   Mw26f
  utensils   PTS2
tax, from whom do earthly monarchs collect   Mw17
topaz   Rev21
treasure buried in a field   Mw13
  grows rusty, where   Mw6
  in heaven, thou shalt have   L18
  never-failing in heaven   L12
  on earth, do not store up for yourself   Mw6
  pots of earthenware to contain their   PCS4
  things old and new   Mw13
treasures of his glory   PE3
  of wisdom and knowledge, are hid   PCo2
  they opened their   Mw2
treasury   J8
  temple   Mw27; Mk12; L21
turquoise   Rev21
woods, scented and costly   Rev18

26   *Migration and Exile*

OLD TESTAMENT

alien, I am become   Ps69
  justice for the   De21
  those who thrust aside the   Ma3
  you must love the   De10
boundaries, God extends your   De12
  of tribal lands   E47
camp, caravan   Is21
captivity of Judah   D5
  years of   Ex13
caravan for your imports   E27
  Ishmaelite   Gen37
  of Dedan   Is21
  plied no longer   Ju5
crossing the River Jordan   Nu35
deportation   Je39ff
deported by Nebuchadnezzar, 4600 Judaeans   Je52
  far from their native land, Israel shall be   Am7
  inhabitants of Damascus   KS16
    of Jerusalem   KS25
  priests brought back to Samaria   KS17
  to Assyria, people of Israel   KS15
    people of Samaria   KS17
  to Babylon   Je39
  to Kir, people of Damascus   KS16
dispersed, gather the   Zp3
Dispersion, the   Zp3
divided, Israel shall no longer be   E37
Egypt, Abram went down to   Gen12
  Jacob's sons went to buy grain in   Gen42
Egyptian not an abomination   De23
enslaved, Israelites   Ex1ff
escape of Moses   Ex2
exile, Ammonite king carried into   Am1

26 MIGRATION AND EXILE

exile beyond Damascus, drive you into   Am5
  deported and go into   Am7
  in Babylon   Ez2
  journey into   E12
  many in   Je29
  of 10,000 fighting men   KS24
  of Jehoiachin   KS25
  she too became an   Na3
  the people of Jerusalem in   KS24
  their glory is carried away into   Ho10
  they have gone into   Mi1
  threat of   Le26
  train of captives into   Na2
exiled captives, roll of   Ne7
  to Kir, the people of Aram   Am1
exiles, column of   Am6
  deported a band of   Am1
  I will assemble the   Mi4
  in Chaldea, brought me to the   E11
  Israelite   D1
  Jewish   D2, 5ff
  of Judah in Babylon   Je28
  take silver and gold from the   Z6
explore the land of Canaan   Nu13
eunuchs deported to Babylon   Je29
fled to Egypt, the remaining people   KS25
foreigner, you may press the   De15
free, let my exiles go   Es45
frontier, Ammonite   De3; Jos12
  Amorite   Jos13
    entry refused at the   Nu21
  Canaanite   Nu34
  Edomite   Jos14; Ju1
    entry refused at the   Nu20
  Moabite   Nu21
  of Cush   E29
  of Israel   Ex23
  of Moab   De2
frontiers of Jerusalem re-established   KS14
  of tribal lands   E47
fugitive, cut off at the crossroads   Ob1

26 MIGRATION AND EXILE

half-breeds shall settle in Ashdod   Z9
Jews which dwelt in Egypt   Je44
journey from Sinai to Edom   Nu9
   Israelite, stages of the   Nu33
   to Canaan, Abram's   Gen12
land flowing with milk and honey   Ex3; E12
   in Egypt, Joseph gave his father   Gen47
   promised   Gen50
lost, rescue the   Zp3
lot, parcelled out Jerusalem by   Ob1
migrated to Asshur, Cush   Gen10
nations, they shall be no more two   E37
Negeb, Abram went from Egypt into the   Gen13
nomads from the dwellings of Jacob   Ma2
outcast, all men call you   Je30
scattered among all peoples   De28
service in the court of Nebuchadnezzar, young men for   D1
settlers from the dwelling of Jacob   Ma2
strange language, people of   Ps114
stranger in the earth   Ps119
   oppress not the   Z7
traveller pitching his tent for a night   Je14
travelling companies   Is21
tribal lands, frontiers of   E47
vagrant, wanderer, Cain a   Gen4
wandered in the wilderness of Beersheba, Hagar   Gen21
   you shall be a   Nu14
wanderers among the nations   Ho9
wilderness, for a long time you lived in the   Jos24
   forty years in the   Nu14
   journey into the   Ex3

NEW TESTAMENT

alien, settled as an   LH11
aliens, earthly monarchs collect tax from   Mw17
   in a foreign land, as   LPF2
     no longer   PE2
Claudius issued an edict that all Jews should leave Rome   A18
deportation to Babylon   Mw1

26 MIGRATION AND EXILE

exiles, as long as we are at home in the   PCS5
leave Rome, all Jews to   A18
outcast, let him be   PG1
  who does not love the Lord   PCF16
refugees in deserts and hills   LH11
tents, living in   LH11
travellers on earth, passing   LH11

27 *Miracles and Angelic Visitations*

OLD TESTAMENT

Aaron's rod turned into a serpent   Ex7
altar was rent in pieces, Jereboam's   KF13
angel appeared to the barren wife   Ju13
  barring Balaam's way   Nu22
  before you, he will send his   Gen24
  destroying   CF21
    the people   SS24
  guardian   Ex23
  in the fiery furnace   D3
  in Zechariah's vision   Z1ff
  of God, as true as   SF27
  reassured Elijah   KS1
  said: I brought you   Ju2
  sat under the tree   Ju6
  sent to save Shadrach, Meshach and Abed-nego   D3
  sent to shut the lions' mouths   D6
  showed himself to Gideon   Ju6
  spoke to Hagar   Gen16
  stood firm, the divine   Ho12
  to cut down the fighting men, the Lord sent an   CS32
  touched Elijah   KF19
  went up with the flame   Ju13
angels, creatures of might   Ps103
  Jacob was met by   Gen32
  of the Lord   Ps35
  on guard   Ps34
  praise him   Ps148
  to guard you   Ps91
breath of life returned   KF17
brightness over the Tabernacle   Nu9ff
bulls, Elijah's miraculous sacrifice of   KF18
burning bush, him who dwells in the   De33
  Lord appeared in the flame of a   Ex3

27 MIRACLES AND ANGELIC VISITATIONS

chariots of fire appeared   KS2
cherub as guardian, a towering   E28
  he rode on a   Ps18
cherubim at the Garden of Eden   Gen3
  face of   E41
  glory of God rose from above the   E9
  lifted their wings   E11
  sound of the wings of   E1, 10
  stood on the right side of the temple   E10
  throned on the   Ps80, 99
  vault over the heads of   E1, 10
cloak, Elijah struck the water with his   KS2
cloud covering the Tabernacle   Nu9ff
  of smoke by day and a bright flame by night   Is4
  of the glory of God   CS6
  of the Lord   Ex40
corpse came to life on touching Elisha's bones   KS13
copious supply of oil   KS4
council of holy ones   Ps89
court of heaven   Job1; Ps82, 89, 92
creation   Gen1
creatures in semblance of human form   E1
day, first   Gen1
dew on the fleece   Ju6
ecstasy, prophetic   Nu11
Elijah was carried to heaven   KS2
Elisha breathed into the child seven times   KS4
  miraculous bones of   KS13
El-roi, Hagar's vision of   Gen16
evil spirit left Saul when David played   SF16
faces, each four-winged creature had four   E1
feeding a hundred men   KS4
fire after the earthquake   KF19
  chariots of   KS2, 6
  fell from heaven   KS1
  from heaven   CS7
  from heaven on the altar   CF21
  from the Lord   Nu11, 16; KF18
  horses of   Ks2, 6
  in the cloud   Ex40
  led them with a glowing   Ps78

27 MIRACLES AND ANGELIC VISITATIONS

fire, not a hair of their head had been singed in the   D3
   sprang from the rock   Ju6
   to light up the night   Ps105
floated, iron   KS6
Gabriel, in Daniel's vision, the Archangel   D10
glory of the Lord appeared   Nu1
gods, sons of   Gen6
heavenly being, Daniel's vision of a   D10
horses of fire appeared   KF2, 6
inscription on the wall at Belshazzar's feast   D5
iron axe-head floated   KS6
kiss of life   KF17; KS4
lion stood with the ass   KF13
living creatures in human form, four   E1
Lord God appeared to Solomon   KF3, 9
low murmuring sound   KF19
lying spirit in the mouths of his prophets   KF22
man, gleaming, in Daniel's vision   D10
members of the court of heaven   Job1
Michael, the Archangel, in Daniel's vision   D10, 12
miracle among you, a great   Jos3
pillar of cloud by day   Ex13; Nu14; Ne9; Ps99
   of fire by night   Ex13; Nu14; Ne9
ravens commanded to feed Elijah   KF17
robe of light   Ps104
Satan incited David to count the people   CF21
seraphim, attendant   Is6
serpent, Aaron's rod turned into a   Ex7
shadow moved backwards on the sun dial of Ahaz   KS20; Is38
signs and portents against Pharaoh   Ne9
sons of God came to present themselves   Job1
spirit alighted on the elders   Nu11
   came forward   KF22
   came into me and stood me on my feet   E2
   Joshua endowed with   Nu27
   lifted Ezekiel up   E8
   of God came upon Azariah   CS15
      took possession of Zechariah   CS24
   of the living creatures was in the wheels   E8
   of the Lord came upon Jahaziel   CS20
      came upon Othniel   Ju3

27 MIRACLES AND ANGELIC VISITATIONS

spirit took possession of Amasi   CF12
still small voice   KF19
sun stayed in mid heaven   Jos10
temple filled with smoke   Is6
vision of a gleaming man   D10
   of the Almighty   Nu24
voice, a still small   KF19
   speaking in the Tent of the Presence   Nu7ff
water divided left and right   KS22
waters were torn apart   Ex14
whirlwind, Lord would take Elijah to heaven in a   KS2
wings, each of the living creatures had four   E1
writing on the wall at Belshazzar's feast   D5

NEW TESTAMENT

all I know is this: once I was blind, now I can see   J9
   we have here is five loaves and two fishes   Mw14
angel, a mighty   Rev5
   a strong   Rev5
   addressed the women   Mw28
   appeared to him in the bush   A7
     to Joseph in a dream   Mw1f
   blew his trumpet   Rev8ff
   Cornelius was directed by a holy   A10, 11
   destroying   LH11
   flying in mid-heaven   Rev14
   through heaven, saying, Woe, woe, woe   Rev8
   from heaven, if an   PG1
   Gabriel was sent to Nazareth   L1
   given the key of the abyss   Rev9
   has spoken to him, others said an   J12
   he will send out his   Mk13
   Jesus, the name given by the   L2
   Michael waged war   Rev12
   now there appeared to him an   L22
   of God, vision in which he saw an   A10
   of light, Satan masquerades as an   PCS11
   of the abyss, Abaddon, Apollyon   Rev9
   of the church at Ephesus   Rev2

27 MIRACLES AND ANGELIC VISITATIONS

angel of the church at Laodicea   Rev3
   at Pergamum   Rev2
   at Philadelphia   Rev3
   at Sardis   Rev3
   at Smyrna   Rev2
   at Thyatira   Rev2
  of the Lord appeared to him in a dream   Mw1
   rolled away the stone   Mw28
   spoke to Philip   A8
   struck him down   A12
   there appeared to him an   L1
   there stood before them an   L2
  opened the prison doors during the night   A5
  or spirit has spoken to him, perhaps an   A23
  rising out of the east   Rev7
  Sadducees deny that there is any   A23
  said, Do not be afraid   L2
  said to me, Write this   Rev19
  said unto them, Fear not: for behold, I bring you tidings   L2
  sent to John   Rev1
  standing in the sun   Rev19
  Stephen's face appeared like the face of an   A6
  there stood by me an   A27
  took up a stone   Rev18
  troubled the water   J5
  welcomed me as if I were an   PG4
  went down to the pool   J5
  with a rainbow round his head   Rev10
  with a sickle   Rev14
  with authority over fire   Rev14
  with great authority   Rev18
  with the keys of the abyss   Rev20
  worship   PCo2
angelic authorities and powers   LPF3
angels, a little lower than the   LH2
  a spectacle unto the world and to   PCF4
  abandoned their proper home   LJu1
  appeared and waited on him   Mw4
  are as the   Mw22
  ascending and descending   J1
  of the four corners of the earth   Rev7

27 MIRACLES AND ANGELIC VISITATIONS

angels, before myriads of   LH12
  being made so much better than the   LH1
  comes in the glory of the Father and his holy   L9
  died and was carried away by the   L16
  dressed in white   A1
  employ no insults   LPS2
  entertained without knowing it   LH13
  followed unnatural lusts   LJu1
  glory of the Father with his   Mw16
    of the holy   Mk8
  he shall put in charge of you   Mw4
  he who was seen by   PTF3
  I charge thee before the elect   PTF5
  in charge of you, he will put his   Mw4
  in blazing fire, mighty   ThS1
  in heaven, not even the   Mw24
    they are like   Mk12
    will not know   Mk13
  in white sitting there   J20
  intervention was real   A12
  law promulgated through   PG3
  long to see, things that   LPF1
  myriads upon myriads of   LJu1
  of God, joy among the   L15
    pay him homage   LH1
    the Son of Man will acknowledge before the   L12
  of the seven churches   Rev1ff
  orders to take care of you, he will give his   L4
  out of my regard for the   PCF11
  raised as far above the   LH1
  Satan's   Rev12
  seen a vision of   L24
  seven, in the presence of God   Rev8, 17, 21
  ten thousand times ten thousand   Rev5
  that he takes to himself, it is not   LH2
  the reapers are   Mw13
  the Son of Man will send out his   Mw13
  they are like   L20
  to judge   PCF6
  tongues of men or of   PCF13
  twelve, at the gates of the city   Rev21

27 MIRACLES AND ANGELIC VISITATIONS

angels, voices of countless   Rev5
   waited on him   Mk1
   who had sinned   LPS2
   will separate the wicked from the good   Mw13
   with seven plagues   Rev15
Apollyon, Abaddon, angel of the abyss   Rev9
archangel Gabriel   L1
   Michael   LJu1; Rev12
archangel's voice, at the sound of the   ThF4
arise, take up thy bed, and walk   Mw9; Mk2; L5
ass speaking with a man's voice   LPS2
baptize you with the Holy Spirit and with fire   Mw3
baptized with the Holy Spirit   A1
blind and crippled came to him, and he healed them   Mw21
   recovered their sight   Mw11; Mk10
burning bush   Mk12; A7
cast out devils   Mw17
celestial beings, not afraid to insult   LPS2
cherubim, carvings of   LH9
cured, she had touched him and been instantly   L8
   them, he laid his hands on them and   L4
dead are raised to life   Mw11
   man sat up and began to speak   L7
   power to raise from the   Mw10; LH11
deaf made to hear   Mw11
death, to be put to, and to be raised again   Mw16
Destroyer, the angel of the abyss   Rev9
destroying angel   PCF10; LH11
devil in debate with Archangel Michael   LJu1
devils came out and went into the pigs   L8
     shouting, You are the Son of God   L4
dumb beast spoke with a human voice   LPS2
   man began to speak   L11
ecstatic utterance, the gift of   PCF12; LPF14
eternal life, God has given us   LJF5
faith has cured you, your   L18
fed the five thousand   Mw14, 16; Mk6; L9; J6
   the four thousand   Mw15f; Mk8
fetters unfastened, found their   A16
Gabriel, Archangel   L1
garment, young man clothed in a long white   Mk16

27 MIRACLES AND ANGELIC VISITATIONS

   garments, two men in dazzling   L24
   gift of God, stir into flame the   PTS1
   gifts of the Holy Spirit   PCF12, 14; PCS6
   God's gift, not a reward   PE2
   guardian angel, it must be his   A12
      angels in heaven, they have their   Mw18
   Holy Ghost, all were filled with the   A4
      and wisdom, seven men full of the   A6
      being sent forth by the   A13
      came upon them, and they spake with tongues   A19
      fell on them   A11
      filled with the   A2
      gifts of the   LH2
      have ye received the   A19
      he shall be filled with the   L1
      he which baptizeth with the   J1
      him that blasphemeth agianst the   L12
      holy men spake as they were moved by the   LPS1
      is come upon you   A1
      it is not ye that speak, but the   Mk13
      Jesus being full of the   L4
      love of God is shed in our hearts by the   PR5
      Paul, filled with the   A13
      Peter, filled with the   A4
      saved us by the renewing of the   Tt3
      sent down from heaven   LPF1
      shall teach you what you ought to say   L12
      the disciples were filled with joy, and with the   A13
      they received the   A8
      thus saith the   A21
      was upon Simeon   L2
      which dwelleth in us   PTS1
      with joy of the   ThF1
      gift of the   LJF2
   Holy Spirit, a share in the   LH6
      all were filled with the   A2; A4
      asking that the converts might receive the   A8
      baptize you with the   Mw3; A1
      bestows on you his   ThF4
      came upon them   A10, 19
      comes on you   A1

27 MIRACLES AND ANGELIC VISITATIONS

Holy Spirit, converts were filled with joy and with the   A13
    descending like a dove   Mw3
    did you receive the   A19
    distributing the gift of the   LH2
    dwelling within us   PTS1
    Elizabeth was filled with the   L1
    fill you, let the   PE5
    for him who slanders the   L12
    found she was in child by the   Mw1
    full of the   L4
    given by God to those obedient to him   L5
    given to those who ask   L11
    giving instructions through the   A1
    God showed his approval by giving the   A15
    he will be filled with the L1
    how God anointed him with the   A10
    impelled by the, spoke the word of God   LPS1
    in the power of the   ThF1
    inspired by the   PR14
    of God, do not grieve the   PE4
    Peter, filled with the   A4
    prevented from delivering the message by the   A16
    receive the   J20
    recommend ourselves by gifts of the   PCS6
    renewing power of the   Tt3
    said, Set Barnabas and Paul apart   A13
    Saul, filled with the   A9, 13
    sent from heaven   LPF1
    spoke to your fathers, how well the   A28
    Stephen, filled with the   A7
    these are the words of the   A21
    to baptize in   J1
    under the influence of the   PCF12
    was poured out   PCF12
    was upon Simeon   L2
    when inspired by the   Mk12
    will come upon you   L1
    will instruct you what to say   L12
    you will receive the gift of the   A2
    your advocate   J14
    Zechariah was filled with the   L1

27 MIRACLES AND ANGELIC VISITATIONS

inspired utterance, the gift of   PR12
Jesus Christ cures you; get up and make your bed   A9
     himself came up and walked along with them   L24
     said to him, Go; your faith has cured you   Mk10
laid his hands on her and she straightened up   L13
     on them and cured them   L4
     upon him and healed him   A28
lame walk   Mw11
language of ecstasy   PCF14
lepers are made clean   Mw11
leprosy left him immediately   Mk1
   was cured immediately   Mw8
life-giving spirit, the last Adam has become a   PCF15
lifted up, as they walked he was   A1
light flashed from the sky all around him   A9
living water   J4, 7
miracle, had been hoping to see some   L23
   workers, God has appointed   PCF12
miracles, a man made known to you through   A2
   among you, when God works   PG3
   and signs, Stephen began to work great   A6
   devils with power to do   Rev16
   faith will bring with it these   Mk16
   false prophets that wrought   Rev19
   in your name, did we not perform   Mw7
   Jews call for   PCF1
   the beast worked great   Rev13
   through Paul God worked singular   A19
miraculous powers, the gift of   PCF12
   signs, by force of   PR15
opened, looking up to heaven, he said, Be   Mk7
passion, showed himself alive after his   A1
plagues, he healed as many as had   Mk3
portent in heaven   Rev12
portents in the sky, I will show   A2
   which God worked among you   A2
power from on high, until ye be endued with   L24
radiance of his coming   ThS2
raiment became shining   Mk9
   was white and glistening   L9
   white as the light   Mw17

27 MIRACLES AND ANGELIC VISITATIONS

raise him up on the last day   J6
raised from the dead, until the Son of Man had been   Mw17
   him from the dead, God   A13; PCo2
     to life on the third day   Mw20
resurrection of the dead, proclaiming the   A4
risen from the dead, remembered when he was   J2
   he is not here: for he is   Mw28
robes, a man in shining   A10
saints raised from sleep, many of God's   Mw27
Saul, Saul, why persecutest thou me?   A9, 26
sick, heal the   Mw10
sign from heaven, demanded of him a   L11
    show them a   Mw16
   Jews require a   PCF1
   of the prophet Jonah, the only   Mw12; L11
   wicked generation demands a   L11
signs and marvels through the apostles   A2
   and miracles to be worked at their hands   A14
   and wonders, wrought among you in   PCS12
   miracles and manifold works of power   LH2
   on earth, I will show   A2
   which God worked among you   A2
sight, he recovered his   L18
   instantly I recovered my   A22
soul and spirit, dividing asunder of   LH4
spirit, a man gifted with the   PCF2
   and wisdom, seven men full of   A6
   both guided by the same   PCS12
   comes out, when an unclean   L11
   coming down from heaven like a dove   J1
   dwells within you, if only God's   PR8
   eager for gifts of the   PCF14
   explores everything   PCF2
   gifts of the   PCF12
   I was caught up by the   Rev1
   I will endue even slaves with a portion of my   A2
   I will pour out on everyone a portion of my   A2
   into the wilderness, Jesus was led by the   Mw4
   Jesus, armed with the power of the   L4
     was then led away by the   Mw4; L4
   measureless God's gift of   J3

27 MIRACLES AND ANGELIC VISITATIONS

spirit of Jesus Christ is given me   PPs1
   of Jesus would not allow them to enter   A16
   of God descended like a dove   Mw3
   ordered to come out   L8
   says expressly   PTF4
   seizes him from time to time   L9
   those who live on the level of the   PR8
spiritual power, carried conviction by   PCF2
staff, Aaron's   LH9
take up your bed and walk   J5
tongues, began to talk in other   A2
   of ecstasy, speaking in   A10
   of men or of angels   PCF13
   the gift of   PCF12
touched the man's ear and healed him   L22
transfiguration, vision of the   Mw17
transfigured, in their presence he was   Mw17; Mk9
trumpets, the angels blew their   Rev8
walked, immediately the girl got up and   Mk5
water became wine   J2
   walking on the   Mw14; Mk6
weep no more; she is not dead: she is asleep   L8
withered arm healed on the sabbath   Mw12

28 *Music*

OLD TESTAMENT

bell, golden, sewn to clothes   Ex28ff
  inscribed 'Holy is the Lord' Z14
Canticles; Song of Songs; Song of Solomon So1ff
castanets SS6
choirs, appointed two great Ne12
cornet SS6; Ps98; D3; Ho5
cymbals SS6; CF13f, 25; CS5, 29; Ez3; Ne12; Ps150
  bronze CF15
dance, daughters of Jephthah Ju11
  girl shows her joy in Je31
  girls of Shiloh Ju21
  on the temple terrace, those who Zp1
  praise his name in the Ps149, 150
dancers chant your praises Ps87
  merry throng of Je31
  moves between the lines of So6
dancing, a time for Ec3
  turned my lament into Ps30
dirge, I will chant over the desert pastures Je9
  sing it as an E32
  those skilled in the Am5
drum SF10
dulcimer D3
fanfare of trumpets KS11; Ps47, 150
fife SF10
flute Job21, 30; Ps150; D3
harp SF10, 16, 18ff; SS6; KF10; CF13ff; CS5, 9, 20, 29; Job21, 30; Ne12; Is5, 16, 23, 30; Ps33, 43, 49, 57, 71, 81, 92, 98, 108, Ps137, 147, 149ff; E26; D3
  of algum wood CS9
  the merry Is24
harpist E33
harpists, ancestor of all Gen4

28 MUSIC

harps, we hanged on the willow   Ps137
horn   CS15; Ps81, 98; D3; Ho5; Z9
jingles, adorn yourselves with   Je31
lament, sing a   Ps30, 56
love song   Is5
lute   SF10; SS6; KF10; CF13ff; CS5, 9, 20, 29; Ne12; Ps57, 71,
    Ps81, 108, 150; Is5, 14; Am5ff
  of algum wood   CS9
  ten-stringed   Ps33, 92, 144
master-singers   CF25
melody of thy viols, I will not hear   Am5
minstrel   KS3; CS35; Ps68
music and singing   D3
  in the house of the Lord   CF6
  of strings   Ps45
  of the heavens   Ps19
  of your lutes, I cannot endure the   Am5
  young men have ceased from their   La5
musical instruments, invent   Am6
   of all sorts   Ec2
   of David   Ne12
musicians   CF6, 9, 15; CS34; E27; Ne4; E33, 40
  apprentice   CF25
  freed from tax   Ez7
organ   Job21, 30; Ps150
pipe   SF10; KF1; Ps81; Is5, 30; Je48; E28; D3
pipers, ancestor of all   Gen4
precentor in charge of music   CF25
procession   Ps68
psalms, honour his name with   Ps135
  praise him with   Ps47
  raise   Ju5; Ps57, 59, 68, 101, 108
  sing   Ps9f, 18. 21, 27, 30, 61, 66, 68, 71, 81, 92, 95, 98, 104ff, 138,
    Ps147, 149
psaltery   SF10; CF25; CS5; Ne12; Ps33, 71, 81, 92, 102, 108, 144, 150;
    D3
ram's horn trumpet   Ex19; Le25; Jos6
reed-pipe   Je48
sackbut   D3
sing a new song   Ps33
sing of thy strength   Ps59

28 MUSIC

sing, the tongue of the dumb shall   Is35
singer   KF10; CF9, 25; CS5, 29; Ez2, 7, 10; Ne7, 10ff; Ps68, 87;
    Ec2; E40
singing and music   D3
  danced for joy to the sound of   CF13
  joy over thee with   Zp3
  women in the palace   Am8
sistrum   Is30
song of all songs   So1
  of Deborah and Barak   Ju5
  of Moses   Ex15; De32
  of the harlot   Is23
  sing praises, sing a new   Is42
songs as on a night of sacred pilgrimage   Is30
  clamour of your   E26
  of thanksgiving, Levites in charge of   Ne12
  of triumph, break into   Is49
  spare me the sound of your   Am5
stringed instruments, chief singer on   H3
strings   Ps150
  instrument of ten   Ps92, 144
tabor   Ps81; Is5
tabret   SF10, 18; Is5, 24, 30; E28
tambourine   Ex15; Ju11; SF18; SS6; CF13; Job21; Ps68, 149ff; Is24, 30
  daughter of Jephthah came out with a   Ju11
  Miriam and all the women danced to the   Ex15
timbrel   SS6; Job21; Ps68, 81
triangle   D3
trumpet   Ex19; Le25; Nu10; Ju3, 7; SF13; SS2, 6, 15, 20; KF1;
    KS9ff; CF13ff; Ez3; Ne4, 12; CS5, 13, 15, 20, 29; Job39;
    Ps47, 81, 98, 150; Is18, 27, 58; Je4, 6, 42, 51;
    E7, 33, Ho5, 8; Joe2; Am2ff; Z9; Zp1
  Ehud sounded   Ju3
  military   Nu31; Je4, 6, 42, 51; Zp1
  of beaten silver   Nu10
  of Gideon   Ju7
  ram's horn   Ex19; Le25; Jos6
  signal calls   Nu10
viol   Is5, 14; Am5ff
zither   D3

28 MUSIC
NEW TESTAMENT

brass, sounding   PCF13
cymbal   PCF13
danced for the guests, daughter of Herodias   Mw14; Mk6
   we have piped unto you, and ye have not   L7
flute   Mw9; PCF14
flute-player   Mw9; Rev18
gong   PCF13
harp   PCF14; Rev5, 15
harper, harpist   Rev14, 18
harps, the sound of   Rev14
hymn, contributes a   PCF14
   Passover   Mw26; Mk14
hymns, sing thankfully in your hart with   PCo3
   songs and psalms, speak to one another in   PE5
   to thy name, sing   PR15
lyre   PCF14
melody in your heart, making   PE5
minstrel   Mw9; Rev18
music and dancing, he heard   L15
musicians   Rev18
pipe   PCF14
piped unto you, we have   L7
pipers   Rev18
psalm, every one of you hath a   PCF14
   stands written in the   A13
psalms, book of   L20; A1
   everything written about me in the   L24
   hymns and songs, speak to one another in   PE5
   merry, let him sing   LJ5
   sing thankfully in your heart with   PCo3
sang his praises, all men   L4
sing and make music in your hearts   PE5
   praises, he should   LJ5
   thy praise in full assembly, I will   LH2
   with the spirit and with the understanding also   PCF14
singing a new song   Rev14
   with grace in your hearts to the Lord   PCo3
song of Moses   Rev15
   of the Lamb   Rev15

28 MUSIC

song, singing a new   Rev5
spiritual songs, psalms, hymns and   PE5
  sing in your heart with   PCo3
trumpet   Mw6, 24; PCF14f; ThF4; LH12; Rev1, 4, 8, 18
  blast   LH12
  call, the last   PCF15
  will sound, for the   PCF15
trumpeter   Rev18
trumpets, a flourish of   Mw6
  angels blew their   Rev8

29 *Penalties, Punishments and Compensation*

OLD TESTAMENT

accidental death, causing   De19
accusation, false   PS69
accusers of Daniel and their families thrown to the lions   D6
adulterers, you make common cause with   Ps50
adultery, on trial for   E16
  penalty for   Le20; De22
  wife suspected of   Nu5
affliction, bread and water of   KF22; 18
arrested, the prophet Jeremiah   Je37
  the prophet Micaiah   KF22
arson, restitution for   Ex22
assault, penalties for   Le24
  restitution for   Ex21
blasphemy, penalties for   Le24
  who speaks, shall be torn to pieces   D3
blood, guilty of shedding   Le17
borrows and does not repay, who   Ps37
bread and water punishment diet   KF22
    for Micaiah   CS18
  of adversity   Is30
  of affliction   CS18
burning as a penalty, following stoning   Nu15; Jos7
    for harbouring forbidden things   Jos7
    for lewdness   Le20ff
chains, Jeremiah released from his   Je40
children punished for the wrongdoing of parents   Nu15; Je31; D6; E18
compensation for wrongdoing   Nu5
condemned to death for not seeking guidance from the Lord   CS15
    for prophesying, Uriah   Je26

299

29 PENALTIES, PUNISHMENTS AND COMPENSATION

confined to Jerusalem   KF2
contention, water of   Nu5
death penalty by hanging   Nu25; De21; Jos8, 10; Est2, 7
  by stoning, offences calling for   De13ff
    for Achan and his family   Jos7
    for blasphemy   Le24
    for breaking the sabbath   Nu15
    for calling up spirits   Le20
    for daughters of Achan   Jos7
    for disobedient sons   De21
    for giving children to Molech   Le20
    for losing virginity before marriage   De22
    for misdemeanours   De22
    for sons of Achan   Jos7
    for worshipping other gods   De17
  for adultery   De22
  for approaching the tabernacle   Nu1
  for breaking house arrest   KF2
  for collecting sticks on the sabbath   Nu15
  for dreamers   De22
  for entering the king's presence unbidden   Est4
  for failing to foretell Nebuchadnezzar's dream   D2
  for kidnap   De24
  for losing virginity   De22
  for miscreants in general   De13
  for murder   Nu35
  for one's own sin only   De24
  for prophesying against the city   Je26
  for prophets in general   De13
  for rape   De22
  for working on the sabbath   Nu15
  for worshipping Baal-peor   Nu25
  for worshipping other gods   De17
  on all the wise men of Babylon   D2
  offences calling for   Ex21ff; Le20; Nu35
  this man must be put to   Je38
disobeying the king's edict, penalty for   Ez6
dungeon   Is24; Je37; La3; Z9
  lost to sight in a   Is42
  where they lie in darkness   Is42
evidence, bearing false   De5, 19

29 PENALTIES, PUNISHMENTS AND COMPENSATION

evidence, withholding   Ke5
eye for eye   Le24
extortion, expiation for   Le6
  put no trust in   Ps62
expiation, rites of   Le4ff
faults, secret   Ps19
fetters, bronze   Je39, 52
  removed from Jeremiah's wrists   Je40
  weighed down with   La3
fire, law of illicit   Le10
  restitution for malicious   Ex22
flogged for prophesying   Je20
  for tampering with the king's edict   E26
  on accusation of transferring allegiance   Je37
  the chief officer had Jeremiah   Je20
flogging, number of strokes permitted   De25
foot for foot   De19
forfeit, your house shall be   D2
fracture for fracture   De24
furnace, fiery, as a place of punishment   D3
gallows, Haman set up   Est5ff
  height of, 75ft or 50cubits   Est7
gaol   Is24
hand for hand   De19
  to be cut off   De25
genitals, penalty for catching hold of   De25
gibbet for hanging   De21; Est5ff
guilty deeds not hidden   Ps69
hanged bodies of the five kings   Jos10
  overnight disposal of   De21
  eunuchs plotting against King Ahauserus   Est2
  for worshipping Baal-peor   Nu25
  on a tree, the plotters were   Est2
  on the gallows that he had himself prepared   Est7
  the king of Ai   Jos8
hanging, penalties calling for   Nu25; De21ff; Jos8, 10
harbouring forbidden things, penalty for   Jos7
homicide, accidental   Nu35
  culpable   Nu35
  sanctuary for   Nu35; De19; Jos20
hung on the gallows, the bodies of Haman's ten sons   Est9

29 PENALTIES, PUNISHMENTS AND COMPENSATION

hung up by the hands, princes were   La5
idolatry, penalties for   Nu25; KF18; KS23; CS14ff, 31
imprisoned for prophesying   Je32
  in a vaulted pit   Je37
  the prophet Jeremiah   Je32ff
kidnap, the penalty for   De24
lash, offered my back to the   Is50
lashes, punish their iniquity with   Ps89
lawlessness and robbery, put an end to   E45
lewdness, penalty for   Le20ff
lies, expiation for   Le6
lion's den as places of punishment and execution   D6
manslaughter   Nu35; De19; Jos20
murder, categories of   Nu35
  on trial for, in Ezekiel's prediction   E16
  sanctuary for   Nu35
penalty for disobeying a royal edict   Ez6
  imposed on the king of Judah   KS18
pillory for every madman who sets up as a prophet   Je29
pit, prisoners out of the   Z9
prison   KF22; CS16, 18; Is24; Je29, 37, 39
  diet   KF22; CS18
  flung him into   E19
  house   CS16
    sit in the darkness of a   Is42
    to bring captives out of   Is42
    to release those in   Is61
    Zedekiah committed to   Je52
prisoners in a dungeon   Is24
punishment for one's own sin only   Je31
  their sin deserves   Ps69
ransom beyond his power to pay   Ps49
rebels, a race of   Is30
  must live in the desert   Ps68
refuge, cities of   Nu35; CF6; Jos20
  mountain   Ps18
renegades   Ps78
restitution for wronging another   Nu5
retribution, High God of   Is59
rod   Pro19, 26, 29
  feels the stroke of his   Is30

29 PENALTIES, PUNISHMENTS AND COMPENSATION

rod, I have felt the   La3
  I will chasten him with a   SS7
  in pickle for the arrogant   Pro19
  struck on the cheek with a   Mi5
ruffians, a band of   Ps22
rumours, penalty for carrying false   Ex23
sabbath, penalties for profaning the   Ex31; Nu15
sanctuary   Ex25ff
  demolish their   De12
  for homicides   Nu35; De19
seduction, penalty for   Ex22
seized, Jeremiah in the Lord's house   Je26
sentence, be just in passing   Ps51
  of death, men under   Ps102
sexual wrongdoing, penalties for   Le20; De22
shed innocent blood, hands that   Pro6
sin whispers to the wicked man   Ps36
sins of my youth, do not remember   Ps25
  unwitting   Ps19
sons punished for the iniquity of their fathers   Nu14
    to the third and fourth generation   Nu31
spare the rod, I will not   SS7
stocks,   Job13; Pro7
  Asa put Hanani in the   CS16
  for every madman who sets up as a prophet   Je29
  the chief officer had Jeremiah put in the   Je20
stolen goods   Ps62
stone you, bring up the mob against you and   E16
stoning, offences calling for   De13ff
thief as your friend   Ps50
  shall be swept away, every   Z5
thresh your bodies with thorns, I will   Ju8
torn to pieces for blasphemy under Nebuchadnezzar   D3
   for failing to foretell Nebuchandnezzar's dream   D2
traitors, no mercy on   Ps59, 78
trial for adultery, Jerusalem in allegory   E16
  for murder, Jerusalem in allegory   E16
  for suspected unfaithfulness   Nu5
truth, water of contention brings out   Nu5
tyrants brought low   Ps107
unfaithfulness, wife suspected of   Nu5

29 PENALTIES, PUNISHMENTS AND COMPENSATION

water of affliction   CS18; Is30
withholding evidence   Le5
witness, bearing false   Ex23

NEW TESTAMENT

anathema, who does not know the Lord, let him be   PCF16
anger cannot promote the justice of God   LJ1
arena, like men condemned to death in the   PCF
Armageddon, assembled the kings at   Rev16
arrested John the Baptist, Herod   Mw4, 14
   Paul, the commandant   A21
bandits crucified with Jesus   Mw27; Mk15
beaten, have done wrong and are   LPF2
   with many stripes, shall be   L12
blasphemy, stone you for your   J10
capital crime, if I have committed any   A25
   offence, I have not found him guilty of any   L23
cast the first stone, let him   J8
chain, prison   PTS1
chained him up for a thousand years   Rev20
chains, arresting men and women and putting them in   A22
   bound beneath the darkness in everlasting   LJu1
   for the sake of the house of Israel   A28
   he had snapped his   Mk5
   Herod put John in   Mw14
   Peter secured by two   A12
   put Jesus in   Mk15
   shackled with two   A21
chastise and release him, I will therefore   L23
condemn not, and ye shall not be condemned   L6
condemned thee, hath no man   J8
   to death, my vote was cast against them   A26
constable put you in jail   L12
cord, made a scourge out of   L12
court, settle out of   L12
eternal fire, paid the penalty in   LJu1
   punishment, they will go to   Mw25
execution, Herod interrogated the guards and ordered their   A12
   led him away to   L23

29 PENALTIES, PUNISHMENTS AND COMPENSATION

fetters and prison bars   LH11
  he had broken his   Mk5
flog a Roman citizen, can you legally   A22
flogged, imprisoned, mobbed   PCS6
  in synagogues, you will be   Mk13
  ordered them to be   A16
  sent for the apostles and had them   A5
  severely, servant who will be   L12
  those who believe   A22
flogging, examine him by   A22
  had to face   LH11
  I propose to let him off with a flogging   L23
forgiveness, for speaking against the Holy Spirit, there is no   Mw12
fortitude, testing of faith breeds   LJ1
gibbet, carried our sins to the   LPF2
  hanging him on a   A5
  put to death by hanging on a   A10
  took him down from the   A13
Great Day, more bearable for Sodom on the   L10
heretic should be warned once and once again   Tt3
imprisoned, more often   PCS11
  spirit, proclamation to the   LPF3
  those who believe   A22
  we prove ourselves when   PCS6
innocent, beyond all doubt this man was   L23
insurrection, Barabbas guilty of   L23
  lay bound with them that had made   Mk15
irons, had him put in   A22
jail, constable put you in   L12
jailer   A16
judge, drag you before the   L12
  yourself. judging your fellow man you   PR2
judged, unbeliever has been   J3
  we are chastened of the Lord, when we are   PCF11
judgement, after the death comes   LH9
  man who puts his faith in him does not come under   J3
  more bearable for Tyre and Sidon than for you   L10
  now is the hour of   J12
  on the living and the dead   LPF4
  when the men of this generation are on trial   L11

29 PENALTIES, PUNISHMENTS AND COMPENSATION

judgement, who commits murder must be brought to   Mw5
  will pay every man for what he has done, God's   PR2
lash, tied him up for the   A22
latter end is worse with them than the beginning   LPS2
murder, theft or sorcery, it must not be for   LPF4
offender, you must forgive the   PCS2
open arrest, to keep Paul under   A24
outlaws, he was counted among the   L22
perdition, man doomed to   ThS2
  waits for them with unsleeping eyes   LPS2
persecute this movement to the death, I implore you   A22
pilfer, tell slaves not to   Tt2
prison bars, fetters and   LH11
  flung them into   A16
  Herod shut John up in   L3
  Jesus heard that John was cast into   Mw4
  John the Baptist was cast in   Mw4; Mk1, 6
  many of the saints did I shut up in   A26
  Peter was kept in   A12
  Saul was sending men and women to   A8
  throw some of you in   Rev2
prisoner, not ashamed to visit a   PTS1
  released unto them one   Mk15
prisoners for punishment, Christians as   A22
  had escaped, assumed that the   A16
public flogging, they gave us a   A16
punishment, God's agents of   PR13
  of eternal ruin   ThS1
  tried by repeated   A26
put to death, I gave my voice against them when they were   A26
  in the body he was   LPF3
    Lazarus, consulted that they might   J12
    the prison keepers   A12
rebels, in custody with the   Mk15
refractory, discipline for the   PTS2
retribution, revealed from heaven, divine   PR1
reward each according to his deeds   Rev2
rod on every son, lays the   LH12
rods, beaten with   PCS11
scourge a man who is Roman, is it lawful for you to   A22
  and to crucify, deliver him to   Mw20

29 PENALTIES, PUNISHMENTS AND COMPENSATION

scourge made of cord   J2
scourging, examined by   A22
sentenced to death, handed over to be   L24
shackled, ordered Paul to be   A21
sin, if your brother commits a   Mw18
slander spoken against the Spirit will not be forgiven   Mw12
stocks, secured their feet in the   A16
stone him, the Jews picked up stones to   J10
   throw the first   J8
stoned, Moses commanded that such should be   J8
   once I was   PCS11
   such women are to be   J8
stripes, approving themselves in   PCS6
strokes, given thirty nine   PCS11
sword of the Spirit   PE6
   with which to smite the nations   Rev19
terrors of judgement to come   ThF1
    God has not destined us for   ThF5
test, do not bring us to the   L11
theft defiles the man   Mk7
thieves crucified with Jesus   Mw27
thongs, tied him up with   A22
tormented day and night for ever   Rev20
   in sulphurous flames   Rev14
torture, condemned the man to   Mw18
whip of cords, Jesus made a   J2
wicked man whom the Lord will destroy   ThS2
witnesses, put to death on the evidence of two or three   LH10
wrath is come upon them to the uttermost   ThF2

30   *Plants*

OLD TESTAMENT

acacia   Ex25f; Is41
  wood, table of   Ex25f
algum   KF8; CS2, 9
almond tree   Gen43; Ec12; e1
   rods of   Gen30
almonds produced by Aaron's staff   Nu17
almug wood , sandalwood   KF8, 10
aloe   Pro7; So4
  trees   Nu24
aloes, powder of   Ps45
apple tree   So2, 8; Joe1
apricot tree   So2, 8
ash tree   Is44
aspen   SS5; CF14
asphodel   So2; Is35
balm   Je8, 46
balsam   Gen43; So6; E27
  as offering   Ex25ff
barley   Ex9; De8; E4, 13, 45; Is28; Je41; Ho3; Joe1
  meal as grain offering   Nu5
bay tree   Ps37
bean   E4
bramble   Is34
briar   Is5, 7, 9, 27, 34, 55; E28; Mi7; Na1
broom bush   KF19; Job30
brushwood, as fire attacks   Ps118
bulrush   Ex2; Is18, 58
bulrushes, ark of   Ex2
box wood   Is41, 60; E27
bush, burning   Ex3
calamus, sweet   Ex30; So4; E27
camel-thorn   Is7, 55

30 PLANTS

camphire   So1, 4
cane, aromatic   Ex30f
caper-bud   Ec2
cassia   Ex30ff; Ps45; Pro7; E27
castor-oil plant   Jon4
cedar   Le14; Nu19; SS5, 7; KS19; CF17; CF1ff, 9; Job40;
       Ps29, 80, 92, 104, 148; So1, 5, 8; Is2, 9, 14, 37, 41,44;
       E17, 23, 27, 31; Am2; Z11
   beside the water   Nu24
   choicest cut down   Je22
   logs   CF14
   of Lebanon   Ju7; KF4f, 9ff
   planks   So8
   plentiful as sycomore fig   KF10
   wood   So1
     without limit   CF22
chestnut   E31
   rods of   Gen30
cinnamon   Ex30ff; Pro7; So2, 4
citrus trees   Le23
coriander   Nu11
corn   Is17, 21, 36, 55, 62; Je31; La2, 5; E36; Ho2, 7ff, 14; Joe2;
       Am8ff; Hg1ff; Z9, 12
   neither, nor figs   Nu20
corn-cockle   Job31
cornfield   SF8
cucumber   Nu11; Je10
cummin   Is28
cypress   Is44, 60
   ark ribs of   Gen6
dill   Is28
ebony   E27
elm   Is60; Ho4
fig, neither, nor corn   Nu20
   leaves, stitched   Gen3
   tree   De8; Nu13; Ju9; SF25, 30; KF4; KS18; Ne13; Ps105;
       Pro27; So2; Is34, 36; Je5, 8; Ho2, 9; Joe1ff; Am4;
       Mi4; Na3; H3; Hg2; Z3
fir tree   SS6; KF5ff; KS19; CS3; So1;Is14, 37, 41, 55, 60;
       E27, 31; Ho14; Na2; Z11
   wood   KF5ff; So1

30 PLANTS

fitch   Is28; E4
flag iris   Ex2, 30; So4; Is19; E27
flax   Ex9; Is19, 42; Ho2
flowers of the field   Ps103
food to animals, green plants given as   Gen1
forest   Ps74, 83, 104; Is44; Ho2
   the high places of a   Je26
   they cut down her   Je46
   trees   E15
fruit trees   Ne9; Ps148
gourd, wild   KS4; Jon4
grapes   Nu13; Ne13
   prohibited for Nazirites   Nu6
   wild   Is5
grass   Is5, 37, 51, 66
   on the roof   Ps129
gum tragacanth   Gen37, 43
hazel   Gen30
heath   Je17
hemlock   Ho10; Am6
henna   So4, 7
   blossom   So1
   bushes   So7
herbs   Is18; La3
   bitter   Nu9
   garden of   KF21
   magic   Job18
hyssop   Ex12; Nu19; KF4; Ps51
ilex   Is44
iris, sweet flag   Ex2, 30; So4; Is19; E27
juniper   KF19; Job30; Je17
leek   Nu11
lentil   Gen25; E4
lign-aloe   Nu24
lily   So2, 4ff; Ho14
   decorative metalwork   KF7
   of the valley   So2
lime, linden or teil tree   Is6
locust bean   KS6; Is1
logs, rafting   KF5
lotus   Job40; Is19

30 PLANTS

mallow   Job6, 24, 30
mandrake   Gen30; So7
majoram   Ex12; Le14; Nu19; KF4
  cleansing ritual of   Nu19
melon   Nu11
millet   E4
mulberry   SS5; FC14; Is40
myrrh   Gen37, 43
myrtle   Ne8; Pro7; Is41, 55; Z1
nettle   Job30; Pro24; So6; Is34; Ho9; Zp2
oak   Ju6; SS18; CF10; Is6, 44; E6, 27; Ho4; Am2; Z11
  at Ophran   Ju6
  burial beneath   Gen35
  of Bashan   Is2
  sacred   Is1
oil tree   Is41
olive   Ex27f, 30ff; Nu28; De6, 8; Jos24; Ne5; Job24; Ps128;
      Is17, 24; Ho14; Am4; Mi6; H3
  leaf, plucked   Gen8
  tree   De24; Ju9; SS15; KS5, 18; CF27; Ne8ff; Job15; Ps52; Is24; Je11;
      Hg2; Z4
  wild   KF6; CF27; Ne8; Is41
    timber of   KF6
  yards   SF8; Ne5
onions   Nu11
palm   De8; Ne8; Is9, 19; Joe1
  carving of   E40ff
  fronds   Le23; So5
  tree, trees   Nu33; Job15; Ps65, 92; So7; Je10
    carvings of   KF6
    city of   Ju1f
    long rows of   Nu24
    of Deborah   Ju4
    of Elim   Ex15
    Vale of   Ju1, 3
papyrus, paper reeds   Is19
pine   KF5f, 9; KS19; CS2; Ps104; Is14, 37, 41, 55, 60; E27; Ho14; Z11
pistachio nut   Gen43
plane tree   E31
    rods from a   Gen30

30 PLANTS

pomegranate   Nu13; De8; SF14; So6, 7, 8; Joe1; Hg2
  decorative carving of   KF7; KS25
  embroidered   Ex28ff
  in flower   So6
  juice of   So8
  neither, nor vines   Nu20
poplar   Gen30; Job40; Is44; Ho4, 14
  rods of   Gen30
reeds   Ex2; Job8, 40; Ps68; Is9, 11, 35, 42; Je51; E29; Ho13
  ark covered with   Gen6
  paper, papyrus   Is19
rose   So2; Is35
  of Sharon   So2
rushes   Job8; So6; Is9, 19, 35
  basket of   Ex2
rye   E9; Is28
saffron   So4
saltwort   Job30; Zp2
sandalwood, almug   KF8, 10
sap, trees full of   Ps92
shittah tree   Is41
  wood   Ex25ff
shrub, neither plant nor   Gen2
spelt, rye wheat   Ex9; Is28; E4
spikenard   So1, 4
stink-wood   Is7
sweet cane   So4; Is43; Je6; E27
sycomore   KF10; CF27; Is9; Am7
  fig   KF10; CF27; CS1, 9; Am7
tamarisk, green   Is44
  tree   SF22, 31
teil tree, lime, linden   Is6
terebinth   Gen12, 18, 35, 49; De11; Jos24; Ju6, 9; SF10; KF13;
     Is1, 6, 57; E6; Ho4
  at Ophrah   Ju6
  great stone beneath   Jos24
  old and propped-up   Ju9
thistle   Je12; Ho10
thistledown   Ps83; Is17
thorn   Is5, 7, 9ff, 27, 33; Je12; E28
  bush   Ju9; Ps58; Ho2, 9, 10

30 PLANTS

tragacanth, gum   Gen37, 43
tree, fruitful   Gen49
  of knowledge   Gen2
  of life   Gen2
  of the forest   Ps96
  planted by the rivers   Ps1
  rank as a spreading   Ps37
trees, cut down for siege works   De20
  cut down their fine   KS3
  cutting at the Jordan   KS6
  Solomon discoursed of   KF4
  that yield food, do not destroy   De20
vine   Ju9; KF4; KS18; Job15;Ps78, 80, 105, 128; So6ff;
      Je6, 8, 31, 48; E15, 17, 19;Joe1ff;
      Is1, 3, 5, 7, 16, 18, 24, 27, 32, 34, 36ff, 61;Ho2, 10, 14;
      Mi1, 4; Na2; Hg2; Z3, 8; Ma3
  ass tethered to a   Gen49
  choice red   Je2
  neither, nor pomegranate   Nu20
  prohibited for the Nazirites   Nu6
  wild   KS4
vines, a land of   De8
vineyard   Gen9; De6, 20, 22; Jos24; Ju14; SF8; KF4, 21; KS5, 18;
      CF27; Ne5, 9; Job24; Ps107; Pro24, 32; Ec2; So1, 7ff;
      Is1. 3. 5. 16, 18, 27, 36ff; Je12, 31f, 35; E19, 28; Ho2;
      Am4f, 9; Na2; Zp1
  Naboth's   KF21
  Noah's   Gen9
watermelon   Nu11
wheat   Ex9; De8; Ju15; SF12; KF5; CS2; Pro27; So7; Is28; Je12,31, 41;
      E4, 27, 45; Joe1; Am5, 8
  harvesting   De8; Ju15; SF6, 12; Je12
willow   Le23; Job40; Ps137; Is15; E17
wormwood   De29; Job30; Pro5; Je9; La3; Am5
  root from which springs   De29

NEW TESTAMENT

aloes   J19
anise   Mw23

30 PLANTS

barley   J6; Rev6
brambles   L6
briars   Mw7; LH6
brushwood   Mk11
burning bush   L20; A7
corn   Mw12f; Mk2, 4; L6, 12, 17; PCF9; PTF5, 9
cummin   Mw23
darnel   Mw13
dill   Mw23
fig tree   Mw21. 24; Mk11, 13; L13, 21; J1; LJ3; Rev6
   casteth untimely figs   Rev6
   which thou cursedst is withered away   Mk11
figs picked from thistles   Mw7
flax   Mw12
flower of the field   LPF1; LJ1
forest set ablaze by a tiny spark   LJ3
fruit, tree known by its   L6
fruits, recognize them by their   Mw7
garden herb, tithes of every   L11
  plant, bigger than any   Mw13
grapes picked from briars   Mw7
grass, all flesh is   LPF1
  do no injury to   Rev9
  flower of the   LJ1
  green, was burnt   Rev8
  withers, the flower falls   LPF1
hedge   Mw21; L14
herbs, all manner of   L11
  becomes greater than all   Mk4
  bringeth forth   LH6
  the greatest among   Mw13
husks that the swine did eat   L15
hyssop   J19; LG9
leaves of the trees serve for the healing of nations   Rev22
lilies of the field   Mw6; L12
marjoram   J19; LH9
mint   Mw23; L11
mulberry tree   L17
mustard seed   Mw13, 17; Mk4; L13, 17
   faith no bigger than a   Mw17; L17
myrrh   L7

30 PLANTS

nard   Mk14; J12
olive, grafted   PR11
   spare the   Rev6
   tree   Rev11
   wild   PR11
palm   J12; Rev7
   branches   J12
pods that the pigs ate   L15
reed, beat him with a   Mw27; Mk15
   bed swept by the wind   Mw11; L7
   in his hand   Mw27
   measuring   Rev11
   snap off the broken   Mw12
rue   L11
seed fell on stony ground   Mw13; Mk4; L8
spikenard   Mk14; J12
sycamine tree   L17
sycomore fig tree   L19
tares   Mw13
thistle   Mw7, 13; Mk4; L6, 8; LH6
thorns and briars, that which beareth   LH6
   crown of   Mw27; Mk15
   do not gather figs of   L6
   grew up and choked the seed   Mk4
   some fell among   Mw13; L8
thyine wood   Rev18
timber set ablaze   LJ3
tree from a mustard seed   L13
   good, yields good fruit   Mw7
   known by its fruit   L6
   of life in John's vision   Rev22
trees, already the axe is laid to the   L3
   that bear no fruit   LJu1
   walking, men like   Mk8
   were burnt, a third of the   Rev8
vine, fruit of the   Mw26; Mk14; L22
   I am the real   J15
   spare the olive and the   Rev6
wheat   Mw3, 13; L3, 16, 22; J12; A27; RCF15; Rev6, 18
woods, scented   Rev18
wormwood   Rev8

31 *Priests and Prophets*

OLD TESTAMENT

anoint him, this is he   SF16
appointed prophet, Elisha   KF19
Ark of the Covenant, custodian of the   SF7
Asherah, four hundred prophets of   KF18
Baal, four hundred and fifty prophets of   KF18
breastplate, kingly   Ex25ff; Le8
chief priest   Ez7
cloak, Elijah's   KS2
chronicles of the seers   CS33
consecration of Aaron   Le8
  of priesthood   Ex29ff
derobed, Aaron   Nu20
destruction of Jerusalem, symbolised by Ezekiel   E5
ecstasy, prophetic   Nu11
ephah in Zechariah's vision   Z5
ephod   SF2, 14, 21ff, 30
  abide without an   Ho3
  carved by Ahijah   SF14
  linen   CF15
    around Samuel   SF2
  priestly garment   Le8
false prophets, Ahab and Zedekiah   Je29
  made fools   Je50
frenzy, Saul fell into   SF18
hair, symbolism of Ezekiel's   E5
hallow the people   Ex19
  yourselves for tomorrow   Jos3
high priest Eliashib   Ne3
    Joshua   Hg1ff; Z3ff
holy people, they shall be called   Is62
Levites enrolled, 38,000   CF23
  provision of land and towns for   E45
man of God came to Eli, a   SF2

31 PRIESTS AND PROPHETS

man of God, do not disturb his bones   KS23
   from Judah   KF13
   from Shemaiah   KF12
Nazirite, a dedicated one   Nu6
  priestly caste   Nu6; Ju13; SF1; La4; Am2
  vow, rules for the special   Nu6
oracle concerning Jerusalem, Ezekiel's   E12
  Solomon's   KF6, 8
pastor   Je2
phylactery upon hand and forehead   Ex13
priest, Aaron derobed   Nu20
  Aaronite   Le1ff
  Abiathar   SS8; KF1ff
  Adaiah   CF9
  Ahimelech   SF21
  Azariah   CF9
  chief   KS25; E37
  deputy chief   KS25
  Eleazar   SF7
  Eli   SF1ff
    a man of God came to   SF2
    were scoundrels, the sons of   SF1f
  from non-Levite classes   KF12
  high, Hilkiah   KS22; Je1
  Jachin   CF9
  Jedaiah   CF9
  Jehoiada   KS11f
  Jehoriarib   CF9
  Maasai   CF9
  Micah's son   Ju17ff
  of Midian   Ex3
  Uriah   KS16
  will pronounce the sentence   De17
  Zadok   SS8; KF1ff
priesthood, consecration of   Ex29ff
  disqualified from, without record of genealogy   Ne7
priestly caste, Nazirite   Ju13
  garments, rules of   E44
priests, arrangement for upkeep of the temple   KS12
  contributions to   E44
  David's sons were   SS8

31 PRIESTS AND PROPHETS

priests deported, brought back to Samaria   KS17
   descendants disqualified   Ez2
   dismissed their foreign wives   Ez10
   families returned from exile   Ez2
   fell by the sword   Ps78
   for Reheboam's hill-shrines   CS11
   freed from tax   Ez7
   land set apart for   E48
   marriage rules for   Le21
   numbers returned from exile   Ne7
   of high places killed   KS23
   of the Lord, you shall be called   Is61
   profaned the sanctuary   Zp3
   put to the sword   SF22
   registration of   CF9
   roster of service   CS8
   rules for drinking   E44
     for hair and beard   E44
     for marriage   E44
   seek the guidance of   De17
   share of offerings   De18
   Solomon's   CS5
   who see no difference between holy and profane   E22
profane and sacred, the difference between   Le10
   both prophet and priest are   Je23
   priests who see no difference between holy and   E22
prophecy inspired with music   CF25
   of Agur   Pro30
   of Lemuel   Pro31
prophesy against Egypt   E30
     Gog   E38
     Seir   E35
     the shepherds   E34
     Tyre   E27
     Zidon   E28
   no more in the name of the Lord or we will kill you   Je11
   over the dry bones   E37
prophet, aged, of Bethel   KF13
   Ahijah   KF11, 14
   appears among you   De13
   came to Ahab   KF20

31 PRIESTS AND PROPHETS

prophet Elijah   KF17ff; KS1ff
   a hairy man   KS1
   carried to heaven   KS2
   fed by ravens   KF17
  Elisha   KF19ff
   took Elijah's mantle   KS2
  Gad   SF22, 24
  Haggai   Ez5
   the Lord's messenger   Hg1
  Hananiah, death of   Je28
  I am no   Am7; Z13
  Iddo, story of the   CS13
  is Saul become a   SF10
  Isaiah   KS19; CS26; Is1ff, 37ff, 39
  Jehu   KF16
  Jeremiah   CS36; Je1ff; D9
   the Lord appointed   Je1
  Micaiah   KF22; CS18
  Moses, never another like   De34
  Nathan   SS7, 12; KF1; CS29
  Oded   CS28
  Shemaiah   CS12
  Shimei   KF1
  stripped of every   Is3
  the Lord will raise a   De18
  used to be called a seer   SF9
  who came from Samaria   KS23
  who speaks for other gods   De18
  will prove mere wind   Je5
  Zedekiah   KF22; CS18
prophetess Deborah   Ju4
  I lay with the   Is8
  Huldah   KS22; CS18
  Noadiah   Ne6
prophetic rapture   SF10
prophets, a company of   SF10, 19
  and priests are frauds, every one of the   Je6, 8
  are prophesying lies in my name   Je14
  came to Elisha   KS2
  do not be deceived by   Je29
  do not listen to your   Je27

31 PRIESTS AND PROPHETS

prophets, do they live forever?   Z1
  false, made fools   Je50
  fifty, followed them   KS2
  four hundred, assembled   KF22; CS18
  from your sons, raised up   Am2
  in rapture   SF19
  massacred by Jezebel   KF18
  no harm, do my   Ps105
  of Baal put to death   KF18ff
  prophesying falsely   Je5
  the sun goes down on the   Mi3
  we have no   Ps74
  were reckless   Zp3
  whether by dreams or urim or   SF28
  who use whitewash instead of plaster   E22
purification of the desecrated house of the Lord   CS29
rapture, they fell into   Sf10, 19
robes, priestly   Ez2; Ne7
rod, Aaron's   Ex7
sacred and common, priests who see no difference between   E22
  and profane, difference between   Le10
sash, priestly   Le8
scion from the root of Jesse   Is11
seer, Gad was David's   CS29; SS24
  Hanani   CS16, 19
  Iddo   CS12
    vision of   CS9
  Samuel   CF9
  used to be called a   SF9
  what is nowadays called a   SF19
seers, the king's   CS35
spirit of Elijah has settled on Elisha   KS2
  of God came upon them   SF19
  of the Lord take possession of you   SF10
supervisor of the house of God   Ne11
teraphim, abide without   Ho3
thummim   Ez2; Ne7
  charm   Le8
  given to Levi   De33
  let the lot be   SF14
tithes and contributions, they defraud God with   Ma3

31 PRIESTS AND PROPHETS

tokens of the Covenant   Ex25ff
urim   SF14, 28; Ez2; Ne7
   charm   Le8
   consulted by Eleazar   Nu27
   given to Levi   De33

NEW TESTAMENT

ambassador of Jesus Christ   Ph1
antichrists have appeared, many   LJF2
apostle and high priest, Jesus Christ   LH3
apostles, he chose twelve   L6
Baptist, John the   Mw3
bishop must be above reproach   PTF3
   must be of unimpeachable character   Tt1
   must not be a newly baptized convert   PTF3
bishopric, let another take his   A1
bishops and deacons at Philippi   PPs1
chief priest   Mw2, 16, 20f, 26ff; Mk8, 10f, 14f; L3, 9, 19f, 22, 24;
       J7, 11f, 18f; A4f, 9, 19, 22f, 25f
   Abiathar   Mk2
   Caiaphas   L3; J11, 18; A4
   Sceva   A19
chief priests, Herod gathered   Mw2
   rejected of the   Mk8
   suffer much from the   Mw16
council of the high priest   A5
deacon   PPs1; PTF3
deaconess must be woman of high principle   PTF3
deacons must be men of high principle   PTF3
   must not be money-grubbers   PTF3
evangelist, do the work of an   PTS4
eyewitnesses of ministers of the word   L1
false prophet, foul spirit from the mouth of the   Rev16
   thrown alive into the lake of fire   Rev19
false prophets, Israel had   LPS2
   just so did their fathers treat   L6
   you have mastery over   LJF4
gospel of the kingdom, preaching the   Mw4

31 PRIESTS AND PROPHETS

herald and apostle, I was appointed   PTF2
high priest   Mw26; Mk2; L1, 3; J11, 18; A4f, 7, 9, 20 22ff;   LH2f, 5, 9
    Aaron   L1; A7; LH5, 9
    Abiathar   Mk2
    Ananias   A23f
    Annas   L3; J18; A4
    apostle and   LH3
    before God   LH2
    Caiaphas   Mw26; L3; J11, 18; A4
    council of the   A5
    in the succession of Melchizedek   LH6
    of good things   LH9
    would you insult God's   A23
Holy Ghost has made you overseers of the flock   A20
Inspiration, do not stifle   ThF5
Interpret ecstatic utterance, the ability to   PCF12
Jerusalem will be trampled down by foreigners   L21
kingdom of God is yours, you who are in need   L6
last day, I will raise him up on the   J6
Levitic priesthood   LH7
meeting of chief priests and lawyers   Mw2
Messias cometh, I know that   J4
ministers of the word   L1
new age, birth pangs of the   Mw24
One who called you is holy   LPF1
oracular spirit, slave-girl possessed by an   A16
    utterance, alarm yourselves at some   ThS2
ordination, not be hasty in   PTF5
ordained you, I have chosen and   J15
phylactery   Mw23
possessed by the power of Elijah   L1
pray everywhere, I will that men   PTF2
    lifting up holy hands to   PTF2
preacher, John the Baptist   Mw3
    ordained a   PTF2
president of the synagogue   Mk5; L8
priest   Mw8; Mk1f; L1, 5, 10, 20; A4; LH2, 7
    Alexander   A4
    allowed to eat the sacred bread   Mk2
    and those whom he consecrates   LH2

31 PRIESTS AND PROPHETS

priest, go and show yourself to the   Mw8; Mk1; L5
  Jonathan   A4
  Melchizedek   LH7
  went past on the other side   L10
  Zechariah   L1, 3, 11
priesthood, become a holy   LPF2
  Levitic   LH7
  of Jesus   LH7
  royal   LPF2
priestly course of Abijah   L1
  service, my   PR15
priests, a deputation of   J1
  accosted him   L20
  alone are allowed to eat sacred bread   L6
  go and show yourselves to the   L17
  have no right to eat at our altar   LH13
  of the sacred tent   LH13
  to serve as   Rev1
prophecies of Isaiah   L3
  shall fail   PCF13
prophecy, above all   PCF14
  daughter who possessed the gift of   A21
  I may have the gift of   PCF13
  in scripture was bound to come true   A1
  of Isaiah, to fulfil the   Mw8
  the gift of   PCF12
prophesied, spoke in tongues of ecstasy and   A19
prophesies, when he prays or   PCF11
prophesy again before many peoples   Rev10
  in your name, did we not   Mw7
  one at a time, you may all   PCF14
  your sons and daughters shall   A2
prophet, a Cretan   Tt1
  Agabus   A11, 21
  and far more than a   L7
  Daniel   Mw24; Mk13
  David spoke as a   A2
  Elijah, Elias   Mw11, L4, 9; J1
  Elisha, Eliseus   L4
  Esaias, Isaiah   Mw3f, 12; Mk1; L4; J1, 12; A8, 28
  has arisen among us, a great   L7

31 PRIESTS AND PROPHETS

prophet, I can see that you are a   J4
  is not recognized in his own country   L4
  is worth more than a man of ecstatic speech   PCF14
  Isaiah, Esaias   Mw3f, 12; Mk1; L4; J1, 12; A8, 28
  Jeremiah, Jeremias, Jeremy   Mw2, 16, 27
  Jesus, this is the   Mw21
  Joel   A2
  Jonah, Jonas   Mw12, 16; L11
  like one of the old prophets, he is a   Mk6
  looked on Jesus as a   Mw21
  of the highest, you shall be called   L1
  people are convinced that John was a   L21
  powerful in speech and action   L24
  sorcerer who posed as a   A13
  to fulfil what the Lord declared through the   Mw1
  we await, are you the   J1
  whom your fathers did not persecute, was there a   A7
  without honour in his own country   J4
prophetess Anna   L2
  who claims to be a   Rev2
prophetic scriptures, disclosed through   PR16
  utterances, do not despise   ThF5
    pointed you out   PTF1
prophets a pattern of patience   LJ5
  a torment, these two   Rev11
  all predicted this present time   A3
  and apostles, I will send them   L11
  and teachers, at Antioch were certain   A13
  answer for the blood of all the   L11
  before you, they persecuted   Mw5
  beware of false   Mw7
  came down from Jerusalem, some   A11
  confirms the message of the   LPS11
  everything written about me in the   L24
  false   Mw7, 24; LPS2
  falsely inspired, many   LJF4
  foretold by the   A26
  God has appointed   PCF12
    spoke through the   LH1
  in the kingdom of God, all the   L13
  in the same way did their fathers treat the   L6

31 PRIESTS AND PROPHETS

prophets, killed their own   ThF2
  madness, put a stop to the   LPS2
  sages and teachers I send you   Mw23
  so persecuted they be   Mw5
  stories of the   LH11
  the doom proclaimed by the   A13
  they have killed my   PR11
  they have Moses and the   L16
  when your fathers murdered   L11
  will come true, all that is written by the   L18
  work will be over   PCF13
quench not the Spirit   ThF5
Righteous One, they killed those who foretold the   A7
ruler of the synagogue   Mk5
seal not the prophecy of this book   Rev22
sermon on the mount   Mw5
scripture has to be fulfilled   J17
shepherds of the church of the Lord   A20
Son of Man will be given up to the chief priest   Mk10
  will have come   Mw10
speak as if you uttered oracles of God   LPF4
spiritual endowment you possess   PTF4
  truths, because we are interpreting   PCF2
steward, God's   Tt1
stewards of the secrets of God   PCF4
temple police, officers of the   L22
wise men, three   Mw2
wonderful works done in thy name   Mw7

32 *Repentance, Hope and Atonement*

OLD TESTAMENT

abuse, let him endure full measure of   La3
alive his own soul, none can keep   Ps22
   the Lord killeth and maketh   SF2
Amen, all the people said   CF16
   the people answered   Ne8
atonement for the offence of Korah   Nu16
   ram of the   Nu5
awe, hold the Lord in   Jos22, 24
beacon in darkness   Ps112
beat them and tore out their hair, I   Ne13
birth again, those long dead to   Is26
bitter draught, drunk with a   Ps60
cheek, let him turn his   La3
comfort ye my people   Is40
commune with your own heart and be still   Ps4
confession, expiation by   KF8
   of Daniel   D9
confusion, let us never be put to   Ps71
conscience smote him, David's   SS24
consolation, cup of   Je16
conversion of Nebuchadnezzar   D4
courage, be of good   Ps31
darkness, a beacon in   Ps112
death in victory, he will swallow up   Is25
defiled my holy place, you have   E5
desolate, no more shall your land be called   Is62
destiny, arise to your   D12
dust, ye that dwell in   Is26
evil befall thee, no   Ps91
expiation by confession   KF8
   for bloodshed   De21
   for the Gibeonites   SS21

32 REPENTANCE, HOPE AND ATONEMENT

expiation, shrine of   CF28
fear of the Lord   Job28
  out them in   Ps9
  therefore will we not   Ps46
forgiveness, supplication for   KF8
forgot the Lord their God, they   Ju3
glory is departed: Ichabod   SF4
God is come into the camp!   SF4
good faith shall be his girdle   Is11
  O God, remember my for my   Ne13
grovel on dunghills   La4
guilt, expiation of   KF2
  for unfaithfulness   Nu5
heal, the hands that smite will   Job5
healed, with his stripes we are   Is53
healing in his wings   Ma4
hear, and your soul shall live   Is55
  me when I call   Ps4
heart, harden not your   Ps95
  he shall strengthen your   Ps31
  I will give them a different   E11, 36
  of stone   E11, 36
  rejoices in the Lord, my   SF2
  that one of broken   Ps34
  the Lord judges by the   SF16
heaven and earth, thou hast made   KS19
  sword of the Lord appears in   Is34
help, from whence cometh my   Ps121
  in trouble, a very present   Ps46
honour me, I will honour those who   SF2
hope in the Lord   Ps31
Ichabod: the glory is departed   SF4
jealous God   Ex34; De4ff; Na1
Jerusalem, a land of comfort   Is33
  shall become a heap of ruins   Je26
kills and gives life, the Lord   SF2
knowledge, fear of the Lord is the beginning of   Pro1
  of the Holy One is understanding   Pro9
laughing-stock, I have become to all nations   La3
lifteth up the beggar from the dunghill   SF2
live, mend his ways and   E18, 33

32 REPENTANCE, HOPE AND ATONEMENT

longing soul, satisfieth the   Ps107
love the Lord thy God   De31
   truth and peace   Z8
mends his ways, when a wicked man   E33
mercy and not sacrifice, I desire   Ho6
   endureth for ever, his   CF16; Ez3; Ps136
   great is his   Ps103
   have   Ps51
   he delighted in   Mi7
   show us thy   Ps85
mourning into gladness, I will turn   Je31
new name, you shall be called a   Is62
peace, dwelling in   Is32
   for the wicked, no   Is48
   make offer of   De20
   man of, Solomon   CF22
   offering on Mount Ebal   Jos8
   the land was at   Jos11; Ju3, 5, 8, 12; CS14
   the world is still at   Z1
   throughout Solomon's reign   KF4
peaceful, cities shall lie   Is32
power belongeth unto God   Ps62
praise, mouth shall show forth thy   Ps51
   the Lord all nations   Ps117
     all the people said   CF16
     let everything that hath breath   Ps150
punish you, though I   Je46
pure lips, I will give all peoples once again   Zp3
purged thy sin   Is6
quicken thou me   Ps119
refuge, the Lord is a sure   Na1
   thou art my only   Je17
reproach, he is filled with   La3
right and just, do what is   Pro21
righteousness cannot save his life   E33
rise again, their bodies will   Is26
rock like ours, the enemy have no   De32
   Lord is my, and my fortress   Ps18
   of his salvation   De32
sanctuary of the Lord   Ho8
saved, who invokes the Lord by name shall be   Joe2

32 REPENTANCE, HOPE AND ATONEMENT

salvation belongeth unto the Lord   Ps3
  from him cometh my   Ps62
  grant us thy   Ps85
  Lord is my   Ps27
seek me, you shall find me   Je29
shame, time to forget the   Is54
sin is purged   Is6
  what man is free from   KF8
sinful ways, gives up his   E18
sinned, we have   D9
sins, remember no more your   Is43
soul, he satisfies the longing   Ps107
  none can keep alive his own   Ps22
still small voice   KF19
strength, God is our   Ps46
supplication for forgiveness   KF8
temptation in the wilderness, the day of   Ps95
thanks, psalm of   CF16
  unto the Lord, give   CF16
transgressions, wipe out   Is43
troubles, former, are forgotten   Is65
trust in princes, put not your   Ps146
  in thee do I put my   Ps7, 16, 71
understanding, knowledge of the Holy One is   Pro9
  to turn from evil is   Job28
unfaithfulness, guilt for   Nu5
ungodly shall perish, way of the   Ps1
vanity, every man is   Ps39
vengeance, a god of   Na1
wait, I say, on the Lord   Ps27
war, never again be trained for   Mi4
warps the judgement, spirit that   Is19
weapons, kindle fires with their discarded   E39
whiter than snow, wash me that I may become   Ps51
wicked, no peace for the   Is48
wisdom, fear of the Lord is   Job28
  first step to   Pro9
wit's end, at their   Ps107
worship, choose here and now whom you will   Jos24
Zion, captive   La1ff
  shall become a ploughed field   Je26

32 REPENTANCE, HOPE AND ATONEMENT

NEW TESTAMENT

abject of mankind, apostles the most   PCF4
advocate, the Holy Spirit   J14f
ambassador, Christ's   PCS5
armour, let Jesus be the   PR13
ask, and ye shall receive   J16
atonement, have now received the   PR5
baptism in token of repentance   L3
baptize you with water for repentance   Mw3
baptized in the River Jordan, confessing their sins   Mw3
   with the Holy Spirit   A11
beam in thine own eye   Mw7
blasphemies, who is this which speaketh   L5
blasphemous, learn not to be   PTF1
blind for three days, Saul was   A9
body of believers united in heart and soul   A4
born anew, you have been   LPF1
brethren pray for us   ThF5
called, but few are chosen, many are   Mw22
carry neither purse not scrip   L10
chains fell away from his wrists   A12
Christ Jesus came into the world to save sinners   PTF1
   we are sure that thou art   J6
Christian, both as a man and as a   Ph1
   speaking the truth as a   PR9
Christians, great rejoicing among all the   A15
   in Rome had news of us   A28
   met their fellow   A16
   there we found fellow   A28
circumcised, not compelled to be   PG2
   uncircumcised man counting as   PR2
clean heart, love which springs from a   PTF1
cock crew, at that moment a   Mw26
comforter, spirit of truth   J15
   which is the Holy Ghost   J14
   will not come, if I go not away   J16
confess our sins, if we   LJ1
   your sins to one another   LJ5
confessing their sins   Mw3

32 REPENTANCE, HOPE AND ATONEMENT

confession that leads to salvation   PR10
conscience enlightened by the Holy Spirit   PR9
    is called as witness   PR2
cross and follow me, take up his   Mw10; Mk10; L9, 14
crucified, the man we once were has been   PR6
cured, if I even touch his clothes I shall be   Mw9; Mk5
day of the Lord, his spirit may be saved on the   PCF5
deliverance, all mankind shall see God's   L3
denied me three times, you will have   J13
die with Christ, did you not   PCo2
died with him, we shall live with him if we   PTS2
disciplined by his Father   LH12
   by the grace of God   Tt2
doubt, wherefore didst thou   Mw14
end of all things is at hand   LPF4
enemies, love your   Mw5
eternal life, heirs to   Tt3
    take hold of   PTF6
    the believer possesses   J6
    the promise of   LJF2
    those who were marked out for   A13
    what should I do to win   Mw19; Mk10; L18
salvation for all who obey him   LH5
everlasting life, he that believeth on me hath   J6
everyone of us shall give account of himself   PR14
everything is possible to one who has faith   Mk9
faith active in love   PG5
  be it unto you, according to your   Mw9
  because of your, so let it be   Mw8
  counted to him as righteousness   PR4; PG3; LJ2
  fight the good fight of   PTF6
  has made thee whole   L17
  holding the mystery of the   PTF3
  hope and love   PCF13
  how little you have   Mw6
  if a man is weak in his   PR14
  is the evidence of things not seen   LH11
  is too small, your   Mw17
  it is not all who have   ThS3
  justified through   PR1, 3, 5
  nowhere have I found such   Mw8

32 REPENTANCE, HOPE AND ATONEMENT

faith on earth, will the Son of Man find   L18
  run the great race of   PTF6
  strong enough to move mountains   PCF13
  the gift of   PCF12
  the shield of   PE6
  through this, you may possess life   J20
  thrown open the gates of   A14
  what is   LH11
  whom resist steadfast in the   LPF5
  with virtue, supplement your   LPS1
Father, I have sinned against heaven and before thee   L15
favour of God, we seek only the   ThF2
fear to have missed his chance   LH4
foolish, disobedient, deceived, we were sometimes   Tt3
forgive my brother, how many times am I to   Mw18
  one another as Christ forgave you   PE4
  us our sins, as we forgive   L11
forgiven us all our sins, he has   PCo2
  who speaks against the Son of Man will be   Mw12
forgiveness of sins, baptism for the   L3
    in whom we have   PCo1
    is now being proclaimed   A13
    repentance bringing the   L24
    that they may receive   A26
fortitude with piety, supplement your   LPS1
found, he was lost, and is   L15
fought the good fight, I have   PTS4
Gentiles, gift of the Holy Spirit poured out even on   A10
give thanks whatever happens   ThF5
glory, in bringing my sons unto   LH2
  of God, all come short of the   PR3
God and money, you cannot serve   Mw6
  forbid that I should boast   PG6
  has chosen what the world counts as folly and weakness   PCF1
  requires, conform with all that   Mw3
  shall call them his sons   Mw5
  who knows their need of   Mw5
gospel, I am not ashamed of the   PR1
Great Day, until the   PTS1
hanged himself, Judas went and   Mw27

32 REPENTANCE, HOPE AND ATONEMENT

Holy Ghost a witness to us   LH10
   abound in hope through the power of the   PR15
   approving ourselves by the   PCS6
   comforter which is the   J14
   made partakers of the   LH6
   my conscience bearing witness to the   PR9
   received the promise of the   A2
   ye shall be baptized with the   A11
  Spirit, conscience enlightened by the   PR9
   he will baptize you with the   Mk1
   says, today, if you hear his voice   LH3
   seal of the promised   PE1
   we had not heard that there is a   A19
   who speaks against the   Mw12
   you will be baptized with the   A11
hope keep you joyful, let   PR12
  of salvation as a helmet   ThF5
  overflow with   PR15
humble folk, go about with   PR15
humbly reckon others better than yourselves   PPs2
hypocrisies, lay aside all   LPF2
immortality, the perishable cannot possess   PCF15
imperishable, raised   PCF15
initiation which you received   LJF2
Jesus of Nazareth, this fellow was with   Mw26
  remember me when you come to your throne   L23
  son of David, have pity on me   L18
judges the secrets of human hearts, God   PR2
kick against the pricks, it is hard for thee to   A26
kingdom of God, a man who looked forward to the   Mk15
   has come close to you   L10
   must pass through hardships to enter the   A14
   no-one who keeps looking back is fit for the   L9
   not far from the   Mk12
  of heaven, I will give you the keys of the   Mw16
   should be thought of in this way   Mw18
knock, and the door will be opened   L11
last day, rise again on the   J11
  shall be first, and the first last   Mw20
lawless deeds are forgiven, happy are those whose   PR4
life and immortality brought to light   PTS1

32 REPENTANCE, HOPE AND ATONEMENT

life, already passed from death to   J5
  of faith, are you living the   PCS13
  to receive it back, lay down my   J10
  vital fragrance that brings   PCS2
lives by the power of God, Christ   PCS13
living water, he would have given you   J4
Lord, I believe; help thou mine unbelief   Mk9
  if thou wilt, thou canst make me clean   Mw8
  lay not this sin to their charge   A7
  Lord, not everyone who calls me   Mw7
love, fidelity and purity, make yourself an example of   PTF4
  greatest of them all is   PCF13
  your enemies, I tell you   Mw5
  your neighbour as yourself   PR13
lower nature, have crucified the   PG5
manner of life may be worthy, so that your   PCo1
mansions, in my Father's house are many   PCo1
many be called, but few chosen   Mw20
  who are first will be last, and the last first   Mk10
mend your ways; take our appeal to heart   PCS13
merciful, I will be   LH8
mercy, disobedient in order that they may receive   PR11
Messiah, followers of the   Mk9
  I now believe that you are the   J11
  not see death until he had seen the   L2
  the Son of God, are you the   Mw26
  wondered whether John was the   L3
mind of Christ, we have the   PCF2
mystery of faith, holding the   PTF3
night is far spent, the day is at hand   PR13
offend thee, if thine eye   Mw18
    if thy hand   Mk9
one shall be taken, the other left   L17
  who is to come, are you the   Mw11
penniless, we own the world   PCS6
perfect joy is now mine   J3
persecution, I extended my   A26
persecutor is preaching the good news, our former   PG1
Peter denied again: and immediately the cock crew   J18
piety with brotherly kindness, supplement your   LPS1
pray for your persecutors   Mw5

32 REPENTANCE, HOPE AND ATONEMENT

pray that you may be spared the hour of testing   L22
prayer is powerful, good man's   LJ5
  turn to   LJ5
present age, evil ways of this   PE2
pure all things are pure, to the   Tt1
purgation of sins   LH1
purifies himself, who has this hope before him   LJF3
put to death those parts of you which belong to the earth   PCo3
race for which we entered, run the   LH12
  in vain, that I did not run my   PPs2
raised to life on the third day   PCF15
rebirth, water of   Tt3
reign with him if we endure   PTS2
religion, live in full observance of   PTF2
  making a show of   Mw6
renewed, day by day we are inwardly   PCS4
renounced the deeds that men hide for shame   PCS4
repent and be baptized in the name of Jesus   A2
  and believe in the gospel   Mk1
  and turn to God, that your sins may be wiped out   A3
  for the kingdom of heaven is at hand   Mw3f
  he commands mankind to   A17
  if someone from the dead visits them they will   L16
  if you do not   Rev2
  ye shall all likewise perish, except ye   L13
repentance and forgiveness, to grant Israel   A5
  baptism as a token of   A13
  before God, I insisted on   A20
  bringing the forgiveness of sins   L24
  called publicly for   Mk6
  I baptize you with water for   Mw3
  John gave baptism in token of   A19
  prove your   Mw3
  to call sinners to   Mw9; Mk2
resurrection, living hope by the   LPF1
  of good and wicked alike   A24
  of the dead, our hope of the   A23
    the true issue is the   A24
  on the last day   J11
  this was the first   Rev20
retribution, warned you to escape from the coming   Mw3; L3

32 REPENTANCE, HOPE AND ATONEMENT

salvation, a sign of your   PPs1
  all men should find   PTF2
  as a helmet   PE6
  author of eternal   LH5
  God destined us for   ThF5
  he who brought us   PTS1
  in the Spirit, God chose you to find   ThS2
Saul, Saul, why persecutest thou me?   A22
save yourselves from this crooked age   A2
saved, everyone who invokes the name of the Lord   PR10
  he that endureth to the end shall be   Mw10, 24
  what must I do to be   A16
  who then can be   L18
  will have all men to be   PTF2
saw the light, my companions   A22
scales fell from his eyes   A9
seal of the Holy Spirit   PE1, 4
secret is this: Christ in you   PCo1
seek and you will find   L11
selected few have received it   PR11
sell your possessions, and give to the poor   Mw19
shine as lights in the world   PPs2
sin, he that is dead is freed from   PR6
  no more, go and   J8
  shall no longer be your   PR6
  shall we persist in   PR6
  slaves of, no longer   PR6
sinful self, destruction of the   PR6
sinless, if we claim to be   LJF1
sinner, God be merciful to me a   L18
  make your hands clean   LJ4
sins and wickedness, dead in your   PE2
  are forgiven you, Jesus said, your   Mw9; L5
  cancelling innumerable   LJ5
  are forgiven through the shedding of his blood   PE1
  confessing their   Mw3
  freed us from our   Rev1
  have been forgiven, because your   LJF2
  he will save his people from   Mw1
  love cancels innumerable   LPF4
soldiers of the light   PR13

32 REPENTANCE, HOPE AND ATONEMENT

Son of God, if you are the   L4
  truly you are the   Mw14
  of Man has come to seek and save what is lost   L19
    hath power on earth to forgive sins   Mw8; Mk2; L5
    will come at the time you least expect him   Mw24; L12
soul, anchor for the   LH6
  from death, rescuing his   LJ5
souls, purified your   LPF1
  salvation of your   LPF1
spirit, do not trust any and every   LJF4
  of God, how may we recognize the   LJF4
  quickened by the   LPF3
  sow seed in the field of   PG6
  vindicated by the   PTF3
spirits of good men made perfect   LH12
  test the   LJF4
standing firm you will win true life   L21
suffer indignity for the sake of the name   A5
sufferings, exalt in our present   PR5
supplications be made for all men   PTF2
sword cannot separate us from the love of Christ   PR8
tell out, my soul, the greatness of the Lord   L1
temple, he threw the money down in the   Mw27
tempted, able to succour them that are   LH2
throne, remember me when you come to your   L23
treasure in heaven, store up   Mw6
trespasses, forgiven all your   PCo2
truth will set you free   J8
turn from these follies to the living God   A14
unbelievers, do not unite yourself with   PCF6
wages of sin is death   PR6
wash away your sins   A22
watch and be sober   ThF5
  and pray, for ye know not when the Son of Man cometh   Mw25; Mk13; L21
water to blood, the power to turn   Rev11
word of God sifts the thoughts of the heart   LH4
worship but do not know, what you   A17
wrong-headed men, rescued from   ThS3
Zion shall come the deliverer, from   PR11

33   *Roads, Paths and Ways*

OLD TESTAMENT

ancient paths, look for the   Je6
  ways   Ps139
byways and unmade roads   Je18
  they take to   Je18
  we take to   La4
cairns, to mark your way built   Je31
causeway at the Upper Pool   Is7
  called the Way of Holiness   Is35
clear boulders to build a highway   Is62
crossroads, do not wait at the   Ob1
  stop at the   Je6
  wisdom stands at the   Ob1
guide them, he shall   Is49
guides lead you astray   Is3
heaps, make thee high   Je31
highway across the desert   Is40
  between Egypt and Assyria   Is19
  build a   Is62
  build up a   Is57
  called the Way of Holiness   Is35
  deserted   Is33
  embankments for the   Is49
  forks, signposted   E21
  the road of the diligent   Pro15
king's highway, we will keep to the   Nu20, 21
main road, we will keep to the   Nu20
path, a level   Ps27
  a tangle of weeds   Pro15
  before me, my messengers to clear a   Ma3
  drink from the torrent beside the   Ps110
  every hill a   Is49
  feet go downwards on the   Pro5
  in the barren desert   Is43

33 ROADS, PATHS AND WAYS

path in the great waters   Ps77
  make sure of the   Je31
  of life   Ps16
  of the sluggard   Pro15
  of thy instruction   Ps119
  prescribed in thy laws   Is26
  shall turn slippery beneath their feet   Je23
  strayed from thy   Ps44
  to death   Pro5
  which no fowl knoweth   Job28
  will be smooth   Je31
  you should take, confused the   Is3
paths drop fatness, thy   Ps65
  familiar with all   Ps139
  look for the ancient   Je6
  known to me, make thy   Ps25
  teach me thy   Ps25
  the ancient ways   Je18
  they do not know   Is42
  they stumble in their   Je18
pilgrimage, a night of sacred   Is30
pilgrims, line of   Ps84
pilgrim's way   Is35
road, if you stray from the   Is30
  lead you back along the   Is37
  make sure of the   Je31
  of no return   Job16
  of the diligent   Pro15
  prepare for my people a   Is62
  start on the right   Pro22
  watch the   Na2
roads, no traveller treads the   Is33
  straighten their twisting   Is42
  they take to unmade   Je18
roadway for passers-by   Is51
signpost, carved   E21
  set up   Je31
streets, we avoid the public   La4
track, clear the   Is57
trackless waste, wandering in a   Ps107
way, build cairns to mark your   Je31

33 ROADS, PATHS AND WAYS

way, dark and slippery   Ps35
  follow it, this is the   Is30
  he made the   Job28
  I lead blind men on their   Is42
  is in the sea, thy   Ps77
  make straight my   Ps5
  misses his   Pro19
  no bird of prey knows the   Job28
  of holiness   Is35
  teach me thy   Ps86
  that leads to good   Je6
  to it, no man knows the   Job28
  wandering in the trackless   Ps107
  where is the   Je6
ways are not your ways, my   Is55
  directed to keep thy statutes   Ps119
  they stumble in the ancient   Je18
waymarks, set up   Je31

NEW TESTAMENT

ends of the earth, away to the   A1
falsifying the straight ways of the Lord   A13
footpath, seed sown along the   Mw13; Mk4; L8
Gentile lands, do not take the road to   Mw10
highway, sat by the   Mk10
  the Lord's   J1
highways, go out on to the   L14
journeys in the dark, he who   J12
make straight the way of the Lord   J1
path, clear a straight   Mw3
  of life, set our feet upon the new   PR6
  some seed fell on the   Mw13; Mk4; L8
paths for your feet, make straight   LH12
  make straight   Mw3; L3
  ruin and misery lie along their   PR3
perdition, on the way to   PCS4
pilgrimage, been to Jerusalem on a   A8
road, abandoned the straight   LPS2

33 ROADS, PATHS AND WAYS

road carpeted with their cloaks   Mk11; L19
  that leads to Gaza   A8
  that leads to life is narrow   Mw7
  the desert   A8
  to Assos, Paul took the   A20
  to Damascus   A9, 22
  to Gentile lands   Mw10
  to Jerusalem   A8, 21
Straight Street, Damascus   A9
way, appointed   L22
  for the Lord, prepare a   Mw3; L3
  forerunner to prepare his   L1
  God himself directs our   ThF3
  I am the   J14
  into the holiest of all   LH9
  narrow is the   Mw7
  not yet made manifest   LH9
  of peace, have they not known   PR3
  of the Lord, make straight the   J1
  that leads to destruction   Mw7
  to perdition   PCS4
  to ruin, those on their   PCF1
  to salvation, those on their   PCF1
ways of the Lord, falsifying the straight   A13
  shall be made smooth, rugged   L3
wayside, some seed fell by the   L8

34 *Rulers, Judges and Lawgivers*

OLD TESTAMENT

annals of Solomon   KF11
  of the kings of Israel   KF15f, 22; KS1, 10, 13ff
  of the kings of Judah   KF15, 22; KS8, 12ff, 20ff
  of the kings of Judah and Israel   CS20, 24f, 27f, 32, 35ff
anoints you prince over Israel, the Lord   SF10
bodyguard, king's   KS25; Je52
canopy, throne   Je43
chapel, the king's   Am7
child king Amon   KS21
    Azariah   KS15
    Joash   KS12
    Josiah   KS22
consort, queen   Ne2
coronet   Is3; E16
counsellor, David's   SS15
court, Bethel is the king's   Am7
  new, of Jehoshaphat   CS20
courtiers   Je36
  retinue of   Je22
crown   SS1, 12; KS11; Ps21, 132; Ls62
  golden   Est7; Ps21
  jewelled   Z9
  lay aside your   E21
  prince Abijah   CS11
  put on Joash's head   KS11
  Queen Vashti's   Est1
  royal Persian and Median   Est1ff, 6
cupbearer, the king's   Ne2
deputy, king's   Je36
diadem   Is28; E21
  kingly   Is62
effigies of kings in the temple   E43
inner court, royal   Est4

34 RULERS, JUDGES AND LAWGIVERS

judge over Israel, Abdon Ju12
   Abimelech Ju8ff; SS11
   Barak Ju4; SF9
   Ehud Ju3; CF7ff
   Eli SF1ff, 14; KF2
   Elon Ju12
   Gideon Ju6ff
   Hoshea, Joshua Ex17, 24; Nu13, 26, 32; De3, 31; Ju2; Jos1ff; KF16; KS23; CF7; Ne8
   Ibzan Ju12
   Jair Ju10; CF2
   Jephthah Ju11f; SF12
   Joshua, Hoshea Ex17, 24; Nu13, 26; 32; De3, 31; Ju2; Jos1ff; KF16; KS23; CF7; Ne8
   Othniel Jos15; Ju1, 3; CF4, 27
   Samson Ju13ff; SF12
     sons of, appointed SF8
   Tola Ju10; CF7
judgement of Solomon KF3
judges appointed by Jehoshaphat CS19
king Abijah of Judah KF14; CS11, 13, 29
  Abijam of Judah KF14
  Abimelech of Gerar Gen20f, 26
    the judge was declared Ju9
  Ahab of Israel KF16ff; KS3, 8ff, 21; CS18, 21ff; Mi6
  Ahasuerus, Xerxes I of Persia Ez4; Est1
  Ahaz of Judah KS15ff; CF3, 8ff; CS27ff; Is1, 7, 14, 38; Ho1; Mi1
  Ahaziah of Israel KF22
    of Judah KS1, 8ff; CF3; CS20ff
  Amaziah of Judah KS12ff; CF3ff; CS24
  Amon of Judah KF22; KS21; CF3; CS18, 33; Ne7; Je1, 25; Zp1
  Arioch of Ellasar Gen14
  Artaxerxes of Persia Ez4ff; Ne2, 5, 13
  Asa of Judah KF15; CF3, 9; CS14, 20ff; Je41
  Azariah, Uzziah, of Judah KS14f; CS26ff; Is1, 6ff; Ho1; Am1; Z14
  Baalis of Ammon Je40
  Baasha of Israel KF15, 21; KS9; CS16; Je41
  Baladan of Babylon KS20; Is39
  Balak of Moab Nu22; Jos24; Ju11; Mi6

34 RULERS, JUDGES AND LAWGIVERS

king Bela of Edom   Gen36
 Belshazzar of Babylon   D5, 7
 Ben-hadad of Syria   KF15, 20; KS6, 8, 13; CS16; Am1
 bombast, give Pharaoh the title   Je46
 Chushan-rishathaim of Aram-naharaim   Ju3
 Cyrus of Persia   CS36; Ez1, 3; Is44; D1, 6, 10
 Darius of Persia   Ez4ff; Ne12; D5ff, 9, 11; Hg1ff; Z1, 7
   made king of the Chaldaeans   D5
 David of the Israelites   Ru4; SF16ff, 29; SS1ff; KF1ff, 8, 11;
     KS8, 11, 14, 17ff; CF2ff, 6, 9ff, 12; CS1ff; Ez3, 8; Ne12;
     Pro1; Ec1; So4; Is7, 9, 16, 22, 29, 37ff, 55; Je13, 17, 21ff,
     Je30, 33, 36; E34, 37; Ho3; Am6, 9; Z12ff
 Eglon of Moab   Ju3
 Elah of Israel   KF4, 16; KS15, 17ff; CF1, 4, 9
 Eliakim, Jehoiakim, of Judah   KS18, 23; CS36; Ne12;   Is22, 36
 Esarhaddon of Assyria   KS19; Ez4; Is37
 Evil-merodach, Ewil-marduk, of Babylon   KS25; Je52
 Hazael of Syria   KF19; KS8ff; CS22; Am1
   anoint to be king of Aram   KF19
 Hezekiah of Judah   KS16ff; CF3ff;CS28ff; Pro25; Is1, 36f, 39;
     Je15, 26; Ho1; Mi1; Zp1
 Hiram, Huram, of Tyre   SS5; KF5, 9ff; CF14; CS2f, 8
 Hophra, Pharaoh   Je44
 Hoshea of Israel   KS15ff
 Ishbosheth of Israel   SS2ff, 23
 Jabin of Canaan   Ju4; SF12; Ps83
 Jareb of Assyria   Ho5, 10
 Jeconiah of Judah   Est2
 Jehoahaz of Israel   KS13ff; CS25
   of Judah   KS23; CS21, 36
 Jehoash of Israel   KS13ff; CS25; Ho1; Am1
 Jehoiachin of Judah   KS24ff; CS36; Je52; E1
 Jehoiakim, Eliakim, of Judah   KS23; CF3; CS36; Je1, 22, 24;
     Je26, 35ff, 45ff, 52; D1
 Jehoram, Joram, of Israel   KS1, 3, 8; CS22
   of Judah   KF15, 22
 Jehoshaphat of Judah   KF15, 22; KS1, 3, 8; CF3; CS17, 19ff
 Jehu of Israel   KF19; KS9f, 13ff; CF2; CS22, 25; Ho1
 Jeroboam I of Israel   KF12ff, 21f; KS3, 9f, 23; CS10
   II of Israel   KS14f; CF5; Ho1; Am1, 7

34 RULERS, JUDGES AND LAWGIVERS

king Joash of Judah   KS11ff; CF3ff, 25; CS18, 23ff
   Joram, Jehoram, of Israel   KS1, 3, 8; CS22
     of Judah   KF15, 22
   Josiah of Judah   KF13; KS21, 23; CS33ff; Je1, 3, 22, 25ff, 35f, 46; Zp1
   Jotham of Judah   KS15; CF3, 5; CS26ff; Is1, 7; Ho1; Mi1
   Maacah of Gath   KF2
   Manasseh of Judah   KS20f; CF3; CS32ff; Je15
   Mattaniah, Zedekiah, of Judah   KS24
   Menahem of Israel   KS15
   Nadab of Israel   KF15
   Nebuchadnezzar, Nebuchadrezzar, of Babylon   KS24; CF6; CS36; Ez1, 5; Ne7; Est2; D1ff; Je21f, 24, 27ff, 32, 34, 37, 39, 43f, 46, Je49, 51ff; E26, 29ff
   Necho, Pharaoh   KS23; CS35ff; Je46
   Omri of Israel   KF16
   Og of Bashan   Nu21; De3, 29ff; Jos2, 9, 12ff; KF4; Ne9; Ps135f
   Pekah of Israel   KS15
   Pekahiah of Israel   KS15
   Pul of Assyria   KS15; CF5
   Reheboam of Judah   KF11; CF3; CS9ff
   Rezin of Aram   KS15ff; Az2; Ne7; Is7ff
   Sargon of Assyria   Is20
   Saul of Edom   Gen36; CF1
     of Israel   SF9ff, 18; SS1ff, 16; CF5, 8ff, 12, 26; Is10
   Sennacherib of Assyria   KS18ff; CS32; Is36ff
   Shallum of Israel   KS15; Je22
   Sihon of the Amorites   Nu21; De1ff, 29ff; Jos2, 9, 12; Ju11; KF4; Ps135f
   Solomon of the Israelites   SS5, 12; KF1ff; KS21, 23; CF3, 6, 14, CF18, 22, 28ff; Ez2; Ne7, 12ff; CS1ff, 10ff, 13, 30, 33ff; Pro1; So1, 3, 8; Je52
   Tirhakah of Cush   KS19; Is37
   Uzziah, Azariah, of Judah   KS14f; CS26ff; Is1, 6ff; Ho1; Am1; Z14
   Xerxes I, Ahasuerus, of Persia   Ez4
   Zechariah of Israel   KS14ff, 18
   Zedekiah, Mattaniah, of Judah   KS24; CS36; Is1, 21, 24, 27, Is29; Je32, 34, 37ff, 44, 49, 51ff
   Zimri of Israel   KF16

34 RULERS, JUDGES AND LAWGIVERS

kingdom with 127 provinces of Persia and Media   Est1, 8
kingdoms of the earth in Daniel's vision   D8
king's advisers   Ne11; Est1
  appointment of   De17
  forest, keeper of   Ne2
  friend   KF4
  garden   Ne3; Je39, 52
  house   Ne3
  laws for Israeli   De17
  of Arabia, tribute of   KF10
  of Midian, capture of   Ju8
  shall present their tribute   Ps72
  table, Mephibosheth had a place at   SS9
law and justice, David maintained   SS8
  of Moses   De27; Jos23; KF2, 8; KS23; CS23; Ez3, 7; Ne8; Ps93, 119; Pro28
laws for Israeli kings   De17
Moses   Ex2ff; Le1ff; Nu1ff; De1ff; Jos1ff; 13, 24; Ju18; SF12; KF8; KS14, 18, 23; CF6, 23, 26; CS23, 25, 33ff; Ez3, 6ff; Ne1, 8ff; Ps77, 99, 103, 106; Is63; Je15; D9; Ma4
palace, Babylonian royal   D4
  in Ashdod   Am3
  in Egypt   Am3
  ivory   Ps45
  of Benhadad   Am1
  of Bozrah   Am1
  of Gaza   Am1
  of Jerusalem   Ne2; Am2
  of Kerioth   Am2
  of Solomon   CS2
  of Tyre   Am1
  Pharaoh's   Je43
  royal   KF16; Am7
Pharaoh   Gen12ff; De11; SF2; KF3, 9, 11; KS17ff, 23; CF4; Ps135ff; So1; Is19, 30, 36; E17, 29f; Je25, 37, 43f, 46ff
  called king bombast   Je46
  the great dragon   E29
pretender to the throne, Adonijah   KF1
prince, appoint Saul   SF9
  Jotham made regent   KS15

34 RULERS, JUDGES AND LAWGIVERS

prince, royal   Je36
princes of Canaan   Ps135
  of Midian captured   Ju7
  of Persia to advise the king   Est1
  of the Philistines, five   SF6
  of Zoan   Is19
provinces under Persian rule   Est1
queen Athalia of Judah   KS8, 11; CF8; CS22ff
  Esther proclaimed   Est2
  mother   Je13, 29
    Hamutal   KS23ff; Je52
    Maacah   CS13
  of Sheba   KF10; CS9
  Vashti of Persia   Est1
regency of Jotham for Azariah   KS15
regent   CS26
reigned, Abijam, 3 years   KF15
  Ahab, 22 years   KF16
  Ahaz, 16 years   KS16; CS28
  Ahaziah of Israel, 2 years   KF22
    of Judah, 1 year   KS8; CS22
  Amaziah, 29 years   KS14; CS25
  Amon, 2 years   KS21; CS33
  Asa, 41 years   KF15
  Athaliah, 7 years   KS11
  Azariah, 52 years   KS15
  Baasha, 24 years   KF15
  David, 40 years over Israel   SS5; KF2; CF29
    7½ years over Judah   SS2
  Elah, 2 years   KF16
  Hezekiah, 29 years   KS18; CS29
  Hoshea, 9 years   KS17
  Ishbosheth, 2 years   SS2
  Jehoahaz, 17 years over Israel   KS13
    3 months over Judah   KS23; CS36
  Jehoiachin, 3 months   KS24; CS36
  Jehoiakim, 11 years   KS23; CS36
  Jehoram, 12 years   KS3
  Jehoshaphat, 25 years   KF22
  Jehu, 28 years   KS10
  Jeroboam I, 22 years   KF14

34 RULERS, JUDGES AND LAWGIVERS

  reigned, Jeroboam II, 41 years   Ks14
    Joash, 40 years   KS12; CS24
    Joram, 8 years   KS8; CS21
    Josiah, 31 years   KS22; CS34
    Jotham, 16 years   KS15; CS27
    Manasseh, 55 years   KS21; CS33
    Menahem, 10 years   KS15
    Nadab, 2 years   KF15
    Omri, 12 years   KF16
    Pekah, 20 years   KS15
    Pekahiah, 2 years   KS15
    Reheboam, 17 years   KF14; CS12
    Saul, 22 years   SF13
    Shallum, 1 month   KS15
    Solomon, 40 years   KF11; CS9
    Uzziah, 52 years   CS26
    Zechariah, 11 years   KS15
    Zedekiah, 11 years   KS24; CS36; Je52
    Zimri, 7 days   KF16
  robe, royal   KF22; CS18; Est5f
  royal children beheaded, seventy   KS10
    palace burnt   Je39, 52
    pavilion   Je43
  sanctuary, king's   Am7
  sceptre   Nu24; Est4; Ps45, 60, 108, 110; Is14; E19
  sea-king   E26
  signet, royal   Est3ff
    of Darius   D6
  throne, royal   KF10, 22; CS18; Ps9, 11, 45, 47, 89, 93, 113, 123, Ps132; Is16, 22; Je43
    canopy of the   Je43
    glorious   Is22
    ivory   KF10
  treasures of the kings of Judah given to their enemies   Je20
  treasuries of Hezekiah   CS32
    of Nebuchadnezzar   D1
  tributes paid to king Solomon   KF4
  vassal of Nebuchadnezzar, Jehoiakim   KS24
  winter-house of king Jeohoiakim   Je36

34 RULERS, JUDGES AND LAWGIVERS

NEW TESTAMENT

administration, the gift of   PR12
Armageddon, assembled the kings at   Rev16
audience chamber   A25
Caesar   Mw22; Mk12; L2f, 20; J19; A11, 17, 25, 27; PPs4
  Augustus   L2; A25, 28
  Claudius   A11
  I appeal to   A25
Caesar's friend, thou art not   J19
captain, chief   Rev6
    governor's   A25
commissioner, royal   PCS11
council   Mk15; L22; A6, 22f
counsellor, Joseph of Arimathaea an honourable   Mk15
crown, given a   Rev6
  golden   Rev4, 9, 14
  let no one rob you or your   Rev3
crowns, on his head were many   Rev19
decree issued by Emperor Augustus   L2
deputy of Achaia   A18
  of Cyprus   A13
diadems, on his head were many   Rev19
elders, to suffer much from the   Mw16
emperor, appealed to the   A26
  Augustus   L2
  Claudius   A18
  decree issued by the   L2
  had no option but to appeal to the   A28
  I have committed no offence against the   A25
  Roman   Mw22; L20; A27
  Tiberius   L3
emperor's laws, flout the   A17
glory and honour, crowned now with   LH2
gospel of the kingdom   Mw9
government and authority, far above all   PE1
  and the authorities, submissive to the   Tt3
governor   J18; A24; PG3
  deputy   LPF2
  Felix   A23f
  Festus   A26

34 RULERS, JUDGES AND LAWGIVERS

governor of Cyprus   A13
  of Damascus   PCS11
  of Judaea   L3
  of Syria   L2
  out of thee shall come a   Mw2
  Porcius Festus   A24
  Roman   Mw27f; Mk15; L20
governors, brought before the   Mw10
Hail, King of the Jews!   Mw27; J19
headquarters, governor's   Mk15
imperial establishment   PPS4
  guard   PPs1
  majesty, Caesar   A25
inquiry, governor's   A25
invisible orders of thrones, sovereigns, authorities   PCo1
iron rod, rule with an   Rev2, 12, 19
judge and lawgiver, there is only one   LJ4
  is the Lord, my   PCF4
  hand you over to the   Mw5
  not, that ye be not judged   Mw7
  or arbitrate, who set you to   L12
  who cared nothing for God or man   L18
judged, you will not be   Mw7
judgement, convince them of divine   J16
  hall, Herod's   A23
    Pilate's   J18
  pass no   Mw7
  seat of Christ   PCS5
  of Gallio   A18
judges of the twelve tribes of Israel   Mw19; L22
judging your fellow man you judge yourself   PR2
jurisdiction of the governor   L20
justice, integrity, pursue   PTF6; PTS2
king Archelaus succeeded Herod   Mw2
  any man who claims to be, is defying Caesar   J19
  Aretas   PCS11
  but Caesar, we have no   J19
    David   Mw1, 9, 12, 15, 20ff; Mk2, 10ff; L1ff, 6, 18, 20; J7;
        A1f, 4, 7, 13, 15; PR1, 4, 11; PTS2; LH4, 11; Rev3, 5, 22
  Herod Agrippa   A12f, 23, 25f
    The Great   Mw2; L1

350

34 RULERS, JUDGES AND LAWGIVERS

  king is your word. My task is to bear witness to the truth   J18
    meant to seize him and proclaim him   J6
    of all worlds   PTF1
    of Egypt   A7
    of Israel, you are   J1
    of Salem   LH7
    of the Jews   Mw2, 27; Mk15; L23; A18f
    over Israel for ever, he will be   L1
    Saul   A13
    Solomon   Mw1, 6, 12; L11f; J10; A7
    who prepared a feast, there was a   Mw22
  kingdom and glory, called you unto his   ThF2
    announcing the good news of the   Mw9
    divided against itself cannot stand   Mk3; L11
    does not belong to this world, my   J18
    of God, can enter the   J3
      come, when will the   L17
      easier... than for a rich man to enter into the   L18
      everyone who forces his way into the   L16
      finds its fulfilment in the   L22
      for of such is the   L18
      for which you are suffering   ThS1
      he went, proclaiming the good news of the   L8
      is nigh at hand   L21
      is not a matter of talk, but of power   PCF4
      man who looked forward to the   L23
      never come into possession of the   PCF6
      seek ye the   L12
      sent them to proclaim the   L9
      some who will not taste death before they have seen the   L9
      spoke freely about the   A19
      spoke to them about the   L9
      spoke urgently about the   A28
      taught about the   A1
      the least is greater than John in the   L7
      those who will never inherit the   PG5
  of heaven, parable of the   Mw20
    who is greatest in the   Mw18
  of his dear Son   PCo1
  parable of the   Mw20
  preserve me unto his heavenly   PTS4

34 RULERS, JUDGES AND LAWGIVERS

kingdom, your Father has chosen to give you the   L12
kingdoms of the world in all their glory   Mw4
   the devil showed him all the   L4
kings, seven   Rev17
   supplication and prayers to be made for   PTF2
   to eat the flesh of   Rev19
   you will be brought before   Mw10
law of Moses   L2; A13, 15, 24, 28; PR2; PG5; PCF9; PCS3; LH10
   teachers of the   L5
lawgiver and judge, there is only one   LJ4
leader must be above reproach   PTF3
Lord of Sabbaoth   PR9
magistrate, chief   A28
magnates   Rev6
marshals   Rev6
master, neither be ye called, for one is your   Mw23
mediator, there is one   PTF2
monarchs from their thrones, he has brought down   L1
officer in the royal service   J4
officials, Herod's chief   Mk6
Pharaoh   A7; PR9; LH11
potentate, who is the blessed and only   PTF6
powers that ruled the world have never known it   PCF2
prince Herod Antipas   Mw14, 22; Mk3, 6, 8, 12;L3, 8, 13, 23; A4
   Lysanias   L3
   of Abilene   L3
   of Galilee   L3
   of Ituraea   L3
   of the kings of the earth   Rev1
   of this world   J14, 16
   of Trachonitis   L3
   Philip   L3
principalities and powers, far above all   PE1
   to be subject to   Tt3
proconsul   A18f
queen Candace, Kandake, of Ethiopia   A8
   of the south   Mw12; L11
remitted the case to Herod   L23
rival king, Jesus   A17
rod of iron, rule with a   Rev2

34 RULERS, JUDGES AND LAWGIVERS

rod, shall come unto you with a   PCF4
Roman emperor   Mk12
rostrum, Herod seated on the   A12
royal chamberlain   A12
  house   Rev1
  priesthood   LPF2
  robes   A12
rule my people Israel   Mw2
rulers are not a terror to good works   PR13
Sanhedrin senate   A5
sceptre of justice   :LH1
sergeants, magistrate's   A16
sovereign, submit yourselves to the   LPF2
tetrarch, Herod Antipas   Mw14, 22; Mk3, 6, 8, 12; L3, 8f, 13, 23; A4
  Lysanias   L3
  of Abilene   L3
  of Galilee   L3
  of Ituraea   L3
  Philip   L3
throne, descendant should sit on his   A2
  Herod sat upon his   A12
  in John's vision   Rev20
  of David   L1
tribunal, emperor's   A25

35 *Sacrificial Procedures*

OLD TESTAMENT

altar, acceptable offerings on my   Is60
   blood-spattered   Je19, E6
     I will demolish their   Mi5
   sacrificial   Ps51
anointing oil, rites of   Ex25ff; Le8
aromatic shell, ingredient of sacred oil   Ex30
balsam as an offering   Ex25ff
bless the sacrifice, Samuel must   SF9
bloodshed, expiation for   De21
bread, sacred   SF21
broth, pour over the rock   Ju6
buffaloes, sacrificial   SS6; Am5
bull as Hannah's sacrifice   SF1
bullocks, sacrificial   E43; Ho12
bulls, sacrificial   Ex24, 29ff; Ju6; CF15; CS29, 35; Ez6, 8; E43, 45
burnt offering   SS6; KF8; KS3, 16; CS1ff, 7ff, 13, 24, 29, 31, 35; Ez3, 8; Ne10; Job1, 42; Ps140; Is43; Je17, 33; Am5; Mi6
   all the beasts of Lebanon are not sufficient   Is40
   at Bethel   Ju21
   at Gibeon   KF3
   by Balaam   Ju21
   by Saul   SF13
   in Ezekiel's vision of the temple   E40, 44
   I will not accept   Je14
   human   KS3
   of strangers   Is56
   rites of   Le6ff
   rules for   Nu28ff
   robbery for   Is61
   sick of   Is1
   to foreign gods   KF11

35 SACRIFICIAL PROCEDURES

candlestick, altar   Nu4; KS4; Je52; D5
  gold   Ex25ff
    seven-branched   Z4
consecrated flesh, if a man is carrying   Hg2
corn, offering of   Le2
David, sacrifice by   SS6
drink offering   Ex29ff; KS16; Ez7; E45; Joe1ff
  of David   CF29
  rites of   Le23
  rules regarding   Nu28
evening slaughter for Passover victims   De16
expiation for bloodshed   De21
  for omissions   Nu15
fat offerings   Je11
fire offering   Ez6
  places, temple   E46
fire-pans, sacrificial   KS25
first born of our sons and cattle, we undertake to bring   Ne10
    sacrifice or redemption of   Ex13
  fruit, day of   Nu28ff
    offering of   Nu18
    sacrifice of   De26
firstling, offering of   Nu18
flagon, altar   Ex25ff; Nu4
  gold   Ex25ff
flesh-hooks, sacrificial   Nu4
food-offering   Le1ff; Nu28ff; SF2
  rites of   Le1ff
  rules for   Nu28ff
frankincense   Ex30ff; Ps72; So3ff; Is60; Je6, 17, 41
  barred for sin-offering   Le5
  omitted for offering   Nu5
freewill offering   Le7, 19; Am4
  rites of   Le7
fruit, holy-gift of   Le19
galbanum, ingredient of sacred oil   Ex30
goats, blood of   Is34
  sacrificial   Le3, 16; Nu7; CS29; Ez6ff; Ps50, 66; E43
gold, offering of   Ex25ff
grain-offering   KF8; KS16; CF21, 23; Ez7; Ne10, 13; Is19, 57; Je14, 17, 33, 41; E46; Joe1ff

35 SACRIFICIAL PROCEDURES

grain-offering, Nazirite   Nu6
    of Manoah   Ju13
    rules for   Nu28ff
guilt-offering   KS12; Ez10
    bring no   Ho4
    in Ezekiel's vision of the temple   E40ff
    rites of   Le5ff
gum resin, ingredient of sacred oil   Ex30
harvest offering, rites of   Le23
   thanksgiving   Ex23
heave-offering, not eat of   De12
    rules regarding   Nu18
holy-gift   KS12; Ne10; E36
    for restitution   Nu5
    of fruit   Le19
    rules for   De12
honey, not to be offered   Le2
hooks, sacrificial flesh   E40
horns of the altar   E43
human sacrifice   Ju11; KS3; Ps106; Is57; Je7, 19, 32; E16, 20; Ho13
    son of the Moabite king for   KS3
incense   Ex25ff; KF3, 9; Ps72, 141; So4; Is43; Je17, 41; Ma1
  burn to their fishing nets   H1
  from Sheba   Je6
  offering of   E16
  put before Levi   De33
  they have burned to vanity   Je18
installation-offering, rites of   Le7ff
kid sacrificed by Gideon   Ju6
  by Manoah   Ju13
kitchens, temple   E46
knives for the sacrifice   Ez1
lamb as whole-offering   SF7
lambs, blood of   Is34
  sacrificial   Ex12; Nu28; De16; SF7; CF29; Ez6, 8; E45
laver, basin, brass   KF7; KS16; CS4
leaven, burn your thank-offering without   Am4
libation, dared to pour   Is57
  of blood   Ps16
Lord of Hosts, sacrifice to the   SF1

35 SACRIFICIAL PROCEDURES

meat-offering   Nu7; KF8; KS3, 16; CS7ff; Ne10ff; Je17, 33; Joe1ff; Am5
  in Ezekiel's vision of the temple   E48
myrrh   Ex30ff; So1, 3ff
oblation, I will not accept   Je14
  in Ezekiel's vision of the temple   E48
  offered to Daniel   D2
odour, soothing   Le1; Nu28
offering, burning to their trawls   H1
  dash from his teeth the loathsome   Z9
  defiled   Ma1
  heave   De12
  Nazirite   Nu6
  of grain   Ex29ff
    dared to present   Is57
  of soothing odour   E6
  of yearling calves   Mi6
  laws of   Je6ff
  sacrificial   Jos8
    rules for   De12
  shared   De12
  they make here is defiled, whatever   Hg2
  whole   De12
oil, anointing   E16
  as an offering   Ex25ff
  barred for sin-offering   Le5
  omitted for offering   Nu5
onycha, ingredient of sacred oil   Ex30
peace-offering   Le4; Nu6; SS6; KF8; KS16; CS31; E45; Am5
  at Bethel   Ju21
  at Gilgal   Sf11
protestation, offering of   Nu5
ram as guilt-offering   Ez10
  kidneys of the   Is34
rams, sacrificial   Ex29ff; CF29; CS29; E43, 45
ripe, offering of first   Nu18
sacred bread   SF21
sacrifice acceptable on my altar   Is56
  at David's altar   CF21;
  at hill-shrines   KF3, 22

35 SACRIFICIAL PROCEDURES

sacrifice at Zoheleth   KF1
  beasts enough for a   Is40
  bring there   De12
  by Abram   Gen15
  by Abraham, Abram   Gen15, Gen22
  by Ahaz   KS16
  by Balaam   Nu23
  by David, abundant   CF29
  by Elkanah   SF1
  by Hezekiah   CS29
  by Jacob   Gen31
  by Job for his sons   Job1
  by Job's companions   Job42
  countless, what are they to me?   Is1
  dash from his mouth the blood of   Z9
  do him service with   Is19
  find fault with your   Ps50
  for the morning, bring your   Am4
  great altar not for   Jos22
    of Gog's horde   E39
  human   Ju11; KS3; Ps106; Is57; J7, 19, 32; E16, 20; Ho13
    bones, he will burn   KF13
  I will not accept   Je14
  in Bozrah   Is34
  in the house of the Lord, all who   Z14
  let them kill   Is29
  look with favour on your   Ps20
  Moabites invited to   Nu25
  mourning   Ps5
  of 100 rams   CS29
  of 200 lambs   CS29
  of 33 bulls   CS35
  of 500 bulls   CS35
  of 670 bulls   CS29
  of 700 oxen   CS15
  of 1,000 lambs   CF29
  of 1,000 oxen   CF29
  of 1,000 rams   CF29
  of 2,600 beasts   Cs35
  of 3,000 sheep   CS29
  of 5,000 beasts   CS35

35 SACRIFICIAL PROCEDURES

sacrifice of 7,000 sheep   KF8
  of 20,000 sheep   KF8
  of 30,000 beasts   CS35
  of 120,000 sheep   CS7
  of beasts beyond reckoning   CS5
  of buffalo   SS6; Am5
  of bull by Gideon   Ju6
  of bullocks   E43
    in Gilgal   Ho12
  of bulls   Ex24, 29ff; CF15; CS29, 35; E43, 45; Ez6
    and rams by David   CF15
  of calves   Mi6
  of cattle   Ho5
  of consecration   Ex29ff
  of fatlings   SS6
  of goats   Le3, 16; Nu7; CS29; Ez6ff; Ps50, 66; E43
  of Isaac, intended   Gen22
  of Jephthah's daughter   Ju11
  of kids   E43
    by Gideon   Ju6
    by Manoah   Ju13
  of lambs   Ex12; Nu28; De16; SF7; CF29; CS29; Ez6; E45;
      Ez6, 8
  of miraculous fire   Ju6; CS7
  of oxen   SS6; KF8; CF8, 29; CS7; Ps66
  of Passover   Ex12; CS35
  of rams   Ex29ff; CF15, 29; CS29; E43, 45; Ez6, 8
  of sheep   CS7, 15, 29; KF8; Is1, 43; E36, 46; Ho5
  offer fat beasts as a   Ps66
  offer thee a willing   Ps54
  offered by Saul   SF13
  only to the Lord   KS5
  Passover   CS7, 35
  rules for   Ex29ff; Le1ff; De12
  sailors offered   Jon1
  sheep and oxen past counting   KF8
  sweet-cane   Is43
  the Lord has prepared a   Zp1
  they brought into contempt   SF2
  thou didst desire   Ps40
  to be made to Daniel   D2

35 SACRIFICIAL PROCEDURES

sacrifice to foreign gods   KF11
   to gods   Ps106
   to gold calves   KF12
   to their nets   H1
   use of salt in   E43
sacrificial beasts for rebuilding temple, 12 he-goats   Ez6
      100 bulls   Ez6
      200 rams   Ez6
      400 lambs   Ez6
   for returning exiles, 12 he-goats   Ez8
      12 bulls   Ez8
      72 lambs   Ez8
      96 rams   Ez8
   feast for the beasts and birds   E39
   implements   Je52
   instruments   E40ff
   procedures   E40ff, 43, 46
salt, covenant of   Nu18
   to accompany offerings   Le2
saucer, sacrificial   Nu4; KS25; CS4, 24; Je52
   of incense   Nu7
shared-offering   SS6; KF8; KS16; CS31; E45
    at Gilgal   SF10
    by Saul   SF13
    of buffaloes   Am5
    on Mount Ebal   Jos8
    rites of   Le3ff
sheaf, offering of   Le3ff
shovel, altar   Ex27ff; KS25
silver, offering of   Ex25ff
sin money   KS12
   offering   KS12; CS29; Ez6, 8; Ne10; Ps40; E45
   in Ezekiel's vision of the temple   E40ff
    Levite   Nu8
    Nazirite   Nu6
    rites of   Le4ff
    rules of   Nu8, 28ff
slaughter of sacrificial bull   Ex29ff
    ram   Ex29ff
smoke-offerings   KF9
snuff-dish, altar   Nu4

35 SACRIFICIAL PROCEDURES

snuffer, altar   KS12, 25; CS4; Je52
soothing offerings to be made to Daniel   D2
spoon, altar   KS25; Je52
   gold   Nu7
   of incense   Nu7
stacte, ingredient of sacred oil   Ex20
sweet odours offered to Daniel   D2
table, altar, and implements   Nu4ff
  sacrificial slaughter   E40ff
thanksgiving, offer a sacrifice of   Am4
thank-offerings   Je17
   rites of   Le7
   without leaven, burn your   Am4
trespass money   KS12
  offering in Ezekiel's vision of the temple   E40
   rites if   Le7
tossing bowl   KS12, 25; CS4; Je52
   silver   Ne7
vessels of the Lord   Is52
  pure offering   Is66
victim, Passover   De16
voluntary-offering, rites of   Le7
votive-offering, rites of   Le7
wafer, Nazirite offering   Nu6
washing, ritual   Ex30ff; Le13
whole-offering   Nu28ff; SS6, 24; KF8, 10; KS3, 5, 16;
      CF16, 21, 29; CS1ff, 8, 13, 24, 29, 31, 35; Ez3, 8; Ne10;
      Job1, 42; Ps40; Je7, 14, 17, 33; E45; Mi6
   altar of   CF6
   at Bethel   Ju21
   at Gilgal   SF10
   bring there   De12
   by Saul   SF13
   do not please me   Je6
   in Ezekiel's vision of the temple   E40ff
   Nazirite   Nu6
   of a sucking lamb   SF7
   of cattle   Le1ff
   of David   CF29
   of Jethro   Ex18
   of Manoah   Ju13

35 SACRIFICIAL PROCEDURES

whole-offering of milch-cows   SF6
    of sheep   Is43
    of the first creature to emerge   Ju11
    of the king's son   KS3
    on Mount Ebal   Jos8
    sated with   Is1
wood-offering   Ne1

NEW TESTAMENT

altar, offered his son on the   LJ2
bread of the Presence   LH9
burnt offerings, to love God is far more than any   Mk12
    thou had no pleasure in   LH10
demons, sacrifice to   PCF10
devils, they sacrifice to   PCF10
frankincense, offered him   Mw2
gold, frankincense and myrrh   Mw2
Holy Spirit, sacrifice consecrated by the   PR15
I require mercy, not sacrifice   Mw12
idols, eating the food sacrificed to   PCF8; Rev2
incense, altar of   LH9
   offering   L1
   the prayers of the saints   Rev5
   to offer the   L1
   we are the   L1
   went up with the prayers   Rev8
lambs, slaughtered   Mk14
myrrh, offered him   Mw2
offering, gave himself up as an   PE5
   laid down by Moses, make the   Mw8; Mk1; L5
   of doves and pigeons   L2
offerings cannot give inward perfection   LH9
Passover lambs being slaughtered   Mk14
prayers of God's people, incense the   Rev5
purification, go through the ritual of   A21
sacred bread, David ate the   Mw12; Mk2; L6
sacrifice, accepting a fragrant offering   PPs4
   and offering thou didst not desire   LH10

35 SACRIFICIAL PROCEDURES

    sacrifice if any life-blood is to crown that   PPs2
       managed to prevent the crowd from offering   A14
       needeth not daily to offer up   LH7
       offered up himself as   LH7
       of the lamb in John's vision   Rev12
       Passover   PCF5
       priest of Jupiter about to offer   A14
       spiritual and eternal   LH9
       their share of the   PCF9
       to devils they   PCF10
       whose fragrance is pleasing to God   PE5
       yourselves as a living   PR12
    sacrificed himself for our sins   PG1; PTF2; Tt2
       to idols, food   Rev2
    sacrifices, a pair of turtle doves or two young pigeons   L2
       cannot give inward perfection   LH9
       for sins, to offer   LH5
       heavenly things require better   LH9
       spiritual   LPF2
       that is far more than any   Mk12
       their blood mingled with their   L13
       to demons   PCF10
       which can never remove sins   LH10
    sacrificial bull   LH9f
      calf   LH9
      death, expiating sin by his   PR3
         justified by Christ's   PR5
      goat   LH9f
      heifer   LH9
      meal   PCF10
    self-mortification, people who go in for   PCo2
    shewbread, David ate the   Mw12; Mk2; L6
      in a material sanctuary   LH9
    sin-offering, animals whose blood is a   LH13
        for himself   LH5
    sins, brought about the purgation of   LH1
      of the people, to expiate the   LH2
    slaughtered, Passover victim   L22

36 Servitude and Tribute

OLD TESTAMENT

act of freedom for slaves   Je34
attendants, the king's   Est2ff
awl to pierce a slave's ear   De15
bondage, fulfilled her term of   Is40
bondmen, takes my sons to be   KS4
bonds, I will burst asunder thy   Na1
butler, Pharaoh's   Gen40
captive, 100,000 Hagarites taken   CF5
   comely women taken   De21
   women and children of Ziklag taken   SF30
captives at Babylon   Ez2
   into exile, the train of   Na2
   of the Philistines forty years   Ju13
   proclaim liberty to   Is61
   returned   Ez2
captivity by their enemies, herded into   Am9
   curse of   De28
   for Israelites for eight years   Ju3
   Gilgal shall go into   Am5
   of Jerusalem   Je1ff
capture the girls of Shilon   Ju21
captured, King Zebekiah   KS25
   the kings of Midian   Ju8
   the princes of Midian   Ju7
cell, measurement of   E40
chains, broke their   Ps107
   prison   Ps149
chamberlains, king's   Est1ff
collar, iron   Ps105
concubines, eunuch in charge of the   Est2
covenant of Zedekiah proclaiming freedom for slaves   Je34
dungeon   La3; Z9
ear pierced with an awl, slave's   De15

36 SERVITUDE AND TRIBUTE

enemies as slaves, to serve your   Je17
enslaved, Canaanites of Asher   Jos17
  of Gezer   Jos16
  of Issashar   Jos17
  Gibeonites by Israelites   Jos9
  Israelites   Ex1ff
escape of Moses   Ex2
eunuch   KS8ff, 18, 20. 23ff; CS18; Is56
  chief Assyrian   KS18
    Babylonian   Je39
    Nebuchadnezzar's   D1
  Ebed-melech   Je38
  Ethiopian   Je38
eunuchs in charge of concubines   Est2
  of women   Est2
  of Judah and Jerusalem   Je34
  royal   Est1ff
  the king's   KS24; KF22; CF28
  to give to his   SF8
  your sons shall be made   KS20
fetters of bronze   Ju16
  on his feet   Ps105
forced labour as peaceful option   De20
  decreed by Ahasuerus   Est10
    by Solomon   KF9, CS8
  for all men of Judah   KF15
  for Ammonites   SS12
  for Canaanites by Manasseh   Jos17
    of Gezer   Jos16
  for inhabitants of Aijalon   Ju1
    of Beth-anath   Ju1
    of Beth-shean   Ju1
    of Canaan   Ju1
    of Dor   Ju1
    of Ibleam   Ju1
    of Kitron   Ju1
    of Megido   Ju1
    of Nahalol   Ju1
    of Shaalbim   Ju1
    of Taanach   Ju1
  for Zion   La1

36 SERVITUDE AND TRIBUTE

gift to Jehoshaphat as tribute   CS17
guard house   Je32f, 37, 39
  tower   Je51
handmaid for a daughter of Belial, count not thine   SF1
  Abigail   SF25
  I am Ruth, thine   Ru3
handmaids, free your   Je34
  pour out my spirit on   Joe2
homage, kings shall pay him   Ps72
hostages taken by Jehoash   KS14; CS25
humble servant, Abigail   SF25
imprisoned, Hoshea by Shalmanezer   KS17
iron chains, collars of   Ps107
  collar   Ps105
  prisoners bound in   Ps107
irons, prisoners'   Ps149
levy, forced   SS20
maid and mistress   Is24
maids for Esther   Est2
manservants, let go free   Je34
master and slave   Is24
mistress and slave-girl   Is24
nails, pare the captive women's   De21
oppressed Israel for thirty years, the Philistines   Ju10
    for twenty years, Sisera   Ju4
pit, Joseph thrown into a   Gen37
pledge, persons held in., to be released   Ne10
prison   Ps88
prisoner, Adoni-bezek taken   Ju1
  bound in irons   Ps107
  David taken   SS21
  groaning   Ps102
  Joseph made   Gen39
  king of Judah taken, by the king of Babylon   KS24
  sets free the   Ps146
prisoners released from the dungeon   Z9
  will take many   D11
puppet, is he a mere   Je22
sell the innocent for silver   Am2, 8
  the poor for a pair of shoes   Am2, 8
servant and master   Is24

36 SERVITUDE AND TRIBUTE

servant, Gehazi   KS4
  honoureth his master   Ma1
  little captive girl   KS5
  of Saul's family   SS8
  Ruth, I am your   Ru3
servants, a spoil to their   Z2
  born in my house   Ec2
  have ruled over us   La5
  pour my spirit upon   Joe2
  slave-girls of   SS6
  will be wicked   Pro29
service in the court of Nebuchadnezzar, young men for   D1
shave captive woman's head   De21
slave, an Egyptian   SF30
  chop wood as a   Jos9
  do not force to surrender a   De23
  draw water as a   Jos9
  eyes of a   Ps123
  freed in seventh year   De15
  goes in fear of his master   Ma1
  I will not be your   Je2
  Joseph as a   Gen37ff
  of slaves   Gen9
  pamper a   Pro29
  pierce the ear of, with an awl   De15
  to command, I am his   SF25
  Tobiah an Ammonite   Ne2
slave-girl, brought back a little   KS5
    displacing her mistress   Pro30
    eyes of a   Ps123
    intercourse with a   Le19
    not treat me as a   Ru2
    of servants   SS6
    Sarai's   Gen46
    the sons of Gideon's   Ju8ff
slave-girls carried off   Na2
    pour out my spirit upon   Joe2
slave-mark, setting a   Job13
slavery, Gibeonites held in   Jos9
  I ransomed you from a land of   Mi6
  sold into   Ps105

36 SERVITUDE AND TRIBUTE

slavery, those who had been freed forced back into   Je34
   was he born in   Je2
slaves, a creditor has come to take my boys as   KS4
   a large number owned by Job   Job1
   a plunder for   Z2
   become rulers   La5
   both men and women, he will seize   SF8
   commerce in   E27
   covenant to proclaim freedom for Hebrew   Je34
   for six years   Ex21
   gift of land to   E46
   Hebrew, to be set free   Je34
   import of   E27
   Israelite   Ex1; Ez2
   male and female, I bought   Ec2
   pour out my spirit upon   Joe2
   ran away   KF2
   redemption of   Le25
   released   Ex21
   rights of   Ex21; Le22, 25
   shall be your   Is45
   to serve your enemies as   Je17
   you may buy   KS5
sold to the king of Aram-naharaim, the Israelites were   Ju3
   to Jabin the Canaanite king, the Israelites were   Ju4
subjection of Israelites to Cusham-rishathaim   Ju3
      to Eglon king of Moab   Ju3
      to Jabin   Ju4
      to Midian   Ju6
      to the king of Aram-naharaim   Ju3
   of Moab to Israel   Ju3
taken prisoner, 200,000 women and children   CS28
taxes, a raiser of   D11
tribute, an officer to extort   D11
   Aramaeans paid to David   CF18
   by Aramaeans   SS8
   Ehud send to pay   Ju3
   from Egypt   Ps68
   Judah put to   KS23
   kings shall present their   Ps72
   Moabites paid   SS8

36 SERVITUDE AND TRIBUTE

  tribute of kings of Arabia   KF10
    of oil to Egypt   Ho12
    paid to Solomon   KF4
  tributary, Hoshea of Assyria   KS17
    the city became a   La1
  tyrants brought low   Ps107
  vassal kingdoms of Babylon   Je34
    kings of Hadadezer   SS10
    of Nebuchadnezzar, Jehoikim   KS24
  whore, barter a boy for a   Joe3
  wives taken in battle   Ju21
  yoke, break the bars of their   E34
    lifted on my neck, his   La1
    is on our necks   La5

NEW TESTAMENT

  allegiance to the Son of God, those who give their   LJF5
  bind you fast, a stranger will   J21
  bond nor free, there is neither, for ye are all one   PG3
  bondage, if a man brings you into   PCS11
    to any man, we were never in   J8
    wanted to bring us into   PG2
  bondmaid   PG4
  bonds, an ambassador in   PE6
  bondwoman   PG4
  branded, caused everyone to be   Rev13
  captive, shall be led away   L21
  captives in Christ's triumphal procession   PCS2
    in his train, he ascended with   PE4
  captivity, my comrades in   PR16
  cargoes of slaves   Rev18
  chains, for the sake of the hope of Israel, I am in   A28
  eunuch, an Ethiopian   A8
  fellow-servant, I am but a   Rev19
  free man, I am not a   PCF9
    men, live as   LPF2
  freedman, the Lord's   PCF7
  handmaiden, regarded the lowliness of his   L1

36 SERVITUDE AND TRIBUTE

homage, if you fall down and do me   Mw4
   to the Lord your God   Mw4
maid answered his knock   A12
   said to Peter   J18
master in heaven, you both have the same   PE6
   sin shall no longer by   PR6
   standeth or falleth by his own, a servant   PR14
masters, be just and fair to your slaves   PCo4
   give up using threats   PE6
   no man can serve two   Mw6; L16
minister, let him who would be great be your   Mw20
pay Caesar what is due to Caesar   L20
prisoner of Jesus Christ   PE3f; Ph1
   of the Lord   PTS1
   whoever is made to be   Rev13
prisoners, to proclaim release for   L4
ransom for many, to give up his life as a   Mw20
registration throughout the Roman world   L2
servant and apostle of Jesus Christ   LPS1
   another man's   PR14
   called in the Lord   PCF7
   cannot serve two masters   Mw6; L16
   centurion had a   L7
   doth he thank that   L17
   God raised up his   A3
   he that is greatest among you shall be your   Mw23
   his discharge in peace, thou givest thy   L2
   I am the Lord's   L1
   ill and near death   L7
   is not greater than his master   J13
   Israel, he hath holpen his   L1
   Jesus thy holy   A4
   judgest another man's   PR14
   not now as a   Ph1
   now lettest thou thy, depart in peace   L2
   of all, he must make himself   Mk9
   of God   LJ1; Rev15
   of Jesus Christ, a good   PTF4
      I should be no   PG1
      Jude   LJu1
      Paul   PR1

36 SERVITUDE AND TRIBUTE

servant of Jesus Christ, who shows himself a   PR14
  of sin, whoever commits sin is a   J8
  of the high priest   Mk14; L22; J18
  of the Jewish people   PR15
  one of my father's paid   L15
  sent to the tenants   Mk12
  suppose one of you has a   L17
  the chief of you like a   L22
  to pass judgement on someone else's   PR14
  to the younger, the elder shall be   PR9
  took upon him the form of a   PPs2
  unto all, made myself   PCF9
  who is the trusty   Mw24
  whoever wants to be great must be your   Mw20; Mk10
  will be cured, say the word and my   L7
  with a message, sent a   L14
servants, accept the authority of your masters   LPF2
  and handmaidens, pour out my spirit on   A2
  at the wedding   J2
  be obedient to your masters   PE6
  called his ten   L19
  gave authority to his   Mk13
  land owner's   Mw21
  met him with the news   J4
  no longer, I call you   J15
  obey in all things your masters   PCo3
  of Christ   PE6
  of the living God   ThF1
  of the supreme God   A16
  of the vineyard owner   L20
  seal the foreheads of his   Rev7
  to be obedient, exhort   Tt2
  to one another in love, be   PG5
  treat me as one of your paid   L15
  under the yoke   PTF6
  whom the master finds alert   L12
serve, Son of Man did not come to be served but to   Mw20; Mk10
  the Lord in ardour of spirit   PR12
service, brothers in Christ's   Rev6
serving-maid, high priest's   Mw26; Mk14; L22
servitude for fear of death   LH2

36 SERVITUDE AND TRIBUTE

slave, Abraham's   PG4
  and freeman, no question here of   PG3; PCo3
  assuming the nature of a   PPs2
  everyone who commits sin is a   J8
  girl who was possessed by an oracular spirit   A16
  in the service of Christ   PCF7
  no longer, but as a son   PG4; Ph1
  of all, must be the willing   Mw20; Mk10
  of two masters, no servant can be   L16
  to the law of sin   PR6f
  when you were called   PCF7
  who commits sin is a   J8
  woman's son born by the course of nature   PG4
slavery, all who wear the yoke of   PTF6
  sold Joseph into   A7
  we have never been in   J8
  woman bearing children into   PG4
slaves, cargoes of   Rev18
  endue with a portion of my spirit   A2
  give obedience to your masters   PCo3
  in God's service   LPF2
  masters, be just and fair to your   PCo4
  not to answer back   Tt2
  obey your earthly masters with fear and trembling   PE6
  of beings which are no gods   PG4
  of Christ   PE6; PCo3
  of corruption, themselves   LPS2
  of righteousness   PR6
  or freemen, whether   PCF12
  to elemental spirits   PG4
  to passions and pleasures   Tt3
  to respect their master   Tt2
steward at the wedding   J2
  to manage his servants   L12
submission, his prayer was heard because of humble   LH5
submit to every institution   LPF2
tax and toll, pay   PR13
  to the Roman emperor   Mk12
taxed, all went to be, each into his own city   L2
  the world to be   L2
taxing, days of the   A5

36 SERVITUDE AND TRIBUTE

taxes, Roman   Mw22; L20
   superintendent of   L19
   this is why you pay   PR13
   to Caesar, opposing the payment of   L23
tenants, vineyard   Mk12
tithe, Abraham gave Melchizedek a   L23
   the people, Levites commanded to   LH7
tithes of every garden herb   L11
   of mint and dill and cummin   Mw23
      and rue   L11
   on all I get, I pay   L18
tribute, does your master pay   Mw17
   to Caesar, is it lawful for us to give   Mw22; Mk12; L20
votive offerings adorn the temple   L21
wait at table   A6
wash his disciples' feet   J13
yoke, bend your neck to my   Mw11
   of slavery   PTF6

37 Sex and Marriage

OLD TESTAMENT

abused her all night   Ju19
adorn yourself like a bride   Is49
adulterer   Is57; Ma3
adulterers are they all   Je9
  the land is full of   Je23
adulteress   Pro2, 5, 7
  loved by another man   Ho3
adulteries, I have seen thins   Je13
adultery   Pro2, 5ff, 22; Je5; E23
  and licence, there is nothing but   Ho4
  do not commit   De5
  on trial for   E16
  penalty for   Le20
  religious   E23
  wife suspected of   Nu5
afterbirth, will eat her own   De28
Aholah, Oholah: Samaria, personification of religious adultery   E23
Aholibah, Oholibah: Jerusalem, personification of religious adultery
     E23
barren, but you shall conceive   Ju13
  made to bear   Ps113
  woman who never bore a child   Is54
  womb never satisfied   Pro30
betroth you to myself forever   Ho2
body, bless the fruit of your   De7
bower, bid the bride leave her   Joe2
bride   Is61ff; Joe2
bridegroom   Ps19; Is61ff; Joe2
  and bride, banish the voice of   Je7
    voice of   Je33
    voices of silenced   Je25
brothel   Je5
canopy, wedding   Ps19
childbirth, death in   Gen35

37 SEX AND MARRIAGE

childbirth, pangs of   Je49
  purification following   Le12
  spirit of a woman in   Je48
  writhing like a woman in   Mi4
conceived, Bathsheba   SS11
  the woman of Shunem   KS4
concubine, Abram's   Gen16
  Gideon's   Ju8
  his, he thrust out to be raped   Ju19
  Saul's, accusations concerning   SS3
  the Levite's   Ju19
concubines, Belshazzar's   D5
  David took more   SS5
  eunuch in charge of the   Est2
  have intercourse with your father's   SS16
  left in charge of the palace   SS15, 20
  Reheboam had sixty   CS11
  Solomon had 300   KF11
courtesan's, Belshazzar's   D5
daughter as Solomon's wife, Pharaoh's   CS8
David and Jonathan, surpassing love   SS1
discharge, bodily   Le15
divorce, foreign wives   Ez10
  note of   De24
  overwhelming cruelty   Ma2
embrace, a time to   Ec3
father and son resort to the same girl   Am2
foreign women, led into sin by   Ne13
fornication, countless acts of   Is57
  overwhelmed her with their   E23
  with male images   E16
  you committed   E16
foster-father   Is49
fruit of your body, bless the   De7
genitals, catches hold of a man's   De25
harem   Je29
harlot, became an   Is1
  fee of a   Mi1
  Israel seen as a   E16
  playing the   Je22ff; E16
  poor forgotten   Is23

37 SEX AND MARRIAGE

harlot, Rahab the   Jos6
  spawn of an adulterer and a   Is57
  thy wife shall be a   Am7
  who keeps company with   Pro29
  whoredoms of the well favoured   Na3
  with the attire of an   Pro7
  your wife shall be a   Am7
harlots came to Solomon for judgement   KF3
harlots' houses   Je5
harlotry, fees for   Mi1
husband, bloody   Ex4
  thou shalt call me   Ho2
incest, forbidden   Le18
intercourse, bring out the man for us to have   Ju19
  David with Bathsheba   SS11
  forbidden with blood relations   Le18
  Israelite men with Moabite women   Nu25
  purification following   Le15
  while still being purified   SS11
  with a slave-girl   Le19
  with your father's concubines   SS16
Ishi, my husband, thou shalt call me   Ho2
labour, anguish of a woman in   Mi4
  pangs of   Is21
  writhing like a woman in   Mi4
lewd conduct, pay the penalty for your   E23
lewdness, penalties for   Le20ff
  your, brought this upon you   E23
licence, city whose name is   Je6
loose woman   Pro2, 5, 7
love, a time to   Ec3
  of women, surpassing the   SS1
  turned to hate   SS13
loved and unloved, first born of wives   De21
  many strange women, Solomon   KF11
lust from boyhood, schooled in   Z13
  image of   E8
man, bring out the   Ju19
marriage, David's   SF15
  forced   De22
  for priests   Le21

37 SEX AND MARRIAGE

marriage gift, Philistine foreskins   SS3
   the sacked city   KF9
   rules in family   De25
   Ruth and Boaz   Ru4
   to foreigners   Ne10
   with foreign wives, enquired into   Ez10
marry while in exile   Je29
marrying foreign women, reviled for   Ne13
menstruation, intercourse forbidden during   Le18
   purification rules concerning   L12, 15
menstruous cloth, cast away   Is30
   woman   La1
   not to come near   E18
miscarriage or untimely birth   Ps144
   priestly curse of   Nu5
mixed blood, separated all who were of   Ne13
mother of all   Gen3
nursing mothers and fathers   Is49
Oholah, Aholah: Samaria, personification of religious adultery   E23
Oholibah, Aholibah: Jerusalem, personification of religious adultery   E23
orgies, watch their naked   H2
pangs of childbirth have gripped her   Je49
paramours   E23
periods, approaching a woman during her   E18
   purification following   SS11
   seclusion during   E18
privy member cut off   De23
procurers, sent out   Is57
prostitute   Gen38; De23; Pro6ff, 23; E23
   Rahab   Jos2
   son of Gilead by a   Ju11
prostitutes, male   De23; KF14ff, 22; KS23; Job36; E23
   came for judgement   KF3
   common   De23
   Samson went with   Ju16
   temple   Ho4
   washed themselves in Ahab's blood   KF22
rape her as you please   Ju19
   in Zion   La5
   of Tamar by Amnon   SS13

37 SEX AND MARRIAGE

raped, the women of Jerusalem   Z14
ravished, the women of Jerusalem   Z14
seed, emission of   De23
   spilled upon the ground   Gen38
seduction, penalty for   Ex22
semen, discharge of   Le15
sex, flaunting your   Na3
sexual organ, severed   De23
   wrongdoing, penalties for   Ex22
sodomites   KF14ff, 22; KS23
spirited woman, Deborah   Ju4
strumpet, your wife shall become a   Am7
temple-prostitute   Gen38; Ho4
testicles, crushed   De23
   ruptured, debarring from altar   Le21
unfaithful to the wife of your youth   Ma2
unfaithfulness, a wife suspected of   Nu5
vice, sprawled in promiscuous   Je2
virgin bosoms pressed   E23
   wife in sackcloth, wailing over the bridegroom of her youth   Joe1
virginity, proof of   De22
wanton for a wife   Ho1
wedding canopy   Ps19
   present of 100 Philistine foreskins   SS3
wedlock, betroth you in lawful   Ho2
whore in Egypt, played the   E23
  Jerusalem personified as a   E16
  playing the   Is1
  seed of the   Is57
whoredom, children of   Ho1
  Ephraim committed   Ho5
  I have seen the lewdness of thy   Je13
  of Jezebel   KS9
  polluted the land with   Je3
  selleth nations through her   Na3
  with daughters of Moab   Nu25
  woman of   Ho1
whorish woman, Jerusalem an imperious   E16
widow, do not oppress the   Z7
  those who wrong the   Ma3
  Zion personified as a   La1

37 SEX AND MARRIAGE

widows and orphans, justice for   De10, 24
widow's weeds   Is47
wife, deserted   Is54
  for Samson   Ju14
  groomsman given Samson's   Ju14
  of your youth, unfaithful to the   Ma2
  Pharaoh's daughter as Solomon's   CS8
  pledged but not taken   De20
  take a wanton for a   Ho1
wives, Abijah had fourteen   CS13
  David took more   SS5
  foreign, to be dismissed   Ez10
  Gideon had many   Ju8
  in battle, capture of   Ju21
  of offending husbands thrown to the lions   D6
  Reheboam had eighteen   CS11
  Solomon had 700   KF11
woman, Deborah was a spirited   Ju4
  in labour, anguish of   Je6, 50
    cry like a   Is42
    gripping his sides like a   Je30
    pangs of a   Is21; Je13, 22
  taken from man   Gen2
  with child when her time is near   Is26
womb, never satisfied, a barren   Pro30ff
  shall I who deliver close the   Is66
  the Lord had shut up her   SF1
women, blessed above, be Jael   Ju5
  in labour   Je31
  surpassing the love of   SS1
  take for yourself   De20
  with child   Je31
  year's preparation for the royal   Est2

NEW TESTAMENT

adulterers and adulteresses   LJ4
  and sinful generations   Mk8
adultery, anyone who marries a divorced woman commits   Mw5
  defiles the man   Mk7

37 SEX AND MARRIAGE

adultery, do not commit   L18; PR2
  eyes full of   LPS2
  free of the law of   PR7
  if a man divorce his wife he commits   Mw19
  in his heart, he has already committed   Mw5
  none who are guilty of   PCF6
  they were told, do not commit   Mw5
  thou shalt not commit   Mw19; PR13; LJ2
  who marries another commits   Mk10; L16
  woman caught in the act of   J8
allure through lusts of the flesh   LPS2
barren, Elizabeth was   L1
  happy are the   L23
  woman, rejoice   PG4
body's desires, obedience to the   PR6
breast that never fed a child, happy the   L23
bride and bridegroom, voice of the   Rev18
bridegroom   Mw9; Mk2; L5
  to whom the bride belongs   J3
  went out to meet the   Mw25
bridegroom's voice, hears the   J3
brother's wife, you have no right to your   Mk6
carouse in broad daylight   LPS2
celibacy, I have no instructions on   PCF2
celibate woman cares for the Lord's business   PCF7
chaste virgin, present you as a   PCS11
chastity for the sake of the kingdom of heaven   Mw19
conceive, Sarah received strength to   LH11
conceived a child by the Holy Spirit   Mw1
  a son in her old age, Elizabeth   L1
concubine, Abraham's   PG4
concupiscence, evil   PCo3
  in the lust of   ThF4
corruption with which lust has infected the world   LPS1
depraved reason, given them up to their own   PR1
dissipation, do not let your minds be dulled by   L21
divorce for cause other than unchastity   Mw19
  Moses gave you permission to   Mw19
divorcement, bill of   Mk10
  let him give her a writing of   Mw5
  writing of   Mw19

37 SEX AND MARRIAGE

divorces his wife, a man who   Mw5; L16
drunk on the wine of fornication   Rev17
effeminate   PCF6
eunuchs of themselves, they had better make   PG5
  there be some   Mw19
fidelity to their plighted word, they show no   PR1
filthy talk, lay aside all   PCo3
fornication, abstain from   ThF4
  among you, it is reported that there is   PCF5
  and indecency not so much as mentioned   PE5
  being filled with   PR1
  committed   LJu1
  defiles the man   Mk7
  drunk on the wine of   Rev17
  encourage them to commit   Rev2
  impurity and indecency belong to lower nature   PG5
  instruct them to abstain from   A15
  let us not commit   PCF10
  put it to death   PCo3
  refuses to repent of her   Rev2
  repented of the   PCS12
  the wine of her   Rev14, 17
  to abstain from   A21
  we be not born of   J8
fornicator, not to eat with a   PCF5
  or idolater, no   PCF6
  sins against his own body   PCF6
fornicators and adulterers, God's judgement will fall upon   LH13
  outside are   Rev22
  perverts, law is aimed at   PTF1
foul cravings, put to death   PCo3
good deeds as befit religious women   PTF2
harlot   Mw21; PCF6
  Rahab   LH11; LJ2
harlots, devoured their living with   L15
  the mother of   Rev17
homosexual perversion   PCF6
husband, a heathen   PCF7
  cannot claim his body as his own   PCF7
  man you are living with is not your   J4
  must not divorce   PCF7

37 SEX AND MARRIAGE

husband must pay honour to the woman's body   LPF3
husbands at home, let them ask their   PCF14
   love your wives   PE5; PCo3
immorality among you, reports of sexual   PCF5
   because there is so much   PCF7
   such as even pagans do not tolerate   PCF5
indecency defiles the man   Mk7
   put to death   PCo3
inordinate affection, mortify your   PCo3
intercourse, exchange of natural for unnatural   PR1
   with her, until her son was born, he had no   Mw1
lasciviousness defiles the man   Mk7
   repented of the   PCS12
   when we walked in   LPF4
learner, a woman must be a   PTF2
lewd fellows of the baser sort   A17
loving his wife, a man loves himself   PE5
lust conceives and gives birth to sin   LJ1
   has infected the world with corruption   LPS1
   not giving way to   ThF4
   put to death   PCo3
lustful eye, if a man looks on a woman with a   Mw5
lusts, deluded by   Pe4
   denying ungodliness and worldly   Tt2
   flee youthful   PTS3
   follow their abominable   LPS2
      their own godless   LJu1
   of our flesh in times past   PE2
      abstain from the   LPF2
   silly women led away with divers   PTS3
male and female all one person in Christ   PG3
males behave indecently with males   PR1
man is the head of the woman   PE5
marriage bond inviolate   LH13
   contract, Joseph desired to set aside   Mw1
   incapable of   Mw19
   is honourable   LH13
   law, obligations of the   PR7
   Mary and Joseph   Mw1
   nature of   Mk10
   Paul's views on   PCF7

37 SEX AND MARRIAGE

marriage renounced for the sake of the kingdom of heaven   Mw19
  they forbid   PTF4
  young widows hanker after   PTF5
married man cares for worldly things   PCF7
  woman aims to please her husband   PCF7
marry again, young widows should   PTF5
  at the resurrection men and woman do not   Mw22
  found that she was in child by the Holy Spirit   Mw11
  if that is the position, it is better not to   Mw19
  than to burn, better to   PCF7
  the men and women of this world   L20
  when they rise from the dead, they do not   Mk12
  will have pain and grief, those who   PCF7
men burn with lust for one another   PR1
moral law, teachers of   PTF1
morality, observe high standards of   PTF2
mother-in-law, Simon Peter's   Mk1; L4
motherhood, woman will be saved through   PTF2
mother's pangs, who never knew a   PG4
pain and grief, those who marry will have   PCF7
pangs that come upon a woman with child   ThF5
passion, lay aside all   PCo3
passions and pleasures, slaves to   Tt3
perversion, the fitting wage of such   PR1
pregnant cried out to be delivered   Rev12
prostitute, Rahab the   LH11; LJ12
prostitutes are entering the kingdom of God   Mw21
resurrection, whose wife is she at the   Mw22; L20
rules of conduct, leads them to break all   PR1
seducers shall wax worse and worse   PTS3
sensual lusts and debauchery a bait   LPS2
sensuality, very clothing contaminate with   LJu1
sexual immorality, I hear reports of   PCF5
shameful passions, God has given them up to   PR1
twain shall be as one flesh   Mw19; Mk10; PE5
unchastity, divorcing for causes other than   Mw5
  only justification for divorce   Mw19
unmarried, I say to the   PCF7
  man cares for the Lord's business   PCF7
  woman dedicated in body as in spirit   PCF7
vice, abandoned themselves to   PE4

37   SEX AND MARRIAGE

vice, no debauchery or   PR13
virgin, espoused to Joseph   L1
  Mary   Mw1; L1
  to present you as a chaste   PCS11
  will conceive and bear a son   Mw1, 5
virginity, decided to preserve his partner in her   PCF7
virgins, male, 144,000   Rev14
  no commandment concerning   PCF7
  which did prophesy, four   A2
wedding feast   L14
  party   L12
  prepared a feast for his son's   Mw22
  supper   Rev19
whore, Babylon the great   Rev17
  judged the great   Rev19
whoremonger nor unclean person hath inheritance   PE5
  men stealers, law is made for   PTF1
whores, the mother of   Rev17
widow, brother shall marry the   Mw22
  given over to self-indulgence   PTF15
widows, status of   PTF5
  weeds   Rev18
  young, should marry again   PTF5
wife, a heathen   PCF7
  cannot claim her body as her own   PCF7
  faithful to his one   PTF3
  man shall leave his father and mother for his   PE5
  must not separate herself   PCF7
  since seven married her, whose will she be?   Mk12
wives and mothers, loving   Tt2
  be subject to your husbands as to the Lord   PE5; PCo3
  chaste and reverent behaviour of their   LPF3
woman learn in silence with all subjection, let a   PTF2
  must not domineer over man   PTF2
  must pay her husband all respect   PE5
  to be a teacher, I do not permit a   PTF2
  with child, pangs that come upon a   ThF5
  who fell into sin   PTF2
  who was living an immoral life   L7
woman's need is man   PCF11
womb, contemplated the deadness of Sarah's   PR4

37 SEX AND MARRIAGE

wombs that never bore a child, happy are the   L23
women burdened with a sinful past   PTS3
  eyes for nothing but   LPS2
  have exchanged natural intercourse with unnatural   PR1
  men who did not defile themselves with   Rev14
  must accept the authority of their husbands   LPF3
  of high principle, deacon's wives   PTF3
  older, should school the younger   Tt2
  Paul's views on   PCF11, 14
  should not address the meeting   PCF14
  should respect the authority of their husbands   Tt2
  who are with child, alas for   L21

38 *Significant Numbers*

OLD TESTAMENT

2 anointed ones   Z4
2 olive branches   Z4
3 cities in the east   De4
3 daughters, Job had   Job42
3 days and 3 nights Jonah was in the fish's belly   Jon1
    darkness   Ex10
    hid in the hills   Jos2
    journey across Nineveh   Jon3
    neither eat nor drink for   Est4
3 men, appoint as emissaries   Jos18
3 things the earth shakes at   Pro30
    there are which are stately in their stride   Pro30
    there are which are too wonderful for me   Pro30
    there are which will never be satisfied   Pro30
3 times a year, to the Presence   De16
4 chariots in Zechariah's vision   Z6
4 things there are which are smallest on earth yet wise   Pro30
    there are which are stately as they move   Pro30
    there are which I do not understand   Pro30
    there are which never say 'enough'   Pro30
    there are which the earth cannot bear   Pro30
5 cities of Egypt speaking the language of Canaan   Is19
5 lords of the Philistines   Jos13
6 days, circuit Jericho   Jos6
    shalt thou work   Le23
6 men with battle-axes, vision of   E8
6 things the Lord hates   Pro6
6 years, set free a slave who has served you   Je34
7 altars of Balaam   Nu23
7 branched candlestick, lamp-stand   Z4
7 days at the tend of the Presence   Le8
    feast at the royal pavilion   Est1
    I stayed dumbfounded   E3

38 SIGNIFICANT NUMBERS

7 days light in one   Is30
   Nile flowed with blood   Ex7
   pilgrim feast   E45
   purge and purify the altar   E43
   they kept the feast   Ne8
   unleavened cakes   Nu28ff
7 ears of corn   Gen41
7 eunuchs in attendance on the king   Es1
7 eyes in the stone in Zechariah's vision   Z4
7 kine, cows   Gen41
7 locks of Samson's hair   Ju16
7 maids picked for Esther   Est2
7 months Israelites shall bury Gog's dead   E39
7 pillars of wisdom   Pro9
7 priests in front of them   Jos6
7 princes of Persia to advise the king   Est1
7 sons grows faint, mother of   Je15
   Job had   Job42
   of that man, hand over   SS21
7 things are detestable to him   Pro6
7 times a day do I praise thee   Ps119
   his wonted brightness, the sun shall shine with   Is30
   pass over him, let   D4
   punishment   Le26
   seven years   Le25
   sprinkle oil   Le8
   sprinkled blood   Nu19
   the child revived by Elijah sneezed   KS4
   the usual heat of the furnace   D3
   wash in the Jordan   KS5
7 tribes remaining   Jos18
7 trumpets of ram's horn   Jos6
7 weeks pilgrim-feast   De16
7 years famine decreed   KS8
   in the hands of Midian   Ju6
   kindle fires with their discarded weapons   E39
   of famine   Gen41
   read the law every   De31
   set free any Hebrew slave within   Je34
   to build the Temple of Solomon   KF6
sevenfold, turn it back on their own heads   Ps79

38 SIGNIFICANT NUMBERS

seventh day blessed   Gen1
   blow the trumpets   Jos6
   closing ceremony   De6
   of rest   Le23
   of the feast   Ju14
   sabbath   De5
   shall do no work on the   Ex23ff
   the battle was joined   KF20
   the boy died   SS12
  year, slaves freed   De15
9 tribes   Nu34
10 commandments   De4ff, 10
10 horns of the beast in Daniel's vision   D8
10 men from nations of every language   Z8
10 years Judah was at peace under Asa   CS14
12 men, choose   Jos3
12 one from each tribe   De1
12 stones, set up   Jos4
thirteenth day, the lot fell on the   Est3
30 daughters of Ibzan   Ju12
30 pieces of silver, wages in Zechariah's oracle   Z11
30 sons of Ibzan   Ju12
30 sons of Jair   Ju10
30 young men to escort Samson   Ju14
40 days and 40 nights, Elijah in the wilderness   KF19
     Moses was up the mountain   De9
      on Mount Sinai   Ex24
   lie on your right side   E4
   Nineveh shall be overthrown   Jon3
   on the mountain   De10
   presented himself, Goliath   SF17
   rain   Hen7
40 sons of Abdon   Ju12
40 years Egyptian cities shall lie derelict   E29
   I was indignant   Ps95
   in the wilderness   Nu14; Am2, 5
   long thou didst sustain them in the wilderness   Ne9
   long was I grieved with this generation   Ps95
   the land was at peace   Ju3, 5, 8, 12
42 children mauled by bears   KS2
42 kinsmen of Ahajiah murdered   KS10

38 SIGNIFICANT NUMBERS

fiftieth year hallowed   Le25
52 days to rebuild the walls of Jerusalem   Ne6
60 cities, inhabitants of, killed by Moses   De3
   of Bashan allotted   Jos13
70 elders of Jerusalem stood in front of the carved idols   E8
70 kings whose thumbs and toes were cut off   Ju1
70 pilgrims murdered   Je41
70 sons of Gideon   Ju8
70 weeks marked out, then shall sin be brought to an end   D9
70 years has passed over Babylon, when a full   Je29
   I will punish Babylon at the end of   Je25
   is the span of life   Ps90
   Israel lay desolate   CS36
   this country shall be a scandal and a horror for   Je25
   to pass while Jerusalem lay in ruins   D9
   Tyre shall be forgotten   Is23
   vented thy wrath   Z1
80 pilgrims waylaid   Je41
80 years if our strength holds   Ps90
   the land was at peace   Ju3
180 days, royal treasures on display   Est1
190 days, lie on your left side   E4
900 chariots of iron   Ju4
1100 pieces of silver to betray Samson   Ju16
1335 days, happy the man who lives to see the completion of   D12
2000 horses I will give you if you can find riders   Is36
3000 men came to take Samson   Ju16
3000 people killed by Levites   Ex32
10,000 men came to Mount Tabor   Ju4
10.000 people stayed   Ju7
22,000 people went back home   Ju7
120,000 who cannot tell their right hand from their left   Jon4
185,000 Assyrians struck dead overnight   Is37

NEW TESTAMENT

2 fishes and five loaves   Mw14; Mk6; L9; J6
2 horns like a lamb's, a beast which had   Rev13
2 prophets a torment to the whole earth   Rev11

389

38 SIGNIFICANT NUMBERS

second death, this is the   Rev2
3 and six in the morning, between   Mw14; Mk6
3 days and three nights in the bowels of the earth   Mw12
    have been with me   Mk8
    I will raise it up in   J2
    in the sea-monster's belly   Mw12
    later, to rise   Mk8
    they found him sitting in the temple after   L2
    to be raised after   Mw27
    with nothing to eat   Mw15
    without sight, and neither did eat nor drink   A9
3 foul spirits like frogs   Rev16
3 times beaten with rods   PCS11
    I begged the Lord to rid me of it   PCS12
    you will disown me   Mw26
third day, God raised him to life on the   A10
    he shall rise again on the   Mk10; L9; PCF15
   heaven, caught up as far as the   PCS12
   hour they crucified him   Mk15
   of living creatures died   Rev8
   of mankind, four angels let loose to kill a   Rev9
   of rivers and springs poisoned   Rev8
   of the earth was burnt   Rev8
   of the sea turned to blood   Rev8
   of the ships foundered   Rev8
   of the stars flung to earth   Rev12
   of the trees were burnt   Rev8
   part of the sun, moon and stars went dark   Rev8
   time Jesus appeared after his resurrection   J21
3½ days, life came into them after   LJ5
3½ years, no rain fell for   LJ5
    the skies never opened   L4
4 angels held bound at the Euphrates   Rev9
    let loose to kill a third of mankind   Rev9
4 corners of the earth   Rev7
4 days, he has been dead   J11
4 living creatures in front of the heavenly throne   Rev4f, 14f, 19
fourth watch of the night he came walking on the water   Mw14; Mk6
5 foolish virgins   Mw25
5 loaves to feed the five thousand   Mw14, 16; Mk6; L9; J6

38 SIGNIFICANT NUMBERS

5 months, Elizabeth lived in seclusion for   L1
   they were allowed to torment for   Rev9
5 times given me the thirty nine strokes   PCS11
5 wise virgins   Mw25
5 words with my understanding, rather speak   PCF14
6 in the morning, between three and   Mw14; Mk6
6 wings, each of the four creatures had   Rev4
sixth hour, there was darkness over the land from the   Mw27; Mk15; L23
   month, Gabriel was sent from God in the   L1
7 angels that stand in the presence of God   Rev8, 17, 21
   with seven plagues   Rev15
7 baskets filled with left-overs   Mw15; Mk8
7 bowls of God's wrath   Rev16f
   of plagues   Rev21
7 churches in the province of Asia   Rev1
7 days, abode in Troas   A20
7 devils cast out from Mary Magdalene   Mk16; L8
7 diadems on the dragon's head   Rev12
7 emperors   Rev17
7 eyes, the lamb had   Rev5
7 flaming torches   Rev4
7 golden bowls of wrath   Rev15ff
   candlesticks   Rev1f
   lamps   Rev1f
   vials   Rev15ff
7 heads, dragon with   Rev12
   of the scarlet beast   Rev13, 17
7 hills on which the woman sits   Rev17
7 horns, the lamb had   Rev5
7 kings of whom five have fallen   Rev17
7 lamps of fire   Rev4
7 loaves to feed the four thousand   Mw15f; Mk8
7 men to deal with these matters, appoint   A6
   of whom Philip was one   A21
7 plagues   Rev15, 21
7 seals   Rev5
7 sons of Sceva   A19
7 spirits before the throne   Rev1
   of God   Rev3ff
7 other spirits more wicked than the first   Mw12; L11

38 SIGNIFICANT NUMBERS

7 stars, he held   Rev1ff
7 thunders spoke   Rev10
7 times am I to forgive my brother   Mw18
    if he trespass against thee   L17
7 trumpets, they were given   Rev8
7 vials of plagues   Rev16f, 21
seventh day, God rested on the   LH4
8 years, bedridden for   A9
ninth hour, from the sixth hour there was darkness until the   Mw2; Mk5; L23
10 days you will suffer cruelly   Rev2
10 horns, beast with   Rev13
  dragon with   Rev12
  of the scarlet beast   Rev17
10 kings not yet begun to reign   Rev17
tenth of the city fell   Rev11
11 were at the table, the   Mk16
12 angels at the holy city   Rev21
12 apostles, called forth unto him the   Mw10, 20; Mk3, 6; L6
12 baskets filled with left-overs   Mw14; Mk6; L9; J6
12 crops of fruit   Rev22
12 foundation stones of the city   Rev21
12 from among his followers, he chose   L6
12 gates of the holy city   Rev21
12 stars, a crown of   Rev12
12 tribes of Israel   Mw19; Rev21
12 years, had an issue of blood for   Mk5
  old daughter dying and revived   L8
  old, when Jesus was, made the pilgrimage   L2
  suffered from haemorrhages   L8
14 days lived in suspense and gone hungry   A27
14 generations from Abraham to David   Mw1
  from David to the carrying away into Babylon   Mw1
  from the carrying away into Babylon to Christ   Mw1
14 years ago was caught up   PCS12
  later I went again to Jerusalem   PG2
18 people on whom the tower fell   L13
24 elders in heaven   Rev4f, 19
24 other thrones in heaven   Rev4f
30 fold, the yield was   Mw13; Mk4
30 pieces of silver   Mw26f

38 SIGNIFICANT NUMBERS

30 years old, when Jesus began his work he was   L3
38 years, crippled for   J5
39 strokes, five times given men   PCS11
40 days and nights he fasted   Mw4
    appeared over a period of   A1
    in the wilderness   Mk1; L4
    led by the Spirit   L4
    tempted by Satan   Mk1; L4
40 in the conspiracy   A23
40 years, God was indignant for   LH3
    old, the healed man was over   A4
    tested in the desert   LH3
42 months, the beast reigned for   Rev13
    will trample the holy city for   Rev11
46 years to build the temple   J2
50 make them sit down in groups of   L9
60 fold, the yield was   Mw13; Mk4
60 years, widow put on the roll at   PTF5
70 cavalrymen, get ready   A23
70 the Lord appointed a further   L10
70 times seven, I say   Mw18
72 the Lord appointed a further   L10
77 times, I say   Mw18
99 sheep that never strayed   Mw18
100 fold, shall receive a   Mw19
    some seed yielded a   Mw13; Mk4; L8
100 sheep, suppose a man has a   Mw18
120 assembled brotherhood   A1
144 cubits high, wall of the holy city   Rev21
153 big fish   J21
200 infantry, get ready   A23
200 miles around, blood flowed   Rev14
200 spearmen, make ready   A23
276 of us were on board   A27
430 years later, a law made   PG3
490 times, I say, forgive your brother   Mw18
500 of our brothers, he appeared to   PCF15
666 the number of the beast   Rev13
1000 years, chained up Satan for a   Rev20
    reigned with Christ for   Rev20
1260 days, holy city trampled underfoot   Rev11

38 SIGNIFICANT NUMBERS

1260 days, woman sustained by God for   Rev12
3000 baptized that day   A2
4000 fed miraculously   M15f; Mk8
5000 fed miraculously   Mw, 16; Mk6; L9; J6
5000 number of believers reached   A4
7000 men who have not knelt to Baal   PR11
7000 people killed by the earthquake in John's vision   Rev11
10,000 times ten thousand angels   Rev5
10,000 words in an unknown tongue   PCF14
12,000 furlongs, the holy city measured   Rev21
12,000 of each of the twelve tribes received the seal   Rev7
23,000 died in one day   PCF10
144,000 received the seal   Rev7
200,000,000 squadrons of cavalry in John's vision   Rev9

39 *Tools and Weapons*

OLD TESTAMENT

anvil Is40ff
armour Ps45; E38
arrow De32; SF20; KS9, 13, 19; Job16, 29, 41; Pro7, 25ff; 1s5, 7, 37, Is49; Je9, 50ff; La3; H3; Ps7, 11, 18, 38, 45, 57, Ps64, 76f, 91, Ps120, 127, 144; E5, 21, 39; Z9
  bronze-tipped Job20; Ps18
axe Ju9; SF13; KF6; KS6; Ps22, 74; Ec10; Is10; Je46; E26
  blunt Ec10
  brushwood Ju9
axehead flew off the handle KS6
awl De15
balance E5
basket Ex2; De23; KS10; Ps81; Je6, 24; Am4, 8
battering-ram E4, 21, 26; Na2
battle-axe Je51; E9
bellows, blacksmith Job32; Je6
birdcage Je5
bit, horse's Is30
bow SF18; SS1; KS6, 13; CS17, 26; Ne4; Job29; Ps37, 46, 78; Is5, 7, 13, 21, 41; Je6, 49ff; E39; Ho1ff, 7; Am2; H3; Z9ff
  steel Job20
  strings Ju16; Ps7, 11, 21
  strung Ps37
breastplate KF22; CS18; Is59
bridle Is30, 37
bucket Is40
buckler KF10; CS23; Ps35; Je46; E23, 26, 38ff
  gold KF10
cage, bird Je5
callipers Is44
catapult, siege CS26
censer E8
chain Is40; D5
chisel Je10

395

39 TOOLS AND WEAPONS

clamps, iron   CF22
cleaver, blunt   Ec10
club   CF11; Job41; Pro25; E21
coat of mail   CS26; Ne4; Is59; Je46, 51
compass, carpenter's   Is44
cord, tent   Je10
coulter, plough   SF13
crook, shepherd's   Ps23; Mi7
dagger   SF17; Job16
dart   SS18; Job41; Pro7
dial, sun   KS20; Is38
engraving tool   Je17
fan, threshing and winnowing   Is41; Je15
fetters, bronze   KS25
file   SF13
fishhook   Job41; E29; Am4; H1
flail   Is28
flesh-hook   SF2
fork   SF2, 13; Is30
gaff, fishing   Job41
gate-bars, bronze   KF4
goad, ox   Ju3; SF13
grappling iron   SS5
graving tool   Is44
habergeon   Job41
hammer   KF6; Is41, 44; Je10, 23, 50
handstave   E39
harpoon   Job41
harrow   Is28
hatchet   Ps74
helmet   CS26; Ps60, 108; Is59; Je46; E23, 27, 38
hinges   KF7
hoe   Is7
hook   Nu33; Jos23; Is19, 37; E29; Am4; H1
horns, iron   KF22; CS18
iron, barbed   Job41
   weapons of   Job20
javelin   SF18ff; Job41
knife   KF18; Ez1; Job16; Pro30; Is18; E5
   flint   Jos5
lance   Je46, 50; E39

39 TOOLS AND WEAPONS

lance, burnished   Je46
lancets   KF18
latchet, shoe   Is5
machine, siege   CS26
mattock   SF13; Is2, 7; Joe3; Mi4
maul   Pro25
millstone   De24; Ju9
nail   Ju4; CS3; Is22, 40; J10
  iron   CF22
net   Job18; Pro1, 29; Ec9; Is19, 51; Je5; E12, 26, 32, 47; Ho7; Mi7; H1
pen   Je8
  iron   Je17
pick   Ps74
plane, carpenter's   Is44
plough, plow, with my heifer   Ju14
ploughshare, plowshare   SF13; Is2; Joe3; Mi4
pruning hook   Is2, 18; Joe3; Mi4
  knife   Is2; Mi4
quiver   SS8; Job39; Ps127; Is22, 49; Je5, 51; La3; H3
  gold   CF18
razor   Ju13; As7; E5
  sharp as a   Ps52
reins   Is11; Je17
ring, iron tethering   D4
rope   Is3, 5; Je10
sabre   Job39, 41; Je6, 50
saw   SS12; CF20; Is10
  stone   KF7
scabbard   Ju47; E21
scales   Is40; Je32; E5, 45
scriber, carpenter's   Is44
shaft   H3
sheath   Je47; E21
shield   SS1; KF10; KS11; CF5; CS9, 11ff, 17, 23, 25ff, 32; Pro30; Is21ff, 37; Je46, 51; Am4; E23, 26ff, 32, 38ff; Na2; Z9
  bossed   Job15
  bronze   CS12
  gold   CS9, 12
shovel   CS4; Is30; Je52

39 TOOLS AND WEAPONS

shuttle Job7
sickle SF13; Je50; Joe3
siege machine CS26
sling SF17; CS26; Job41; Pro26; Z9
spear Nu25; SF13, 17ff, 26; SS1ff, 21; KF18; KS11; CF11; CS11ff, 23, CS25ff; Ne4; Job39, 41; Ps35, 46, 57; Is2; Je6, 46; E39; Joe3; Mi4; Na2ff; H3
  fish Job41
spike, iron Am1
spiked weapons CS33
sundial KS20; Is38
sword Nu31; De13, 20, 28; Jos5ff, 19; Ju7; SF13, 17ff, 25; SS20; KF3, 18ff; KS6, 19; CF5, 10; Ne4; Job33, 39; Ps7, 22, 31, 34, Ps37, 41, 49,37, 44ff, 55, 57, 63ff, 76, 78, 89, 144, 149; Pro5, 25, Pro30; D11; Is1ff, 13ff, 21ff, 27, 51, 65ff; La1f, 4ff;Naff; Zp2; Hg2; Z9, 11, Z13; E5ff, 11ff, 14, 16ff, 21, 23ff, 28ff, 35, 38ff; Ho1ff, 7,11, 13; Joe2ff; Am1, 4, 7, 9; Mi4ff; Je2, 5ff, 9, 11ff, Je14ff, 18ff, 24ff, 29, 31ff, 38ff, 44, 46ff
target, buckler, gold KF10
tent-peg Ju4
thong, sandal Is5
threshing instruments, iron Am1
throwing-stick E39
tongs, smith's Is44
tools, iron KF6
traces, harness Je2, 5
traps, metal toothed Job18, 41
weapons, discarded E39
wheel E1ff, 10ff; D7
  potter's Je18
whip Is10
yoke De22, 28; SF6; KF19; Is10, 14, 30, 47; Je2, 5, 27, 30, 51; La1, 3, 5; Ho10ff; Mi2; Na1
  cords and bars of a Je27

NEW TESTAMENT

anchor A27; LH6
armour L11

39 TOOLS AND WEAPONS

axe   Mw3; L3
balances, pair of   Rev6
basket   Mw4ff; Mk6, 8; J6; A9; PCS11
bit   LJ3
bridle   LJ3; Rev14
bucket   Mw13; J4
chain   Mw14; Mk5, 15; A21, 26, 28; PE6; PTS2; LJu1
chains and fetters   L8
compass, ship's   A28
cord   L5
cudgel   Mw26; Mk14; L22
fan, winnowing   Mw3; L3
fetters   Mk5; L8
gibbet   A5, 13; LPF2
goad   A26
hook   Mw17
javelin   J19
lance   J19
latchet, shoe   J1
millstone   Mw18; Mk9; L17; Rev18
nail   J20
needle   Mk10; L18
net   Mw4, 13; Mk1; L5; J21
oars   Mk6
pen   LJT1
plough, plow   L9
rope   A27
saw, sawdust   Mw7
scales, pair of   Rev6
sheath   J18
shovel   Mw3; L3
sickle   Mk4
spear   J19
stave   Mw26; Mk14; L22
sword   Mw10, 26; Mk14; L2, 21f; J18; A12, 16; PR8; PE6; LH4, 11
  two-edged   LH4
yoke   A15; PTF6; Ph5

40 *Trades, Professions and Industry*

OLD TESTAMENT

accountant   Ne13
adjutant-general   CS34; Is36; Je36, 52
administrators, appointed Shedrach, Meshach and Abednego   D2
ambassador   CS35; Is18; Je49; Ob1
  Pharaoh's   Is30
apothecary   CS16; Ne3; Ec10
archer, bowman   Gen21; SS11; CF10; CS14, 35; Ps55, 78; Is21;
     Je4, 51; Am2
army officer   De1; SF14, 17, 26; SS2ff, 8, 17f; KF1f, 9, 11, 14f, 22;
     KS1, 4f, 8f, 11, 15, 18, 22, 25; CF13, 18ff, 27ff; CS16f,21,
     CS25, 32; Is3, 20, 22, 36, 59; Je36f, 39f, 43, 52ff; E17, 23
armourer   KS24
artificer   Is3
  Egyptian   Is19
assayer   Je6
astrologer   Is47; D2, 4ff
baker   Je37; Ho7
  Pharaoh's   Gen40
barber   E5
beggar   Ps109
blacksmith   Gen4; SF13; Job32; Is44
  master   Gen4
  none to be found   SF13
brick-kiln   SS12; Je43; Na3
bricks   Gen11
bronze worker   KF7
builder   KF5; KS12, 22; CS34; Ne4; Ps81, 127; E27
burnishing   Is21
captain, army   SS4; KF9, 22; KS1, 11, 25; CS23; Is3, 59;
     Je39ff, 43, 51ff; D3, 11
  ship's   Jon1
carder   Is19

40 TRADES, PROFESSIONS AND INDUSTRY

carding, weaving and spinning   Is19
carpenter   SS5; KS12, 22; CF14, 22; CS24, 34; Ez3; Is41, 44;
    Je24, 29; Z1
carving, wood   KF6
caulker, calker   E27
cavalryman   Ex14; SF8; KF9, 20; Ne2; D11; H1
chamberlain   KS23; Est1ff
chancellor   Ez4
charmer, diviner   Is19
  snake   Ps58
chief constable, Babylonian   D3
  governor in the house of the Lord   Je20
  minister   CS28
  officer in the house of the Lord   Je20
chiefs of the province   Ne11
churn   Pro30
cisterns hewn from rock   De6; Ne9
clay ground for metal casting   KF7
  potter's   Is29, 41, 45, 64; Je18
clerk   CF26; CS26, 34
commander, army   De1; SF14, 26; SS2ff, 8, 17, 19;
    KF1f, 4, 9, 11, 15, 19; KS4ff; CF18ff, 25, 27; CS16, 26, 32;
    Is20; Je51ff; E17, 23; Na3; Z10
commissioners to bring young virgins to the king   Est2
comptroller of the household   KF4, 16, 18; KS10, 15, 18; CS26, 28;
    Is22, 36
confectioners   SF8
constable, chief   D3
cook,   SF8
coppersmith, master   Gen4
counsellor   CF27; D3
courier   CS30
  with the king's writ   Est3ff
courtiers of King Darius   D6
  of King Solomon   CS9
craftsmen   Ex31ff; Nu31; KF7; KS24; CS2, 24; Is44; Je10, 24, 29;
    Ho8, 13
  metal   KF7; CS2, 24
  skilled   Ex31
  who work in gold   Nu31
crucible, metal refining   Os12; Pro17, 27; E22

40 TRADES, PROFESSIONS AND INDUSTRY

cupbearer   KF10; CS9
customs officer   KF10
dancer   So6
dealer, animal   Z11
district officer   KF20
doctor of law   Ez7; Ne8
door keepers   Ne7, 10, 13; SS4; CF9, 15, 23; CS23, 34; Ez2, 7, 10; Je35
    guild of   Ez2
dresser of vines and figs   KS25; CF27; CS26; Is61; Je39, 52; Joe1; Am7
dukes of Edom   CF1
elders, called together   KS22
   consulted by Reheboam   KF12
   by Solomon   KF8
   of the people   Je19, 26
   of Israel   E20
   summoned   Joe1ff
embalming   Gen50; Am6
embassy sent to David   CF14
engineer   CS26
engraver   CS2
ensign   Z9
envoy   SS10; KF20; KS20
   David's   CF19
   from Babylon   Is39
   sent by the Nile   Is18
eunuch, chief   KS25l Je39
executioner   Is10
farmer, husbandman   Gen4; KS25; CS26; Je14, 31, 51ff; Joe1; Am1, 5; Z13
feller, timber   Is14
fining pot for silver   Pro17, 27
fisherman   Is19; Je16; E26, 47
flax-dresser   Is19
flock-master   Na3
footman   Je12
foreman   KF5
   building   KS12, 22; CS34
forge   Is54
founder, metal   Je51

40 TRADES, PROFESSIONS AND INDUSTRY

foundry   KF7; CS4
fowler   Je5; Ps91, 124; Pro6; Ho9
fuller   KS18; Is36; Ma3
fuller's soap   Ma3
furnace, smelting   De4; Pro17, 27; Is48, 54; Je6; La5; E1,   22; Ma4
gaoler, jailer   Is10
gate-keeper   SS18; Ne3, 7, 11ff
gilder   Is40
glazed earthenware   Pro26
goldsmith   Ne3; Is40f, 46; Je10, 51
governor   Ez2, 5, 8; Ne3, 8; Je30, 41, 51; E23; Z9, 12
   assassination of the   Je41
   chief temple   Je20
   city   CS34
   for Israel, out of Bethlehem shall come a   Mi5
   Gedaliah appointed   KS25
   of Judah   Ne5; Hg1
   of the citadel   Ne7
   of the city   KF22; KS10, 23
   provincial Babylonian   D3
     Persian   Est1, 3ff, 9
   regional   KF4
   selected from their own number   Je30
grape-gatherer   Je6, 49; Ob1
grinding corn   La5
guard   SS8, 13, 25, 20; KF1; KS10; CF9, 18; D1
guild of doorkeepers   Ez2
   linen workers   CF4
handmill   Je25
haulier   KF5; CS2ff
helmsman   E27
herald   D3; Is52; Je49; Ob1; Na1; H2
   Nebuchadnezzar's   D3
herdsman   Gen4; SF21; Am1, 7
hewer of wood   Is10; Je46
high commissioner   Ez4
hired labourer   Is16; Ma3
hireling   Is21
horse-leach   Pro30
horseman   CS16; E38ff

40 TRADES, PROFESSIONS AND INDUSTRY

hunter   Gen10, 25; Job15; Ps22, 91; Pro6, 12; Is13, 24; Je16, 48; La1; Ho12; Mi7
husbandman, farmer   Gen4; Je14, 31, 51ff; Joe1; Am5; Z13
ivory, working in   KF22; CS9; Ps45; So5; E27; Am3, 6
judge   Ju4, 10, 12, 15; CS19; Ez7; D3; Mi4
  Babylonian   D3
keeper of the royal forests   Ne2
  of the royal threshold   Est2
  of the wardrobe   KS22
king's adviser   Ne11
  friend   CF27
labourer   KF5, 11; KS25; Is21; Je39, 52; Hg1
  building   KF5
  gangs, in charge of   KF11
leech   Pro30
levies, commander of forced   KF12
lime burning   Is33
linen worker   CF4
logging, raft   KF5
loom, web severed from   E37
magistrate   CF23, 26; Ne2, 4, 12ff; Ez9
mariner   E27; Jon1
marksman   Ps78
mason   KF5; KS12, 22; CF14, 22; CS24; Is54; Ez3
melting pot   Pro17
    for silver   Pro27
merchant   CS9; Ne3, 13; So3; E27; Ho12
messenger   Je51; Na2
metal worker   KF7; CS2, 24
mill, noise of the   Ec12
millstone   Is47; Je25
mine, silver   Job28
minister, chief   D6
minstrel   KS31 CS35
money-lender   Ps109
mould, bronze   KF7
musician   CS34; Ez7; Ne4; E33, 40
nurse, children's   SS4; KS11; CS22; Is49
oarsman   E27
officer in charge of the Lord's house   Je29
officers deported to Babylon   Je29

40 TRADES, PROFESSIONS AND INDUSTRY

officers in charge of the foremen   KF9
  of Elam   Je49
  of Judah and Jerusalem   Je29, 34
  of the house of the Lord   Je36
  of the king of Babylon   Je39
outrunner   KF1
oven, baker's   Ho7
overseer   Ne11
paint, house   Je22
perfumer   Ne3; Ec10; SF8
physician   CS16; Je8
pilot, ship's   E27
ploughman, plowman   Ps129; Is28, 61; Je14, 31, 51; Am9
porter   CF26; CS34; Ne4
potter   CF4; Ps2; Is29ff, 41, 45, 64; Je18ff; La4; Z11
potter's wheel   Je18
precentor   Ne11
prefect, Babylonian   D3, 6
pressing oil or wine   KS6; Ne13; Job24; Pro3; Is5, 16, 63;
        La1; Joe3; Z14
quarry, stone   Jos7; Ec10; Is50
  at Shebarim   Jos7
quarryman   KF5; CS2; Ec10
quartermaster   SF17; Je51
reaper   Ks4; Je9, 50; Am2, 9
recorder   KS18; Is36
refiner, metal   Je6, 9; Ma3
regent, Daniel appointed   D2
  Jotham appointed   CS26
regional governors   KF10
runner   Je4
sailor   E27; Jon1
saltpit   Zp2
satraps, Babylonian   D3, 6
  king's   Est3ff, 9
  royal   Ez8
sawyer   Is10
scribe   SS20; KS12, 22; CF2; CS26, 34; Ne8, 12; Ps45; Is33, 66;
        Je8, 36; Ez4, 7
  the king's   Est3
sculptor   CF22

40 TRADES, PROFESSIONS AND INDUSTRY

sea of cast metal   KF7
seaman   KF9
seamster   Ex26ff
secretary   CF2; CS34; Ez4
   of state   KF4; KS18; CF18; CS34; Is36
secretaries, the king's   Est3ff
shambles, slaughter-house   Is14; Je12
shearer   Is53
sheep breeder, sheep master   KS3
   farmer, shepherd   Gen4, 29; KS3; Job24; Ps23, 28, 49, Ps78ff, 95, 100; So1; E34; Ho12; Am1, 3; Is13, 31, 38, 40, Is44, 56, 61, 63; Je2, 6, 10, 12, 14, 25, 31, 33, 43, 49ff; Mi5, 7; Na3; Zp2; Z10f, 13
sheriff, Babylonian   D3
shield-bearer   CS14
shipmaster   Jon1
silversmith   Ju17; Pro25
singer   KF10; CF9; CS5, 29; Ez2, 7, 10; Ne7, 10ff; Ec2
sledge threshing   Is28
smelting furnace   De4; Je11
smith   KS24; Is44, 54; Je24, 29; Z1
snake-charmer   Ps58; Ec10
soldering   Is40
soldier   Ex14; SF13; SS10; KF1; KS3, 13; CS16, 25; Is31, 36; Je4, 46; E38ff; D11; Ho1; Am2; Na3; Z10
spinner   Is19
staff officer   E23
steward   Is22
stone cutter   KS12
   cutting craft   Ex31
stonemason   SS5
stone squarer   KF5
   worker   CS2
straw for bricks   Ex5
superintendent of the enforced levy   KF4
   of the regional governors   KF4
tablet engraving   Je17
teacher   Ps119; Is50
temple-servitor   Ez2, 7, 8; Ne3, 7, 10ff
tiller of the soil   Z13

40 TRADES, PROFESSIONS AND INDUSTRY

timber feller   KF5; CS2; Is14
trader   CS9
treasurer   Ez1, 7; Is22
   Babylonian   D3
treasury   KS20
tutor   KS10; CF27
vagabond   Ps109
viceroy   Je51; E23
   of Babylon   D3, 6
   of Jehoshaphat   KF22
vine and fig dresser   KS25; CF27; CS26; Ls61; Je39, 52; Joe1; Am7
vintager   Am9; Ob1
wardrobe, keeper of the   CS34
watchman   SS18; KS9; So3, 5; Ps127, 130; Is1, 21, 24, 52, 56,
     Is62; Je6, 31; E3, 33; Ho9
weaver   Job7; Is19, 38
wheel, potter's   Je18
winepress   Is5, 16, 63; Je48; La1; Ho9; Joe3
   hewn out of rock   Is5
wine-vats, the king's   Z14
woodcutter   Ec10; Je46
woodman   CS2; Ps74
woodworker   CS2; Ps74
worker in stone   CS2
   in wood   CS2
work-gangs in Egypt   Ex1
wreathenwork, metal   KS25
wrought iron   E27

NEW TESTAMENT

advocate   A24
ambassador   PE6
ambassage, envoy   L14
architect   LH11
assayer   LPF1
athlete   PTS2
attendant, court   Mw14
baker   Mw16
beloved physician, Luke   PC04

40 TRADES, PROFESSIONS AND INDUSTRY

bishop   PTF3
bleacher   Mk9
boxer   PCF9
builder   A4; PCF3; LH11; LPF2
  master   PCF3
captain, army   J18
  of the temple   L22; A4f
  ship's   A27; Mk6
carpenter   Mw13; Mk6
centurion   Mw8
chamberlain   A12; PR16
clerk, town   A19
collector of taxes   Mw17
constable   Mw5
controller of the temple   A4f
coppersmith   PTS4
counsellor   L23
craftsmanship and design, an image shaped by   A17
craftsmen of any trade   Rev18
  provided a great deal of employment for   A19
deacon, deaconess   PTF3
deputy governor   A18; LPF2
doctor   Mk2; L8; PCo4
  of law   Mw5, 8f, 12, 16, 20f, 23; Mk1ff, 10ff, 14; L2, 5, 9, 15, 20, 22; J8; A4ff, 23
doorkeeper   J10
employment, engage in honest   Tt3
envoy   L14
executioner   Mk6
farmer   PTS2
fellow-worker   ThF3
fisherman   Mw4; Mk1; L5
flute player   Mw9; Rev18
fuller   Mk9
gardener   J15, 20
governor   Mw10; PCS11; PG4; LPF2
harpist   Rev14, 18
herald   Mw11; Mk1; PTS1
husbandman   Mw21; Mk12; L20; J15; PTS2; LJ5
innkeeper   K10
jailer   A16

40 TRADES, PROFESSIONS AND INDUSTRY

judge   Mw5; L18; A13
keeper, prison   A5, 12
labourer   Mw20; PTF5; PTS2; LJ5
  is worthy of his hire   L10
landlord   Mw20
land owner   L15
lawyer   Mw2, 9, 15, 23, 26; Mk2, 7, 9, 12, 14f; L5, 7, 10f, 14, L19f, 23; Tt3
magistrate   L12; A16f; Tt3
master builder   PCF3
merchant   Mw13
messenger   J13
mill, sound of the   Rev18
millstone   Mw18; Mk9; L17; Rev18
minister   Mk10
minstrel   Mw9
money changer   Mw21
  lender   L7
musician   Rev18
necessities of life, must produce the   Tt3
nurse, children's   ThF2
occupations, see that they engage in honourable   Tt3
officer, magistrate's   A16
  of the temple   L22
orator   A24
pastor   Pe4
pay for his own labour, each will get his own   PCF3
  the worker earns his   L10
physician   Mw9; Mk2; L8; PCo4
  beloved   PCo4
piper   Rev18
ploughman, plowman   PCF9
police   J18; A5
  temple   L22; J7
porter   Mk3; J10
potter   PR9; Rev2
president of the synagogue   Mw9; L8
proconsul   A18f
publican   Mw5, 18, 21; L3, 5, 15, 18f
rabbi   Mw23
reaper   Mw13

40 TRADES, PROFESSIONS AND INDUSTRY

sailor   A27; Rev18
schoolmaster   PG3
scribe   Mw2, 5, 7ff, 12f, 15, 17, 20, 23, 26; Mk1f, 7ff, 14f;
     L5, 9, 11, 15, 20, 22, 23; J8; A4, 6, 23
sea-captain   A27; Rev18
sergeant, magistrate's   A16
silversmith   A19
shambles, meat-market   PCF10
shepherd   Mw9, 25f; Mk6, 14; L2; J10; A8, 20; LPF2, 5; LJu1
ship-master   Rev18
shipmen   A27f
soldier   Mw8; L3, 7; J18f; A12, 21, 27f; PTS2
steward   Mw20; L8, 12, 16; J2; PCF4; PTS2
superintendent of taxes   L19
swineherd   Mk6
tanner   A9f
tax-gatherer   Mw5, 9ff, 18, 21; Mk2; L3, 5, 7, 15, 18
teacher   Mw23; Mk9; L2; PR12, 16; PE4; PTF1; PTS1f; LH5; LPS2;
     LJF2
  of the law   Mw13; L5
tent-maker   A18
town clerk   A19
tutor   PG3
vine dresser   L13
  grower   Mw21; Mk12; L20
wages you never paid   LJ5
warder, prison   A5, 12, 16
work, he who will not, shall not eat   ThS3
  quietly for a living   ThS3
worked for a living night and day   ThF2
worker earns his pay   PTF5

41 *Trading, Import and Export*

OLD TESTAMENT

agents, trading   Is23
baggage-train   Is10, 29; D11
borrowing   Pro22
business   Ps107
  timidity in   Pro11
buyer   Pro20; E7
  and seller   Is24
camels laden with spice   Is60
cargo   E27
caravan, trading   Gen37; Is21; E27
commerce in goats   E27
  in precious stones   E27
  in sheep   E27
  in spice   E27
  in wine   E27
  in wool   E27
  land of   E16ff
  Tarshish a source of your   E27
convoy, traders'   Is60
customs officer   KF10
custom tax   E24
dealer in animals   Z11
  in cloth   E27
  in silver wiped out   Zp1
discount   Pro28
export   KF10
fair, trading   E27
goods taken in pledge   H2
harbour of Tarshish, trading   Us23
import from Ophir   KF10
  of almug wood   KF10
  of balm   E27
  of balsam   E27
  of bronze   E27

41 TRADING, IMPORT AND EXPORT

import of calamus   E27
  of cassia   E27
  of chariots   KF10; CS1
  of ebony   E27
  of gold   KF10
  of honey   E27
  of horses   KF10; CS1
  of ivory   E27
  of oil   E27
  of precious stones   KF10
  of slaves   E27
  of spices   KF10
  of sweet cane   E27
  of syrup   E27
  of wheat   E27
  of wrought iron   E27
  via Tarshish   E27
imported, chariots from Egypt   KF10; CS1
  horses from Egypt and Coa   KF10; CS1
interest   Pro28
land purchase   Le25; Je32
lending   Pro22, 28
levies on merchandise   CS9
loan, pledges for   De24
lost property, rules regarding   De22
market of Tyre   E27
  your wares, ships to   E27
  place   Is23, 59
merchandise of Ethiopia   Is45
  of Tyre   Is23
    will be plundered   E26
merchant   CS9; Ne3, 13; So3; Is47; E27; Ho12
  princes of Tyre   Is23
merchants, city of   E17
  Nubian   Is45
  of Lower Town at Jerusalem   Zp1
  of Sidon   Is23
  of Tarshish   E38
merchantmen ships   KF22; CS9
money lender   Ps109
  lending, rules regarding   Ex22

41 TRADING, IMPORT AND EXPORT

port of entry   Is23
property exchange   Ru4
return on merchandise   Ec11
sabbath, buying and selling merchandise on   Ne10, 13
sale and valuation of property   Le25, 27
seller   Pro20; E7
ships for trade with Tarshish   CS20
  of Tarshish, merchant   Is2, 23
  trading   CS8, 20
spice, camels laden with   Is62
stolen goods   Ps62
timber licence   Ez3
tithe of all produce   Le27; De12, 14; CS31; Ne10, 13; Ma3
trade at Tyre, profit of   Is23
  foreign   KF10
  in gold   E27
  in precious stones   E27
  of nations, their revenue   Is23
trader   CS9; Z11, 14
traders, house of Jacob crowded with   Is2
  of Tarshish   E38
  of Tyre, the most honoured men on earth   Is23
trading partners   Job41
  quarters in Damascus   KF20
traffic, a land of   E17
tribute and custom   KF10; Ez4
wares of Damascus, forty camel loads   KS8
  sea-going ships to market your staple   E27

NEW TESTAMENT

accounts, produce your   L16
bill, write thy   L16
bought and sold in the temple   Mw21; Mk11; L19
business, be not slothful in   PR12
  keep calm and look after your own   ThF4
  overreach his brother in   ThF4
buy or sell, no one allowed to   Rev13
buying and selling in the temple   Mw21; Mk11; L19; J2

41 TRADING, IMPORT AND EXPORT

cargoes, no longer buys their   Rev18
  of flour   Rev18
  of gold and silver   Rev18
  of horses and chariots   Rev18
  of marble   Rev18
  of oil   Rev18
  of perfume   Rev18
  of sheep and cattle   Rev18
  of slaves   Rev18
  of spice   Rev18
  of wheat   Rev18
  of wine   Rev18
cash, turned his share into   L15
corn dumped in the sea   A27
creditor, there was a certain   L7
custom-house   Mk2; L5
dealers in cattle, sheep and pigeons   J2
  in pigeons   Mw21; Mk11; J2
  in purple fabric   A16
  in the temple   Mw21; Mk11; L19; J2
debtors, creditor who had two   L7
  one by one, summoned his master's   L16
deposit, put money on   L19
goods, rich in the world's   PTF6
interest, on deposit for   L19
market place, standing idle in the   Mw20
    turn my father's house into a   J2
merchandise, brass   Rev18
  house of   J2
  no man buyeth their   Rev18
merchant   Mw13
  princes of the world   Rev18
merchants grown rich on her bloated wealth   Rev18
  of the earth   Rev18
money changer   Mw21; Mk11; J2
  lender   L7
partners in payments and receipts   PPs4
pence, why was this not sold for three hundred   Mk14; J12
profit each had made, to see what   L19
profits distributed to all in need   A4
property in land or houses, all who had   A4

41 TRADING, IMPORT AND EXPORT

rich, he was very successful, for he was very   L18
sale, you thought God's gift was for   A8
sell everything you have and distribute to the poor   L18
sellers of doves   Mk11
selling and buying in the temple, drove out all who were
       Mw21
sold and bought in the temple   Mw21; Mk11; L19
tables of the money-changers   Mw21
trade with this, gave them a pound, saying   L19
traded by sea, those who   Rev18
   with five talents   Mw25
traders in all these wares   Rev18
   temple   L19
   were once the merchant princes   Rev18
trading and making money   LJ4
usury, I should have received mine own with   Mw25; L19
wares, traders in all these   Rev18
wheat, lost cargo of   A28

42 *Transport, Vehicles and Vessels*

OLD TESTAMENT

ark, Noah's   Gen6ff
  of acacia, shittim wood   De10
  of bulrushes   Ex2
  of the Covenant   De10, 31
ass   Gen49; Nu22; Jos6, 15; Ju10, 12, 19; SF9, 16, 25, 27;   SS16ff;
       KF13; KS4, 7; CF5, 12, 27; CS28; Ez2; Ne7; Job1, 24, 42;
       Pro26; Is21, 30; E23; Z9, 14
  laden   Ju19
axle, axle-tree, bronze   KF7
baggage train   Is110, 29; D11
beasts of burden   Is46
bier,   SS3; CS16
bit, horse's   Is30
bridle   Ps32; Pro26; Is30, 37
camel   Gen 24, 31, 37; Ex9; Le11; De14; Ju8ff; SF27, 30; KF4, 10;
       KS8; CF5, 12, 27; CS9; Ez2; Ne7; Est8; Job1, 42; Is21, 30, 60,
       Is66; Je2, 49; E25; Z14
canal, Chebar, Kebar   E1, 43
canvas sail   E27
captain, ship's   Jon1
caravan, camel   Gen37
  trading   Is21; E27
carriage   Is10, 46
cart for the Ark of God   SS6; CF13
  ox   SF6
  rope   Is5
cartwheel   Is28
caulking, ship's seams   E27
chariot   Ex14; Jos11, 17; Ju1, 4; SF8f; SS1, 15; KF1, 4, 9f, 20, 22;
       KS5ff, 13; CF18; CS1, 14, 16; Ps20, 68, 104; So6;
       Is2, 5, 21, 31, 36f, 43, 66; Je4, 17, 22, 46, 50ff;
       E23, 26ff, 39; D11; Ho10; Joe2; Mi1, 5; Na2f; H3, 10;
       Hg2; Z6, 9
  lining for a   E27

42 TRANSPORT, VEHICLES AND VESSELS

chariot of cedar wood   So3
  two-horsed   Is21
  wheel   Ps77
  wheels like the whirlwind   Is5
chariots   countless   Is37
  like a whirlwind   Is66
  no end to their   Is2
  of fire   KS6
convoy, traders'   Is60
crown, bronze trolley   KF7
deck, ship's   E27
dhows of Arabia   Is2
dromedary   KF4; Est8; Is60, 66; Je2
felloes, wheel   KF7
flanges, bronze trolley   KF7
fleet, Solomon's   KF9
galley   Is33
goad, ox   Ju3; SF13
handles, bronze trolley   KF7
harness   Je46; Mi1
  chariot   KF18
  ox   SS24
haulier   KF5; CS2ff
helmsman   E27
horse   Ex9; Jos11; SS15; KF4, 9ff, 20; KS5ff; Ez2; Est6, 8; Job39; Ps20, 32ff, 76, 147; Pro21, 26; Is2, 5, 21, 30ff, 43, 63, 66; Je4, 6, 8, 11ff, 17, 22, 46, 50f; E23, 26ff, 38ff; Ho1, 14; Joe2; Am6; Mi5; Na2f; H1, 3; Hg2; Z1, 6, 9, 12, 14
hub, wheel   E1
Jehu drives furiously   KS9
jetty, offshore piles   E27
litter   Is66
  of Solomon   So3
mariner   E27; Jon1
mast   Pro23; Is33
  of cedar   E27
mule   SS13, 18; KF1, 10; CF12; Ez2; Ne7; Est8; Ps32; Is66; E27; Z14
naves, wheel   KF7
oars, galley   Is33

42 TRANSPORT, VEHICLES AND VESSELS

oars of oak   E27
oarsman   E27
outrunner   KF1
overboard, thrown, to lighten the ship   Jon1
  throw me   Jon1
oxen, draught   KF1, 4, 8, 19; Ne5; Job1; Ps8, 66; Is7, 22, 30; E1; Am6
pack animals   KS3
palanquin head-rest, gold   So3
  lining, leather   So3
  of King Solomon   So3
  poles, silver   So3
  seat of purple stuff
pilot, ship's   E27
raft of logs   KF5; CS2
reins   Is11; Je17; Ho11
rigging, ship's   Pro23; Is33
rim, wheel   E1
rope, cart   SF19; Is3, 5; Je10
rowers   E27
saddle, ass   KF2, 13
saddlecloth   Ju5; E27
  woollen   E27
sail, canvas   Is33; E27
    blue and purple   E27
    patterned linen   E27
sailor   E27; Jon1
seaman   KF9
seams, caulking ship's   E27
ships   Ps104; Pro30; Is60; E27
  from Tarshish, trading   E27
  go to sea in   Ps107
  laden with merchandise   Pro31
  merchantmen   KF10; CS8f, 20
  of Chittim   D11
  of Solomon's fleet   KF9
  of Tarshish   Is2, 23
  of Tyre   Z9
  of war   D11
  stately   Is60
  swift   Job9

42 TRANSPORT, VEHICLES AND VESSELS

ships trading   CS8f, 20; Is2, 23; E27
  wrecked by the east wind   Ps48
shipmaster   Jon1
ship's company   E27
shipwreck   KF22
skiff, reed-built   Job9
sledge, threshing   Job9
spacecraft of Ezekiel's vision   E1, 10
spokes, wheel   KF7
stables   KF4, 10; Est7; E25
swivel-pins, metal trolley   KF6
tacklings, ship's rigging   Is33
tyres, tires, round like the moon   Is3
trolley, bronze   KF7; KS16, 25; CS4; Je27, 52
undersetters, base   KF7
vessels, Arab   Je49
  of bulrushes   Is18
  of reeds   Is18
wagon   Nu7; SF6; Is66; E23; Am2
  covered   Nu7
wheel   E1ff, 10ff; D7; Na3
  within a wheel   E1, 10
wheels, bronze trolley   KF7
  by the four living creatures   E1, 10
  of the cherubim   E10
  with eyes   E1, 10
wheel-forks, bronze trolley   KF7
whip   Pro26; Na3
yoke, draught   De22, 28; SF6; KF19; Is10, 14, 30, 47;
    Je2, 5, 27, 30f, 51; La1, 3, 5; Ho10f; Mi2; Na1

NEW TESTAMENT

abandon ship, the sailors tried to   A27
adrift on the open sea   PCS11
anchor   A27
  safe and sure   LH6
  weighing   A27
anchors dropped from the stern   A27
  from the bows, lay out   A27

42 TRANSPORT, VEHICLES AND VESSELS

anchors slipped the   A27
ark, Noah's   Mw24; L17; LH11; LPF3
ass   Mw21; L13f; J12; LPS2
boat   Mw13, 15; J6
   battling with a head-wind in a rough sea   Mw14
   beside them, he climbed into the   Mk6
   cut the ropes of the   A27
   fishing   Mw4
   he sat in the   Mk4
   Jesus got into the   Mw8; J21
     withdrew quietly by   Mw14
   lowered the ship's   A27
   ran into a heavy squall   L8
   set off privately by   Mk6
   ship's, dropped away   A27
   to save Jesus from being crushed by the crowd   Mk3
boats, he got into one of the   L5
bow, lay out anchors from the   A27
   stuck fast   A27
cargo ship to unload at Tyre   A21
carriage   A21
   sitting in his   A8
captain, ship's   A27; Rev18
cast ashore on a rugged coast   A27
Castor and Pollux, ship of Alexandria   A28
chariot, sitting in his   A8
chariots and horses, cargoes of   Rev18
donkey   Mw21; L13f; J12
   Jesus found a   J12
dropped four anchors from the stern   A27
foresail set to the wind   A27
gear, the ship's   A27
harbour, Cretan   A27
   exposed to south-west and north-west   A27
   unsuitable for wintering   A27
head to wind, impossible to keep the   A27
helm, large ship turned by a small   LJ3
hoisted aboard the ship's boat   A27
jettisoned the ship's gear   A27
lashings of the steering paddles   A27
lightened the ship by dumping the corn at sea   A27

42 TRANSPORT, VEHICLES AND VESSELS

mainsail, lowered the   A27
on board, two hundred and seventy six of us   A27
overboard, those who can swim should jump   A27
rope   A27
rowing, toiling in   Mk6
rudder   LJ3
  bands   A27
run before the wind   A27
sail-cloth, sheet of   A10f
sailed under the lee of Clauda, Crete and Cyprus   A27
sailing with you, the lives of all who are   A27
sailor   A27; Rev18
sea-captain   Rev18
set sail for Syria   A18
ship aground, ran the   A27
  and cargo, loss of the   A27
  and sat on the sea, he entered the   Mk4
  ashore, planned to run the   A27
  bound for Phoenicia   A21
  cast the net on the right hand side of the   J21
  covered with the waves   Mw8
  departed privately by   Mk6
  embarked in a   A27
  found in Patara   A21
  had wintered in the island   A28
  he entered into a   Mw9; L8; J6
  in the midst of the sea   Mw14
  Jesus went into a   Mw13
  master   Rev18
  named Castor and Pollux   A28
  owner   A27
  running before the wind   A27
  sailed for Assos   A20
  set sail in a   A28
  should wait on him, a small   Mk3
  to unload at Tyre   A21
  turned about by a small helm   LJ3
  undergirded the   A27
  waves beat on the   Mk4
shipmen   A27
ships at sea, all who had   Rev18

42 TRANSPORT, VEHICLES AND VESSELS

ships boat, lowered the   A27
  fishing   Mw4
  foundered, a third of the   Rev8
  gear, jettisoned the   A27
  standing by the lake   L5
shipwreck   A27; PCS11
sounded and found twenty fathoms   A27
steering-paddles, lashings of the   A27
stern, dropped anchors from the   A27
  pounded by the breakers   A27
tackle, tackling, ship's   A27
tempest, tossed in the   A27
undergirded the ship   A27
vessel bound for Italy, an Alexandrian   A27
voyage, risky to continue with the   A27
  will be disastrous   A27
weighing anchor   A27

43 *Treachery and Trickery*

OLD TESTAMENT

abandoned camp, the Aramaeans   KS7
accused the Jews, Chaldaeans   D3
adversaries for Solomon, Hadad and Rezon   KF11
affections, stifling their natural   Am1
allies, former, march you to the frontier   Ob1
ambush   Ps10, 17, 59
   by Jeroboam   CS13
anger of Moses for dissidents   Nu16
apostate Israel   Je3
armed bands roaming the countryside   Je40, 42
arrogance of Jacob, I loathe the   Am6
bait, let her be   SF18
bandits   KF11
beards, shaved off half their   SS10
beast, do not behave like a   SS13
betray the survivors, do not   Ob1
betrayal of Samson by Delilah   Ju16
blood on your robe   Je2
blood-guilt rests on Saul   SS21
booty of asses, camels and sheep   CF5
   of Jericho   Jos6
bribe for the king of Assyria   KS16
   her priests give direction in return for a   Mi3
   they take a   Am5
bribed to utter a prophecy   Ne6
bribery of officials   Ez4
brigands will defile Israel   E7
brutish, pastors are become   Je10
bullies and robbers, the common people are   E22
burnt goodly castles   Nu31
cage, drew him into a   E19
captured from Jerusalem, the royal treasures   KS14
cave, robbers'   Je1
caves and holes, the people hid in   SF13

423

43 TREACHERY AND TRICKERY

chains, all her great men thrown into   Na3
changed sides, Abner   SS3
    the Hebrews   SF14
charge brought against the Israelites   Ez4
cheated, Israel by Assyria   KS15
  Menahem by Pul   KS15
confederates mislead you   Ob1
conspiracy against Amaziah   CS25
  against Joram   KS9
    Pekah   KS15
    Pekahiah   KS15
    Zechariah   KS15
  of Absalom   SS13ff
  of King Amon's courtiers   KS21
  of Zimri   KF16
conspirators killed by the people   KS21
court, destitute thrust out of   Am5
day of vengeance on their enemies   Est7
deceitful above all things, the heart is   Je17
deceived, the witch of En-dor   SF28
decoy you, they will   Ju2
demand of Ben-hadad on Ahab   KF20
demolished, the walls of Jerusalem   Je52
den of robbers? is this house become a   Je7
deprived of rank, the Queen Mother   KF15
destitute thrust out of court   Am5
destroyed, Jerusalem   Je52
destroyer of the Gentiles   Je4
disguise: Ahab   CS18
  ashes upon his face   KF20
  inhabitants of Gibeon   Jos19
  Jeroboam's wife   KF14
  Saul   SF28
  the king of Israel   KF22
  with a bandage   KF20
dissidents, anger of Moses for   Nu16
enter the city, show us how to   Ju1
evidence, bearing false   De5, 19
exterminate the people of Judah, made up my mind to   Je44
false accusation   KF21
  evidence   De19

43 TREACHERY AND TRICKERY

false tongue   Pro6
  witness   Pro6
    by Jezebel   KF21
faults, secret   Ps19
fled the country, Hadad   KF11
flight, put to, by the men of Ai   Jos7
    for taking forbidden things   Jos7
flotsam on the water, swept away like   Ho10
forgery of Ahab's name by Jezebel   KF21
forgetting the ties of kinship   Am1
fools and blockheads one and all   Je10
forbidden plunder   Jos7
foul play, victim of   D11
fraud, fill their master's house with violence and   Zp1
freebooters   KF11
gall, judgement turned into   Am6
garments, cut off half their   SS10
gazing-stock, make thee as a   Na3
grain, he will take a tenth of your   SF8
gossip   Pro11ff, 18, 20, 26
harbourer of forbidden things   Jos7
hid among rocks, the people   SF13
  among the baggage, Saul   SF10
  in a pit, covered and strewn   SS17
  in a well   SS17
  in pits and cisterns   SF13
  in the fields, David   SF20
hidden beneath a mantle   Ju4
  beneath a rug, Sisera lay   Ju4
  Joash, the one surviving prince   KS11
honesty twisted like briars   Mi7
humiliated, David's envoys were   SS10
hunt their kinsmen down   Am1
intimidation of Nehemiah   Ne2ff
intrigue, he will seize the kingdom by   D11
judgement for rewards, the judge who gives   Mi7
  turned into gall   Am6
  turned to wormwood   Am5
justice, hateful, you who make   Mi3
  her rulers sell   Mi3
  you have turned into poison   Am6

43 TREACHERY AND TRICKERY

lay in wait for Samson, the people of Gaza   Ju16
lie in wait in the vineyards   Ju21
   on the hill-top   Ju9
  upon lie, they invent   Ps35
lies, Ephraim compasseth me about with   Ho11
looted, Aramaean gold   KS7
lot, her nobles were shared out by   Na3
lunatic, David acted like a   SF21
lured to their death, the prophets of Baal   KS10
mad, feigned himself   SF21
mislead you, confederates   Ob1
mock a hunchback, brutes who would   Ps35
net   Ps9ff, 35, 57, 66, 140
  cast over him, caught in its meshes   E17
  drives his kinsmen like a hunter into the   Mi7
  spread out, you have been a   Ho5
  to catch my feet   La1
panic of Aramaeans at Samaria   KS7
pastors are become brutish   Je10
persecute the guiltless, you   Am5
perverse and crooked generation   De32
pit they have dug to catch me   Je18
  trap   Ps7, 9, 35; Ec10
    dug in my path   Ps57
     muddy   Ps40
pledge, garments seized in   Am2
plunder, men that lust for   Ps76
  of Egypt   Ex3
  of Jericho forbidden   Jos7
  taken from you, shared out   Z14
plundered, house of the Lord to supply bribes   KS16
  houses of Jerusalem   Z14
plunderers, gave them over to   KS17
  the Lord made them prey to   Ju2
poison, you have turned justice into   Am6
prayer of Vengeance   La3
pretence to be a mourner   SS14
  to be ill   SS13
pricks in your eyes   Nu33
provoke me to anger, Jews   E8
pulled down, the walls of Jerusalem   Je52

43 TREACHERY AND TRICKERY

raiders, the Lord made them prey to   Je52
ransom, hold men to   Am5
realm of wickedness, Edom   Ma1
rebellion against Assyria   KS18
  against the house of David   KF12
    Israel   KS3
    king of Assyria   KS18
    Nebuchadnezzar   KS24
  of Reheboam   KF11
rebels, a race of   Is30
  must live in the desert   Ps68
relapse into deeper corruption, they would   Ju2
renegades   Ps78
revenge plotted on Shimei   KF2
revolt against Joash   KS24
    Nebuchadnezzar   KS24
reward, judgement given for   Mi7
rifled, house of Jerusalem   Z14
robbed all who passed that way   Ju9
robbers' cave   Je1
  do you think that this house is a   Je7
  is this house become a den of   Je7
  lying in wait   Ho6
  shall enter my secret place and defile it   E7
  who gave Israel to the   Is42
robe, blood on the corner of your   Je2
ruffians, a band of   Ps22
rug rolled up in a bed   SF19
ruin, their feats lure them to   Ps69
rumour, alive with   Ps55
  upon rumour   E7
rumours, carrying false   Ex23
ruse, Zebel resorted to   Ju9
scandal, alive with   Ps55
scoundrel, Sheba   SS20
scoundrels, Eli's sons were   SF1ff
  surrounded the house   Ju19
secret agents like Locusts   Na3
sell justices, her rulers   Mi3
slander   Ec7
slanders, neighbours walk with   Je9

43 TREACHERY AND TRICKERY

slippery as oil, their words are   Ps55
smoke from a chimney, they shall disappear like   Ho13
snare   Ps18, 64, 69, 91
   for your feet, your own kith and kin lay a   Ob1
   in the very temple of God   Ho9
   to entrap you   Jos23
   you have been a   Ho5
snares they have hidden for my feet   Je18
sow the wind and reap the whirlwind   Ho8
spies, Absalom sent throughout Israel   SS15
   as numerous as stars   Na3
   on the roof   Jos2
   sent to Bethel   Ju1
spite, the public square is never free from   Ps55
spoil, enjoy the use of   De20
   treasures of Judah carried to Babylon as   Je20
sport, enjoy the use of   De20
spy out the country of Laish   Ju18
   the land, five fighting men of Dan   Ju18
staff of reed to the house of Israel   E29
steal, shall not   De5
stumbling block   Is57; E14
   blocks I will lay before this people   Je6
tax levied on the poor   Am5
test Solomon, the Queen of Sheba came to   KF10
thickets, the people hid in   SF13
thief as your friend   Ps50
thieves or robbers come by night   Ob1
   they break into houses, they are   Ho7
thirty pieces of silver   Z11
threat to Ahab by Ben-hadad   KF20
ties of kinship, forgetting   Am1
tithe, bring within three days   Am4
traitor, friends turned   La1
   in his over-confidence   H2
   of Bethel let free   Ju1
traitors   Ps59, 78
   no mercy on   Ps59
   will lay their plots   D11
transgressors, clan chosen as   Jos7
trap, David has walked into a   Sf23

43 TREACHERY AND TRICKERY

trap, deadly, to catch men   Je5
  for him while speaking amicably, plans a   Je9
  they will shut you fast in the   Ju2
traps for the righteous   Is29
  hidden   Ps140
treachery committed against the God of Israel   Jos22
  of Achan, remember the   Jos22
  of Jehu to Ahaziah and Jehoram   KS9
  of Jezebel   KF21
  of Joab against Amasa   SS20
  Sisera's death through   Ju4
treason! Athalia cried   KS11; CS23
tribute of grain extorted from the poor   Am5
trickery by the citizens of Ai   Jos8
  by the inhabitants of Gibeon   Jos9
  of Benjamites by feigned retreat of the Israelites   Ju20
  of Darius into condemning Daniel   D6
  of David by Joab   SS14
  of Eglon by Ehud   Ju3
  of Isaac by Jacob   Gen27
  of Isaac by Rebecca   Gen27
  of Jacob by Laban   Gen29
  of Joshua by the Gibeonites   Jos9
  of Naaman by Gahazi   KS5
  of Shechem by Jacob's sons   Gen34
  of Sisera by Jael   Ju4
  of the king of Israel by a prophet   KF20
tricks, Midianites with their crafty   Nu25
tyrants brought low   Ps107
vengeance, Jeremiah's prayer of   La3
  on Jezebel, I will take   KS9
  on their enemies, a day of   Est7
  this is the day of   Je46
violence and fraud, who fill their master's house with   Zp1
warning against Joab   KF2
well, hid in the   SS17
whip for your backs, they will be a   Jos23
whirlwind, reap the   Ho8
wicked counsellor, from you has come forth a   Na1
  generation, this   De1
  go down to Sheol in peace   Job21

43 TREACHERY AND TRICKERY

wicked men move boundary stones   Job24
    reap what is not theirs   Job24
wickedness, realm of   Ma1
    rid Israel of   De17
wormwood, judgement turned to   Am5

NEW TESTAMENT

abuse and persecution, I had met him with   PTF1
    with abuse, do not repay   LPF3
ambush, the son of Paul's sister heard of the   A23
    to kill Paul, planned an   A25
anger against his brother, anyone who nurses   Mw5
arrested, John the Baptist   Mw4
arrogant, boastful and abusive, men will be   PTS3
bad men all hate the light   J3
bandit, Barabbas was a   J18
    do you take me for a   Mk14
betray brother to death, brother shall   Mk13
    Jesus, Judas went to the chief priests to   Mk14
    you, even your parents and brothers will   L21
betrayed, alas for him by whom the Son of Man is   L22
    into the hands of men, Son of Man shall be   Mw17
blaspheme, compelled them to   A26
blasphemous fellow, who is this   L5
blasphemy, put off all   PCo3
blood-money   Mw27
burst open so that his entrails poured out   A1
busybodies, we hear there are   ThS3
charlatans will make progress   PTS3
common cause against the Messiah, rulers made   A4
condemn yourself as unworthy of eternal life   A13
conflicts and quarrels, what causes   LJ4
crafty rogues, dupes of   PE4
crucified, handed Jesus over to be   J19
    the Lord of glory, powers that ruled the world   PCF2
damnation, in danger of eternal   Mk3
day of the Lord will come   LPS3
deadly sin, there is such a thing as   LJF5

43 TREACHERY AND TRICKERY

defraud his brother, let no man   ThF4
den of thieves, made my house a   Mw21; Mk11; L19
denied the Holy One, ye   A3
deny me thrice, thou shalt   Mw26; Mk14; L22
destruction, they are heading for   PPS3
dregs of humanity, we are treated as   PCF4
  of the populace, recruited from   A17
enemy, he is the   ThS2
envy, rivalry, and malevolence, they are one mass of   PR1
evil doer, root out the   PCF5
  for evil, never render   PR12; ThF5; LPF3
  love of money is the root of all   PTF6
  men shall wax worse and worse   PTS3
extortioners   PCF5
faith, lopped off for lack of   PR11
false apostles   PCS11
  witness against Jesus   Mw26
fight against the Holy Spirit, you always   A7
frame a charge against him, they wanted to   Mw12
Gentiles, Herod and Pilate conspired with the   A4
get thee behind me Satan   Mw16
godless and wicked age   Mk8
gossips and busybodies   PTF5
greed, ruthlessness, defiles the man   Mk7
ground their teeth with fury   A7
hate your enemy, they were told   Mw5
hated me without reason   J15
heathen men to crucify him, you used   A2
hypocrites love to pray where all can see them   Mw6
idle, they learn to be   PTF5
idling their time away   ThS3
impious and sinful, law is aimed at the   PTF1
infuriated, the whole congregation were   L4
injustice, filled with every kind of   PR1
jeered at him, 'Hail, king of the Jews!'   Mw27
Judas said to Jesus, 'Rabbi', and kissed him   Mk14
  would you betray the Son of Man with a kiss?   L22
judgement, terrifying expectation of   LH10
justice is mine, I will repay   LH10
kidnappers, liars, perjurers, law is aimed at   PTF1
kill himself, the jailer intended to   A16

43 TREACHERY AND TRICKERY

killed with the sword, he that killeth with the sword   Rev13
kiss, betrayed with a   Mw26; Mk14; L22
law of sin, a slave to the   PR7
liars and perjurers, law is made for   PTF1
libellously report me, as some   PR3
lied to the Holy Spirit   A5
lying in wait, a party more than forty strong are   A23
malice and deceit, away with all   LPF2
   and envy, our days were passed in   Tt3
   defiles the man   Mk7
   filled with every kind of rapacity and   PR1
misdeeds, responsible for other people's   PTF5
mocked him, the men surrounding Jesus   L22
    the soldiers   L23
   maltreated and spat upon, the Son of Man will be   L18
murderer, everyone who hates his brother is a   LJF3
oath not to eat or drink until they had killed Paul   A23
offence, the Pharisees have taken great   Mw15
perdition, an evident token of   PPs1
   going to   Rev17
persecuted the church of God, I   PCF15; PG1
persecution was started against Paul and Barnabas   A13
persecutor of the church in pious zeal   PPs3
perverse generation, what an unbelieving and   L9
pestilent fellow, Paul   A24
pilfer from the common purse, Judas used to   J12
plot laid against Paul   A20
poisoned their minds against Christians   A14
pretence and jealousy, away with all   LPF2
pretext of a closer investigation to do away with him   A23
property of widows, men who eat up the   Mk12
quarrels, a contentious temper, belong to the lower nature   PG5
   and conflicts, what causes   LJ4
rabble rousers   A17
railing with railing, not rendering   LPF3
rascal, swindler, son of the devil   A13
rebellion against God, the final   ThS2
   as in those days of   LH3
renounce their faith, tried to make them   A26
retribution, day of   PR2

43 TREACHERY AND TRICKERY

retribution, God's agents of   PR13
  has come, thy day of   Rev11
  has overtaken them   ThF2
  the fury of   PR2
  who warned you to escape from the coming   Mw3
riot in the daytime, count it pleasure to   LPS2
  run the risk of being charged with   A19
robber, Barabbas was a   J18
robber's cave, making my house a   Mw21; Mk11; L19
  fell into the hands of   L10
  have met dangers from   PCS11
root out the evil-doer from your community   PCF5
ruin and perdition, plunge men into   PTF6
ruthless greed nothing less than idolatry   PCo3
scandal, bishop may not be exposed to   PTF3
  deaconesses who will not talk   PTF3
  monger   PR1; PTS3; Tt2
scum of the earth, we are treated as   PCF4
sin, anything which does not arise from conviction is   PR14
  entered the world through Adam   PR5
  is death, the wages of   PR6
  it was the woman who fell into   PTF2
  Jews and Greeks alike are all under the power of   PR3
  lust conceives   LJ1
  not all sin is deadly   LJF5
  the sting of death is   PCF15
  wages of   PR6
sinfulness, deception of   ThS2
  their deliberate choice, make   ThS2
sinners, Jesus came into the world to save   PTF1
sins, elders who commit   PTF5
    you being dead in your   PCo2
sham apostles   PCS1
  Christians   PG2
shipwreck of their faith   PTF1
slander, base suspicions, quibbles which give rise to   PTF6
slandered by those who claim to be Jews   Rev2
slanderer, any Christian who is a   PCF5
  or swindler, no   PCF6
slaughter, the day has come for   LJ5
Son of God, he has claimed to be   J19

43 TREACHERY AND TRICKERY

Son of God, throw yourself down, if you are the   L4
spitefully, pray for those who treat you   L6
strife or vainglory, let nothing be done through   PPs2
stumbling block and retribution   PP11
   be placed in a brother's way, that no   PR14
   before the children, Balaam cast   Rev2
   to me, you are a   Mw16
   to the Jews and folly to the Greeks   PCF1
   to them that are weak   PCF8
  stone, I lay in Sion a   PR9
swindler, any Christian who is a   PCF5
  you rascal   A13
swindlers, no slanderers or   PCF6
  pagans who are   PCF5
terrorists   A21
test, conspired to put the Spirit to the   A5
  you are not to put the Lord your God to the   Mw4
thief, at what hour would come   Mw24
  come as a   LPs3
  come upon you like a   Rev3
  in the night   ThF5
  Judas was a   J12
  must give up stealing   PE4
  or robber climbs in some other way   J10
thieves, a den of   Mw21; Mk11; L19
  break in   Mw6
  fell among   L10
  or grabbers, no   PCF6
threatenings, Saul breathing out   A9
trespasses and sins, who were dead in   PE2
tricked him, saw the astrologers had   Mw2
unbelief, acted ignorantly in   PTF1
vengeance, cup of God's   Rev14
  fierce wine of his   Rev16
  has come, the great day of   Rev6
  is mine, I will repay, saith the Lord   PR12; LH10
venom, the tongue is charged with deadly   LJ3
viper's brood, you   Mw3
whisperers and scandal-mongers   PR1
wicked and godless age   Mk8
  Christ died for the   PR5

43 TREACHERY AND TRICKERY

wicked, fiery darts of the   PE6
  men and charlatans will make progress   PTS3
wickedness of men, retribution falling on   PR1
  the secret power of   ThS2
  this present age of   PG1
  will be revealed in human form   ThS2
widows, men who eat up the property of   Mk12; L20
wrath of God, seven golden bowls full of the   Rev15
  winepress of   Rev19
wrong for wrong, see that no one pays back   ThF5; LPF3
wrongs you, do not set yourself against the man who   Mw5
Zion, a stone to trip over, here I lay in   PR9

44 *Violence, Murder and Massacre*

OLD TESTAMENT

alive, in the nations of patrimony leave no creature   De20
   neither man nor woman did David bring back   SF27
assassinated, the governor of Judah   Je41
behead Elisha, the king sent to   KS10
beheaded, seventy sons of Ahab   KS10
blind and lame killed by David   SS5
blood, marked with   Le8, 14
   Nile turned to   Ex7
   of the Covenant   Ex24
   waters turned to   Ex4, 7
body flung into a pit, Absalom's   SS18
bound with new ropes, Samson   Ju15ff
branding   Is3
breath, did not leave alive any that drew   Jos11
burning as a penalty   Le20ff; Jos7; D3
   torches tied to jackals' tails   Ju15
burnt after stoning   Jos7; Nu15
   by Pharaoh, Gezer   KF9
   city of Jericho   Jos6
   every town within reach of the Israelites   Ju20
   Gibeah in revenge   Ju20
   harbourers of forbidden things   Jos7
   house of the Lord   KS25
   Jerusalem   KS25
   occupants of the castle of Shechem   Ju9
   Samson's wife and her father   Ju15
   thousand men and women   Ju15
butchered on a stone, sons of Gideon   Ju9
cannibalism under siege   KS6
children burnt as sacrifice to Baalim   Le20; KS17; CS28; Is57; E16, 23
   eaten under siege   KS6
   given in pledge for food   Ne5

44 VIOLENCE, MURDER AND MASSACRE

children, keep alive for yourselves   De20
  punished for their father's crime   Nu14, 31; Je31; E18; D6
  put to death   Ex1, 31; Nu21, 31; De2ff, 20ff, 23; Jos6ff;
      Ju1, 9, 11, 18, 20ff; SF7, 15, 22, 27; KF11; KS8, 10, 15, 25;
      D6, 20; Am1
  thrown to the lions   D6
corpses, the ground was strewn with   Ju9
cracked, the skull of Abimelech   Ju9
crime after crime of Gaza and Tyre   Am1
    of Israel   Am2
crushed by the city wall, 27,000 men   KF20
cut off, great toes and thumbs of Adoni-bezek   Ju1
    of seventy kings   Ju1
  head of Goliath   SF17
    of Ishbosheth   SS4
    of Saul   SF31; CF10
  heads of the Midianite princes   Ju7
  his hands and feet   SS4
  out your right eyes as a covenant   SF11
  the oxen to pieces, Saul in his anger   SF11
  up limb by limb, the concubine   Ju19
dash to the ground their children   KS8; Is13; Ho13; Na3
death penalty   Ex21ff; Le20, 24; Nu1, 15, 25, 35;
    De13ff, 17, 21f, 24; Jos7f, 10; KF2; D2; Est2, 4ff; Je26;
  for mercy killing   SS1
  put to, any who had not gone up at Mizpah   Ju21
  the scoundrels of Gibeah   Ju20
despoiled, Solomon's temple   KS16
destroy those you have taken prisoner   KS6
destroyed by the Chaldaeans, Jerusalem was   CS36
  every male in the country KF11
destruction, let an order be made for their   Est3
died, 20,000 men in the forest of Ephron   SS18
ear, blood on the   Le8, 14
eaten by dogs, Jezebel shall be   KF21
exterminate all Jews, orders sent out to   Est3ff
  inhabitants of the whole country   Jos9
  you, the Lord's delight to   De28
eyes, gouge out your own   SF11
  gouged out, Samson's   Ju16
  put out, Zedekiah's   KS25; Je39, 52

44 VIOLENCE, MURDER AND MASSACRE

fell in battle, 500,000 Israelites   CS13
  through the window, Ahaziah   KS1
    Jezebel   KS9
fire consumed the officer and fifty men   KS1
    thousand men and women in the castle   Ju9
  set over his head   KF16
    to Jericho   Jos6
    to Jerusalem   KS25
    to their fortresses   KS8
  the city destroyed with   SF30
flogged and put to death, those remaining at Jerusalem   KS25; Je52
flogging   De25; Je20, 37; E26
food for birds and dogs, Baasha's family   KF16
    House of Ahab   KF21
    The people   KF14
foreskins, Philistine, taken by way of vengeance   SF18; SS3
furnace, thrown into the blazing   D3
Goliath's head, David took   SF17
gouge out your eyes as a condition of surrender   SF11
    Zedekiah's eyes   KS25
hamstrung the chariot horses, David   SS8; CF18
hand cut off   De25
hanged, bodies of the five kings   Jos10
  king of Ai   Jos8
  the seven sons of Saul   SS21
head caught in an oak tree, Absalom's   SS18
humiliation of David's envoys   CF19
hung up by the hands   La5
hurl them to death   SS21
killed, 10 sons of Haman   Est9
  20 men by Jonathan   SF14
  30 men for their clothes, by Samson   Ju14
  85 priests by Doeg   SF22
  200 Philistines for their foreskins, by David   SF18
  360 followers of Abner   SS2
  600 Philistines with an ox-goad   Ju3
  700 Aramaeans in chariots   SS10
  800 men by the Jews in Susa   Est9
  4,000 Israelites on the field   SF4
  7,000 charioteers   CF19

44 VIOLENCE, MURDER AND MASSACRE

killed, 10,000 men of Seir   CS25
  10,000 Moabites   Ju3
  18,000 Benjamites   Ju20
  18,000 in the Valley of Salt   CF18
  18,000 Israelites   Ju20
  22,000 Aramaeans   SS8; CF18
  22,000 Israelites   Ju20
  25,000 Benjamites   Ju20
  30,000 Israelite foot-soldiers   SF4
  40,000 horsemen   SS10
  40,000 infantry   CF19
  42,000 at the fords of Jordan   Ju12
  75,000 enemies of the Jews   Est9
  100,000 infantry in one day   CS28
  120,000 troops in one day   CS28
  Agag by Samuel   SF15
  Ahab in battle   KF22
  Ahaziah by Jehu   CS22
  all oxen, asses and sheep of Nob   SF22
  Amaziah at Lachish   CS25
  Amnon, when Absalom said 'strike'   SS13
  blind and lame by David   SS5
  by a lion, the man of God   KF13
  by the flames, the men carrying Shadrach, Meshach and Abednego   D3
  children and babes in arms of Nob   SF22
  Elah by Zimri   KF16
  Ephraimites unable to pronounce 'Shibboleth'   Ju12
  every creature, by Benjamites   Ju20
  every Midianite boy, by Moses   Nu31
  family of Jeroboam, by Baasha   KF15
  governor of the Philistines   SF13
  herdsmen by the army   CS14
  Joab at the altar   KF2
  Joash by his servants   CS24
  Joram's brothers by Joram   CS21
  Jehoram by Jehu   KS9
  kings of Midian by Gideon   Ju8
  Mattan at the altar   CS23
  men and women of Nob   SF22
  Nadab by Baasha   KF15

44 VIOLENCE, MURDER AND MASSACRE

killed, newborn Israelite boys to be   Ex1
  Pekah by Hoshea   KS15
  Pekahiah by Pekah   KS15
  priests of high places   KS23
  Shallum by Menachim   KS15
  Zechariah by Shallum   KS15
lawlessness and robbery, put an end to   E45
lion's den, thrown into the   D6
little ones, massacre of   Nu31; De2ff
      Shimei by Solomon   KF2
  keep for yourselves the female   Nu31; De20
massacre, indiscriminate, ordered by Moses   Ex32
  of 30,000 inhabitants of Judah   CS25
    all the ministers of Baal   KS10
    Amorites by Saul   SF11
    Judaean officers   CS24
    inhabitants of Gibeah by Israelites   Ju20
      of Jericho by Joshua   Jos6
    men of Penuel by Gideon   Ju8
    people of Laish by Danites   Ju18
      of Shechem by Abimelech   Ju9
    population of the whole region by Joshua   Jos6
    prophets by Jezebel   KF18
    quiet and carefree people of Laish   Ju18
measured for slaughter: two cord's length put to death; one   cord's length spared   SS8
merciless annihalation by Joshua   Jos11
  killing, death for   SS1
messenger, killing the   SS1
mortally wounded, Ahaziah by Jehu   KS9
murder, categories of   Nu35
  of 42 kinsmen of Ahaziah   KS10
    70 brothers of Abimelech   Ju9
    70 princes by their guardians   KS10
    80 pilgrims   Je41
    Abel by Cain   Gen4
    Abimelech's brothers   Ju9
    Amon by his courtiers   KS21
    Egyptian by Moses   Ex2
    Ben-hadad by Hazael   KS8
    Eglon king of Moab   Ju3

44 VIOLENCE, MURDER AND MASSACRE

murder of Gedaliah and others at Mizpah   KS25
    Sennacherib by his sons   KS15
    Sisera with a tent-peg   Ju4
    the Levite's concubine   Ju20
    Uriah the Hittite   SS12
    sanctuary for   Nu35
nailed to the temple of Dagon, Saul's skull   CF10
  to the wall, the body of Saul   SF31
necks of the five kings, all the troops put their feet on the   Jos10
outrage committed by Israel   Jos7
parricide ordered by Moses   Ex32
pity, have no, put him to death   De13
plunder their possessions   Est3
pregnant women ripped open by Menahem   Ks15
priests fell by the sword   Ps78
prophets massacred by Jezebel   KF18
put to death, 31 kings by Joshua   Jos12
    all Amelekites by Saul   SF15
    all of Ahaba's house   KS10
    Amaziah by conspirators   KS14
    Adonijah by Solomon   KF2
    entire household of Ahab   KS10
    nobles of Judah   Je39, 52
    people of Gezer by Pharaoh   KF9
    prophets of Baal by Elijah   KF18ff
    Queen Athalia by Jehoiada   CS23
    Rezin by the king of Assyria   KS16
    servants who had killed Joash   CS25
    temple guardians at Jerusalem   Je52
raiding the country, David left no one alive   SF27
ravaged, the territory by Menahem   KS15
razed by the Chaldaeans, Jerusalem   CS36
  to the ground every fortified town   KS3
    the city of Rabbah   SS11
ripping open pregnant women   KS8, 15; Am1
rod, punishment with   SS7; Pro129, 26, 29; Is30; La3; Mi5
sack of Jerusalem   Je52
slain before the altars of Baal, Mattan was   KS11
  before his eyes, the sons of Zedekiah   KS25; Je39, 52
slaughter by Joshua of all at Ai   Jos8

44 VIOLENCE, MURDER AND MASSACRE

  slaughter by Joshua of all at Bethel   Jos8
        Debir   Jos10
        Eglon   Jos10
        Hazor   Jos11
        Hebron   Jos10
        Jericho   Jos6
        Lachish   Jos10
        Libnah   Jos10
        Makkedah   Jos10
        Shephelah   Jos10
        from Kadesh-barnea to Gaza   Jos10
        in the land of Goshen   Jos10
        the Negeb   Jos10
        the villages   Jos10
    of Amorites   Jos10
      beasts of Jericho   Jos6
      every living soul   Jos11
      every living thing   Jos10
      the population of the whole region   Jos10
      women and children   Jos8
  commanded by Moses:
    indiscriminate   Ex32
    of all in the cities   De2, 3
      Amorites   Nu21
      Bashanites   Nu21
      Canaanites   Nu21
      children   De2, 3
        except girl virgins to keep   Nu31
      friends and neighbours   Ex32
      Midianites   Nu31
      women   Nu31; De2, 3
  of two out of every three prisoners, by David   SS8
    42 kinsmen of Ahaziah by Jehu   KS10
  of 1,000 men with an ass's jawbone, by Samson   Ju15
    10,000 at Bezek, by the Israelites   Ju1
    18,000 Edomites by David   SS8
    Agag, by Samuel   SF15
    all inhabitants, except the virgins to keep   Ju21
    Ammonites by the Israelites   Ju11
    children and babes in arms, by Saul at Samuel's instigation
        SF15

44 VIOLENCE, MURDER AND MASSACRE

slaughter of herds and flocks, by Samuel
   newborn boys, ordered by Pharaoh   Ex1
   men and women of Jabesh-gilead, by the Israelites   Ju21
   ministers of Baal, by Jehu   KS10
   people of Jerusalem, by Judahites   Ju1
   Philistines, the Israelites kept up the   SF7
   prophets of Baal, by Elijah   KF18
spare no one   SF15
spoil their good land   KS3
sticks drove against Absalom's body, three stout   SS18
stoned to death, Achan, his family, and animals   Jos7
     Adoram   KF12
     disobedient sons   De21
     Hadoram   CS10
     Naboth   KF21
     Zechariah   CS24
stoning   Le20, 24; Nu15; De13f, 17, 21ff; Jos7; KF12, 21; CS24;
     E16
  David threatened with   SF30
strewn with their dead, the road was   SF17
struck down, 185,000 Assyrian soldiers   KS19
   in the face, Micaiah by Zedekiah   KF22; CS18
suffocated, Ben-hadad by Hazael   KS8
suicide, Saul fell on his sword   CF10
sword, driven into Eglon's belly   Ju3
  put to the, all the men, women and children   SF15
     enemies of the Jews   Est9
     every living thing in the city of priests   SF22
     infants and sucklings   SF15
     inhabitants of Bethel   Ju1
       of Gibeah   Ju20
       of Laish   Ju18
     the whole army of Sisera   Ju4
     their young men   KS8
  Saul fell on his   SF31
tear your bodies with briars   Ju8
terror, threat of sudden   Le26
thresh your bodies with thorns   Ju8
thrown bound into the furnace, Shadrach, Meshach and Abednego   D3
  down from the window, Jezebel was   KS9

44 VIOLENCE, MURDER AND MASSACRE

thrown into the Nile, every newborn baby to be   Ex1
   over a cliff, 10,000 men were   CS25
     to the lions, Daniel   D6
       Daniel's accusers, their wives and children   D6
thumbs and toes, blood on   Le8, 14
     of Adoni-bezek cut off   Ju1
trampled to death, the lieutenant   KS7
vengeance, foreskins of the Philistines taken in   SF18
victims of fire and sword, captivity and pillage   D11
wounded in the belly, Saul was   SF31

NEW TESTAMENT

bandit, do you take me for a   L22
beat him, they   L22
beaten with many stripes   L12
beheaded for the sake of God's word   Rev20
   James, Herod   A12
   John the Baptist, Herod   Mw14; Mk6; L9
blindfolded him, they   L22
bound, Jesus was sent   J18
broke their legs, the soldiers   J19
cane, beat him about the head with a   Mk15
chains, Jesus was put in   Mw27; Mk15
   Herod put John in   Mw14
   men and women put in   A22
   Peter was secured by two   A12
   shackled with two   A21
condemned to death, my vote cast against them   A26
cross and save yourself, come down from the   Mk15
crucified, handed him over to be   Mk15
   him at the place called The Skull, Golgotha   L23
   Jesus   Mw27; Mk15f; L23; J19
   with Jesus, two thieves   Mw27
crucifixion   Mw23, 26f; Mk15f; L2f; A2
crucify and kill him, you used heathen men to   A2
   him, they shouted all the louder   Mw27
   some of them you will kill and   Mw23
cut off the ear of the high priest's servant   Mk14; L22; J18
dart, thrust through with a   LH12

44 VIOLENCE, MURDER AND MASSACRE

deadly fume that kills   PCS2
death, clamouring for Paul's   A21
  Jesus put to   Mw27; Mk15; L23; J19
  should be put to   Mk14
  they shall put him to   L18
done to death, blood of all who had been   Rev18
drunk with the blood of God's people   Rev17
execution, Herod interrogated the guards and ordered their   A12
eye for eye, tooth for tooth, they were told   Mw5
flog a Roman citizen? can you legally   A22
  him and kill him, they will   L18
  some of them you will   Mw23
flogged, had the apostles   A5
  imprisoned, mobbed   PCS6
  ordered to be   A16
  Pilate had Jesus   Mw27; Mk15; J19
flogging, examine him by   A22
furnace, thrown into the blazing   Mw13
gibbet, hanging on a   A5
  put to death on a   A10
head in a charger, John the Baptist's   Mw14
irons, had him put in   A22
kill one another, to make men   Rev6
  Paul, conspired to   A23
  the heir, let us   L20
  the prisoners for fear that any should escape   A27
lash, tied him up for the   A22
maltreat them and stone them, a move to   A14
martyr Stephen, the blood of thy   A22
massacre of all children in Bethlehem, Herod ordered   Mw2
mocked, flogged and crucified, hand him over to be   Mw20
murder and treachery, they are one mass of   PR1
  defiles the man   Mk7
  of Stephen   A7
murderer, begged the release of a   A3
murderers, law aimed at   PTF1
  outside are   Rev22
murders, work of the flesh   PG5
persecute this movement to the death   A22
  you, they will   J15

44 VIOLENCE, MURDER AND MASSACRE

persecution, beginning of violent   A8
pierced his side with a spear   J19
prison, beheaded John the Baptist in   Mw4; Mk1, 6; L3
    cast in, Paul and Silas   A16
    Herod shut John the Baptist in   Mw4; Mk1, 6; L3
    Peter kept in   A12
    Saul sending men and women to   A8
prisoners for punishment, Christians were   A22
public flogging, though we are Roman citizens, they gave us   A16
put to death on the evidence of two or three   LH10
       the Son of Man to be   Mk8
       without pity   LH10
rods, beaten with   PCS11
sawn in two, they were   LH11
scourge a Roman citizen? is it legal to   A22
    and to crucify, deliver him to   Mw20
    him, they shall   L18
scourged, Paul   A22
    took Jesus to be   Mw27; Mk15; J19
scourging, examined by   A22
shackled, Paul was   A21
    Peter was   A12
slaughtered for God's word   Rev6
stabbed his side with a lance   J19
stocks, secured their feet in   A16
stone him, the Jews picked up stones to   J10
   us, the people will   L20
   you for your blasphemy   J10
stoned by the people, fear of being   A5
   even an animal must be   LH12
   I was   PCS11
   Paul, the crowds   A14
   Stephen, they   A7
   such women are to be   J8
   they were   LH11
stones to cast at him, they took up   J8
strike him on the mouth, ordered his attendant to   A23
strokes, given thirty nine   PCS11
struck at the high priest's servant and cut off his ear   Mw26
   him on the face, one of the police   J18

44 VIOLENCE, MURDER AND MASSACRE

sword, all who take the, die by the   Mw26
  death by the   LH11
  fall by the   L21
  put to the   LH11
thongs, tied him up with   A22
torture, condemned the man to   Mw18

45 Wars, Battles and Armies

OLD TESTAMENT

adjutant-general   KF4; KS18, 22, 25; CF18; Is36; Je36, 52
    Seraiah   SS8
    Sheva   SS20
advance, beckon with arm upraised to the   Is13
ambush, for the citizens of Ai   Jos8
    set all round Gibeah   Ju20
    for the Benjamites   Ju20
archer   CF10; CS14, 35; Ps55; Je4, 51; Am2
    Ishmael was a skilled   Gen21
    archers shot down from the walls   SS11
armour   SF14, 17, 31; KF10, 22; CS18; Ps45; E38
    washed of blood   KF22
armour-bearers   CF10ff
    Joab's   SS18
armoury   KS20; CS11; Ne3; Is39
    Hezekiah's   Is39
arms, call your troops to   Joe3
    capable of bearing, 470,000 in Judah   CF21
        1,100,000 in Israel   CF21
army, 232 young men of Ahab   KF20
    600 men mustered by Saul   SF13
    600 men under Hittai   SS15
    1,000 men from Maacah   SS10
    1,000 men to be with Jonathan   SF13
    2,000 men to be with Saul   SF13
    3,000 men of Benjamine   CF12
    3,000 men picked by Saul   SF13
    3,000 picked men to search fo David   SF26
    3,700 men of Jehoiada   CF12
    4,600 men of Levi   CF12
    6,000 horses of the Philistines   SF13
    6,800 men of Judah   CF12
    7,000 Israelites of Ahab   KF20

45 WARS, BATTLES AND ARMIES

army, 7,100 men of Simeon   CF12
  10,000 soldiers from Judah   SF15
  12,000 men from Tob   SS10
  17,200 men of Jediael   CF7
  18,000 men of Mansseh   CF12
  20,800 men of Ephraim   CF7
  26,000 men of Asher   CF7
  28,600 men of Dan   CF12
  30,000 chariots of the Philistines   SF13
  30,000 levied men under Solomon   KF5
  30,000 men from Judah   SF11
  30,000 men under David   SS6
  36,000 men of Izrahiah   CF7
  37,000 men of Naphtali   CF12
  40,000 men of Asher   CF12
  44,760 men of Reuben and Gad   CF5
  50,000 men of Zebulun   CF12
  120,000 men from east of Jordan   CF12
  180,000 chosen warriors under Reheboam   KF12; CS11
  180,000 men of Jehozabad   CS17
  200,000 foot soldiers at Telaim   SF15
  200,000 men of Amasiah   CS17
  200,000 men of Eliad   CS17
  280,000 men of Benjamin   CS14
  280,000 men of Johananan   CS17
  300,000 men from Israel   SF11
  300,000 men from Judah   CS14
  300,000 men of Adnach   CS17
  300,000 men of Amaziah   CS25
  375,500 men of Uzziah   CS26
  400,000 men of Abijah   CS13
  500,000 men capable of bearing arms   SS24
  800,000 men capable of bearing arms   SS24
  1,000,000 men of Zerah   CS14
  angel struck down the Syrian   Is37
  Babylonian   Je39; E26
  Chaldaean   Je37
  conscripted of the Israelites   Nu1ff
  Edomite   Nu20
  goest not forth with the   Ps108
  greater than yours   De20

45 WARS, BATTLES AND ARMIES

army into battle, thou dost no longer lead our   Ps44
   king is not saved by a great   Ps33
     of the north and a vast   D11
   kings have fled headlong with their   Ps68
   of Gog   E38
   of Nebuchadnezzar,   Je52
   Pharaoh's   Je37
     drowned   Ex14
   Philistines mustered their   SF28
   round you like a wall   Is29
   with banners, terrible as an   So6
   units of 50   SF8
     of 100 and 1,000   SS18
     of 1,000   SF8
   victory by Gideon's   Ju8
arrow   De32; SF20; KS9, 13, 19; Job16, 29, 41; Pro7, 25ff; Is5, 7, 37, 49; Je9, 50ff; La3; H3; Z9; Ps7, 11, 18, 38, 45, 57, 64, 76f, 91, 120, Ps127, 144; E5, 21, 39
   bronze-tipped   Job20; Ps18
   drunk with blood   De32
arsenal   Je50
attack on Amalekites by David   SF30
     Bethel by Joseph   Ju1
     Bezek by Judah and Simeon   Ju1
     Canaan, with Judah leading   Ju1
     Debir by Judah   Ju1
     Gath by Hazael   KS12
     Gibeon by Amorites   Jos10
     Israel by Aradites   Nu21
       by Ben-hadad   KF20
       by eastern tribes   Ju6
       by Eglon   Ju3
       by Hazael   KS10
     Jerusalem by Judah   Ju1
     Judah by Aram   KS15
       by Assyrians   KS18
     Kiriath-arba by Judah   Ju1
     Kiriath-sepher by Judah   Ju1
     Hebron by Judah and Caleb   Ju1
     Midianite camp by Gideon   Ju7
     Nadab by Maasha   KF15

45 WARS, BATTLES AND ARMIES

attack on Pekahiah by Pekah   KS15
   quiet and carefree people of Laish by Danites   Ju18
   Shallum by Menahem   KS15
   Shechem by Abimelech   Ju9
   Thebez by Abimelech   Ju9
   Zephath by Judah and Simeon   Ju1
  through the wilderness of Edom   KS3
avenge the outrage of Gibeah   Ju20
bait, let her be   SF18
banners, an army with   So6
barracks   Ne3
bastions, battering-rams against your   Na2
battering on a leaning wall   Ps62
battering-ram   E4, 21, 26; Na2
battle array, countless host in   Joe2
  between Abner and Joab   SS2
   David and Isgobosheth   SS2
   Israel and Amorites   Nu21
    and Aradites   Nu21
    and Bashanites   Nu21
    and Benjamites   Ju20
    and Edomites   Nu20; Ob1
    and Judah   KS14
    and Midianites   Nu31
    and Sihon   De2
   Joshua and Amalek   Ex17
   Judah and Canaanites   Ju1ff
  did not die in   Is22
  in the forest of Ephron   SS18
  Lord brought disaster in every   Ju2
   mighty in   Ps24
  Lord's prowess on the field of   Z14
  Moabites, do not provoke to   De2
  no longer lead our armies into   Ps44
  of Ephraim, David fought the Israelites in the   SS18
  of Jericho, Joshua's army in the   Jos6
  Philistines advancing to   SF7
   mustered for   SF4
  roused the frenzy of   Is42
  tramp the muddy ways in   Z10
  war-cries on the day of   Am1

45 WARS, BATTLES AND ARMIES

battle, will not save them by Ho1
battle-axe Je51; E9
battle-cry Je4; E21; Ho5; Zp1
   he will raise Is42
   signal for the Nu31
battlefield with shouting, Saul made for the SF14
battlements Ps84; E27
  laid in ruins Zp3
battle-quarters Ps76
beacon, fire the Je6
  for the nations Is42
  upon the top of a mountain Is30
bell, war-horse Z14
besieged, Jabesh-gilead by Nahash the Ammonite SF11
  Jerusalem by Nebuchadnezzar KS24ff
  Thebez by Abimelech Ju9
bodyguard, captain of the king's KS25; Je39ff
  scattered E12
bow SF18; SS1; KS6, 13; CS17, 26; Ne4; Job29; Ps37, 46, 78;
     Is5, 7, 13, 21, 41; Je6, 49ff; La1ff; E39; Am2; H3; Z9ff
  steel Job20
  strings Ju16; Ps7, 11, 21
  strung Ps37
bowman Ps78
breached, the wall of Jerusalem by Jehoash KS14
breastplate KF22; CS18; Is59
brigandine Je46, 51
buckler KF10; CS23; Ps35; So4; Je46; E23, 26, 38ff
  gold Ec9
burnt by the Israelites, every town within reach Ju20
  in revenge, the city of Gibeah Ju20
  the standing corn of the Philistines Ju15
camp, army Joe2
captain KF9; KS1, 11, 25; Je51
  of bodyguard KS25; Je39ff
  of chariots KF22
  of companies Is59
  of fifty KS1; Is3
  of guard Je43, 52
  of hundred KS11; CS23
  of raiding parties SS4

45 WARS, BATTLES AND ARMIES

captured, Amaziah by Jehoash   KS14
  1,700 horses   SS8
  20,000 foot soldiers   SS8
catapult, siege   CS26
cavalier   E23
cavalry   KF9, 20; Ne2; D11; H1
  escort of   Ne2
  he will make them serve in   SF8
  horses   KF4
  Pharaoh's   Ex14
champion, the Philistine Goliath   SF17
chariot, chariots   Is31, 36, 43; Je4, 17, 22, 46, 50ff; E23, 26ff, 39;
    Ho10; Joe2; Na3; Z6, 9
  burn their   Jos11
  captured by David, 1,000   CF1
  commanders   KF9; KS8; CS21
  countless   Is37
  horses of Pharaoh   So1
    of Solomon, 40,000   KF4
  like a whirlwind   Is66
  no end to their   Is2
  of Ammi-nadib   So6
  of iron, Canaanite   Jos17; Ju1, 4
  of Pharaoh   Ex14
  of Solomon   KF1, 4, 10; CS1
  of Zerah, 300   CS14
  ten left to Jehoahaz   KS13
  towns   KF10; CS1, 9
  two-horsed   Is21
  washed of blood   KF22
cheer when the trumpets sound   Nu10
club   CF11; Job41; Pro25; E21
coat of mail   CS26; Ne4; Is59; Je46, 51
commander, Aramis   KS5
  Banaiah   KF2, 4
  Hananiah   CS26
  Joab   SS8; CF18, 27
  of Ben-hadad   KF15; CS16
  of cavalry   KF9
  of chariots   KF9
  of Hedadezer   CF19

45 WARS, BATTLES AND ARMIES

commander of Hezekiah   CS32
   of Jabin's forces   Ju4
   of units   De1
   Sisera   Ju4
   squadron   E17
commander-in-chief, Abner   SF17; SS2ff; KF2
   Amasa   SS17, 19
   Assyrian   KS18
   Babylonian   Je51ff
   David's   KF1ff, 11
   flogged and put to death   KS25
   Ner   SF26
   Sargon's   Is20
   Saul's   SF14
   shall I speak for you to the   KS4
conscription, military   Nu31ff
   of young men   Nu1
dagger   SF17; Job16
dart   SS18; Job41; Pro7
defeat of Aramaeans   KF20
   of Joram by Edomites   KS8; CS21
   of Midianites   Ju8
deserted, men of Manasseh   CF12
enemy   Ps25, 27, 30ff, 35, 37, 44, 55ff, 60, 68, 78, 89, 97, 107, 110, 118,
       Ps127, 139, 143
   of all, none could withstand them   Jos21
   the sea closed over their   Ps78
   vengeance on my   Is1
engine of war   E26
ensign on an hill   Is30
enter the city, show us how to   Ju1
envoys, David's to the Ammonites   SS10
   from Babylon   KS20
   from Ben-hadad   KF20
   sent to Ahab   KF20
escort, armed   Je39
   for Absalom, 50 men   SS15
   of cavalry   Ne2
   officers of the   KF14
   warrior   So3
eunuch in charge of the fighting men   KS25

45 WARS, BATTLES AND ARMIES

Field of Blades   SS2
fighting men, Solomon's   KF9
   the Israelites were Solomon's   CS8
   eunuch in charge of the   Je52
fire, set to Jerusalem   Ju1
   set to Laish   Ju18
firebrands   Pro26; Is50
flight, one man can put a thousand to   Jos23
flint, make knives of   Jos5
fort   E4, 17, 21
fortifications, strengthen your   Na3
fortified cities captured   Ne9
   Ramah   KF15
fortress   D11
   razed   Ho10; Mi5
forts built around Jerusalem   KS25
   ruined   Is32
   siege   Is29
garrison   Je51; E26
  David established   CF18
    stationed   SS8
  Philistine   SF10
grappling-iron   SS5
guard   SS8, 15, 20; KF1
  duty on the gate   CF9
  house   Je32ff, 37, 39
  Jehu's   KS10
  Nebuchadnezzar's   D1
  room   KF14; CS12
  tower   Je51
habergeon, suit of armour   Ne4; Job41
handstave   E39
hate, a time to   Ec3
helmet   CS26; Ps60, 108; Is59; Je46; E23, 27, 38
hid in the fields, David   SF20
holy war, declare a   Joe3
horses and chariots, a great number of   Jos11
  hamstring their   Jos11
  I will give you 2,000 if you can find riders   KS18
  Solomon had 12,000   KF10; CS1
  squadrons of   Joe2

45 WARS, BATTLES AND ARMIES

horsemen   KF1; CS16; Je4, 46; E38ff; D11; Ho1; Am2; Na3; Z10
   in their thousands   Is31
   only fifty left to Jehoahaz   KS13
   rely on Egypt for   Is36
infantry, Aramaeans had 20,000   SS10
   countless as sand   SF13
   Jehoahaz left with 10,000   KS13
   Pharaoh's   Ex14
invasion of Israel by Assyrians   KS17
iron, barbed   Job41
   weapons of   Job20
javelin   SF18ff; Job41
   of Phinehas   Nu25
jawbone of an ass used as a weapon   Ju15
Jericho, collapse of the walls under siege   Jos6
killed in battle, 500,000 Israelites   CS13
   in one day, 120,000 troops   CS28
knife   KF18; Ez1; Job16; Pro30; Is18; E5
   flint   Jos5
lance   Je46, 50; E39
   burnished   Je46
lieutenant   KF9; KS9ff, 15
line of battle   SF17; KF20
machine, siege   CS26
mantelet, siege screen set in place   E4; Na2
march-past, David's army   SS18
marksman   Ps78
maul   Pro25
mercenary army of Aramaeans   SS10
   of 100,000 Israelites   CS25
   troops in Egypt   Je46
military service, conscription for   Nu1, 31ff; Jos4
   exemption from   De24
millstone thrown from the castle   De24; Ju9
mount, siege   Is29; D11
munition, keep the   Na2
muster, sound of the   Je4
mustered, 32 kings with their chariots   KF20
nail, hammered through Sisera's head   Ju4
navy   KF10

45 WARS, BATTLES AND ARMIES

night attack on the Philistines   SF14
officer in charge of 100   CF28; CS25
     of 1,000   CF13, 28; CS17, 25
  of the guard   Je37
officers dressed in blue or purple   E23
  over units of 100 and 1,000   SS18
outrunners   KF1
ox-goad as a weapon   Ju3
panic I spread before you   Jos24
  fled in, Midianites   Ju7
     Philistines   SF7
  that drove them out, not your sword   Jos24
  threat of   Le26
  will throw nations into   De7
panic-stricken, the whole country was   Jos2
plunder by Jehoshaphat and his men   Cs20
  Chaldaeans raided the camels for   Job1
  of camels and sheep   CS14
  of cities of Bashan   De3
  of city of Heshbon   De2
  of everything in the city   De20
  of houses in Jerusalem   Z14
  of Midianites   Nu31
  of Shechem's city   Gen34
  of treasures of Jerusalem taken to Egypt   CS12
  taken from you, shared out   Z14
  they turned to   SF14
post, I will stand at my   H2
quartermaster   SF17; Je51
quiver   SS8; Job39; Ps127; Is22, 49; Je5, 51; La3; H3
  gold   CF18
raided, Jerusalem by Jehoash   KS14
  the country, David   SF27
raiding parties from the Philistine camp   SF13
rampart   KF21; Ps91
ram's horn trumpet   Ex19
    at Jericho   Jos6
rebellion of Absalom   SS13ff
recaptured, cities taken by Ben-hadad   KS13
red, shields gleaming   Na2
reinforcements, Pharaoh sent to help Assyria   KS23

45 WARS, BATTLES AND ARMIES

rescued all the Amalekite prisoners   SF30
revenge by Gideon   Ju8
   on Abner   SS3
   on the Amalekites   SF15
revolt, the Hebrews were in   SF13
rifled, the houses of Jerusalem   Z14
roll, Saul's men called the   SF14
routed by the Philistines   SF4
   by the men of Israel at Gilboa   SF31
ruffians, a band of   Ps22
ruin, leave as a mound   De13
sabre   Job39, 41; Je6, 50
scabbard   SF17; Je47; E21
scarlet, their soldiers are all in   Na2
sentry   SS13
sentry-duty   Ne7
shaft, spear   H3
sheath   Je47; E21
shield   SS1; KF10; KS11; CF5; CS9, 11ff, 17, 23, 25ff, 32; Pro30; Is21ff, 37; Je46, 51; Am4; E23, 26ff, 32, 38ff; Na2; Z9
   bossed   Job15
   bronze   CS12
   gold   CS9, 12
shield-bearer   SF17; CS14
shields, burnish your   Is21
   of mighty men   S04
   of their warriors are gleaming red   Na2
   screen of   E26
shout, the whole army at Jericho   Jos6
   when the trumpets sound   Nu10
siege, Chaldaeans raised the   Je37
   closing in   Na2
   dire straits during the   Je19
   draw water for the   Na3
   laid to Tirzah   KF16
   machine   CS26
   mount   D11
   Nebuchadnezzar laid to Jerusalem   Je37, 52; D1
   of Jerusalem by Assyrians   CS32
   of Rabbah   SS11

45 WARS, BATTLES AND ARMIES

siege of Samaria   KS6, 17ff
  raise against Jerusalem   Je6
  ramp   SS20; KS19; Is37; Je6, 32ff; E4, 17, 21, 26; D11
  towers   Is23
  works   Ec9; Is29; H1
signal post on a hill   Is30
single combat   SS2
sling   SF12; CS26; Job41; Pro26; Z9
slingers   KS3
spear   Nu25; SF13, 17ff, 26; SS1ff, 21; KF18; KS11; CF11;
    CS11ff, 23, 25ff; Ne4; Job39, 41; Ps35, 46, 57; Is2; Je6, 4;
    E39; Joe3; Mi4; Na2ff; H3
  of Phinehas, transfixed by the   Nu25
spies sent out from Shittim   Jos1
spiked weapons   CS33
spoil from your enemies, share with your kinsmen   Jos22
  of Midian cities   Nu31
  of silver and gold   Na2
spy out all the land   De1
squadrons of Gomer and Beth-togarmah   E38ff
  of horse   Joe2; Na2
  of Moab   Nu24
  of the king of Jerusalem scattered   E12, 17
standard bearer   Is10
  march under the   Nu2
  planted as a token of vistory   Ps74
  raise the   Is13; Je51
  raised, how long must I see the   Je4
  stronghold   Ps31
surrender of Jehoiachin   KS24
  of the Hagarites   CF5
surrounded, Dothan by the Aramaeans   KS6
survey the country   Jos18
sword   Nu31; De13, 20, 28; Jos5ff, 19; Ju7; SF13, 17ff, 25; SS20;
    KF3, 18ff; KS6, 19; CF5, 10; Ne4; Job33, 39; Ps7, 22, 37, 44ff,
    Ps55, 57, 63ff, 76, 78, 89, 144, 149; Pro5, 25, 30; La1f, 4ff;
    Is1ff, 13ff, 21ff, 27, 31, 34, 37, 41, Is49, 51, 65ff; E5ff, 11ff, 14,
    E16ff, 21, 23ff, 28ff, 35, 38ff; Je2, 5ff, 9, 11ff, 14ff, 18ff, 24ff,
    Je29, 31ff, 38ff, 44, 46ff; D11; Joe2ff; Am1, 4, 7, 9; Mi4ff;
    Na2ff; Zp2; Hg2; Z9,11,13
  Balaam slain with the   Nu31

45 WARS, BATTLES AND ARMIES

sword, curse of the   De28
  devoured with the   Is1
  drawn in front of Joshua   Jos5
  of Ehud   Ju3
  of Gideon   Ju7
  people of Leshem put to the   Jos19
  put all males to the   De13
  put inhabitants to the   De13
  ready at his side, each with his   So3
  young and old put to the   Jos6
swords, 400,000 Israelites with   Ju20
swordsmen, Solomon's escort skilled   So3
  king of Moab took 700   Ks3
target, buckler, of gold   KF10
tent peg hammered through Sisera's head   Ju4
throwing-stick   E39
tower of strength   Ps9, 18, 20
trench, front line   SF17
troops of horses   Am4
trumpet and battle-cry, a day of   Zp1
  call   Je4, 6, 42, 52
  signal for battle-cry   Nu31
undefended city of Ai burnt   Jos8
undermining the city walls   SS20
vengeance, day of   Is61
  exacted on the Midianites   Nu31
  granted me   Ps18
  on killers of Ishbosheth   SS4
victory assured   Le26
  his right hand and holy arm have won him   Ps98
  is the fruit of long planning   Pro11
  of Gideon over the Midianites   Ju8
  praise of your   Ps20
  standards as a token of   Ps74
war any more, neither shall they learn   Is2
  book of the Lord   Nu21
  broke out, none had spear or sword   SF13
    once again   SS21
  declare a holy   Joe3
  fit for, at eighty-five   Jos14
  houses of David and Saul at   SS2ff

45 WARS, BATTLES AND ARMIES

war, Israel with Judah   KF15
   let us solemnly declare   Je6
   never again be trained for   Mi4
   on Israel, the king of Aram making   KS6
   Philistines collected their forces for   SF17
   revel in   Ps68
   stamps out   Ps46
   teach each succeeding generation how to make   Ju3
   time for peace, a time for   Ec3
   trains my hands for   Ps144
   waged by David's men at Keilah against the Philistines   SF23
war-cry, war-cries, on the day of battle, amid   Am1ff
   men of Esrael and Judah raised   SF17
   the Philistines raised   SF17
war-horse   E23; Joe2; Z9ff, 14
   inscribed bells on the   Z14
   plunges into battle   Je8
warrior and soldier, every   Is3
   bull-calf of all nations   Ps68
   chieftain   E32
   endowed with princely qualities, David   Ps89
   shall not save himself   Am2
   to keep you safe   Zp3
warriors, confidence of returning   Mi2
   flung into the sea   E27
   ruthless   E32
   served as   E27
   sharp arrows in store for you   Ps120
   trusted in the number of your   Ho10
watchman   So3, 5; E3, 33; Ho9
watch-tower   KS9, 17ff, 25; Is5, 21, 32; Je52; E4, 17, 21, 26
   erected on every side   KS25
   take position on the   H2
weapons, discarded   E39

NEW TESTAMENT

active service, a soldier on   PTS2
adversary the devil   LPF5
armies, Jerusalem encircled by   L21

45 WARS, BATTLES AND ARMIES

armies of heaven   Rev19
  of the beast   Rev19
armour, let Jesus be the   PR13
  of God   PE6
  of righteousness   PCS6
  on which a man relies   L11
  put on our   PR13
  which God provides, put on the   PE6
arms, carries off the   L11
army at his own expense, serving in the   PCF9
  then came I with an   A23
arrows, flaming   PE6
Augustan cohort   A27
barracks   A21ff
battle of God, day of   Rev16
  who shall prepare himself to the   PCF14
  without first sitting down to consider   L14
battles, there shall be   Mk13
bow, rider held a   Rev6
breastplate   PE6; Rev6
  of faith and love   ThF5
breastplates, fiery red, blue and sulphur yellow   Rev9
captain, army   J18; A21
  of the guard   A28
cavalry, squadron of   Rev9
cavalrymen, seventy   A23
centurion   Mw8, 27; Mk15; L7, 23; A10, 21ff, 27
chariots and horses, cargoes of   Rev18
  rushing to battle, noise of   Rev9
chief captain   A23
coat of mail   A23; PE6; ThF5
    armed with faith and love for   ThF5
cohort, Augustan   A27
  Italian   A10
  officer commanding the   A21
commandant   A21ff
  Claudius   A23
commanders and fighting men, to eat the flesh of   Rev19
  Herod's   Mk6
commanding officer   A24; PTS2
comrade-in-arms   Ph1

45 WARS, BATTLES AND ARMIES

conquerors, we are more than   PR8
darts, fiery   PE6
detachment of soldiers, Judas took a   J18
envoys and asks for terms, he sends   L14
escort for Paul, a safe   A23
fight gallantly armed with faith   PTF1
force of soldiers came down at the double   A21
guard, Herod's   MK6
  post   A12
  sentry   A12
  Pilate's   Mw28
helmet   PE6
  hope of salvation for   ThF5
horsemen, seventy   A23
horses and chariots rushing to battle   Rev9
  equipped for battle   Rev9
infantry, two hundred   A23
insurrections, when you hear of wars and   L21
Italian cohort   A10
light-armed troops, 200   A23
messenger, the centurion's   A10
military guard, in prison under   A12
nation shall rise against nation, and kingdom against kingdom   L21
officer commanding   A21, 24; PTS2
orderly, military   A10
peace, have they not know the way of   PR3
quaternion of soldiers   A12
rode forth, conquering and to conquer   Rev6
sentry   A12
shield   PE6
siege-works, your enemies will put up   L19
slaughter one another, to make men   Rev6
soldier   Mw8; Mk6; L3, 7, 23; J18f; A27f
  fellow   Ph1
  like a good   PTS2
soldiers, a force of   A21
  a man set under authority, having under me   L7
  asleep between two   A12
  consternation among the   A12
  of Herod's guard   Mk6

45 WARS, BATTLES AND ARMIES

soldiers of Pontius Pilate   Mw27f; Mk15
   of the light   PR13
   the governor's   A23
   two hundred   A23
spearmen, two hundred   A23
spies, sent forth   L20
squadrons of cavalry   Rev9
sword, cuts more keenly than a two-edged   LH4
   given a great   Rev6
   held power of the   PR13
   remnants were slain with the   Rev19
   sharp two-edged   Rev1
   the right to kill by   Rev6
   to kill, who takes the   Rev13
   two-edged, out of his mouth a   Rev1f
trench about thee, enemies cast a   L19
troop commander   J18
troops, Herod's   L23
trumpet call for battle   PCF14
victorious, to him who is   Rev2
victory is mine; I have conquered the world   J16
war broke out in heaven   Rev12
   going to make   L14
   I shall make   Rev2
   came of your lusts   LJ4
weapons of righteousness, we wield   PCS6, 10

46 Water, Wells and Rivers

OLD TESTAMENT

brook, Kidron   KF15; KS23; CS15, 29ff
  of Cherith   KF17
  of Gaash   SS23
  of the willows   Is15
  The, land boundary   E48
canal, Chebar, Kebar   E1, 43
cataract   Ps42
cistern at Secu, the great   SF19
  cracked   Je2
  drink water from your own   Pro5
  each drink water from his own   KS18; Is36
  for the waters of the Old Pool   Is22
  hewn out for themselves   Je2
  rock-hewn   De6; Ne9; Je2
  Uzziah dug many   CS26
  wheel broken at the   Ec12
conduit of the Upper Pool   KS18; Is7, 36
  Hezekiah built, to carry water to Jerusalem   KS20
damned its rivers   E31
deep waters   Ps104
dew   De32, 33; Job38; Ps133; Pro3, 19; So5; Is18; D4ff; Ho6, 13ff
ditch for the water at the Old Pool   Is22
  irrigation   Ps65
flood   Ps24, 29, 69, 88
  land swept by   Is28
  Noah's   Gen6ff; Ps104; Is54
  overwhelming   Is28
  used to rise from the ground   Gen2
fords of the Arnon   Is16
  of the Jordan   Jos; Ju3, 12
  of the wilderness   SS15ff
fountain of life   Ps36

46 WATER, WELLS AND RIVERS

fountain, pitcher broken at the   Ec12
   to remove impurity   Z13
   sealed   So4
   spring from the Lord's house   Joe3
   troubled   Pro25
furrow, water   Ps65
gorge, Kidron   SS15; KF2, 15
   of Arnon   Nu21ff
   of Eshcol   Nu32
   of Kanah   Jos16ff
   of Shittim   Joe3
   of the Arabah   Am6
   of the Arabim   Is16
   of Zared   Nu21
irrigation   Ec2; Is58; Je31; E17
Kebar, Chebar canal   E1, 43
marshes, salt   E47
mist and fog   Ps105, 135; Is44; Je10, 51; Ho6, 13; Joe2; Zp1
ocean   Ps8, 77, 93, 148
   depths   Is51
   primeval   E26
polluted, the water is   KS2
   well   Pro25
ponds for fish   Is19
pool, artificial at Jerusalem   Ne3
   Great, at Gibeon   Je41
   in Hebron   SS4
   King's   SS12; Ne2
   Lower   Is22
     of Caleb   Jos15
   of Gibeon   SS2
   of Jerusalem   KS20
     Upper   KS18
   of Rabbah   SS12
   of Samaria   KF22
   of Shelah   Ne3
   of Siloah   Ne3
   of Sirah   SS3
   of water, you must give me   Jos15
   Old   Is22

46 WATER, WELLS AND RIVERS

pool, Upper   Is36
  at Jerusalem   Is36
  of Caleb   Jos15
pools in Heshbon   So7
  of Caleb   Ju1
  saltpans and swamps   E47
rain   Gen7; Le26; De11; KF17, 18; Ps65, 68, 72, 78, 135;
      Pro16, 25f, 28; Ez10; Ec11ff; Is4, 55; Je5, 10, 18, 51;
      E13, 38; Ho6; Am4; Z10
  forty days   Gen7
ravine of Kerith   KF17
ravines of Gaash   SS23; CF11
reservoir   Ne3
River Arnon   KS10; Is16; Je48
  Chebar, Kebar   E1, 3, 10, 43
  Euphrates   De1; Jos1, 24; SS8ff; KF4, 14; KS23; CF5, 18ff; CS9m 35;
      Is7ff; Je2, 13, 46, 51; Mi7; Z10
    flooding of the   Is8
    Great Bend of the   SS10
  Gihon   CS32
  Gozan   KS17; CF5
  Habor   KS17ff
  Jordan   De9, 27; Jos1ff, 13, 16, 22; SS2, 16, 24; KF2, 17;   KS5ff, 10;
      CF12, 19; Ps114; Is9; Je12, 50
    at the time of harvest   Jos3
    divided the waters of the   Jos3
    swelling of the   Je50
  Kadesh   E47
  Kebar, Chebar   E1, 3, 10, 43
  Kidron   SS15; KF2, 15; KS23; CS15, 29ff; Je31
  Kishon   Ju5
  Nephtoah   Jos15
  Nile   Ex1; Is18ff, 63; E29ff, 32; Am8ff; Na3; Z10
    rising like the   Le46
  Shihor   Je2
  Shiloah   Is8
  sluices opened   Ne2
  The   Ps72, 80, 89; Is11; Je2
  Tigris   D10
  which flows towards Ahava   Ez8
river-crossings   Je51

46 WATER, WELLS AND RIVERS

rivers among the sand-dunes   Is41
  dammed   E31
  dries up   Ps74
  in the barren desert   Is43
  of Babylon   Ps137
  of Cush   Is18
  of Ethiopia   Is18
  run into the sea   Ec1
saltpans, swamps and pools   E47
sea   Ps65ff, 68, 72, 78, 80, 89, 96, 98, 135; Pro8, 23
  and its waves roared   Je31
  Chinneroth   Jos12ff
  churned up by the four winds   D7
  closed over them   Ps106
  Dead   Nu34; De3; Jos3, 12, 15, 18; CS20; E39
  divided   Ps78
  Egyptian   Is11
  Great   Nu34; Jos1, 9, 15; E47ff
  he gathered them   Ps33
  Kinnereth   Jos12ff
  Mediterranean   Jos1, 9, 15; E47ff
  of Arabah   De3ff; Jos3, 12; KS14
  of Joppa   Ez3
  of Reeds   KF9; Ne9; Ps106; Je49
  of the Plain   KS14
  Red   Nu33; De1; Jos24; KF9; Ne9; Ps106, 136; Je49
    by way of the   Nu14, 21
    divided   Ex14
    locusts blown into the   Ex10
    towards the, by way of the wilderness   Ex13
  suck the abundance of the   De33
  the surging   Ps89
  Western   De34; Ps139
sea-bed   Ps18
sluices and ponds for fish   Is19
  of the rivers opened   Na2
spring at Jericho   KS2
  channels for the   Ps74
  Dragon   Ne2
  drink from your own   Pro5
  muddied   Pro25

46 WATER, WELLS AND RIVERS

spring, pitcher shattered at the   Ec12
  of Fright   Ju7
  of Lehi   Ju15
  of living water   Je2
  of Meribah   Nu20
  of Nephtoah   Jos15
springs, blocked by Hezekiah   CS32
  bubbling   Is35, 49
    in a thirsty land   Is35
  from parched land   Ps107
  land of   De8
  of Jordan   Ps42
  stop up their   KS3
  turn dry land into   Is41
  twelve, of Elim   Ex15; Nu33
streams blocked by Hezekiah   CS32
  from Lebanon   So4
  from the rock   Ps78
  land of   De8
  of Egypt   Is27, 37
    dried up all the   Is37
  of Judah   Joe3
  of the Euphrates   Is27
  of thy delights   Ps36
  of Ulai   D8
  out of the cliff   Ps78
  place of rivers and broad   Is33
  run into the sea   Ec1
  running   Ps42
  turbulent in flood   Je46
swamp if Libnath   Jos19
swamps, pools and saltpans   E47
torrent beside the path   Ps110
  channels for the   Ps74
  of Egypt   Nu34; Jos14; KF8; KS24; Is27
  of Kishon   Ju4; Ps83
  swept over us   Ps124
torrents, cool rain streaming in   Je18
  in dry land   Is35
  pour down the hill-side   Mi1
water, bitter, that causes the curse   Nu5

46 WATER, WELLS AND RIVERS

water from the rock   Ne9; Nu20; Is48
  from the temple in Ezekiel's vision   E47
  I purify this   KS2
  lustral   Nu8
  of contention   Nu5
  of Jordan cut off   Jos9
  of Meribah   Nu20
  piled up like a bank   Jos3
  polluted   KS2
  poured out before the Lord   SF7
  purifying   Nu8
  spring of living   Je2
  undrinkable   Ps78
water-channels dried up   Joe1
watercourse, planted beside the   Ps1
water-hole of Vaheb   Nu21
waters above the mountains   Gen6; Ps104
  deep   Ps104
  dividing the   Is63
  gathered   Gen1
  I am come into deep   Ps69
  land of   De8
  made sweet   Ex15
  of Babylon   Ps137
  of comfort   Ps23
  of Dimon   Is15
  of Meribah   Ps81, 106; E47
  of Meribah-by-Kadesh   De32
  of Nimrim   Is15
  risen   Ps69
  roar of mighty   Is17
  teem, let the   Gen1
  turned to blood   Ex7
water-spouts   Ps148
watery depths   Ps71
well by the gate of Bethlehem   CF11
  drink out of thine own   Pro5
  in Hagar's vision   Gen16
  jump into, to escape arrest   Pro28
  keeps its water fresh   Je6
  of Abimelech   Gen21

46 WATER, WELLS AND RIVERS

well of Abraham   Gen21, 26
  of Beersheba   Gen21
  of Esek   Gen26
  of Hagar   Gen21
  of Horeb   Ex17
  of Isaac   Gen26
  of living water   So4
  of Massah   Ex17
  of Meribah   Ex17; Nu20
  of Moses   Ex17
  of Reheboth   Gen26
  of Secu, the great   SF19
  of Shibah   Gen26
  of Sitnah   Gen26
  of the Living One of Vision   Gen16, 25
  of wisdom   Pro18
  tainted   Pro25
  wheel broken at the   Ec12
wells, I have dug   Is37
  in the valleys   Is41
  of salvation   Is12
  stop all their   KS3

NEW TESTAMENT

brook, Kedron, Cedron   J18
cross-currents, caught between   A27
deluge upon the world of godless men   LPS2f
flood, Noah's   Mw24; L17; LPS2f
fountain   LJ3
fountains, star fell upon   Rev8
lake, a heavy squall struck the   L8
  casting a net into the   Mw4
  of Gennesaret   L5
  walking on the   Mw14; Mk6; J6
lake-side, began to teach by the   Mk4
    Jesus sat by the   Mw13
      went to the   MK2f
mist   LJ4; LPS2
ocean where the great whore sat   Rev17
pool at the sheep market   J5

471

46 WATER, WELLS AND RIVERS

pool of Siloam   J9
quicksand   A27
rain   Mw5; Mk4; L4, 8, 12; A14, 28; LH6; LJ5
river, Euphrates   Rev9, 16
  Jordan   Mw3; Mk1; L4; J1, 3, 10
  of the water of life in John's vision   Rev21
rivers and springs, a third of   Rev8
     turned into blood   Rev16
  have met dangers from   PCS11
  of living water   J7
riverside, went outside the city gate to the   A16
rushing waters, voice like   Rev1
sea, battling with a rough   Mw14
  better for him to be thrown into the   L17
  dangers of   PCS11
  drowned in the depths of the   Mw18
  every living thing died in the   Rev16
  fierce waves of the   LJu1
  head-wind at   A27
  Jesus walking on the   Mw14; Mk6; J6
  of Adria   A27
  of Galilee   Mw4, 15; Mk1, 7; J6
  of glass   Rev4
  of Tiberius   J6, 21
  Red   A7; PCF10; LH11
  roar and surge of the   L21
  ruffled by the wind, a heaving   LJ1
  saw a beast rising out of the   Rev13
  side, Jesus sat by the   Mw13
    began to teach by the   Mk4
  thrown into the   Mk9
  turned to blood   Rev8, 16
  walking on the   Mw14; Mk6; J6
shallows, running on to the   A27
spring, always welling up, an inner   J4
  called Jacob's Well   J4
springs, a third of rivers and   Rev8, 16
  of the water of life   Rev7, 21
  that give no water   LPS2
tempest, tossed in the   A27
water, does a fountain gush with both fresh and brackish   LJ3

46 WATER, WELLS AND RIVERS

water, Jesus walking on the   Mw14; Mk6; J6
  of life   J4; Rev7
  of the Euphrates dried up   Rev16
  poisoned   Rev8
  Samaritan woman came to draw   J4
  springs of life   Rev21
  streams of living   J7
  turned into wine   J2
  walked on the   Mw14; Mk6; J6
waters, voice like rushing   Rev1
waves, tossed by the, whirled about   PE4
well, donkey or ox falls into a   L14
  Jacob's   J4
  Jesus sat down by the   J4
wells without water   LPS2

47 *Weather*

OLD TESTAMENT

cloud   Ps18, 147; Pro8, 16
  and dense fog   Joe2; Zp1
  and wind without rain   Pro25
  darkens the dawn with thick   Am4
  dispersed like   Is44
  drop dew   Pro3
  heavy with rain   Ec11
  no bigger than a man's hand   KF18
  out of the sea, ariseth a little   KF18
  poured water   Ps77
  with flashes of fire   E1
cloud-banks   Is14
cloudburst   Is30
cloud-masses   Job26
dew   Job38; Ps133; Pro3; Ho6, 13ff
  drenched with   So5; D4ff
  heavens withhold their   Hg1
  heavy at harvest time   Is18
  nor rain, neither   KF17
  skies drip with   De33
  upon the grass   Pro19
  words distil like   De32
drought, scorching   Is25
dust, curse of   De28
dust-storm   Ps78
earth shakes, the heavens shudder   Joe2
earthquake   KF19; Is29; E38; Am1
east wind, cruel blast   Is27
    locusts carried by   Ex10
    rolled back the Red Sea   Ex14
fire and hail   Ex9
fog   Ps105; Joe2; Zp1
frost   Job38; Ps147

47 WEATHER

frost at night   Je36
frozen, the water stands   PS147
gale   Ps148
hail   Job38; Ps78, 105, 148; Is32; Hg2
  sweeping storm of   Is28
hailstones   E38
  as hard as rock   E13
  the Lord hurled great   Jos10
hailstorm   Ex9
hoar-frost   Ps147
hurricane   Pro1; E38; Jon1
ice   Job6, 38
  crystals of   Ps148
  sheet of   E1
lightning   Ps18, 77, 97, 144; D10
  out of the fire   E1
  with rain   Je10, 51
mist, a dissolving   Is44
  from the ends of the earth   Ps135; Je10, 51
  morning   Ho6, 13
murk and gloom, a day of   Zp1
rain and tempest   Is4
  at the proper time   Le26
  both autumn and spring   De11
  cloud   Pro16
  clouds full of   Ec11ff
  falling on crops   Ps72
  forty days   Gen7
  gives or holds back   Pro25ff
  I hear the sound of coming   KF18
  in the autumn   Z10
  in the spring   Z10
  killed vines and figs with torrential   Ps78
  makes the earth blossom   Is55
  nor dew, neither   KF17
  of autumn and spring, showers in their turn   Je5
  of heaven   De11
  opens rifts for the   Ps135
  refresh the land with   Ps68
  shivering, the people sat in heavy   Ez10
  streaming in torrents, cool   Je18

47 WEATHER

rain, sweeping   Pro28
   teeming   E38
   torrential   E13
   torrents of   Ps78
   visit the earth with   Ps65
   with lightning   Je10, 51
rainbow   Gen9, E1
scorching wind blew up from the east   Jon4
showers, abundant rain   Am4
   like spring rains   Ho6
   watering the earth   Ps72
   withheld   Am4
skies, unfurled the   Je10
smoke in the wind   Ps68
snow   SS23; CF11; Job6, 24, 37ff; Ps51, 148; Pro25ff, 31;   Is1, 55; Je18; La4; D7
   at harvest   Pro25
   in summer   Pro26
snowflakes   Ps68
spring rains that water the earth   Ho6
storm   Is17, 21; Na1
   and rain   Is4
   at sea   Ps107; Jon1
   icy   Is25
   ride out the   H2
   wind   E1
storm-clouds   Z10
storm-winds of the south   Z9
tempest   Ps83, 91; Is4, 28ff, 32, 54; Am1
   blowing up a mighty   Je25
   of rain and hailstones   Is30
   shelter from the   Is25
thunder   Ps68, 81, 104; Is17, 29; Am4
   and rain   SF12
thundered long and loud   SF7
   the skies   Ps77
west wind dispersing locusts   Ex10
whirlwind   Ps77; Pro1, 10; Is5, 17, 21, 40; Je23, 30; E1; D11; Ho13; Am1; Na1; H3; Z7
   of the south   Z9
   sows the wind and reaps the   Ho8

47 WEATHER

wild and stormy, the weather grew   Ju19
wind, cruel blast of the east   Is27
  east   Ps48
    bringing locusts   Ex10
    rolled back the Red Sea   Ex14
  fine as dust before the   Ps18
  from his storehouses   Je10
  from the Lord   Nu11
  let loose   Ps78
  mighty   Gen1
  north   Pro25
  out of his storehouses   Ps135
  smoke in the   Ps68
  sows the, and reaps the whirlwind   Ho8
  south, he drove   Ps78
  voice of the Lord   Ps29
  west, dispersing locusts   Ex10
winds of heaven, the four   Z2

NEW TESTAMENT

battling with a head-wind and a rough sea   Mw14
breeze sprang up, a southerly   A27
cloud appeared, casting its shadow over them   Mk9
  banking up in the west   L12
  cast a shadow over them   L9
  pillar of   PCF10
  removed him from their sight   A1
  white, in John's vision   Rev14
clouds carried away by the wind   LJu1
  he is coming with the   Rev1
  of heaven   Mw24
  that are carried with a tempest   LPS2
earthquake   Mw27f; Mk13; L21, 23
eclipse of the sun   Mw27; Mk15; L23
Euroclydon: the fierce north-east wind   A27
fair weather   Mw16
fierce wind, the north-eastern   A27
four winds, gather his chosen from the   Mk13
gale, like figs shaken down by a   Rev6

47 WEATHER

gales, ships driven by strong   LJ3
hail, a storm of   Rev11
  fire and blood   Rev8
hailstones weighing perhaps a hundredweight   Rev16
head-wind and a rough sea, battling with a   Mw14
    labouring against a   Mk6
head-winds at sea   A27
heat wave when the wind is from the south   L12
heavy weather, making   A27
ice, a sheet of   Rev4
lightning   Mw24; Rev8
  and thunder   Rev16
  fell from heaven   L10
  flash that lights up the earth   L17
  from the throne   Rev4
mist seen for a while and then dispersing   LJ4
  driven by a storm   LPS2
rain, a sign of   L12
  down came the   LJ5
  from heaven, he sends you   A14
  it was cold and had started to   A28
  may fall, shut up the sky so that no   Rev11
  none for three years and six months   L4
  on the honest and the dishonest   Mw5
  prayed that there should be no   LJ5
  when earth drinks in the   LH6
  when you see cloud banking up in the west   L12
rainbow round the angel's head   Rev10
  round the throne   Rev4
rains, autumn and spring   LJ5
red sky in the evening   Mw16
    in the morning   Mw16
shower, there cometh a   L12
sign of rain in the west   L12
signs of the times, can ye not discern   Mw16
sky turned black   Rev6
snow, white as   Mk9
southerly breeze sprang up   A27
squall, a heavy   Mk4; L8
storm arose on the lake, a great   Mw8
  mists driven by a   LPS2

47 WEATHER

storm of wind on the lake   L8
  subsided and all was calm   L8
  was raging, a great   A27
strong wind was blowing and the sea was rough   J6
tempest, clouds that are carried with a   LPS2
  exceedingly tossed with a   A27
thunder, peals of   Rev4, 8
  some said it was   J12
thunders spoke, seven   Rev10
whirlwind   LH12
wind, a noise like that of a strong driving   A2
  a rushing mighty   A2
  and the sea obey him, even the   Mk4
  and waves, he gives his orders to the   L8
  bloweth where it listeth   J3
  in the south forecasting a heat-wave   L12
  set the foresail to the   A27
  south, sprang up   A27f
winds, angels holding back the four   Rev7
winter, pray that it may not be   Mw24
  try to get here before   PTS4

48 *Weights, Measures and Coins*

OLD TESTAMENT

acres, vineyard of five   Is5
balances   E5; Am8
   falsifying the   Am8
   the wicked   Mi6
bath as measure of wine and oil   CS2
   fixed measure   E45
   of oil, one hundred   Ez7
   of water   KF7
   of wine   Is5
breadth and length of Jerusalem   Z2
bushel, accursed short   Mi6
   giving short measure in the   Am8
   honest   E45
   of barley   Ru2
   of seed   Is5
   of soil   Is40
   ten of seed, yielding only a peck   Is5
cab, kab, quarter, of locust beans   KS6
cubits, buildings, detailed measurements in   KF6ff
   capital, height in   Je52
   dagger, length in   Ju3
   flying scroll in Zechariah's vision, dimensions in   Z5
   gallows, height in   Est5
   Goliath, height in   SF17
   house measurements in   CS3
   land measurements in   Nu35
   long   E40
   measuring-rod in   E40ff
   Nebuchadnezzar's golden image, dimensions in   D3
   new temple, dimensions in   Ez6
   temple pillar, circumference in   Je52
     height in   Je52
   wall of Jerusalem repaired, length in   Ne3

48 WEIGHTS, MEASURES AND COINS

darics, 10,000 given   CF29
drachmas, drams, gold contributions to fabric fund   Ez2; Ne7
  gold contributions to rebuilding funds   Ne7
    golden bowls of 1,000   Ez8
ephah, fixed standard   E45
  making small dishonestly   Am8
  measure of barley meal   Nu5
    of flour   Le24; Nu15, 28; Ju6
    of grapes   Is5
    of manna   Ex16
    of meal   SF17
    of parched grain   SF17
feet, measure of height, Egyptian opponent   CF11
      gallows   Est5
      Goliath   SF17
    of Nebuchadnezzar's golden image   D3
gallon, honest   E45
  of wine   Is5
gerah as measure of silver   Nu18
  as money   Nu3
  as prescribed weight of gold   CF28
  as sacred standard   Le27
  as standard weight   E45
head taller, Saul was a   SF9
height of gallows   Est5
  of Goliath   SF17
hin as measure of oil   Nu15, 28; E45
    of water   E4
    of wine   Le23
homer as measure of barley   Ho3
    of bread   SF16
    of seed   Is5
  standard measure   E45
inches, sword measured in   Ju3
kab, cab, quarter, of locust beans   KS6
kor as fixed measure   E45
  as measure of barley   CS27
    of flour   KF4ff
    of grain   CS2
    of meal   KF4ff
    of oil   KF4

48 WEIGHTS, MEASURES AND COINS

kor as measure of wheat   KF4ff; CS27; Ez7
maneh, fixed measure   E45
measure fixed for barley, oil and wheat   E45
  infamous false   Mi6
  keep true   Le19
  of corn   Hg2
  of wine   Ho3; Hg2
  use only perfect   De25
measurements of new temple   Ez6
  of pillar   KS25
  of platform   CS6
  of sanctuary land   E45
  of Solomon's buildings   CS3
  of temple in Ezekiel's vision   E40ff
  shall be honest   E45
measuring-line   Ziff
measuring-rod   E40
mina, fixed measure   E45
minas of gold   KF10
  of silver contributed for fabric fund   Ne7
      contributed for rebuilding fund   Ez2; Ne7
omer, measure   Ex16
overweight in the silver, taking   Am8
peck, ten bushels of seed returning only a   Is5
pieces of silver   Ju16ff; Ho3
pounds of gold   KF10
reed, measuring   E40ff
rod, measuring   E40ff
scales   Je32; E5, 45; Ho12; Am8
  can I connive at false   Mi6
  hills in a pair of   Is40
  moisture on the   Is40
  tilted fraudulently   Am8
shekel as standard weight   E45
  royal standard   SS14
  sacred standard   Nu3
  to buy flour or barley   KS7
shekels, gold   Nu31; KF10; KS5
    buckler, weight in   CS9
    earrings, weight of   Ju8
    for altar site   CF21

48 WEIGHTS, MEASURES AND COINS

shekels, gold, shield, weight of   CS9
  silver   KF10; Je32
    daily toll of   Ne5
    dishes given   Nu7ff
    import value of horses and chariots   CS1
    levy of   KS15
    price of siege food in   KS6
    quarter as present   SF9
    weight of prescribed   CF28
  annual offering of a third   Ne10
  making great   Am8
  of bronze   SS21
  of hair   SS14
  personal value in   Le27
  quarter cab of locust beans for five   KS6
  standard recognized by merchants   Gen23
  to sharpen axe, goad, ploughshare or mattock   SF13
  weight of daily food ration   E4
    of iron spear head   SF17
    of suit of armour   SF17
silverlings, pieces of silver   Is7
span, measurement used with cubits   SF17
talents, bronze   CF29
  gold   KF9f; CF22, 29; Ez8
    annual receipt of   KF10
    crown of Milcom in   SS12; CF29
    fine of   CS36
    penalty of   KS18
  iron   CF29
  lead   Z5
  silver   KF16, 20; KS5; CF22, 29; Ez7f
    fine of   CS36
    for hire of chariots   CF19
    land price in   KF16
    paid to Pul by Menahem   KS15
    penalty of   KS18
    to be paid for destruction of Jews   Est3
    tribute of   CS27
    weight of silver vessels in   Ez8
weights and measures, Levites responsible for   CF23
  can I connive at a bag of light   Mi6

48 WEIGHTS, MEASURES AND COINS

weights, use true   De25

NEW TESTAMENT

balances, pair of   Rev6
bank, paid into the   L19
breadth and length and height and depth   Pe3
bushel, candle under a   Mw5; Mk4; L11
bushels of wheat, a thousand   L16
coins, poor widow dropped in two tiny   Mk12; L21
   scattered the money-changers'   J2
cubit, add to his stature one   Mw6; L12
cubits, one hundred and forty four   Rev21
   two hundred   J21
denarii, three hundred   Mk14; J12
   two hundred   Mk6; J6
denarius for a day's work   Mw20
deposit, why did you not put my money on   L19
fathoms, sounding   A27
farthing   Mw5, 10; Mk12; L12
   until you have paid the uttermost   Mw5; L12
farthings, are not five sparrows sold for two   L12
firkin   J2
foot to his height, who can add a   Mw6; L12
fund, temple   Mw27
furlongs   Mw14
  fifteen   J11
  sixteen hundred   Rev14
  three score   L24
  twelve thousand   Rev21
gallons, jars of twenty and thirty   J2
  thousand   L16
hundredweight, hailstones weighing perhaps a   Rev16
  half a   Mw13; L13; J19
interest, on deposit for   L19
measuring-rod   Rev11, 21
measures of meal, three   Mw13
  of oil, a hundred   L16
  of wheat, a hundred   L16
mile, go with him two   Mw5

48 WEIGHTS, MEASURES AND COINS

miles, seven from Emmaus to Jerusalem   L24
  two from Bethany to Jerusalem   J11
mite, until thou hast paid the very last   L12
  widow's   Mk12; L21
money changers   Mw21
  take no   L9
pence, fifty   L7
  five hundred   L7
  three hundred   Mk14; J12
  two   L10
penny a day agreed with the labourers   Mw20
  bring me a   Mw22; Mk12; L20
  measure of wheat for a   Rev6
  three measures of barley for a   Rev6
pennyworth, two hundred   Mk6; J6
pound, gave them each a   L19
  weight, a hundred   J19
  thirty, perfume worth   Mk14; J12
  twenty, are we to spend   Mk6
    would not buy enough bread   J6
quart of flour   Rev6
quarts of barley-meal, three   Rev6
silver coin in a fish's mouth   Mw17
  piece, show me a   Mw22; Mk12; L20
  pieces, fifty   L7
    fifty thousand   A19
    five hundred   L7
    ten   L15
    thirty   Mw26f
    two   L10
scales, a pair of   Rev6
tables of the money changers   Mw21
talent   Mw25
  every hailstone about the weight of a   Rev16
thirty pieces of silver   Mw26f
toll, tax or   Mw17
two pence, sparrows sold five for   L12
usury   L19

APPENDIX A *Personal Names*

OLD TESTAMENT

Aaron (brother of Moses)
　　Ex4ff; Le1ff; Nu1ff, 12, 20; De9f; Jos24; Ju20; SF12; CF6, 12, 15;
　　CS31,35; Ez7; Ps77, 99, 105f, 115, 118, 133, 135; Mi6
(a Levite) CF23ff
Abagtha Est1
Abda KF4; Ne11
Abdeel Je36
Abdi CF6; CS29; Ez10
Adiel CF5
Abdon (a judge) Ju12
　(son of Jehiel) CF8ff
　(son of Micah) CS34
　(son of Shimei) CF8
Abednego D1ff
Abel Gen4
Abi KS18
Abia CF3
Abiah SF8; CF6f, 24; Ne10,12
Abi-albon SS23
Abiasaph Ex6
Abiathar SS8, 15; SF22, 29ff; KF1; CF15ff, 27
Abida Gen25; CF1
Abidan Nu1, 7ff
Abiel SF9, 14; CF11
Abiezer Jos17; Ju8; SS23; CF7, 11, 27
Abigail SS2ff, 17; SF25, 27, 30; CF2
Abihail Nu3ff;CF2, 5; CS11; Est2
Abihu Ex6, 24ff; Le10; Nu26; CF6, 24
Abijah KF14; CS11, 13, 29
Abijam KF14
Abimael Gen10; CF1
Abimelech (king of Gerar)　Gen20f, 26
　(a judge) Ju8ff; SS11
Abinadab SF7, 16ff; SS6;　CF2, 8f, 13
Abinoam Ju4
Abiram Nu6, 26; De11; KF16; Ps106
Abishag KF1f
Abishai SF26; SS2, 10, 21ff; CF2, 11, 18
Abishalom KF15
Abishua CF6, 8; Ez7
Abishur CF2

APPENDIX A PERSONAL NAMES

Abital SS3; CF3
Abitub CF8
Abner SF14, 17, 20, 26; SS2ff; KF2; CF26ff
Abraham (Abram) Gen12ff, 17ff; DE1, 6, 34;Jos24; Ks13; CF1;
    Ne9; Ps47, 105; Is29, 41, 51, 63; Je33; E33; Mi7
Absalom SF3, 13ff; KF1ff; CF3; CS11
Achan Jos7
Achar CF2
Achbor (Akbor) Gen36; KS22; CF1; Je26, 36
Achish SF21, 27ff; KF2
Achsah Jos15; Ju1; CF2
Achzib Mi1
Adah Gen4, 36
Adaiah KS22; CF6, 8ff; CS23; Ez10; Ne11
Adalia Est9
Adam Gen2; CF1
Abdeel Gen25; CF1
Addar CF8
Ader CF8
Adiel CF4, 9, 27
Adin Ez2, 8; Ne7, 10
Adina CF11
Adlai CF27
Admatha Est1
Adna Ez10; Ne12
Adnah CS17
Adoni-bezek Ju1
Adonijah SS3; KF1ff; CF3; CS17; Ne10
Adonikam Ez2, 8; Ne7
Adoniram KF4ff
Adoni-zedek Jos10
Adoram SS20; KF12
Adrammelech KS19; Is37
Adriel SF15; SS21
Agag Nu24; SF15
Agee SS23
Agur Pro30
Ahab (king of Israel) KF16ff; KS3, 8ff, 21; CS18, 21ff; Mi6
  (prophet reviled by Jeremiah) Je29
Aharah CF8
Aharhel CF4
Ahasbai SS23
Ahasuerus Ez4; Est1ff; D9
Ahaz KS15ff; CF3, 8ff; CS27f; Is1, 7, 14, 38; Ho1; Mi1
Ahaziah (king of Israel) KF22
  (King of Judah) KS1, 8ff; CF3; CS20ff

487

APPENDIX A PERSONAL NAMES

Ahban CF2
Aher CF7
Ahi CF5, 7
Ahiah CF8; Ne10
Ahiam SS23; CF11
Ahian CF7
Ahiezer Nu1, 7fff; CF12
Ahihud Nu34; CF8
Ahijah SF14; KF4, 11, 14ff, 21; KS9; CF2, 11; CS9ff
Ahikam KS22; CS34; Je26, 39f, 43
Ahilud SS8, 20; KF4
Ahimaaz SF14; SS15ff; KF4; CF6
Ahiman Nu13; Jos15; Ju1; CF9
Ahimelech SF21f, 26, 30; SS8; CF18, 24
Ahimoth CF6
Ahinadab KF4
Ahinoam SF14, 25, 27, 30; SS2ff; CF3
Ahio SS6; CF8f, 13
Ahira Nu1, 7ff
Ahiram Nu26
Ahisamach Ex31ff
Ahishahar CF7
Ahishar KF4
Ahithophel CF27
Ahitophel SS15ff, 23
Ahitub SF14, 22; SS8; CF6, 9, 18; Ez7; Ne11
Ahlai CF2, 11
Ahoah CF8
Aholiab Ex31ff
Ahumai CF4
Ahuzam CF4
Ahuzath Gen26
Ahzai Ne11
Aiah Gen36; SS3, 21; CF1
Akan Gen 36; CF1
Akbor (Achbor) Gen36; KS22; CF1; Je26, 36
Akkub CF3, 9; Ez2; Ne7f,11ff
Alemeth CF7ff
Aliah CF1
Allon CF4
Almodad Gen10; CF1
Alvah Gen36
Amal CF7
Amalek Gen36; Ex17; SS8; CF1
Amariah CS19, 31; CF6, 23ff; Ez7, 10; Ne10ff; Zp1
Amasa SS17ff; KF2; CF2; CS28

APPENDIX A PERSONAL NAMES

Amasai (Amashai, Amashsai) (son of Azarel) Ne11
  (son of Gershom) CF6, 15; CS29
Amasiah CS17
Amaziah (king of Judah) KS12ff; CF3ff; CS24ff
  (priest of Bethel) Am7
  (son of Hilkiah) CF6
Ami Ez2
Ammi (Lo-ammi) Ho2
Amittai Jon1
Ammiel Nu13; SS9, 17; CF3,26
Ammihud Nu1, 7ff, 34; CF7, 9
Ammihur SS13
Amminadab Ex6; Nu1, 7ff; CF2, 6, 15; Ru4
Aminadib SO6
Ammishaddai Nu1, 7ff
Ammizabad CF27
Amnon SF3, 13; CF3ff
Amok Ne12
Amon KF22; KS21; CF3; CS18,33; Ne7; Je1, 25; Zp1
Amos Am1ff, 7
Amoz KS19; CS26, 32; Is1ff, 13, 21, 37ff
Amram Ex6; Nu3ff; CF1, 6, 23ff; Ez10
Amraphel Gen14
Amzi CF6; Ne11
Anah Gen36; CF1
Anaiah Ne8, 10
Anak Nu13; De9; Jos15; Ju1
Anan Ne10
Anani CF3
Ananiah Ne3
Anath Ju4
Ananthoth Ne10; SS23; CF7
Aner Gen14
Aniam CF7
Antothiah CF8
Anub CF4
Aphiah SF9
Aphses CF24
Ara CF7
Arad CF8
Arah CF7; Ez2; Ne6ff
Aram Gen10, 22; KS13;CF1f,7
Aran Gen36; CF1
Araunah SS24
Arba Jos14
Ard Gen46; Nu26

APPENDIX A PERSONAL NAMES

Ardon CF2
Areli Gen46; Nu26
Aridai Est9
Aridatha Est9
Ariel Ez8
Arioch (king of Ellasar) Gen14
  (captain of royal bodyguard) D2
Arisai Est9
Armoni SS21
Arnan CF3
Arod Nu26
Arodi Gen46
Arphaxad Gen10f; CF1
Artaxerxes Ez4ff; Ne2, 5, 13
Arza KF16
Asa KF15; CF3, 9; CS14, 20ff; Je41
Asahel SS2ff, 23; CF2, 11, 27; CS17, 31
Asaiah KS22; CF4, 6, 9, 15; CS34
Asaph (Levite musician) CF6, 9, 15ff, 25; CS5, 20, 29, 35; Ez2ff; Ne7, 11ff
  (father of Joah, secretary of state) KS18; Is36
  (keeper of the royal forests) Ne2
Asareel CF4
Asarelah CF25
Asenath Gen41, 46
Ashbel Gen46; Nu26; CF8
Asher Gen30, 35; Ex1; Nu1, 7ff; De27, 33; Ju1, 6ff; CF2, 7
Ashkenaz Gen10; CF1
Ashpenaz D1
Ashvath CF7
Asiel CF4
Asnah Ez2
Asnappar (Osnappar) Ez4
Aspatha Est9
Asshur CF1ff
Asriel Nu26; Jos17
Asshar Gen41
Asshurim Gen25
Assir Ex6; CF6
Atarah CF2
Ater Ez2; Ne7, 10
Athiah Ne11
Athaliah KS8, 11; CF8; CS22ff
Athlai Ez10
Attai CF2, 12; CS11
Azaliah KS22; CS34
Azaniah Ne10

490

APPENDIX A PERSONAL NAMES

Azareel CF12, 25, 27; Ez10
Azarel Ne11ff
Azariah (Abed-nego) D1ff
  (Jezaniah, son of Hoshaiah) Je42ff
  (Levite priest) CS26, 29, 31; Ne3, 7f, 10, 12
  (son of Ahimaaz) CF6
  (son of Jehalelel) CS29
  (son of Jehoshaphat) CS21
  (son of Jehu) Ez7
  (son of Jeroham) CS23
  (son of Johanan) CF6
  (son of Kilkiah) CF6
  (son of Nathan) KF4
  (son of Obed) CS15, 23
  (son of Zadok) KF4
  (son of Zephaniah) CF6
  (Uzziah, king of Judah) KS14
Azaz CF5
Azaziah CF27; CS31
Azbuk Ne3
Azel CF8ff
Azgad Ez2, 8; Ne7, 10
Aziza Ez10
Azmoth SS23; CF8ff, 11, 27
Azriel CF5, 27; Je36
Azrikam CF3, 8ff; CS28; Ne11
Azubah KF22; CF2; CS20
Azzan Nu34
Baal CF5 8ff
Baal-hanan Gen36; CF1, 27
Baalis Je40
Baana KF4; Ne3
Baanah SS4, 23; KF4; CF11; Ez2; Ne7, 10
Baara CF8
Baaseia CF6
Baasha KF15, 21; KS9; CS16; Je41
Bakbakkar CF9
Bakbuk Ez2; Ne7
Bakbukiah Ne11f
Balaam Nu22; De23; Jos13, 24; Ne13; Mi6
Baladan KS20; Is39
Balak Nu22; Jos24; Ju11; Mi6
Bani SS23; CF6, 9; Ez2, 8, 10; Ne3, 8ff
Barak Ju4; SF9
Barakel (Barachel) Job32
Bariah CF3

APPENDIX A PERSONAL NAMES

Barkos Ez2; Ne7
Baruch Ne3, 10f; Je32, 36, 43, 45
Barzillai SS17f; KF2; Ne7
Basemath Gen26, 36, 38
Basmath KF4
Bathsheba SS11; KF1ff; CF3
Bathshua CF2
Bavai Ne3
Bazluth (Bazlith) Ez2; Ne7
Bealiah CF12
Bebai Ez2, 8, 10; Ne7, 10
Becher Gen46; Nu26; CF7
Bechorath SF9
Bedad Gen36; CF1
Badan CF7
Beeliada CF14
Beera CF7
Beerah CF5
Beeri Gen26; Ho1
Beeroth CF11
Bela Gen14, 36, 46; Nu26; CF1, 5, 7f
Belshazzar D5, 7
Belteshazzar (Daniel) D1ff
Ben-abinadab KF4
Benaiah SS8, 20f; KF1ff; CF4, 11, 15, 18, 27; CS20, 31; Ez10; E11
Ben-ammi Gen19
Ben-dekar KF4
Ben-geber KF4
Ben-gershom Ju17
Ben-hadad KF15, 20; KS6, 8, 13; CS16; Am1
Ben-hana CF4
Ben-hayil CS17
Ben-hesed KF4
Ben-hur KF4
Beninu Ne10
Benjamin (a priest) Ez10; Ne3, 12
  (Ben-oni) (son of Jacob) Gen35, 42ff;Ex1; Nu1, 7ff; De27, 33; SF10ff; CF2, 7f, 11; Ez1; Je6; Ho5; Ob1
  (son of Bilhan) CF7
Beno CF24
Benob SS21
Ben-oni (Benjamin) Gen35
Ben-zoheth CF4
Beor Gen36; Nu22; De23; Jos13, 24; CF1; Mi6
Bera Gen14
Berachah CF12

APPENDIX A PERSONAL NAMES

Berachiah CF6
Bered CF7
Beri CF7
Beriah Gen46; Nu26; CF7f,23ff
Besai Ez2; Ne7
Besodiah Ne3
Beth-rapha CF4
Bethuel Gen22, 24, 28
Bezai Ez2; Ne7, 10
Bezalel Ex31f; CF2;CS1; Ez10
Bezer CF7
Bichri SS20
Bidkar KS9
Bigtha Est1
Bigthan (Bigthana) Est2
Bigvai Ez2, 8; Ne7, 10
Bildad Job2, 8, 18, 25, 42
Bilgai Ne10
Bilgah CF24; Ne12
Bilhah Gen29, 35, 46
Bilhan CF1, 7
Bilshan Ne7
Bimhal CF7
Binea CF8f
Binnui Ez3, 8,10; Ne3,7,10, 12
Birsha Gen14
Birzavith CF7
Bithiah CF4
Biztha Est1
Boaz CF2; Ru2ff
Bocheru CF8f
Bohan Jos15
Bukki Nu34; CF6; Ez7
Bukkiah CF25
Bunah CF2
Bunni Ne9f
Buz Gen22; CF5
Buzi Ez1
Cain Gen4
Calcol CF2
Caleb Nu13, 26, 32f; De1; Jos14f, 21; Ju1, 3; CF2, 4, 6
Canaan Gen9f; CF1
Caphtor De2
Carcas Est1
Careah (Kareah) KS25
Carmi Gen46; Ex6; Nu26;   Jos7; CF2f, 5

APPENDIX A PERSONAL NAMES

Carshena Est1
Chenaanah KF22
Cheran Gen36; CF1
Chileab SS3
Chilion Ru1f
Chimham (Kimham) SS19; Je41
Col-hozeh Ne3, 11
Conaniah CS31, 35
Coniah Je22
Coz CF4
Cozbi Nu25
Cush Gen10; KS19; CF1
Cushan-rishathaim (Chushan-rishathaim) Ju3
Cushi Je36; Zp1
Cyrus CS36; Ez1, 3; Is44; D1, 6, 10
Dalaiah CF3
Daliah CF4
Dalphon Est9
Dan Gen30, 35, 46; Ex1; Nu1, 7ff; De27, 33; Jos19; CF2, 7
Daniel (a priest) Ne10
   (Danel) (Belteshazzar) E14, 28; D1ff
   (family of Ithamar) Ez8
   (son of David) CF3
Darda KF4; CF2
Darius Ez4ff; Ne12; D5f, 9, 11; Hg1ff; Z1, 7
Darkon Ne7
Darlon Ez2
Dathan Nu16, 26;De11; Ps106
David Ru4; SF16ff, 29; SS1ff; KF1ff, 8, 11, 14, 17ff; CF2f, 6, 9f, 12; Cs1ff;
      Ez3, 8; Ne12; Pro1; Ec1; So4; Is7,9, 16, 22, 29, 37ff, 55;
      Je13, 17, 21ff, 33, 33, 36; E34, 37; Ho3; Am6, 9; Z12ff
Debir Jos10, 15
Deborah Gen35; Ju4
Dedan Gen10, 25; CF1
Delaiah CF24; Ez2; Ne6ff;Je36
Delilah Ju16
Diblaim Ho1
Dibri Le24
Diklah Gen10; CF1
Dinah Gen30, 34, 46
Diphath CF1
Dishan Gen36; CF1
Dishon Gen36; CF1
Dodai CF27
Dodavahu CS20

APPENDIX A PERSONAL NAMES

Dodo Ju10; SS23; CF11
Doeg SF21
Dumah Gen25; CF1; Is21
Ebal Gen36; CF1
Ebed Ez8
Ebed-melech Je38ff
Eber Gen10; CF1, 8; Ne12
Ebiasah CF6, 9, 26
Eden CS29, 31
Eder CF23
Edom (Esau) Gen36
Edrei De1
Eglah SS3; CF3
Eglon Ju3
Ehi Gen46
Ehud Ju3; CF7ff
Eker CF2
Ekron SF5ff
Eladah CF7
Elah (an Edomite) Gen36
  (chief in Edom) CF1
  (father of Shimei) KF4
  (king of Israel) KF16; KS15, 17ff
  (son of Caleb) CF4
  (son of Uzzi) CF9
Elam Gen10; CF1, 8, 26; Ez2, 8, 10; Ne7, 10, 12; Is22
Elasah CF2, 8f; Ez10; Je29
Eldaah Gen25; CF1
Eldad Nu11
Elead CF7
Eleazar (family of Parosh)   Ez10; Ne12
  (son of Aaron) Ex6, 27;   Le10; Nu20, 25; De10; Jos14, 17, 21, 24;
      Ju20; CF6, 9; Ez7, 8
  (son of Abinadab) SF7
  (son of Dodai) CF27
  (son of Dodo) SS23
  (son of Mahli) CF23ff
Elhanan SS21f; CF11, 20
Eli SF1ff; CF11, 20
Eliab Nu1, 7ff, 16, 26; De1; SF16ff; CF2, 6, 12ff; CS11
Eliad CS17
Eliada SS5; KF11; CF3
Eliah CF8
Eliahba SS23; CF11
Eliakim KS18, 23; CS36;   Ne12; Is22, 36
Eliam SS11, 23

APPENDIX A PERSONAL NAMES

Eliasaph Nu1, 3, 7ff
Eliashib CF3, 24; Ez10; Ne3, 12ff
Eliathan CF25
Elidad Nu34
Eliel CF5f, 8, 11f, 15; CS31
Elienai CF8
Eliezer (a Levite) Ez8
  (a priest) CF15; Ez10
  (of Damascus) Gen15
  (son of Becher) CF7
  (son of Dodavahu) CS20
  (son of Moses) Ex18; CF23, 26ff
Elihoenai Ez8
Elihu (son of Barakel) Job32ff
  (son of Shemaiah) CF26ff
  (son of Tohu) SF1
Elijah (family of Elam) Ez10
  (family of Immer) Ez10
  (the prophet) KF17ff; KS1ff,9; CS21; Ma4
Elika SS23
Elimelech Ru1ff
Elionai CF3f, 7, 26; Ez10; Ne12
Eliphal CF11
Eliphaz (son of Esau) Gen36; CF1
  (Job's friend) Job2, 4, 15, 22, 42
Eliphelehu CF15
Eliphelet CF3, 8, 14; Ez8, 10
Elisha KF19; KS2ff, 13
Elishah Gen10; CF1
Elishama (a priest) CS17
  (adjutant-general) Je36
  (son of Ammihud) Nu1, 7f; CF7
  (son of David) SS5; KS5;
  (son of Jekamiah) CF2ff
Elishaphat CS23
Elisheba Ex6
Elishua SS5; CF14
Elizaphan Nu3ff, 34; CF15; CS29
Elizur Nu1. 7ff
Elkanah Ex6; SF1; CF6, 9, 12; CS28
Elnaam CF11
Elnathan KS24; Ez8; Je26, 36
Elon (a Hittite) Gen26, 30, 46
  (a Zebulunite) Nu26
  (one of the judges) Ju12
Elpaal CF8

APPENDIX A PERSONAL NAMES

Elpelet CF14
Elphelet SS5, 23
Eluzai CF12
Elzabad CF12, 26
Elzaphan Ex6
Elzaphon Le10
Emim Gen14
Enan Ni1, 7f
Enoch (son of Cain) Gen4
  (son of Jared) Gen5; CF1, 5
  (son of Midian) Gen25
  (son of Reuben) Gen46;Ex6; Nu26
Enosh (Enos) Gen4; CF1
Ephah Gen25; CF1ff
Ephai (Ophai) Je40
Epher Gen25; CF1, 4ff
Ephlal CF2
Ephod Nu34
Ephraim Gen41, 46; Nu1, 7ff, 26; De33; Jos16; Ju1ff; CF2,7; Is9; Je7, 31; E37; Ho4, 11, 13
Ephrath CF2
Ephrathah CF2, 4
Ephron Gen23
Er Gen38, 46; Nu26; CF2, 4
Eran Nu26
Eri Gen46; Nu26
Esarhaddon KS19; Ez4; Is37
Esau Gen25f, 33, 36; Jos24; CF1; Je49; Ob1; Ma1
Eshbaal CF8ff
Eshban Gen36
Eshbani CF1
Eshcol Gen14
Eshek CF8
Eshtemoa CF4
Eshton CF4
Esther (Hadassah) Est2ff
Etam CF4
Etha KF4
Ethan CF2, 6, 15
Ethbaal KF16ff
Ethan CF4
Ethni CF6
Eve Gen3
Evi Nu31
Evil-merodach (Ewil-marduk) KS25; Je52
Ezbai CF11

APPENDIX A PERSONAL NAMES

Ezbon Gen46; CF7
Ezekiel E1, 24
Ezer Gen36; CF1, 4, 7, 12; Ne3, 12
Ezra CF4; Ez7; Ne8, 12
Ezrai Ne12
Ezri CF27
Gabbai Ne11
Gad (son of Jacob) Gen30, 35, 46; Ex1; Nu1; De27. 33; CF2, 5
  (the prophet) SF22, 24; CF21, 29; CS29
Gaddi Nu13
Gaddiel Nu13
Gadi KS15
Gaham Gen32
Gahar Ez2; Ne7
Galal CF9; Ne11
Gamaliel Nu1, 7ff
Gamul CF24
Gareb SS23; CF11
Gashmu (Geshem) Ne6
Gatam Gen36; CF1
Gaza De2
Gazez CF2
Gazzam Ez2; Ne7
Geber KF4
Gedaliah ('a great man') KS25; Je52
  (a priest) Ez10
  (son of Ahikam) Je39ff
  (son of Amariah) Zp1
  (son of Jeduthun) CF25
  (son of Pashhur) Je38
Gedor CF8f
Gehazi KS4, 8
Gemalli Nu13
Gemariah Je29, 36
Genubath KF11
Gera (a Benjamite) SS16f; KF2; CF8
  (grandson of Benjamin)   Gen46; Ju3
Gershom Ex2, 18; Ju18; CF6, 15, 23, 26; Ez8
Gershon Gen46; Ex6; Nu33ff; CF6, 23; CS29
Gesham CF2
Geshem (Cashmu) Ne2, 6
Geshur CF2
Gether Gen10; CF1
Geuel Nu13
Gibbar Ez2
Gibeon Ne7

APPENDIX A PERSONAL NAMES

Giddalti CF25
Giddel Ez2; Ne7
Gideon Ju6ff
Gilalai Ne12
Gilead Nu26,36,Jos17;CF2,5ff
Ginath KF16
Ginnethon Ne10, 12
Gishpa Ne11
Gog CF5; E38ff
Goliath SF17, 21; SS21; CF20
Gomer (son of Japheth) Gen10; CF1
 (wife of Hosea) Ho1
Guni Gen46; Nu26; CF5, 7
Haahashtari CF4
Habakkuk H1
Habaziniah Je35
Hacaliah (Hachaliah) Ne1, 10
Hadad Gen25, 36; KF11; CF1
Hadadezer SS8, 10; KF11; CF18f
Hadar Gen36
Hadassah (Esther) Est2ff
Hadlai CS28
Hadoram Gen10; CF1, 18; CS10
Hagab Ez2
Hagabah Ez2; Ne7
Hagar Gen16, 21, 25
Haggai Ez5; Hg1f
Haggedolim Ne11
Haggeri CF11
Haggi Gen46; Nu26
Haggiah CF6
Haggith SS3; KF1ff; CF3
Hakkatan Ez8
Hakkoz (Koz) CF24; Ne3, 7
Hakupha Ez2; Ne7
Hallohesh Be3, 10
Ham Gen5ff; CF1
Haman Est3ff, 9
Hammedatha Est3,9
Hammoleketh CF7
Hamor Gen33f; Jos29; Ju9
Hamuel CF4
Hamul Gen46; Nu26; CF2
Hamutal KS23ff; Je52
Hanamel Je32
Hanan (son of Igdaliah) Je35

APPENDIX A PERSONAL NAMES

Hanan (son of Shashak) CF8f, 11; Ez2; Ne7f, 10, 13
Hananel (Hananeel) Je31
Hanani (a priest) Ne12
  (father of Jehu) CS16, 19; KF16
  (brother of Nehemiah) Ne1,7
  (family of Immer) Ez10
  (son of Heman) CF25
Hananiah (a chief) Ne10
  (a priest) Ne12
  (a prophet) Je28, 36ff
  (family of Bebai) Ez10
  (governor of the citadel) Ne7
  (king's commander) CS26
  (Shadrach) D1ff
  (son of Heman) CF25
  (son of Shashak) CF8
  (son of Shelemiah) Ne3
  (son of Zerubbabel) CF3
Haniel CF7
Hannah SF1ff
Hanniel Nu34
Hanun SS10; CF19; Ne3
Haran Gen11; CF2
Harbona Est1, 7
Hareph CF2
Harhaiah Ne3
Harhas KS22
Harhur Ez2; Ne7
Harif Ne7
Harim CF24; Ez10; Ne3, 7, 10, 12
Hariph Ne10
Harnepher CF7
Harosheth Ju4
Harsha Ez2; Ne7
Harum CF4
Harumaph Ne3
Haruz KS21
Hasadiah CF3
Hashabiah CF6, 9, 25ff; CS35; Ez8; Ne3, 10ff
Hashabnah Ne10
Hashabniah Ne3, 9
Hashbaddanah Ne8
Hashem SS23; CF11
Hashhub Ne11
Hashum Ez2, 10; Ne7f, 10
Hasrah CS34

APPENDIX A PERSONAL NAMES

Hassenaah Ne3
Hassenuah CF9
Hasshub CF9; Ne3, 10
Hassophereth Ez2
Hasupha Ez2; Ne7
Hathach Est4
Hathath CF4
Hatipha Ez2; Ne7
Hatita Ez2; Ne7
Hattil Ez2; Ne7
Hattush CF3; Ez8; Ne3, 10, 12
Havilah Gen10; CF1
Hazael KF19; KS8ff; CS22; Am1
Hazaiah Ne11
Hazarmoth Gen10; CF1
Hazelelponi CF4
Hazo Gen22
Heber Gen46; Nu26; Ju4; CF4f
Hebron Ex6; Nu3ff; CF6, 15, 23ff
Hegai (Hege) Est2
Helah CF4
Heldai CF27; Z6
Heled SS23; CF11
Helek Nu26; Jos17
Helem Z6
Helez SS23; CF2, 11, 27
Helkai Ne12
Helon Nu1, 7ff
Hemam Gen36
Heman KF4; CF2, 6, 15, 25; CS5, 29, 35
Hemdan Gen36
Hen Z6
Henadad Ez3; Ne3, 10
Hepher Nu26; Jos17; CF4, 11
Hephzi-bah KS21
Heresh CF9
Heth Gen10; CF1
Hezeki CF8
Hezekiah (Hizkiah) (family of Ater) Ez2; Ne7, 10
  (king of Judah) KS16ff; CF3ff; CS28ff; Pro25; Is1, 36f, 39; Je15, 26;
     Ho1; Mi1; Zp1
Hezion KF15
Hezir CF24; Ne10
Hezrai SS23
Hezro CF11
Hezron Gen46; Ex6; Nu26; Ru4; CF2f, 5

APPENDIX A PERSONAL NAMES

Hiddai SS23
Hiel KF16
Hilkiah (comptroller) KS18; Is22, 36
  (father of Gemariah) Je29
  (father of Jeremiah) Je1
  (high priest) KS22; CF9; CS34f; Ne11
  (son of Hosah) CF26
  (son of Shallum) CF6; Ez7; Ne8
Hillel Ju12
Hirah Gen38
Hiram (king of Tyre) SS5; KF5, 9ff; CF14; CS2f, 8
  (craftsman) KF7; CS2ff
Hizkiah (Hezekiah) Zp1
Hobab Ju4
Hobaiah Ne7
Hod CF7
Hodaiah CF3
Hodaviah (Hodiah) CF4f, 9; Ez2f; Ne8ff
Hodesh CF8
Hodiah (Hodaviah) CF4f, 9; Ez2f; Ne8ff
Hodvah Ne7
Hoglah Nu26ff, 36; Jos17
Hoham Jos10
Homam CF1
Hophni SF1ff
Hophra (Pharaoh) Je44
Horam Jos10
Hori Gen36; Nu13; CF1
Horonaim SS13
Hosah CF16, 26
Hosea Ho1ff
Hoshaiah Ne12; Je42ff
Hoshama CF3
Hoshea (a chief) Ne10
   (king of Israel) KS15ff
   (son of Azaziah) CF27
   (son of Elah) KS15ff
Hotham CF7, 11
Hothir CF25
Hul Gen14; CF1
Huldah KS22; CS34
Hupham Nu26
Huppah CF24
Huppim Gen46
Hur Ex17, 31; Nu31; CF2ff; CS1; Ne3
Hurai CF11

APPENDIX A PERSONAL NAMES

Huram CF8
  (Hiram) (king of Tyre) SS5; KF5, 9ff;CF14;CS2f, 8
  (craftsman) KF7; CS2ff
Huri CF5
Hushai SS15ff; KF4; CF27
Husham Gen36; CF1
Hushim Gen46; CF7
Huzzab Na2
Ibhar SS5; CF3, 14
Ibneiah CF9
Ibri CF24
Ibzan Ju12
Ichabod SF4, 14
Idbash CF4
Iddo (a chief) Ez8
  (father of Aminadab) KF4
  (father of Berechaiah) Z1
  (seer) CS9, 12
  (son of Joah) CF6
  (son of Zechariah) CF27; Ez5; Ne12
Igal Nu13; SS23
Igdaliah Je35
Igeal CF3
Ikkesh SS23; CF11
Imla CS18
Imlah KF22
Immer CF9, 24; Ez2, 10; Ne3, 7, 11; Je20
Imna Nu26; CF7
Imnah Gen46; CF7; CS31
Imrah CF7
Imri CF9; Ne3
Iob Gen46
Iphedeiah CF8
Ira SS20ff; CF11, 27
Irad Gen4
Iram Gen36; CF1
Iri CF7
Irijah Je37
Ir-nahash CF4
Iru CF4
Isaac Gen17, 21f, 27; De1, 6, 4; Jos24; KS13; CF1; Ps105; Je33; Am7
Isaiah (a Benjamite) Ne11
  (family of Merari) Ez8
  (the prophet) KS19; CS26, 32; Is1ff, 13, 20, 37ff
  (son of Athalia) Ez8
  (son of Hananiah) CF3

APPENDIX A PERSONAL NAMES

Isaiah (son of Rehabiah) CF26
Iscah Gen11
Ishbah CF4
Ishbak Gen25; CF1
Ishbosheth SS2ff, 23
Ishhod CF7
Ishi CF2, 4ff
Ishma CF4
Ismachiah CS31
Ishmael (son of Abraham)   Gen16ff, 25; CF1; Ps55
  (son of Azel) CF8ff
  (son of Jehohanan) CS23
  (son of Nethaniah) KS25; Je40ff
  (son of Pashhur) Ez10
Ishmaiah CF12, 27
Ishmerai CF8
Ishpan CF8
Ishuah Gen46
Ishui Gen46
Ishvah CF7
Ishvi Nu26; CF7
Ishyo SF14
Ispah CF8
Israel (Jacob) Gen32, 46; Ex32; F1, 5; Ez8
Issachar Gen30, 35, 46; Ex1; Nu1ff; De27; CF2, 26
Isshiah CF7, 12, 23ff
Isshijah Ez10
Ithali CF11
Ithamar Ex6, 27ff; Le10; CF6, 24; Ez8
Ithiel Ne11; Pro30
Ithmah CF11
Ithra SS17
Ithran Gen36; CF1, 7
Ithream SS3; CF3
Ittai SS15ff
Izhar Ex6; Nu3ff, 16; CF6, 23ff
Izrahiah CF7; Ne12
Izri Cf25
Izziah Ez10
Jakobah CF4
Jaalah Ez2; Ne7
Jaanai CF5
Jaare-oregim SS21
Jaasiel CF27
Jaasau Ez10
Jaazaniah (army captain)   KS25

APPENDIX A PERSONAL NAMES

Jaazaniah (son of Azzur) E11
  (son of Jeremiah) Je35
  (son of Shaphan) E8
Jaaziah CF24
Jaaziel CF15ff
Jabal Gen4
Jabesh KS15
Jabez CF4
Jabin Jos11; Ju4; SF12; Ps83
Jachin Gen46; Ex6; Nu26; CF9, 24
Jacob Gen25, 29ff, 37, 42ff; Ex1; De1, 6, 32, 34; Jos24; SF12; KS13;
    CF1; Ps20, 22, 44, 46f, 53, 59, 75f, 81, 84f, 94, 99, 105, 132,
    135, 146ff; Is2, 8f, 14, 17, 27, 29, 40ff, 48ff, 58ff,65; Je2, 5, 10,
    30f, 33, 46, 51; La1ff; E20, 28, 37, 39; Ho12; Am3, 6ff; Ob1; Mi1ff, 7;
    Ma1f
Jada CF2
Jaddai Ez10
Jaddua Ne10, 12
Jadon Ne3
Jael Ju4
Jahath CF4, 6, 23ff; CS34
Jahaziel CF12, 16, 23ff; CS20; Ez8
Jahdai CF2
Jahdiel CF5
Jahdo CF5
Jahleel Gen46; Nu26
Jahmai CF7
Jahzeel Gen46; Nu26
Jahzerah CF9
Jahziel CF7
Jair (a judge) Ju10; CF2
  (father of Elhanan) SS21; CF20
  (son of Manasseh) De3;KF4
  (son of Shimei) Est2
Jakeh Pro30
Jakim CF8, 24
Jalam Gen36; CF1
Jalon CF4
Jamin (a Levite) Ne8
  (son of Ram) CF2
  (son of Simeon) Gen46; Ex6; Nu26; CF4
Jamlech CF4
Japheth Gen5ff; CF1
Jaffia Jos10; SS5; CF3, 14
Japhlet CF7
Jarah CF9

APPENDIX A PERSONAL NAMES

Jareb Ho5, 10
Jared Gen5; CF1
Jaresiah CF8
Jarha CF2
Jarib CF4; Ez8, 10
Jaroah CF5
Jashen SS23
Jashobeam CF12, 27
Jashoboam CF11
Jashub Nu26; CF7; Ez10
Jasiel CF11
Jathniel CF26
Javan Gen10; CF1
Jaziz CF27
Jeaterai CF6
Jecoliah KS15; CS26
Jeconiah ('a prisoner') CF3
  ('king of Judah') Est2
  (son of Jehoiakim) Je24, 27
Jedaiah (a priest) Ez2
  (returned exile) Z6
  (son of Harumaph) Ne3,7,11ff
  (son of Shimri) CF4, 9, 24
Jediael CF7, 11, 26
Jedidah KS22
Jedidiah SS12
Jeduthun CF9, 16, 25; CS5, 29, 35; Ne11
Jeezer Nu26
Jehaleel CF4
Jehdeiah CF24
Jehezekel CF24
Jehiah CF15
Jehiel (a tutor) CF27
  (father of Abdon) CF8ff, 23
  (father of Obadiah) Ez8
  (father of Shecaniah) Ez10
  (Levite musician) CF15ff
  (Levite storeman) CF26, 29
Jehoaddah CF8
Jehoaddan CS25
Jehoaddin KS14
Jehoahaz CS21, 25, 36
Jehoash KS13ff; CS25; Ho1; Am1
Jehohanan (a priest) Ne12
  (family of Bebai) Ez10
  (father of Azariah) CS28

APPENDIX A PERSONAL NAMES

Jehohanan (son of Meshelemiah) CF26
Jehoahaz (king of Israel)   KS13ff; CS25
  (king of Judah) KS23; CS21, 36
Jehoiachin KS24ff; CS36; Je52; E1
Jehoiada (a priest) KS11f;   CS22ff; Je29
  (father of Benaiah) SS8, 20ff; KF1ff; CF11f, 18, 27
Jehoiakim (Eliakim) KS23; CF3; CS36; Je1, 22, 24, 26, 35ff, 45ff, 52; D1
Jehoiarib CF9, 24
Jehonadab KS10
Jehonathan CS17; Ne12
Jehoram (a priest) CS17
  (king of Israel) KS1, 3, 8; CS22
  (Joram) (king of Judah)   KF15, 22
Jehoshaphat (a priest) CF15
  (father of Jehu) KS9
  (king of Judah) KF15, 22; KS1, 3, 8; CF3;   CS17, 19ff
  (secretary of state) SS8, 20; KF4; CF18
Jehosheba KS11; CS22
Jehozabad KS12; CF26; CS17, 24
Jehozadak (Josedech) CF6; Hg1ff; Z6
Jehu (charioteer king of Israel) KS9ff, 13ff; CF2; CS22, 25; Ho1
  (son of Anathoth) CF12
  (son of Hanani) KF16, 19; CS19ff
  (son of Josibiah) CF4
Jehubbah CF7
Jehucal Je37
Jehudi Je36
Jeiel CF5, 15f; CS20, 26, 29, 35; Ez8, 10
Jekameam CF23ff
Jekamiah CF2ff
Jekuthiel CF4
Jeleth Gen36
Jemimah Job42
Jemuel Gen46; Ex6
Jephthah Ju11; SF12
Jephunneh Nu26, 34; De1; Jos14ff, 21; CF4, 6ff
Jerah Gen10; CF1
Jerahmeel CF2, 24; Je36
Jerai CF26
Jered CF4
Jeremai Ez10
Jeremiah (a Gadite) CF12
  (father of Hamutal) KS23ff; Je52
  (father of Jaazaniah) Je35
  (of Gederah) CF12
  (of Manasseh) CF5

507

APPENDIX A PERSONAL NAMES

Jeremiah (the prophet) CS35f; Ez1; Ne10, 12; Je1, 7, 11, 14, 18ff, 26ff, 36ff, 40, 42ff, 49, 51; D9
Jeremoth CF7ff, 23, 25; Ez10
Jeriah CF23ff
Jeribai CF11
Jeriel CF7
Jerimoth CF7, 12, 25, 27; CS11, 31
Jerioth CF2
Jeroboam I (king of Israel) KF11f, 21; KS3, 9f, 23; CS10
  II (king of Israel) KS14f; CF5; Ho1; Am1, 7
Jeroham (a Benjamite) CF8f, 12
  (father of Adaiah Ne11
  (father of Azareel) CF27
  (father of Azariah CS23
  (father of Elkanah) SF1;CF6
Jerubbaal (Gideon) Ju6ff;SF12
Jerubbesheth SS11
Jeshebeab CF24
Jesher CF2
Jeshishai CF5
Jeshohaiah CF4
Jeshua (Joshua) (son of Azania) Ne9f
  (son of Jozadak) Ez10
  (Levite official) CF24; CS31; Ez2ff; Ne7f, 12
Jeshurun (Jesurun) De32f; Is44
Jesimiel CF4
Jesse Ru4; SF16ff; CF2, 10; CS11; Ps72; Is11
Jether Ju8; KF2; CF2, 4
Jetheth CF11
Jethro Ex3, 18Jetur Gen25; CF1
Jeuel CF9
Jeush Gen36; CF1, 7ff, 23; CS11
Jeuz CF8
Jezaniah (Azariah) Je40, 42
Jezebel KF16ff, 21; KS9
Jezer Gen46; Nu26; CF7
Jeziel CF12
Jezliah CF8
Jezoar CF4
Jezreel CF4; Ho1ff
Jibsam CF7
Jidalph Gen22
Jieil CF11
Joab (commander) SF26; SS2ff; KF1ff, 11, 18ff, 26ff; CF2, 11
  (craftsman) CF4; Ez2,8; Ne7

APPENDIX A PERSONAL NAMES

Joah KS18; CF6, 26; CS29, 34; Is36
Joahaz CS34
Joash (king of Judah) KF22; KS11ff; CF3ff, 25; CS18
  (of Ophrah) Ju6ff
  (son of Becher) CF7
  (son of Shemaah) CF12
  (storeman) CF27
Job Job1ff; E14
Jobab Gen10, 36; Jos11; CF1, 8
Jochebed Ex6; Nu26
Joed Ne11
Joel (a priest) Ez10
  (son of Azariah) CF15;CS29
  (son of Laddan) CF23, 26ff
  (son of Pethuel) Joe1
  (son of Samuel) SF8; CF4ff
  (son of Zichri) Ne11
  (warrior of David) CF11
Johohanan Ne6
Joiada Ne3, 12ff
Joiakim Ne12
Joiarib Ez8; Ne11ff
Jokim CF4
Jokshan Gen25; CF1
Joktan Gen10; CF1
Jonadab SS13; Je35
Jonah KS14; Jon1ff
Jonathan (a scribe) Je37
  (son of Abiathar) SS15; KF1
  (son of Adin) Ez8
  (son of Gershom) Ju18
  (son of Jada) CF2
  (son of Joiada Ne12
  (son of Kareah) KS25; Je40
  (son of Saul) SF13f, 19; SS1ff; CF8ff
  (son of Shage) CF11
  (son of Shammah) SS23
  (son of Shimeai) SS21
  (son of Uzziah) CF27
Jorah Ez2
Jorai CF5
Joram (king of Judah) KF15,22
  (son of Isaiah) CF26
  (son of Toi) SS8
Jorkoam CF2

APPENDIX A PERSONAL NAMES

Josabad CF12
Josedech (Jehozadak) Hg1f;Z6
Joseph (a priest) Ne12
  (family of Binnui) Ez10
  (son of Asaph) CF25
  (son of Israel) Gen30ff; Ez1; Nu1ff, 13; De27, 33; CF2, 5, 7; Ps77, 81,
     Ps105; E37; Am5ff
Joshah CF4
Joshaphat CF11
Joshaviah CF11
Joshbekashah CF25
Joshua (Hoshea) (son of Nun)
     Ex17, 24; Nu13, 26, 32; De1, 3, 31; Ju2; Jos1ff; KF16; KS23;
     CF7; Ne8
  (Jeshua, a Levite) Ne7, 12
  (son of Jehozadak) Z3, 6; Hg1f
Josiah (king of Judah) KF13; KS21, 23; CS33ff; Je1, 3, 22, 25ff, 35ff, 46;
     Zp1
  (son of Amon) CF3
  (son of Zephaniah) Z6
Josibiah CF4
Josiphiah Ez8
Jotham (king of Judah) KS15; CF3, 5; CS26ff; Is1, 7; Ho1; Mi1
  (son of Jahdai) CF2
  (son of Jerubbaal) Ju9
Jozabad CS31, 35; Ez8, 10; Ne8, 11
Jozachar KS12
Jozadak Ez3, 5, 10
Jubal Gen4
Jucal Je38
Judah (a Levite) Ne12
  (son of Hassenuah) Ne11
  (son of Jacob) Gen29ff; Ex1; Nu1, 7ff; De27; Ju1; Ru4; CF2, 5, 10;
     Ez1,10; Is48, 65; E37; Ob1
Judith Gen26
Juphunneh Nu13
Jushab-hesed CF3
Kabzeel SS23
Kadmiel Ez2ff; Ne7, 9f, 12
Kalcol KF4
Kallai Ne12
Kareah (Careah) KS25; Je40ff
Kedar Geb25; CF1
Kedemah Gen25; CF1
Kedorlaomer Gen14
Kehaniah CF26

APPENDIX A PERSONAL NAMES

Keilah CF4
Kelaiah (Kelita) Ez10
Kelub CF4, 27
Kemuel Gen22; Nu34; CS18
Kenaanah CF15
Kenan Gen5; CF1
Kenani Ne9
Kenaniah CF15
Kenaz Gen36; Jos15; Ju3; CF1, 4
Karen-happuch Job42
Keros Ez2; Ne7
Kesed Gen22
Keturah Gen25; CF1
Keziah Job42
Kimham (Chimham) SS19; Je41
Kir Is22
Kir-hareseth KS3
Kish (father of Saul) SF9f, 14; SS21; CF12
  (father of Shimei) Est2
  (son of Abdi) CS29
  (son of Jehiel) CF8ff
  (son of Mahli) CF23
  (son of Ner) CF8
Kishi CF6
Kislon Nu34
Kittim Gen10; CF1
Kohath Gen46; Ex6; Nu3ff; CF6, 15, 23; CS29,34
Kolaiah Ne11; Je29
Korah Gen36; Ex6; Nu16;   CF1ff, 6, 9
Kore CF9, 26; CS31
Koz (Hakkoz) Ne3, 7
Kushaiah CF15
Laadah CF4
Laadan CF7, 23, 26
Laban Gen24ff
Lael Nu3ff
Lahad CF4
Lahmi CF20
Laish SF25; SS21
Lamech Gen4ff; CF1
Lappidoth Ju4
Leah Gen29ff; Ru4
Lebanah Ez2; Ne7
Lebo-hamath KF8
Lemuel Pro31
Letushim Gen25

APPENDIX A PERSONAL NAMES

Leummim Gen25
Levi Gen29ff; Ex1; De2; CF2, 6, 23; Ez8; Ps135; Z12; Ma2
Libni Ex6; Nu3ff; CF6
Likhi CF7
Lo-ammi (Ammi) Ho1
Lo-ruhama (Ru-hamah) Ho1
Lot Gen11ff; De2; Ps83
Lotan CF1
Lud Gen10; CF1
Luz Gen48
Maabarah Is10
Maacah (concubine of Caleb) CF2
  (father of Shephatiah) CF27
  (grandmother of Asa) KF15; CS15
  (king of Gath) KF2
  (mother of Abijah) CS13
  (mother of Absolom) SS3; CF3
  (son of Reumah) Gen22
  (wife of Jehiel) CF8
  (wife of Machir) CF7
  (wife of Reheboam) CS11
Maadai Ez10
Maadiah Ne12
Maai Ne12
Maasai CF9
Maaseiah (Mahseiah) (a chief) Ne10
  (a clerk) CS26
  (a governor) CS34
  (a priest) Ez10; Ne8, 12; Je21, 37
  (father of Neriah) Je32, 51
  (son of Ahaz) CS28
  (son of Adaiah) CS23
  (son of Baruch) Ne11
  (son of Shallum) Je35
  (temple musician) CF15
Maaz CF2
Maaziah CF24; Ne10
Machbanai CF12
Machi Nu13
Machie Jos13, 17
Machir (son of Amiel) SS9, 17
  (son of Manasseh) Nu26f, 36; De3; CF2, 7
Madai Gen10; CF1
Magdiel Gen36; CF1

APPENDIX A PERSONAL NAMES

Magog Gen10; CF1
Magor-missabib (Pashhur) Je20
Magpiash Ne10
Mahalah CF7
Mahalaleel Ne11
Mahalalel Gen5; CF1
Mahalath Gen28; CS11
Maharai CF27
Mahasham CF8
Mahath CF6; CS29, 31
Mahazioth CF25
Mahlah Nu26ff, 36; Jos17
Mahli Ex6; Nu3ff; CF6, 23; Ez8
Mahlon Ru1ff
Mahol KF4
Maknadebai Ez10
Malachi Ma1
Malcham CF8
Malchiah (district ruler) Ne3
  (father of Pashhur) Je21, 38
  (Melichu, a priest) CF9; Ez10; Ne8, 10ff
  (temple musician) CF6
  (temple official) CF24
Malchiel Gen46; Nu26; CF7
Malchiram CF3
Malluch (a priest) Ez; Ne10, 12
  (son of Hashabiah) CF6
Mamre Gen14
Manahath Gen36; CF1
Manasseh (family of Hashum) Ez10
  (king of Judah) KS20f; CF3; CS32ff; Je15
  (son of Joseph and Asenath) Gen41, 46, 48, 50; Nu1, 7ff, 26; De3, 29, 33;
    Jos1ff, 12f, 16ff; Ju1f; KF4
Manoah Ju13
Maoch SF27
Maon CF2
Mara (Naomi) Ru1
Mareshah CF2
Marsena Est1
Mash Gen10; CF1
Massa Gen25; CF1
Matred Gen36; CF1
Matri SF10
Mattan KS11; CS23; Je38
Mattaniah (a Levite) CF9; CS20, 29; Ne11f

APPENDIX A PERSONAL NAMES

Mattaniah (family of Pahath-moab) Ez10
  (Zedekiah, king of Judah) KS24
  (son of Heman) CF25
Mattenai Ez10; Ne12
Mattithiah CF9, 15ff, 25; Ez10; Ne8
Medad Nu11
Medan Gen25; CF1
Mehetabel Gen36; CF1; Ne6
Mehida Ez2; Ne7
Mehir CF4
Mehujael Gen4
Mehuman Est1
Meinim Ez2
Melatiah Ne3
Melchizedek Gen14; Ps110
Melech CF8ff
Melichu (Malluch) Ne10, 12
Melzar D1
Memucan Est1
Manahem KS15
Meonothai CF4
Mephibosheph (son of Jonathan) SS21
  (son of Saul) SS4, 9,16,19, 21
Merab SF14, 18; SS21
Meraiah Ne12
Meraioth CF6, 9; Ez7; Ne11ff
Merari Gen46; Ex6; Nu3ff; CF6, 9, 15, 23ff;
Mered CF4
Meremoth Ez8; Ne3, 10, 12
Meres Est1
Meribaal CF8ff
Merodach-baladan KS20; Is39
Mesh CF2, 8
Mesha KS3
Meshach (Mishael) (exile) D1ff
  (son of Japheth) Gen10; CF1
Meshelemiah CF9, 26
Meshezabek (Meshezabeel) Ne3, 10ff
Meshillemith CF9
Meshillemoth CS28; Ne11
Meshobab CF4
Meshullam (a Gadite) CF5
  (adjutant-general) KS22
  (family of Kodath) CS34
  (gatekeeper) Ne12
  (priest) Ne10

APPENDIX A PERSONAL NAMES

Meshullam (prominent citizen) Ez8, 10; Ne12
  (son of Berechiah) Ne3, 6, 8
  (son of Elpaal CF8
  (son of Hodaviah) CF9
  (son of Joed) Ne11
  (son of Meshillemith) CF9
  (son of Zadok) Ne11
  (son of Zerubbabel) CF3
Meshullemeth KS21
Methuselah Gen5; CF1
Methushael Gen4
Meunim Ez12; Ne7
Mibhar CF11
Mibsam Gen25; CF1, 4
Mibzar Gen36; CF1
Mica SS9; CF9; Ne10ff
Micah (father of Abdon) CS34
  (from Ephraim) Ju17ff
  (of Moresheth) Je26; Mi1
  (son of Meribbaal) CF8ff
  (son of Shimei) CF5
  (son of Uzziel) CF23ff
  (son of Zabdi) Ne11
Michael (a Gadite) CF5
  (father of Omri) CF27
  (father of Sethur) Nu13
  (father of Zebadiah) Ez8
  (son of Baaseiah) CF6
  (son of Beriah) CF8
  (son of David) CS21
  (son of Izrahiah) CF7
Micaiah (father of Akbor)KS22
  (officer) CS17
  (son of Gemariah) Je36
  (son of Imla) KF22; CS18
  (son of Zaccur) Ne12
Michal SF14, 18; SS3; CF15
Micri CF9
Midian Gen25ff; Ju6ff; CF1; Ps83; Is10
Mijamin CF24;Ez10; Ne10, 12
Mikloth CF8ff
Mikneiah CF15
Milalai Ne12
Milcah Gen11ff; Nu26ff, 36; Jos17
Miniamin CS31; Ne12

APPENDIX A PERSONAL NAMES

Miriam (daughter of Bithia) CF4
  (sister of Moses) Ex15; Nu12; CF6; Mi6
Mirmah CF8
Mishael (a priest) Ne8
  (Meshach) (exile) D1ff
  (son of Uzziel) Ex6; Le10
Misham CF8
Mishma Gen25; CF1, 4
Mishmannah CF12
Mispar Ez2
Mispereth Ne7
Mithredath Ez1, 4
Mizram CF1
Mizraim Gen10
Mizzah Gen36; CF1
Moab Gen19; CF4
Moadiah Ne12
Molid CF2
Mordecai (a chief) Ez2; Ne7
  (son of Jair) Est2ff
Moses Ex2ff; Le1ff; Nu1ff;   De1ff; Jos1ff, 13, 24; Ju18; SF12; KF8;
        KS14, 18, 23; CF6, 23, 26; CS23, 25, 33ff; Ez3, 6ff; Ne1,8ff;
        Ps77, 99, 103, 106; Is63; Je15; D9; Mi6; Ma4
Moza CF2, 8ff
Muppim Gen46
Mushi Ex6; CF6, 23
Naam CF4
Naamah Gen4; KF14; CS12
Naaman Gen46; Nu26; KS5; CF8
Naarah CF4
Naarai CF11
Nabal SF25, 27, 30; SS2ff
Naboth KF21; KS9
Nadab Ex6, 24ff; Le10; Nu26; KF15; CF2, 6, 8ff, 24
Naham CF4
Nahamani Ne7
Naharai SS23; CF11
Nahash SF11; SF10,17; CF19
Nahath CF1, 6; CS31
Nahbi Nu13
Naheth Gen36
Nahor Gen11ff; Jos24
Nahori CF1
Nahshon Ex6; Nu1, 7ff; Ru4; CF2
Nahum Na1
Naomi Ru1ff

APPENDIX A PERSONAL NAMES

Naphish Gen25; CF1
Naphtali Gen30ff; Ex1; Nu1,7ff; De27, 33; Ju1ff; KF7
Nathan SS5, 7, 12, 23; KF1,4; CF2ff, 11, 14, 17, 29; CS9, 29; Ez8, 10; Z12
Nathan-melek KS23
Neariah CF3ff
Nebai (Nobai) Ne10
Nebaioth Gen25ff; CF1
Nebat KF11, 16ff, 21ff; KS3, 9f, 13, 17, 23; CS9f, 13
Nebo Ez10
Nebuchadnezzar (Nebuchadrezzar) KS24; CF6; CS36; Ez1, 5; Ne7; Est2;
    Je21f, 24, 27ff, 32, 34, 37, 39, 43ff, 46, 49, 51ff; E26, 29ff; D1ff
Nebusarsekim Je39
Nebushazban Je39
Nebuzaradan KS25; Je39f, 41, 43, 52
Necho KS23; CS35ff; Je46
Nebadiah CF3
Nehemiah Ez2; Ne1, 3, 7f, 10, 12
Nehum Ne7
Nehushta KS24
Nekoda Ez2; Ne7
Nemuel Nu26; CF4
Nepheg Ex6; SS5; CF3, 14
Nephishesim (Nephushesim) Ne7
Ner SF14, 26; SS2ff; KF2; CF8ff
Nergalsarezer (Nergal-sharezer) Je39
Neriah Je32, 36, 43, 45, 51
Nethaneel NU1ff, 7ff; CF2, 15, 24, 26; CS17, 35; Ez10; Ne12
Nethaniah KS25; CF25; CS17; Je36, 40ff
Netophah CF11
Neziah Ez2; Ne7
Nimrod Gen10; CF1; Mi5
Nimshi KF19; KS9; CS22
Noadiah Ez8; Ne6
Noah (daughter of Zelophehad) Nu26ff, 36; Jos17
  (the patriarch) Gen5ff; CF1; Is54; E14
Nobai (Nebai) Ne10
Nogah CF3, 14
Nohah CF8
Nun Nu13, 26; De1; Jos1; Ju2; KF16; CF7; Ne8
Obadiah (a Gadite) CF12, 27
  (a Levite) CS34
  (a priest) Ne10, 12
  (a prophet) Ob1
  (comptroller) KF18ff; CS17
  (son of Arnan) CF3

APPENDIX A PERSONAL NAMES

Obadiah (son of Azel) CF8ff
  (son of Izrahiah) CF7
  (son of Jehiel) Ez8
  (son of Shemaiah) CF9
Obal Gen10
Obed Ru4; CF2, 11, 26; CS23
Obed-edom SS6; CF13, 15ff, 26; CS25
Obil CF27
Ocran Nu1, 7ff
Oded CS15, 28
Og Nu21; De3, 29ff; Jos2, 9, 12ff; KF4; Ne9; Ps135f
Ohad Gen46; Ex6
Ohel CF3
Oholibamah Gen36; CF1
Omar Gen36; CF1
Omri KF16; KS8; CF7 9, 27; CS22; Mi6
On Nu16
Onam Gen36; CF1ff
Onan Gen38; Nu26; CF2
Ophai (Ephai) Je40
Ophir Gen10; CF1
Ophrah CF4
Oreb Ju7; Ps83
Oren CF2
Ornan CF21; CS3
Orpah Ru1
Osnappar (Asnappar) Ez4
Othni CF26
Othniel Jos15; Ju1, 3; CF4, 27
Ozem CF2
Ozni Nu26
Paarai SS23
Padon Ez2; Ne7
Pagiel Nu1, 7ff
Pahath-moab Ez2, 8, 10; Ne3, 7, 10
Palal Ne3
Pallu Gen46; Ex6; Nu26; CF5
Palti Nu13; SF25
Paltiel Nu34; SS3
Parmashta Est9
Parnach Nu34
Parosh Ez2, 8, 10; Ne3, 7, 10
Parshandatha Est9
Paruah KF4
Pasach CF7

APPENDIX A PERSONAL NAMES

Paseah (Phaseah) CF4; Ez2; Ne3, 7
Pashhur (Pashur) (a priest) Ez2, 10; Ne7, 10
 (chief officer) Je20
 (son of Malchiah) CF9; Je21,38
Pedahel Nu34
Pedahzur Nu, 7ff
Pedaiah KS23; CF27; Ne3, 8, 11, 13
Pekah KS15ff; CS28; Is7
Pekahiah KS15
Pelaiah CF3; Ne8, 10
Pelaliah Ne11
Pelatiah CF3ff; Ne10; E11
Peleg Gen10ff; CF1
Pelet CF2, 12
Peleth Nu16; CF2
Peninnah SF1
Penuel CF4, 8
Pethuel Joe1
Peresh CF7
Perez Gen38; Nu26; Ru4; CF2ff, 9, 27; Ne11
Perida Ne7
Peruda Ez2
Pethahiah CF24; Ez10; Ne9, 11
Peulthai CF26
Pharaoh (title) Gen12ff; De11; KF3, 9, 11; KS17ff, 23; CF4; Ps135ff; So1;
    Is19, 30, 36; Je25, 27, 43f, 47
Phaseah (paseah) Ne3, 7
Phicol Gen21ff
Phinehas (son of Eleazar) Ex6; Nu25, 31; Jos22, 24; Ju20; CF6, 9; Ez7ff;
    Ps106
 (son of Eli) SF1ff, 14
Pildash Gen22
Pilha Ne10
Piltai Ne12
Pinon Gen36; CF1
Piram Jos10
Pispah CF7
Pithon CF8ff
Pochereth-hazzebaim Ez2; Ne7
Poratha Est9
Potiphar Gen37
Potiphera Gen41ff
Pue Gen46; Nu26;Ju10; CF7
Puah Ex1
Pul KS15; CF5
Purah Ju7

APPENDIX A PERSONAL NAMES

Put Gen10; CF1
Putiel Ex6
Queen of Sheba KF10; CS9
Raama CF1
Raamah Gen10
Rab-mag Je39
Rab-saris KS18; Je39
Rab-shakeh KS18; Is36
Rachel (Rahel) Gen29ff; Ru4; SF10; Je31
Raddai CF2
Rahab Jos2
Raham CF2
Rakem CF7
Ram Ru4; CF2; Job32
Ramiah Ez10
Rapha CF8
Raphah CF8
Raphu Nu13
Reaia CF5
Reaiah CF2, 4; Ez2; Ne7
Reba Nu31
Rebecca Gen22ff
Rechab SS4; KS10; Ne3; Je35
Reelaiah Ez2
Regem CF2
Regem-melech Z7
Rehabiah CF23f, 26
Rehob Ne10
Rehoboam KF11; CF3; CS9ff
Rehum Ez2, 4; Ne3, 10, 12
Rei KF1
Rekem Nu31; CF2
Remaliah KS15ff; CS28; Is7ff
Rephael CF26
Rephah CF7
Rephaiah CF3ff, 7, 9; Ne3
Reshaph CF7
Reu Gen11; CF1
Reuben Gen29ff; Ez1; Nu1, 7ff, 26; De11, 27, 33; Jos14; CF2, 5
Reuel Gen36; Nu1, 7ff; CF1, 9
Reumah Gen22
Rezia CF7
Rezin KS15ff; Ez2; Ne7; Is7ff
Rezon KF11
Ribai SS23; CF11
Rimmon SS4

APPENDIX A PERSONAL NAMES

Rinnah CF4
Riphath Gen10
Rizpah SS3, 21
Rodanim Gen10; CF1
Rohgah CF7
Romamti-ezer CF25
Rosh Gen46
Ru-hamah (Lo-ruhamah) Ho2
Ruth Ru1ff
Sabta CF1
Sabtah Gen10
Sabtecha Gen10; CF1
Sacar CF11, 26
Sallai (Sallu) CF9; Ne11ff
Salma CF2
Salmon Ru4
Salu Nu25
Samgar-nebo Je39
Samlah Gen36; CF1
Samson Ju13ff; SF12
Samuel (son of Ammihud)   Nu34
   (son of Elkanah) SF1ff, 19, 28; CF6, 9, 26, 29; CS35; Ps99; Je15
   (his ghost) SF28
   (son of Tolah) CF7
Sanballat Ne2, 4ff, 13
Saph SS21
Sarah Gen17ff; Is51
Sarai Gen11ff
Saraph CF4
Sargon Is20
Sarsechim Je39
Saul (first king of Israel) SF9ff; SS1ff, 16; CF5,8f, 12, 26; Is10
   (king of Edom) Gen36; CF1
   (son of Simeon) Ex6; Nu26; CF4
   (son of Uzziah) CF6
Seba Gen10; CF1
Segub KF16; CF2
Seir Gen36; CF1
Seled CF2
Semachiah CF26
Sennacherib KS18ff; CS32; Is36ff
Seorim CF24
Serah Gen46; Nu26; CF7
Seraiah (adjutant general) SS8
   (chief priest) KS25; Ne12; Je52
   (quarter master) Je51

APPENDIX A PERSONAL NAMES

Seraiah (son of Azariah) CF6; Ez7
  (son of Azriel) Je36
  (son of Hilkiah) Ne11
  (son of Kenaz) CF4
  (son of Tamhumeth) Je40
  (tribal leader) Ez2; Ne10
Sered Gen46; Nu26
Serug Gen11; CF1
Seth (Sheth) Gen4; CF1
Sethur Nu13
Shaaph CF2
Shaashgaz Est2
Shabbethai Ne8, 11
Shachia CF8
Shadrach Diff
Shaharaim CF8
Shallum (doorkeeper) CF9; Ez2; Ne7
  (king of Israel) KS15; Je22
  (father of Hezekiah) CS28
  (son of Hallohesh) Ne3
  (son of Josiah) CF3
  (son of Naphtali CF7
  (son of Tikvah) KS22; CS34
  (son of Sisamai) CF2
  (son of Zadok) CF6; Ez7
  (uncle of Jeremiah) Je32, 35
Shallun Ne3
Shalmai Ez2; Ne7
Shalman Ho10
Shalmaneser KS17ff
Shama CF11
Shamed CF8
Shamer CF6
Shamgar Ju3
Shamhuth CF27
Shamir CF24
Shamlai Ez2
Shamma CF7
Shammah Gen36; SF16ff; SS23; CF1
Shammai CF2, 4
Shammoth CF11
Shammua (son of David) CF14
  (son of Galal) Ne11ff
  (son of Zaccur) Nu13
Shamsherai CF8
Shapham CF5

APPENDIX A PERSONAL NAMES

Shaphan (adjutant-general) KS22, 25; Je36
  (father of Ahikam) Je26, 39f, 43
  (father of Elasah) Je29
  (father of Jaazaniah) E8
  (son of Azaliah) CS34
Shaphat Nu13; KF19; KS3; CF3, 5, 27
Sharai Ex10
Sharar SS23
Sharezer (Sherezer) KS19; Is37; Z7
Shashak CF8
Shashal Ez10
Shavsha CF12
Sheal Ez10
Shealtiel (father of Zerubbabel) Ez3ff; Ne12; Hg1f
  (son of Jeconiah) CF3
Sheariah CF8
Sheba Gen10ff; SS20; CF1, 5
Shebaniah CF15; Ne9f, 12
Sheber CF2
Shebna KS18; Is22, 36
Shecaniah (a priest) Ne12
  (father of Hattush) Ez8
  (father of Jahaziel) Ez8
  (father of Shemaiah) CF3; Ne3
  (son of Arah) Ne6
  (son of Obadiah) CF3, 24; CS31
Shechem Gen33ff; Nu26; Jos17ff; CF7
Shedeur Nu1, 7ff
Shehariah CF8
Shelah Gen10ff; Nu26; CF1f, 4
Shelemiah (doorkeeper) CF26; Ne3
  (father of Jehucal) Je37f
  (father of Nethaniah) Je36
  (a priest) Ne13
Sheleph Gen10; CF1
Shelesh CF7
Shelomi Nu34
Shelomith (daughter of Dibri) Le24
  (daughter of Rehoboam) CS11
  (daughter of Zerubbabel) CF3
  (son of Josiphiah) Ez8
Shelomoth CF23f, 26
Shelumiel Nu1, 7ff
Shem Gen5ff; CF1
Shema CF2, 5, 8; Ne8
Shemaah CF12

APPENDIX A PERSONAL NAMES

Shemaiah (a clerk) CF24
  (a Levite) CS17, 29, 31, 35
  ('man of God') KF12
  (a priest) Ez10; Ne10, 12
  ('prominent man') Ez8
  (a prophet) CS12; Je29
  (father of Delaiah) Je36
  (father of Shimri) CF4
  (father of Uriah) Je26
  (son of Delaiah) Ne6
  (son of Elizaphan) CF15
  (son of Hasshub) CF9; Ne11
  (son of Joel) CF5
  (son of Mattanaiah) Ne12
  (son of Meshelemaiah)CF26
  (son of Shecaniah) CF3;Ne3
Shemariah CF12; CS11; Ez10
Shemeber Gen14
Shemer KF16
Shemida Nu26; Jos17; CF7
Shemiramoth CF15ff; CS17
Shenazzar CF3
Shephatiah (a Haruphite)CF12
  (a tribal leader) Ez2, 8; Ne7
  (son of David) SS3; CF3
  (son of Jehoshaphat) CS21
  (son of Maacah) CF27
  (son of Mahalalel) Ne11
  (son of Mattan) Je38
  (son of Reuel) CF9
Shephi CF1
Shepho Gen36
Shephuphan CF8
Sherah CF7
Sherebiah Ez8; Ne8f, 12
Sheresh CF7
Sheshai Nu13; Jos15; Ju1
Sheshan CF2
Sheshbazzar Ez1
Sheth (Seth) CF1
Shethar Est1
Shethar-bozenai Ez5
Sheva CF2
Shilhi KF22; CS20
Shillem Gen46; Nu26
Shiloh SF14

APPENDIX A PERSONAL NAMES

Shilshah CF7
Shimea CF2ff, 6, 8
Shimeah SS13
Shimeai SS21
Shimeam CF9
Shimeath KS12; CS24
Shimei (a Levite) CS29, 32; Ez10
  (a tribal leader) CF8
  (opponent of Adonijah) KF1
  (of Ramah) CF27
  (son of Gerah) SS16; KF2
  (son of Gershon) Ex6; Nu3; CF6, 23; Z12
  (son of Gog) CF5
  (son of Jahath) CF6
  (son of Jeduthun) CF25
  (son of Kish) Est2
  (son of Libni) CF6
  (son of Pedaiah) CF3
  (son of Zaccur) CF4
Shimon CF4
Shimpath CF8
Shimri CF4, 11, 26; CS29
Shimrith CS24
Shimron Gen46; Nu27; CF7
Shimshai Ez4
Shinab Gen14
Shinar Gen14
Shiphi CF4
Shiphtan Nu34
Shiprah Ex1
Shisha KF4
Shishak KF11, 14; CS12
Shitrai CF27
Shiza CF11
Shobab SS5; CF2ff, 14
Shobach SS5
Shobai Ez2; Ne7
Shobal Gen36; CF1, 4
Shobek NE10
Shobi SS17
Shoham CF24
Shomer KS12; CF7
Shophach CF19
Shua CF7
Shuah Gen25; CF1, 4
Shual CF7

525

APPENDIX A PERSONAL NAMES

Shubael CF23ff
Shuham Nu26
Shuni Gen46; Nu26
Shupham Nu26
Shethelah Nu26; CF7
Sia Ne7
Siaha Ez2
Sibbecai CF27
Sibbechai SS21; CF20
Sidon Gen10; CF1
Simeon (family of Harim) Ez10
  (son of Jacob) Gen29ff; Ex1; Nu1; De27; Jos19; Ju1; CF2, 4
Sippai CF20
Sisamai CF2
Sisera (army commander) Ju4f; SF12; Ps83
  (temple servitor) Ez2; Ne7
Sithri Ex6
Sodi Nu13
Solomon SS5, 12; KF1ff; KS21, 23; CF3, 6, 14, 18, 22, 28ff; CS1ff, 10f,
      CS13, 30, 33ff; Ez2; Ne7, 12ff; Pro1; So1, 3, 8; Je52
Sophereth Ne7
Sotai Ez2; Ne7
Suah CF7
Susi Nu13
Tabbaoth Ez2; Ne7
Tabeal Is7
Tabeel Ez4
Tabrimmon KF15
Tahan Nu26; CF7
Tahash Gen22
Tahath CF6ff
Tahpenes KF11
Tahrea CF9
Talmai Nu13; Jos15; Ju1; SS3, 13; CF3
Talmon CF9; Ez2; Ne7, 11ff
Tamar (daughter of Absalom) SS14
  (daughter-in-law of Judah) Gen38; Ru4; CF2ff
  (sister of Absalom) SS13
Tanhumeth KS25; Je40
Taphath KF4
Tappuah CF2
Tarea CF8
Tarshish Gen10; CF1, 7; Est1
Tartan KS18; Is20
Tattenai Ez5
Tebah Gen22

APPENDIX A PERSONAL NAMES

Tebaliah CF26
Tehinnah CF4
Tekoa CF11
Telah CF7
Telem Ez10
Temah Ez2; Ne7
Teman Gen25ff; CF1
Temeni CF4
Terah Gen11; Jos24; CF1
Teresh Est2
Tibni KF16
Tidal Gen14
Tiglath-pileser (Tilgat-pilneser) Ks15ff; CF5; CS28
Tikvah KS22; CS34
Tilon CF4
Timna Gen36; CF1
Tiras Gen10; CF1
Tirhakah KS19; Is37
Tirhanah CF2
Tiria CF4
Tirzah Nu26ff, 36; Jos17
Toah CF6
Tob-adonijah CS17
Togarmah Gen10; CF1
Tohu SF1
Toi SS8
Tola (son of Issachar) Gen46; Nu26
　(a judge) J10; CF7
Tou CF18
Tubal CF1
Tubal-cain Gen4
Ucal Pro30 Uel Ez10
Ulam CF7ff
Ulla CF7
Unni CF15; Ne12
Ur CF11
Uri Ex31ff; KF4; CF2; CS1; Ez10
Uriah (Urijah)(a Hittite) SS1, 23; KF15; CF11
　(a priest) Ks16; Ez8; Ne3, 8; Is8
　(a prophet) Je26
Uriel CF6, 15; CS13
Uthai CF9; Ez8
Uz Gen10ff; CF1
Uzai Ne3
Uzal Gen10; CF1
Uzza CF6, 8, 13; Ez2; Ne11ff

APPENDIX A PERSONAL NAMES

Uzzah SS6
Uzzi CF6f 9; Ez7; Ne11ff
Uzzia CF11
Uzziah (family of Immer) Ez10
  (Azariah) (king of Judah) KS15; CS26ff; Is1,6ff; Ho1; Am1; Z14
  (son of Uriel) CF6
  (son of Zechariah) Ne11
Uzziel Ex6; Le10; Nu3ff; CF4, 6ff, 15, 23ff; CS29; Ne3
Vaizatha (Vajezatha) Est9
Vashti Est1ff
Vophsi Nu13
Zabad CF2, 7,11; CS24; Ez10
Zabbai Ez10; Ne3
Zabbud KF4
Zabdi Jos7; CF8, 27; Ne11
Zabdiel CF27; Ne11
Zabud KF4
Zaccai Ez2; Ne7
Zaccur Nu13; CF4, 24ff;   Ne10, 12ff
Zacher CF8
Zadok (accountant) Ne13
  (chief at Jerusalem) Ne3,10
  (officer of tribes) CF27
  (the priest) SS8, 15ff; KF1ff; CF6.9.15f, 18; Ez7; Ne11; E40, 48
  (warrior of David) CF12
Zaham CS11
Zalaph Ne3
Zalmunna Ju8; Ps83
Zaphenath-paneah (Joseph) Gen14
Zaphon Ju12
Zattu Ez2, 8, 10; Ne7, 10
Zavan Gen36; CF1
Zaza CF2
Zebadiah CF8, 12; CS17;   Ez8,   10
Zebah Ju8; Ps83
Zebediah CF26ff; CS19
Zebidah KS23
Zebina Ez10
Zeboyim Gen14
Zebul Ju9
Zebulun Gen30ff; Ex1; Nu1, 7ff; De27, 33; Jos19; Ju1, 4, 6; CF2
Zechariah (a Merarite) CF15
  (a priest) CF15ff; CS35;   Ne8,   12
  (a Reubenite) CF5
  (family of Elam) Ez10
  (family of Kohath) CS34

APPENDIX A PERSONAL NAMES

Zechariah (family of Parosh) Ez8
  (father of Abijah) CS29
  (king of Israel) KS14f, 18
  (king's officer) CS17
  (of Manasseh) CF27
  (official at Jerusalem) Ne11
  (son of Bebai) Ez8
  (son of Benauah) CS20
  (son of Hosah) CF26
  (son of Isshiah) CF24
  (son of Jeberechiah) Is8
  (son of Jehiel) CF9
  (son of Jehoiada) CS24
  (son of Jehoshaphat) CS21
  (son of Meshalemia) CF
  (the prophet) CS26; Ez5; Z1, 7
Zedekiah (Mattaniah) (king of Judah) KS24; CS36; Je1, 21, 24, 27, 29, 32, 34, Je37ff, 44, 49, 51ff
  (a priest) Ne10
  (son of Hananiah) Je36
  (son of Josiah) CF3
  (son of Kenaanah) KF22; CS18
  (son of Maaseiah) Je29
Zeeb Ju7; Ps83
Zelek SS23; CF11
Zelophedad Nu36
Zelophehad Jos17; CF1
Zemira CF7
Zephaniah KS25; Je21, 29, 7, 52; Zp1; Z6
Zephi CF1
Zepho Gen36
Zephon Nu26
Zerah Gen36ff; Nu26; Jos7; CF1, 4, 6, 9, 27; CS14; Ne11
Zerahiah CF6; Ez7ff
Zeresh Est5ff
Zereth CF4
Zeruah KF11
Zerubbabel CF3; Ez2ff; Ne7, 12; Hg1ff; Z4
Zeruiah SF26; SS2, 8, 14ff; KF2; CF2, 11, 18, 27
Zetham CF23, 26
Zethan CF7
Zethar Est1
Zia CF5
Ziba SS9, 16, 19
Zibeon Gen36; CF1
Zibia CF8

APPENDIX A PERSONAL NAMES

Zibiah KS12; CS24
Zichri Ex6; CF8ff, 26ff; CS23, 28; Ne11ff
Ziha Ex2; Ne7, 11
Zillah Gen4
Zilpah Gen29ff
Zilthai CF8
Zimmah CF6
Zimran Gen25; CF1
Zimri (king of Israel) KF16; KS9
  (son of Jarah) CF9
  (son of Jehoaddah) CF8
  (son of Salu) Nu25
  (son of Zerah) CF2
Ziph CF4
Ziphah CF4
Ziphion Gen46
Zippor Nu22; Jos24; Ju11
Zipporah Ex2ff, 18
Ziza CF4, 23; Cs11
Zobebah CF4
Zohar Gen23ff; Ex6
Zoheth CF4
Zophah CF7
Zophai CF6
Zophar Job2, 11, 20, 42
Zuar Nu1, 7ff
Zuph SF1; CF6
Zur Nu25, 31; CF8ff
Zuriel Nu3ff
Zurishaddae Nu1, 7ff
Zuzim Gen14

NEW TESTAMENT

Aaron L1; A7; LH, 9
Abel Mw23; L11; LH11, 12
Abiathar Mk2
Abijah (Abia) Mw1; L1
Abiud Mw1
Abraham Mw1, 8, 22; Mk12; L1, 3, 13, 16, 19f; J8; A3, 7, 13; PR9, 11;
    PCS11; PG3f; LH2, 6f, 11; LJ2; LPF3
Achaicus PCF16
Achaz (Ahaz) Mw1
Achim Mw1

APPENDIX A PERSONAL NAMES

Adam L3; PR5; PCF15; PTF2; LJu1
Addi L3
Aeneas A9
Agabus A11, 21
Agar (Hagar) PG4
Agrippa A25f
Ahaz (Achaz) Mw1
Alexander (a coppersmith) A19; PTS4
 (a disciple) PTF1
 (a priest) A4
 (son of Simon) Mk15
Alphaeus (father of James) Mw10; Mk3; L6; A1
 (father of Levi) Mk2
Aminadab (Amminadab) Mw1; L3
Amon Mw1
Amos L3
Ampliatus (Amplias) PR16
Ananias (who cured Saul) A9, 22
 (who dropped dead) A5
 (high priest) A23f
Andrew Mw4, 10; Mk1, 3, 12; L6; J1, 6, 12; A1
Andronicus PR16
Anna L2
Annas L3; J18; A4
Antipas Rev2
Apelles PR16
Apollos A18f; PCF1, 3f,16; Tt3
Apphia Ph1
Aquila A18; PR16; PCF16; PTS4
Aram (Arni) L3
 (Ram) Mw1
Archelaus Mw2
Archippus PCo4; Ph1
Aretas PCS11
Aristarchus A19f, 27; PCo4; Ph1
Aristobolus PR16
Arni (Aram) L3
Arphaxad (Arpachsad) L3
Artemas Tt3
Asa (Asher) Mw1; L2
Asyncritus PR16
Augustus Caesar L2; A25
Azariah (Ozias) Mw1
Azor Mw1
Balaam LPS2; LJu1; Rev2
Balak Rev2

531

APPENDIX A PERSONAL NAMES

Barabbas (Bar-Abbas) Mw27; Mk15; L23; J18
Barak LH11
Bar-Jesus (Elymas) A13
Bar-Jona (Simon Peter) Mw16
Barnabas A9,11ff; PCF9; PG2
Barsabbas (Joseph Justus) A1
Bartholomew Mw10; Mk3; L6; A1
Bartimaeus Mk10
Beor (Bosor) LPS2
Berachiah (Barachias) Mw23
Bernice A25f
Blastus A12
Boanerges (James and John) Mk3
Boaz (Booz) Mw1; L3; LPS2
Caesar (title) Mw22; L2f, 20; J19; A11, 17, 25, 27; PPs4
Caiaphas Mw26; L3; J11, 18; A4
Cain LH11; LJF3; LJu1
Cainan (son of Arphaxad) L3
  (son of Enosh) L3
Candace (Kandake) A8
Carpus PTS4
Cephas (Simon Peter) J1; PCF1, 3, 9, 15; PG1f
Chloe PCF1
Chuza L8
Cis (Kish) A13
Claudia PTS4
Claudius Caesar A11
  Lysias (commandant) A23
Clement PPS4
Cleopas L24
Cleophas (Clopas) J19
Cornelius A10
Cosam L3
Crescens PTS4
Crispus A18; PCF1
Cyrinius (Quirinius) L2
Damaris A17
Daniel Mw24; Mk13
David Mw1, 9, 12, 15, 20ff; Mk2, 10ff; L1ff, 6, 18, 20; A1f, 4, 7, 15; PR1, 4, 11; PTS2; LH4, 11; Rev3, 5, 22
Demas PCO4; PTS4; Ph1
Demetrius A19; LJT1
Didymus (Thomas the twin) J11, 20f
Dionysius A17
Diotrephes LJT1
Dorcas (Tabitha) A9

APPENDIX A PERSONAL NAMES

Drusilla A24
Eber (Heber) L3
Eleazar Mw1
Eliakim Mw1; L3
Elias (Elijah) Mw11, 16f, 27; Mk6, 8f, 15; L1, 4, 9; J1; PR11
Eliezer L3
Elijah (Elias) Mw11.16f, 27;Mk6, 8f, 15; L1, 4, 9; J1; PR11
Elisha (Eliseus) L4
Eliud Mw1
Elizabeth (Elisabeth) L1
Elmadam (Elmodam) L3
Elymus (Bar-Jesus) A13
Enoch L3; LH11; LJu1
Enosh (Enos) L3
Epaenetus PR16
Epaphras PCo1, 4; Ph1
Epaphroditus PPs2, 4
Er L3
Erastus A19; PR116; PTS4
Esaias (Isaiah) Mw3f, 8, 12f, 15; Mk7; L3f; J1,12; A8; PR9f
Esau PR9; LH11f
Esli L3
Esrom (Hezron) Mw1; L3
Eubulus PTS4
Eunice PTS1
Euodia (Euodias) PPS4
Eutychus A20
Eve PCS11; PTF2
Ezekias (Hezekiah) Mw1
Felix A23ff
Festus (Porcius) A25
Fortunatus PCF16
Gaius A19f; PR16; PCF1;   LJT1
Gallio A18
Gamaliel A5, 22
Gideon (Gedeon) LH11
Gog Rev20
Hagar PG4
Heber (Eber) L3
Heli L3
Hermas PR16
Hermes PR16
Hermogenes PTS1
Herod (Agrippa) A12f, 23, 25f
   (Antipas the Tetrarch) Mw14, 22; Mk3, 6, 8, 12; L3, 8f, 13, 23; A4
   (the Great) Mw2; L1

533

APPENDIX A PERSONAL NAMES

Herodias Mw14; Mk6; L3
Herodion PR16
Hezekiah (Ezekias) Mw1
Hezron (Esrom) Mw1; L3
Hosea (Osee) PR9
Hymenaeus PTF1; PTS2
Isaac Mw1, 8, 12; Mk12; L3, 13, 20; A3, 7; PR9; PG4; LH11; LJ2
Isaiah (Esais) Mw3f, 8, 12f, 15, 26; Mk1, 7; L3f; J1, 12; A8, 28; PR9f, 15
Jacob (grandfather of Jesus) Mw1
  (son of Isaac) Mw8, 22; Mk12; L1, 3, 13, 20; J4; A3, 7; PR9, 11; LH11
Jairus L8
Jambres PTS3
James (brother of Jesus) Mw13; Mk6; PG1
  (brother of John) Mw4, 10, 17; Mk1, 3, 5, 9f, 13f; L5f, 8f; A1, 12, 15, 21;
      PCF15; PG2; LJ1
  (brother of Joseph) Mk15f
  (brother of Jude) LJu1
  (son of Alphaeus) Mw10; Mk3; L6; A1
Jannai (Janna) L3
Jannes PTS3
Jared L3
Jason A17; PR16
Jeconiah (Jechonias) Mw1
Jehosphaphat (Josaphat)Mw1
Jephthah (Jephthae) LH11
Jeremiah (Jeremias) (Jeremy) Mw2, 16, 27
Jesse Mw1; L3; A13; PR15
Jeremiah (Jeremias) (Jeremy) Mw2, 16, 27
Jesse Mw1; L3; A13; PR15
Jesus Bar-Abbas Mw27
  Christ Mw1ff; Mk1ff; L1ff; J1ff; A1ff; PR1ff; PCF1ff PCS1ff;
      PG1ff; PE1ff; PPs1ff; PCo1ff; ThF1ff; ThS1f; PTF1ff; PTS1ff;
      Tt1ff; Ph1;LH2ff; LJ1ff; LPF1ff; LPS1ff; LJF1ff; LJS1; LJT1; LJu1;
      Rev1, 11, 14, 17, 19f, 22
  Justus PCo4
Jezebel Rev2
Joanna (Johanan) (father of Joda) L3
  (wife of Chuza) L8, 24
Job LJ5
Joda (Juda) L3
Joel A2
Johanan (Joanna) L3
John (Jon, Jonah, Jonas) (father of Simon Peter) Mw16; J1, 21
  (the Baptist) Mw2ff, 9, 11, 14, 16f; Mk1, 6, 8, 11; L1, 3, 5, 7, 9, 11, 16, 20,
      Mk22; J1, 3, 5, 10; A1, 11, 13, 18, 19
  (the Evangelist) Mw4, 10,17; Mk1, 3ff, 9f, 13f; L5f, 8f; A1, 3f, 8, 12f;

APPENDIX A PERSONAL NAMES

John (the Evangelist) PG2; LJF1; LJS1; Rev1, 22
   Mark A12, 15
Jonah (Jonas) Mw12, 16; L11
Jonam L3
Jonathan A4
Joram Mw1
Jorim L3
Josaphat (Jehoshaphat) Mw1
Jose (Joshua) L3
Josech (Joseph) L3
Joseph (Joses) (brother of Jesus) Mw13; Mk6
   (father of Jesus) Mw1; L1ff; J1, 6
   (of Arimathaea) Mw27; Mk15; L23; J19
   (son of Jacob) J4; A7; LH11
   (son of Jonam) L3
   (Josech) (son of Juda) L3
   (Joses) (son of Mary) Mk15
   (son of Mattathiah) L3
   Barnabas (Joses) A4
   Barsabbas (Justus) A1
Joses (Joseph) (Barnabas) A4
   (brother of Jesus) Mw13; Mk6
   (son of Mary) Mk15
Joshua (Jose) (Father of Er)L3
   (son of Nun) A7; LH4
Josiah (Josias) Mw1
Jotham (Joatham) Mw1
Juda (Joda) L3
Judah (Juda) (son of Joseph) L3
   (Judas) (son of Jacob) Mw1; L3
Judas (Juda) (brother of Jesus) Mw13; Mk6
   (resident of Damascus) A5
   (revolutionary) A5
   (Judah) (son of Jacob) Mw1; L3
   (son of James) L6; J14; A1
   Barsabbas A15
   Iscariot Mw10, 26f; Mk3, 14; L6, 22; J6, 12f, 18;A1
Jude LJu1
Julia (Julias) (Junias) PR16
Julius (centurion) A27
Junias (Julia) Julias) PR16
Justus (Jesus Justus) PCo4
   (Joseph Barsabbas) A1
   (Titius) A18
Kandake (Candace) A8

APPENDIX A PERSONAL NAMES

Kish (Cis) A13
Korah (Core) LJu1
Lamech L3
Lazarus J11f; L16
Lebbaeus (Thaddaeus) Mw10
Levi (son of Alphaeus) Mk2
  (son of Jacob) LH7
  (son of Melchi) L3
  (son of Symeon) L3
  (tax gatherer) L5
Linus PTS4
Lois PTS1
Lot L17; LPS2
Lucas (Luke) PCS13; PCo4; PTS4; Ph1
Lucius A13; PR16
Luke (Lucas) PCS13; PCo4; PTS4; Ph1
Lydia A16
Lysianus L3
Lysias A24
Maath L3
Magog Rev20
Mahalaleel (Maleleel) L3
Malchus J18
Manaen A13
Manasseh (Manasses) Mw1
Mark (Marcus) PCo4; PTS4; LPF5; Ph1
Martha L10; J11f
Mary (convert in Asia) PR16
  (mother of James) Mw27f; Mk15f
  (mother of Jesus) Mw1f, 13; Mk6; L1f, 24; J2; A1
  (mother of John Mark) A12
  (of Magdala) Mw27f; Mk15f; L8, 24; J19f
  (sister of Martha and Lazarus) L10 J11f
  (wife of Clopas) J19
Mathusala (Methuselah) L3
Matthan Mw1
Matthat (father of Heli) L3
  (father of Jorim) L3
Mattathia L3
Mattathiah (Mattathias) (father of Joseph) L3
  (father of Maath) L3
Matthew Mw9f; Mk3; L6; A1
Matthias A1
Melchi (father of Levi) L3
  (father of Neri) L3
Melchizedeck (Melchisedec) LH5ff

APPENDIX A PERSONAL NAMES

Melea L3
Menan (Menna) L3
Methuselah (Mathusala) L3
Michael (archangel) LJu1;   Rev12
Mnason A21
Moses Mw8, 17, 19, 22f; Mk1, 7, 9, 12; L2, 5, 9, 16, 20, 24; J1, 3, 5ff;
    A3, 6f, 13, 15, 21, 26; PR5, 9f; PCF9f; PCS3; PTS3; LH3, 7, 10ff;
Naaman L4
Naasson (Nahshon) Mw1; L3
Naggai (Nagge) L3
Nahor (Nachor) L3
Nahshon (Naasson) Mw1; L3
Nahum (Naum) L3
Narcussus PR16
Nathan L3
Nathanael J1, 21
Naum (Nahum) L3
Nereus PR16
Neri L3
Nicanor A6
Nicodemus J3, 7, 19
Nicolas A6
Noah (Noe) Mw24; L3, 17; LH11; LPF3; LPS2
Nympha (Nymphas) PCo4
Obed Mw1; L3
Olympas PR16
Onesimus PCo4; Ph1
Onesiphorus PTS1
Osee (Hosea) PR9
Ozias (Azariah) Mw1
Parmenias A6
Patrobas PR16
Paul (formerly Saul) A13ff; PR1; PCF1, 3, 16; PCS1, 10; PG1; PE1, 3;
    PPs1; PCo1, 4; ThF1f; ThS1, 3; PTF1; PTS1; Ph1; LPS3
Peleg (Phalec) L3
Perez (Phares) (Pharez) Mw1; L3
Persis PR16; LJu1; Rev15
Peter (Simon) (Cephas) Mw4, 8, 10, 14ff, 26; Mk3, 5, 8ff, 13f, 16; L5f, 8f, 12, 22;
    J18, 20f; A1ff, 8f, 11f, 15; PG1f; LPF1; LPS1
Phalec (Peleg) L3
Phanuel L2
Pharaoh (title) A7; PR9; LH11
Phares (Perez) (Pharez) Mw1; L3
Philemon Ph1
Philetus PTS2
Philip (apostle) Mw10; Mk3; L6; J1, 6, 12, 14; A1

537

APPENDIX A PERSONAL NAMES

Philip (brother of Herod) Mw14; Mk6; L3
  (the Evangelist) A6, 8, 21
Philologus PR16
Phlegon PR16
Phoebe (Phebe) PR16
Phygelus PTS1
Pilate (Pontius) Mw27; Mk15; L3, 13, 23; J18f; A3f, 13; PTF6
Porcius Festus A24f
Priscilla (Prisca) A18;
Prochorus A6
Publius A28
Pudens PTS4
Pyrrhus A20
Quartus L2
Quirinius (Cyrinius) L2
Rachel Mw2
Ragau (Reu) L3
Rahab (Rachab) (mother of Salma) Mw1
  (prostitute at Jericho) LH11; LJ2
Ram (Aram) Mw1
Rebecca (Rebekah) PR9
Reheboam (Roboam) Mw1
Reu (Ragau) L3
Rhesa L3
Rhoda A12
Roboam (Reheboam) Mw1
Rufus Mk15; PR16
Ruth Mw1
Sadoc (Zadok) Mw1
Sala (Shelah) L3
Salathiel (Shealtiel) Mw1; L3
Salma (Salmon) Mw1
Salome (daughter of Mary) Mk15f
  (daughter of Herodias)   Mw14; Mk6
Samson LH11
Samuel A3, 13; LH11
Sapphira A5
Sarah (sara) PR4, 9; LH11; LPF3
Saruch (Serug) L3
Saul (king of Israel) A13
  (Paul) A7ff
Sceva A19
Secundus A20
Sem (Shem) L3
Semein (Semei) L3
Sergius Paulus A13

APPENDIX A PERSONAL NAMES

Serug (Saruch) L3
Seth L3
Shealtiel (Salathiel) Mw1; L3
Shem (SeM) L3
Shelah (Sala) L3
Silas A15, 17f
Silvanus PCS1; ThF1; ThS1; LPF5
Simeon (Symeon) (father of Levi) L3
  (Niger) A13, 15
  (of 'Nunc Dimittis') L2
Simon (a leper) Mw26; Mk14
  (a magician) A8
  (a Pharisee) L7
  (a tanner) A9f
  (a Zealot) Mw10; Mk3; L6;A1
  (brother of Jesus) Mw13; Mk6
  (carried the cross) Mw27; Mk15; L23
  Iscariot (father of Judas) J6, 13
  Peter (Cephas) (Bar-jona) Mw4, 10, 16f; Mk1,3, 14; L4ff, 22, 24; J1, 6;
      J13, 18, 20f; A10f; LPS1
Solomon Mw1, 6, 12; L11f; J10; A7
Sopater A20
Sosipater PR16
Sosthenes A18; PVF1
Stachys PR16
Stephen A6, 8, 11, 22
Stephanas PCF1, 16
Susanna L8
Symeon (Simeon) L3
Syntyche PPs4
Tabitha (Dorcas) A9
Tamar (Thamar) Mw1
Terah (Thara) L3
Tertius PR16
Tertullus A24
Thaddaeus (Lebbaeus) Mw10; Mk3
Thara (Terah) L3
Theophilus L1; A1
Theudas A5
Thomas (Didymus the Twin) Mw10; Mk3; L6; J11, 4, 20f; A1
Tiberius L3
Timaeus Mk10
Timon A6
Timothy (Timotheus) A16ff; PR16; PCF4, 16; PCS1; PPs1f; PCo1; ThF1, 3;
      ThS1; PTF1, 6; Ph1; Tt1, 3
Theophilus A1

APPENDIX A PERSONAL NAMES

Titius Justus A18
Titus PCS2, 7f, 12f; PG2; PTS4; Tt1, 3
Trophimus A20f; PTS4
Tryphaena PR16
Tryphosa PR16
Tychicus A20; PE6; PCo4; PTS4; Tt3
Tyrannus A19
Urban (Urbane) PR16
Uriah (Urias) Mw1
Zacchaeus L19
Zacharias (Zechariah) (father of John the Baptist) L1, 3, 11
   (father of Berachiah) Mw23
Zadok (Sadoc) Mw1
Zarah (Zara) Mw1
Zebedee Mw4, 10, 20 26f; Mk1, 3, 10; L5; J21
Zechariah (Zacharias) (father of John the Baptist) L1, 3, 11
   (father of Berachiah) Mw23
Zelotes (Simon called) L6
Zenas Tt3
Zerubbabel (Zorobabel) (Father of Abiud) Mw1
   (father of Rhesa) L3

APPENDIX B *Place Names*

OLD TESTAMENT

Aabah De1
Abarim Nu33; Je22
  Mount Nu27; De32
  Valley of E39
Abdon Jos19, 21; CF6
Abel-beth-maacah SS20; KF15; KS15
  -keramim Ju11
  -mayim CS16
  -meholag KF4, 19
  -meholah Ju7
  -mizraim Gen50
  -shittim Nu33
Accad Gen10
Acco Jos19; Ju1
Achor, Vale of Jos7, 15; Is65; Ho2
Achzib Jos15, 19; Ju1
Adadah Jos15
Adam Jos3
Adamah Jos19
Adami-nekeb Jos19
Addan Ez2
Addar Jos15
Addon Ne7
Adithaim Jos15
Admah Gen10, 14; De29; Is15; Ho6, 11
Adoraim CS11
Adullam Jos12, 15; CS11; Ne11
  Cave of SF22; SS23; CF11; Mi1
Adummim Jos15, 18
Ahava Ez8
  River Ez8
Ahlab Ju1
Ai Gen12f; Jos7ff, 12; Ez2; Ne7; Je49
Aiah Ne11
Aijalon Jos19, 21; Ju1, 12; SF14; CF6, 8; CS11, 28
  Vale of Jos10
Ain Nu34; Jos15, 19, 21; CF4
Akrabbim Ju1; Jos15
Akshaph Jos11ff, 19
Alamellech Jos19

541

APPENDIX B PLACE NAMES

Almon Jos21
Alemeth CF6
Almon-diblathaim Nu33
Aloth KF4
Alush Nu33
Amad Jos19
Amalek Nu24; CF18; Ps83
Amalekite land Gen14
Amam Jos15
Amana, Mount So4
Ammah, Hill of SS2
Ammon SS11; KF14; CS12; Ne13; Ps83; Is11; Je9, 27, 41, 49; E25; Am1; Zp2
Amonite land Gen 11
Anab Jos11, 15
Anaharath Jos19
Ananiah Ne11
Anath Ju3
Anathoth Jos21; KF26; CF6, 11ff, 27; Ez2; Ne7, 11; Is10; Je1, 11, 32
Anem CF6
Aner CF6
Anim Jos15
Aphak Jos19
Aphek Jos12f,15;SF4,29;KF20
 -in-Sharon Jos12
Aphekah Jos15
Aphik Ju1
Aphrah Mi1
Ar Nu21ff; De2; Is15
Arab Jos15
Arabah Jos11f, 18; SF23, 30; SS4; KS25;Je39, 52; E47; Z14
 Gorge of the Am6
 Sea of De4; Jos3, 12; KS14
Arabia KF10; Job39; Is2, 21; Je25; E27
Arabim, Gorge of Is15
Arad Nu21, 33; Jos12; Ju1
Aram SS15; KF10ff; KS3f, 6ff; 12ff; CS16, 22, 28; Is7, 17, 22; E16; Ho12; Am1; Z9
 -naharaim De23; Ju3; CF19
 -zobah CF19
Ararah Jos15
Ararat Gen8; KS19;Is37; Je51
Argob De3; KF4; KS15
Arieh KS15
Ariel Is29
Arnon, Fords of Is16

APPENDIX B PLACE NAMES

Arnon, Gorge of Nu22ff; De22ff; Jos12ff; KS10
  River Ju11; KS10; Je48
Aroer Nu32; De2, 3; Jos12, 13; Ju11; SF30; SS24; KS10; CF5, 11;
    Is17; Je48
Arpad KS18; Is10, 36ff; Je49
Aruboth KF4
Arvad E27
Asal (Azal) Z14
Ashan Jos15, 19, 21; CF4, 6
Ashbea CF4
Ashdod Jos11, 13, 15; SF5ff; CS26; Ne13; Is20; Je25; Am1, 3; Zp2; Z9
  -pisgah Jos12
Asher Jos17, 19; KF4; E48
Ashkelon Jos13; Ju1, 14;   Je25, 47; Am1; Zp2; Z9
Ashkenaz (Ashchenaz) Je51
Ashnah Jos15
Asshur Gen2, 10, 25; Nu24; Ps83; E27
Ashtaroth De1; Jos9, 12ff; CF6, 11
Ashterothikarnaim Gen14
Ashtoreth SF31
Assyria Nu24; KS15ff; CF5ff; CS28,30ff; Ez4ff;Is8,10ff, 19ff, 27ff, 30ff,
    Is36ff; Je2, 50; E31f; Ho5, 7ff, 14; Mi5, 7; Na3; Zp2; Z10
Ataroth Nu32; Jos16; CF2
  -addar Jos16, 18
Athak SF30
Atharim Nu21
Atroth-shopham Nu32
Ava (Avva) KS17
Aven E30; Ho10
  Vale of Am1
Avith Gen36; CF1
Avvim Jos18
Azal (asal) Z14
Azekah Jos10, 15; SF17; CS11; Ne11; Je34
Azmon Nu34; Jos15
Aznoth-tabor Jos19
Baal CF4
  Heights of Nu22
  of Break-through (Baal-perazim) SS5; CF14
Baalah Jos15; CF13
  Mount Jos15
Baalath Jos19; KF9; CS8
  -beer Jos19
  -judah SS6
Baal-gad Jos12ff
  -hamon So8

APPENDIX B PLACE NAMES

Baal-hazor SS13
 -hermon CF5
   Mount Ju3
 -meon Nu32; E25
 -peor De4
 -perazim SS5; CF14
 -shalisha KS4
 -zephon Ex14; Nu33
Babel Gen10f
Babylon KS17, 20 24ff; CS32f, 36; Ez1ff; Ne7, 13; Est2; Ps87, 137;
    Is13ff, 21, 39, 43, 47ff, 52;Je20f, 24, 27, 29, 32, 34, 36ff, 46, 49ff;
    E12, 17, 19, 21, 24, 26, 29ff, 32; D1ff; Mi4; Z2, 6
Bahurim SS3, 16, 19, 23; KF2; CF11
Baither Jos15
Bajith Is15
Balah Jos19
Bamoth Nu21
 -baal Jos13
Barhum SS23
Bashan Nu21; De1, 3, 29; Jos9, 12ff, 17, 20; KF4; KS10; CF5ff; Ne9;
    Ps22, 68; Is2, 33; Je22, 50; E27; Am4; Na1; Mi7
Bath-gallim Is10
 -rabbim
Bealoth Jos15
Be-ashtarah Jos21
Be-ashtaroth Jos21
Beer Ju9
  Waterhole of Nu21
 -elim Is15
 -lahai-roi Gen16
Beeroth Jos9,18; SS4,23; Ne7
 -bene-jaakan De10
Beersheba Gen21, 26; Jos15, 19; Ju20; SF8; SF24; KF19; KS12, 23;
    CF4; CS19, 24, 30; Ne11; Am5, 8
Ben-hadad Je49
Bene-barak Jos19
 -jaakan Nu33
Benjamin, land of SF7; SS2, 21ff; KF4; CF27; Ps80; Je1, 6, 17, 32ff; E48
Ben-hinnom, Valley of Jos15, 18; KS23; CS28, 33; Je7, 19, 32
Beon Nu32
Berakah, Valley of CS20
Bered Gen16
Berothai SS8
Berutha (Berothah) E47
Besor, Ravine of SF30
 -barah Ju7

APPENDIX B PLACE NAMES

Besor -beel-meon Jos13
 -birei CF4
 -car SF7
 -dagon Jos15, 19
 -diblathaim Je48
 -eden KS19; Is37; Am1
Bethel Gen12f, 28, 35; Jos7, 12, 16, 18; Ju1ff, 20ff; SF10; KF12, 16; KS2, 10, 17, 23; CF7; CS13, 25; Ez2; Ne7,11; Je48; Ho10, 12; Am3f, 7
 hill country of SF13
 -sharezer Z7
Beth-emek Jos19
Bether, Mountains of So2
Beth-ezel Mi1
 -gader CF2
Beth-gamul Je48
 -gilgal Ne12
 -haggan KS9
 -hakkarem (haccarem) Ne3; Je6
 -hanan KF4
 -haram Jos13
 -hoglah Jos15, 18
 -horon Jos18,21; SF13; CF6
  Lower Jos16, 18; KF9; CF7; CS8
  Pass of Jos10
  Upper Jos16; CF7; CS8
 -jeshimoth Nu33; Jos12ff; E25
 -joab CF2
 -lebaoth Jos19
Bethlehem Gen35; Jos15, 19; Ju12, 17ff; Ru1; SF16f, 20; SS2, 21ff; CF2, 4, 11; Ez2; Ne7; Je41; Mi5
Beth-maacah KS25; Je40
 -marcaboth Jos19; CF4
 -meon Je48
 -millo Ju9
 -nimrah Nu32; Jos13
 -pazzez Jos19
 -pelet Jos15; SS23; Ne11
 -peor De3, 34; Jos13
 -rehob Ju18; SS10
 -shan SF31
 -shean os17; Ju1; KF4; CF7
 -shemesh Jos15, 19, 21; Ju1; SF6; KF4; KS14; CF6; CS25, 28; Je43
 -shittah Ju7
 -taoouah Jos15
 -togarmah E38

APPENDIX B PLACE NAMES

Bethuel SF30; CF4
Bethul Jos19
Beth-zur Jos15; CF2; CS11; Ne3
Betonim Jos13
Beulah (Israel) Is62
Beyond-Euphrates Ez4f, 7; Ne2ff
Bezek Ju1; SF11
Bezer-in-the-wilderness De4; Jos20ff; CF6
Bileam CF6
Bilhah CF4
Bithron SS2
Bizjothjoh Jos15
Blessing (Berakah), Valley of CS20
Bohan, Stone of Jos18
Bokim Ju2
Borashan SF30
Bozez, Rock of SF14
Bozkath Jos15; KS22
Bozrah Gen36; CF1; Is34, 63; Je48ff; Am1; Mi2
Bramble-bush (Seneh) Rock SF14
Bubastis E30
Buz Je25
Cabbon Jos15
Cabul Jos19; KF9
Cain Nu24; Jos15
Calah Gen10
Calneh Am6
Calno Is10
Canaan Gen12, 15, 17, 23; Ex6, 16; Nu13ff; De1ff; Jos14ff; Ps135, 195ff;
    Is19, 23; E16; Ob1; Zp2
Caphtor Je47; Am9
Carchemish CS35; Is10; Je46
Carem Jos15
Carmel Jos15, 19; SF15, 25, 27, 30; SS2ff, 23; CF11; So7
    Je46, 50; Am1, 9; Mi7; Na1
  Mount KF18; KS2; Am1
Casiphia Ez8
Chaldea (Chaldaea) Gen11; Je32, 50ff; E1, 11, 16
Chebar (Kebar) River E1, 3, 10, 43;
Chemosh (Kemosh) Je48
Chephar-haamonai Jos18
Cherith Brook KF17
Cherub (Kerub) Ne7
Chilmad E27
Chub E30
Chinneroth (Kinnereth), Sea of Jos12

APPENDIX **B** PLACE NAMES

Chittim (Kittim) Nu24; Is23; E27; D11
Cilicia E27
City of David (Zion) SS5; KF8ff, 22; KS9, 12, 24ff; CF11, 15; CS8, 16, 21, 25,
    CS27ff; Ne3, 12; Is22
  of the Sun (Heliopolis) Is19
Coa KF10; CS1
Crier's Spring Ju15
Culom Jos15
Cush Gen2; Is11, 18, 20, 37; E29ff, 38ff; Na3; Zp3
Cushan H3
Cuthah Ks17
Dabbesheth Jos19
Daberah Jos21
Daberath Jos19; CF6
Damascus Gen4; SS8; KF11, 15; KS8, 14, 16; CF18; CS16, 24, 28;
    So7; Is7f, 10, 17; Je49; E27, 47; Am1, 5; Z9
Dan Gen14; De34; Jos19; Ju18; SS24; KF12, 15; KS10; CS16, 30; Je4, 8;
    E27, 48; Am8
  Camp of Ju18
Dannah Jos15
David, City of (Zion) SS5; KF8ff, 22; KS9, 12, 14ff; CF11, 15; CS8, 16, 21,25,
    CS27ff; Ne3, 12; Is22
Dead Sea Gen14; Nu34; De3; Jos3, 12, 15,18; CS20; E39
Debir Jos11ff, 21; Ju1; CF6
Dedan Is21; Je22, 49; E25, 27, 38
Diblah (Diblath) E6
Dibon Nu21, 32; Jos13; Ne11; Is15; Je48
  -gad Nu33
Dilan Jos15
Dinhabah Gen36; CF1
Dimnah Jos21
Dimon Is15
  Waters of Is15
Dimonah Jos15
Dividing Rock SF23
Dizahab De1
Dophkah De1
Dor Jos11ff, 17; Ju1; KF4; CF7
Dothan Gen37; KS6
Dragon Spring (Well) Ne2
Dumah Jos15
Dura, Plain of D3
Ebal, Mount De11, 26, 27; Jos8
Ebed Ju9
Eben-ezer SF4, 7
Eber Nu24

APPENDIX B PLACE NAMES

Ebez Jos19
Ebronah Nu33
Ecbatana Ez6
Eden Gen2; E27, 31, 36; Is51; Am1
  garden in Gen2
Eder Jos15
Edom Nu20, 24, 33; Ju11; SS8; KF9, 11, 22; KS3, 8, 16; CF1, 18; CS8, 20f, 25;
      Ps60, 76, 83, 108, 137; Is11, 34, 63; Je9, 25, 27, Je40, 49; La4;
      E25, 27, 32, 35ff; D11; Am1ff, 9; Ob1; Joe3; Ma1
Edomite land Gen32
Edrei Nu21; De3; Jos12ff, 19
Eglaim Is15
Eglath-shelishiyah Je48
Eglon Jos10f, 15
Egypt Gen12, 37, 39ff, 45ff, 50; Ex1ff, 17ff, 22f, 32ff; Jos13, 24; Ju2;
    SF2, 12, 15, 27; KF3ff, 9ff; KS17, 23ff; CS1ff, 9ff, 26, 35ff; Ne9;
    Ps68, 78, 80ff, 87, 105ff, Ps114, 135; Pro7; Is11, 19ff, 23, 27,
    Is30ff, 36ff, 43, 45, 52; Je2, 9, 11, 16, 23ff, 26, 31f, 34, 37, 41f, 46;
    E17, 19ff, 23, 27, 29ff; D11; Ho2, 7ff, 11ff; Joe3; Am2ff, 8ff; Mi6ff;
    Na3; Hg2; Z10, 14
  Torrent of Nu34; Jos15; KF8; KS24; Is27
Ekron Jos13, 15, 19; Ju1; SF5ff, 17; KS1; Je25; Am1; Zp2; Z9
Elah, Vale of SF17, 21
Elam Gen14; Ez2; Ne7; Is11, 21; Je25, 49; E32; D8
Elaph Jos18
Elath De2; KF9; KS14, 16
El-berith Ju9
Elealeh Nu32; Is15ff; Je48
El-Elohey-Israel Gen33
Elim Ex16; Nu33
Elishah E27
Ellasar Gen14
Elon Jos19; KF4
  -bez aanannim Jos19; Ju4
Eloth KF9; CS8, 26
El-paran Gen14
Eltekeh Jos19, 21
Eltekon Jos15
Eltolad Jos15, 19
Emek-achor Ho2
  -keziz Jos18
Enam Jos15
En-dor Jos17; SF28
  -eglaim E47
  -gannim Jos15, 19, 21
  -gedi Jos15; SF23ff; CS20; So1; E47

APPENDIX B PLACE NAMES

-haddah Jos19
-hakkore Ju15
-harod Ju7; SF29; Ps83
-hazor Jos19
-mishpat Gen14
Enoch City Gen14
Enrimmon Ne11
En-rogel Jos15,18; SS17; KF1
 -shemesh Jos15, 18
 -tappuah Jos17
Ephah Is60
Ephes-dammin SF17
Ephraim Jos19ff,24; SS2, 13, 18; CF27; CS13, 15, 17, 19, 25, 30, 34; Ps60, 78, 80, 108; Is7, 17, 28; Je31, 50; E48; Ho5ff, 14; Ob1; Z9ff
Ephraim, hill country of Ju2ff, 7ff, 17; SF1, 9; KF4, 12; CF6
 Mount Je4
 territory of De34
Ephrathah (Ephratah) Gen35; Jos15; Ru4; Ps132; Mi5
Ephron SS13, 18; CS13
 Mount Jos15
Erech Gen10; Ez4
Esau, Mount of Ob1
Esech Gen10
Esek Gen26
Eshan Jos15
Eshcol, Gorge of Nu13; De1
Eshtaol, Jos15, 19; Ju13, 18
Eshtemoa Jos21;SF30; CF4,6
Eshtemoh Jos15
Etam Jos15; Ju15; CF4; CS11
 Rock of Ju15
Etham Nu33
Ether Jos15, 19
Ethiopia Est1, 8; Job28; Is18, 20, 43, 45; E29ff, 38; Na3; Zp3
Euphrates River Gen2; Nu22; De11; Jos1, 24; SS8, 10; KF4, 14; KS23; CF5, 18ff; CS9, 35; Ps72, 80, 89; Is7ff, 27; Je2, 13, 46, 51; Mi7, 10
 great bend of the CF19
Evi Jos13
Ezem Jos15, 19; CF4
Ezion-geber Nu33; De2; KF9, 22; CS8, 20
Far House SS15
Field of the Blades SS2
of the Watchers (Zophim) Nu23
Fuller's Field KS18; Is7, 36

549

APPENDIX B PLACE NAMES

Gaal Ju9
Gaash, Mount Jos24; Ju2
  Ravines of SS23; CF11
Gaba Jos18
Gad SS24;KS10; Je49; E48
Gaiam-in-Galilee Jos12
Galilee Jos12, 20; KS15; CF6; Is9
Gallim Jos15; SF25; Is10
Galud, Mount Ju7
Gammad E27
Gareb, Hill of Je31
Gath Jos11, 13; SF5ff, 17, 2127; SS21; KF2;KS12; CF8, 18, 20;CS11,26;
       Am6; Mi1
  -hepher Jos19; KS14
  -rimmon Jos19, 21; CF6
Gaza Gen10; Jos11,13,15; Ju1, 6, 16; SF6; KF4; KS18; CF7; Je25,47;
       Am1; Zp2; Z9
Geba Jos18, 21; SF13ff; KF15; KS23; CF6, 8; CS16; Ez2; Ne7, 11ff;
       Is10; Z14
Gebal Ps83; E27
Gebalites, land of the Jos13
Gebbim (Gebim) Is10
Geder Jos12
Gederah Jos15; CF4, 12
Gederoth Jos15; CS28
Gedor Jos15; CF4, 12
Ge-harashim CF4; Ne11
Geliloth Jos22
Gerar Gen10, 20, 26; CS14
Gerizim, Mount De11, 27; Jos8; Ju9
Geshur SS3, 13ff; CF3
Geshurite country Jos13
Gezer Jos10, 12, 16, 21; Ju1; KF9; CF6ff, 14, 20
Giah SS2
Gebbethon Jos19, 21; KF15ff
Gibea CF2
Gibeah Jos15, 18; Ju19; SF10ff, 22ff; SS23; CF11; CS13; Is10; Ho5, 9ff
Gibeath-haaraloth Jos5
Gibeon Jos9, 18, 21; SS2, 20; KF9; CF8ff, 14, 21; Ne3; Je28, 41
  Great Stone of SS20
  Vale of Is28
Gihon KF1
  River CS32ff
Gilboa SF28
  Mount SF31; SS1; CF10
Gilead Gen31; Nu32; De2, 4, 34; Jos12ff, 17, 20; Ju10, 20; SS2, 17, 24;

550

APPENDIX B PLACE NAMES

Gilead   KF2, 4, 17; KS10, 15; CF2, 5ff, 26ff; Ps60, 108; Je8, 22, 46, 50; E47; Ho6, 12; Am1; Ob1; Mi7; Z10
  Mount So4, 6
Gilgal De11; Jos4ff, 14; Ju2; SF10ff; SS19; KS2, 4; Ho4, 9; Am4ff; Mi6
  camp of Jos9ff
Giloh Jos15; SS15
Gilron River Gen2
Gimzo CS28
Girgashite land Gen15
Gittah-hepher Jos19
Gittaim SS4; Ne11
Goath Je31
Gob SS21
Gog's Horde, Valley of E39
Golan De4; Jos20ff; CF6
Gomer E38
Gomorrah Gen10ff, 18ff; De29; Is1, 13; Je23, 49ff; Am4; Zp2
Goshen Gen45f; Jos11, 15
Goyim Gen14
Gozan KS17ff; Is37
  River KS17; CF5
Great Pool in Gibeon Je41
  Sea Nu34; Jos1, 9, 15; E47ff
Greece (Grecia; Javan) Is66; D8, 10ff; Z9
Gudgodah De10
Gur KS9
  -baal CS26
Habor CF5
  River KS17ff
Hachilah, Hill of SF23ff
Hadad-rimmon Z12
Hadashah Jos15
Hadid Ez2; Ne7, 11
Hadrach Z9
Hakkephirim Ne6
Halah KS17ff; CF5
Hali Jos19
Halhul Jos15
Ham, lands of Ps78, 105ff
  villages of Nu32
Hamath SS8; KF8; KS14, 17ff, 24ff; CF18; CS8; Ps76; Is10ff, 36; Je39, 49; E47; Am6; Z9
Hammath Jos19
Hammon Jos19; CF6
  -dor Jos21
Hamonah E39

551

APPENDIX B PLACE NAMES

Hamon-gog, Valley of   E39
Hananiah Ne3
Hanes Is30
Hannathon Jos19
Hapharaim Jos19
Hara CF5
Haradeh Nu33
Harim Ne7; Ez2
Harod SS23; CF11
Harosheth-of-the-Gentiles Ju4
Harran (Haran) Gen11f, 27; KS19; Is37; E27
Hashmonah Nu33
Hauran E47
Havilah Gen2, 25; SF1
Havvoth-jair Nu32; De3; Jos13; Ju10; CF2
Hazar-addar Nu34
  -enan Nu34; E47
  -gaddah Jos15
  -hatticon E47
Hazar-shual Jos15, 19; CF4; Ne11
  -susah Jos19
  -susim CF4
Hazazon-tamar Gen14; CF20
Hazer Je49
Hazeroth Nu11, 33; De1
Hazor Jos11ff, 15, 19; Ju4; SF12; KF9; Ne11
  -hadattah Jos15
Hebron Gen13, 23, 37; Jos10ff, 20; Ju1, 16; SF30; SS2ff, 15; KF2; CF2ff, 11ff; CS11
Helam SS10
Helbah Ju1
Helbon E27
Heleph Jos19
Heliopolis (City of the Sun) Is19
Helkath Jos19, 21
Hena KS18ff; Is37
Hepher Jos12; KF4
Hephzi-bah (Jerusalem) Is62
Heres, Mount Ju1,8
Hermon, Mount De3; Jos11ff; CF5; Ps42, 89, 133; So4
Heshbon Nu21, 32; De1f, 29; Jos9, 12ff, 21; Ju11; CF6; Ne9; So7; Is15ff; Je48ff
Heshmon Jos15
Hethlon E47ff
Hezron Jos15
Hiddekel River (Tigris) D10
Hilen CF6

APPENDIX B PLACE NAMES

Hill of God SF10
Hinnom, Valley of   Jos15; Ne11
  Valley of the Sons of CS33
Hittite country Jos1
  land Gen15
Hivite land Gen15
Hobah Gen14
Holon Jos15, 21; Je48
Hor, Mount Nu20, 23ff; De32
Horeb Ex3; CS5; Ps106; Ma4
  Mount Ex33; KF8, 19; De1, 18
Horem Jos19
Horesh SF23
Hor-haggidgad Nu33
Hormah Nu14, 21; De1; Jos12, 15, 19; Ju1; SF30; CF4
Horonaim Is15; Je48
Hosah Jos19
Hukok Jos19; CF6
Humtah Jos15
Hur Jos13
Hushah SS21; CF4, 20
Ibleam Jos17; Ju1; KS9, 15
Idalah Jos19
Idumea (Edom) Is34; E35
Ijon (Iyyon) SS24; KF15; KS15; CS16
Immer Ez2; Ne7
India Est1, 8
Ionia (Javan) E27
Ir-melach Jos15
Iron Jos15
Irpeel Jos18
Ir-shemesh Jos19
Israel Ex2ff, 9, 11f, 14ff, 37f, 32, 34, 39; Le4, 10, 16f, 20, 22, 25; Nu1, 3f,
    Nu7, 10f, 16, 18ff, 31f, 36; De1f, 4ff, 9f, 13, 17ff, 25ff, 29,31ff;
    Jos1, 3ff, 7ff, 13f,21ff; SF1ff; SS1ff; KF1ff; KS1ff; CF1ff; CS1ff;
    Ez1ff; Ne13; Ps22, 25, 41, 50, 53, 68ff, 71ff, 76, 78, 83, 89, 98,
    Ps105ff, 114ff, 118, 121ff, 125, 129ff, 135ff, 147; Pro1; Ec1; So3;
    Is1, 4ff,   7ff, 14, 17, 19, 21, 24, 27, 30ff, 34, 40ff, 43ff, 52, 54,
    Is56ff, 60, 63; Je2ff, 5, 9ff, 12ff, 17ff, 23ff, 27ff, 34f, 37ff, 45ff, 48ff;
    La2; E4, 6ff, 17, 9ff, 25, 27ff, 33ff, 38ff, 43, 45, 47ff; D9;Ho1ff;
    Joe2ff; Am1ff; Ob1; Mi1ff, 5ff; Na2;   Zp3; Z8ff, 12; Ma1, 4
Issachar Jos17; KF4; CS30; E48
Ithnan Jos15
Ittah-kazin Jos19
Ivvah KS18; Is37
Iye-abarim Nu21, 33

APPENDIX B PLACE NAMES

Iyim Nu33; Jos15
Iyyon (Ijon) SS24; KF15; KS15; CS16
Izalla E27
Jaar Ps132
Jabbok Nu21
  ford of the   Gen32
  Gorge De2; Jos12
  River Ju11
Jabesh SF31
  -gilead Ju21; SF11, 31; SS2; CF10
Jabez CF2
Jabneel Jos15, 19
Jabneh CS26
Jacob Mi3, 5; Na2
Jagur Jos15
Jahaz Nu21; De2; Jos13, 21; Ju11; Is15; Je48
Jahazah Je48
Jahzah CF6
Janim Jos15
Janoah Jos15; KS15
Japhia Jos19
Jarkon Jos19
Jarmuth Jos10, 12, 15, 21; Ne11
Jashub Jos17
Jattir Jos15, 21; SF30; CF6
Jaudi KS14
Javan (Ionia) Is66; E27
Jaw-bone Hill (Ramath-lehi) Ju15
Jazer Nu21, 32; Jos13, 21; SS24; CF6, 26; Is16; Je48
Jearim, Mount Jos15
Jebus (Jerusalem) Jos18; Ju19; CF11
Jebusite land Gen15
Jehoshaphat, Valley of   Joe3
Jehovah-jireh Gen22
  -shalom Ju6
  -shammah E48
Jehud Jos19
Jericho Nu22, 33; Jos2, 6, 12, 16, 18, 24; SS10; KF16; KS2, 25; CF6, 19;
        CS28; Ez2; Ne3, 7; Je39, 52
  Valley of   De34
Jeruel CS20
Jerusalem Jos10, 12, 14, 18; Ju1, 19; SS5, 10, 24; KF2ff, 9ff; KS9, 12, 18;
        KS22ff; CF3, 6, 8ff, 11, 19; CS1ff; Ez1ff; Ne1ff, 11ff; Est2; Ps51,
        Ps68, 79, 102, 116, 122, 125, 135, 137, 147; Ec1; So1, 3, 5ff, 8;
        Is1ff, 7, 10, 22, 14, 27ff, 30ff, 36ff, 40ff, 52, 59ff, 62ff; Je1ff, 9, 11,
        Je13ff, 17ff, 23ff, 27, 29, 32ff, 39ff, 42, 44, 51ff; La1f, 4; E4ff, 8,

APPENDIX B PLACE NAMES

Jerusalem (continued) E11ff, 21ff, 26, 33, 36; D1, 5ff, 9; Joe2ff; Am1ff; Ob1;
  Mi1, 3ff; Zp1, 3; Z1ff, 7ff, 12ff; Ma2ff
Jeshanah SF7; CS13
Jeshimon Nu23; SF23, 26
Jeshua Ne11
Jetur CF5
Jezreel Jos15, 19; SF25ff; SS2ff; KF4, 18ff; KS8ff; CF3; CS22
  Vale of Jos17; Ju6; Ho1
Jiphtah Jos15
  -el, Valley of Jos19
Jithlah Jos19
Jogbehah Nu32; Ju8
Jokdeam Jos15
Jokmeam KF4; CF6
Joknean Jos19, 21
  -in-Carmel Jos12
Joktheel Jos15; KS14
Joppa Jos19; CS2; Ez3; Jon1
  Sea of Ez3
Jordan CF6; Je12, 49; E47; Z11
  fords of the Jos2; Ju3,7,12
  mouth of the Jos15
  Plain of Gen13; De3; SS18; KF7
  River Gen50; Nu22, 32ff; De9, 27; Jos1, 13, 16, 19, 22; Ju11; SS2, 16,
     SS19, 24; KF2, 17; KS2, 5ff, 10; CF12, 19; Ps114; Je12, 50
  Spring of Ps42
  Vale of SF31
Joseph, district of KF11
  land of Z10
Jotbah KS21
Jotbathah Nu33; De10
Judah De34; Ru1; SS2ff, 24; KF12, 19ff; KS1ff; CF2ff; CS10ff; Ez1ff;
     Ne1ff, 11; Est2; Ps60, 68ff, 76, 97, 108, 114; Pro25; Is1ff, 5, 7ff, 19, 22,
     Is25, 28, 36, 40; Je1ff, 7, 9, 11, 13ff, Je17ff, 26ff, 30ff, 36ff, 42, 44ff,
     Je49ff; La1ff, 5; E4, 8ff, 21, 26ff, 48; D1, 5, 9; Ho1, 4ff, 12; Joe3;
     Am1ff, 7; Ob1; Mi1, 5ff; Zp1, 2; Hg1ff; Z1ff, 8ff, 12, 14; Ma2ff
  country of Jos11, 20
  land of SF22, 30
  wilderness of Ju1, 15
Juttah Jos15, 21
Kabzeel Jos15; CF11
Kadesh Gen14; Nu20, 33; Ju11; SS24; Ps29
  River E47
  -barnea Nu32, 34; De1, 9; Jos14ff
Kadmonite land Gen15
Kambul Je51

APPENDIX B PLACE NAMES

Kamon Ju10
Kanah Jos19
  Gorge of Jos16ff
Kanneh E27
Karka Jos15
Karkor Ju8
Karnaim Am6
Kartah Jos21
Kartan Jos21
Kattah Jos19
Kebar (Chebar), River E1, 3, 10, 43
Kedar Ps120; So1; Is21, 42, 60; Je2, 49
Kedemoth De2; Jos13, 21; CF6
Kedesh Jos12, 15, 19ff; KS15; CF6
Kehelathah Nu33
Keilah Jos15; SF23; Ne3
Kekabzeel Ne11
Kemosh (Chemosh) Je48
Kenath CF2
  villages of Nu32
Kenite land Gen15; Nu24
Kenizzite land Gen15
Kephar-ammoni Jos18
Kephirah Jos9, 18; Ez2
Kereth Zp2
Kerioth Am2
  -hezron Jos15
Kerith, Ravine of KF17
Kerub (Cherub) Ez2; Ne7
Kesalon Jos15
Kesil Jos15
Kesulloth (Cheshulloth) Jos19
Kibroth-hattaavah Nu11, 33; De9
Kibzaim Jos21
Kidon CF13
Kidron Brook KF15
  Gorge SS15; KF15; KS23; CS15. 29ff
  River KF2, 15; KS23; Je31
Kinah Jos15
King's Pool Ne2
  Valley Gen14
Kinnereth (Chinneroth) Nu34; De3; Jos11, 19; KF15
  Sea of Jos12ff
Kir KS16; Is15; Am1, 9
  -hareseth Is16
  -heres Je48

APPENDIX B PLACE NAMES

Kiriathaim (Kirjathaim) Nu32; Jos13; CF6; Je48; E25
Kiriath (Kirjath-arba) Gen23; Jos14ff, 20; Ju1; Ne11
  -baal Jos15, 18
  -huzoth Nu22
  -jearim Jos9, 15, 18; Ju18; SF7; CF2, 13; CS1; Ez2; Ne7; Je26
  -sannah Jos15
  -sepher Jos15; Ju1
Kirioth (Kerioth) Je48
Kishion Jos19
Kisloth (Chisloth) -tabor Jos19
Kishon Jos21; KF18
  River Ju4ff
Kishon, Torrent of Ps83
Kithlish Jos15
Kitron Ju1
Kittim (Chittim) Nu24; Is23; Je2; E27
Koa E23
Kozeba CF4
Kun (Chun) CF18
Laban De1
Lachish Jos10, 12, 15; KS14, 18; CS11, 25, 32; Ne11; Is36; Mi1
Lahir KS19; Is37
Lahmas Jos15
Laish Ju18; Is10
Lakkum Jos19
Lasha Gen10
Lebanon De1, 11; Jos1, 9; KF5, 9; KS19; CF5; CS8; Ez3; Ps29, 72, 92,
    Ps104; So3ff, 7; Is2, 10, 29, 33, 35, 37, 40, 60; Je18, 22; E17, 27,
    E31; Ho14; Na1; H2; Z10ff
  Mount Ju3
  Vale of Jos11f
Lebaoth Jos15
Lebo-hamath Nu13, 34; Jos13; Ju3; KS14; CF13; E47; Am6
Lebonah Ju21
Lecah CF4
Lehi Ju15; SS23
  Hollow of Ju15
Leshem Jos19
Levi E48
Libnah Nu33; Jos12, 15, 21; KS8, 19, 23; CF6; Is37ff
  Swamp of Jos19
Libya E30, 38; Na3
Lod CF8; Ez2; Ne7, 11
Lo-debar Jos13; SS9, 17; Am6
Lower Beth-horon KF9
  Pool Is22

APPENDIX B PLACE NAMES

Lower Town of Jerusalem (Maktesh) Zp1
Lubim (Libya) Na3
Lud (Lydia) Is66; E27, 30
Luhith Is15; Je48
Luz Gen28; Jos16, 18; Ju1
Lydia (Lud) Is66; E27, 30
Maacah SS10; CF19
Maarath Jos15
Machbenah CF2
Machir Ju5
Machpelah Gen23, 25, 50
Madmannah Jos15; CF2
Madmen Je48
Madmenah Is10
Madon Jos11ff
Magbish Ez2
Magog E38ff
Mahanaim Gen32; Jos13, 21; SS2, 17, 19; KF2, 4; CF6
Mahaneh-dan Ju13, 18
Makaz KF4
Makheloth Nu33
Makkedah Jos10, 12, 15
Maktesh (Lower Town of Jerusalem) Z91
Mamre Gen13, 23
Manach Jos15
Manahath CF8
Manasseh CS15, 30, 34; Ps60, 108; E48
 land of KS10
 territory of De34
Maon Jos15
 wilderness of SF23ff
Marah Ex15; Nu33
Maralah Jos19
Mareshah Jos15; CF4; CS11, 14, 20; Mi1
Maroth Mi1
Mashal CF6
Masrekah Gen36; CF1
Massa Pro30f
Massah De6, 9; Ps95
Mecherah CF11
Meconah Ne11
Medeba Nu21; Jos13; CF19; Is15
Medes, City of the KS17
Media KS17ff; Is21; Est1; E27; D8
 Province of Ez6
Mediterranean Jos9; Ps80, 89; E47ff

APPENDIX B PLACE NAMES

Megiddo Jos12, 17; Ju1; KF4, 9; KS9; CF7
  Vale of CS35; Z12
Mehalbeh Jos19
Meholah SS21
Meholoah SF18
Memphis Ho9
Mephaath Jos13, 21; CF6; Je48
Merathaim Je50
Meribah Nu20
  Waters of Ps81, 95, 106
  -by-kadesh De32; E47ff
Merom, Waters of Jos11
Mesha Gen10
Meshech Ps120; E27, 32, 38f
Meshek Is66
Mesopotamia Ju3
Metheg-ha-ammah SS8
Me-zahab Gen36; CF1
Michmas Ez2; N7
Michmash Ne11; Is10
  Pass of SF13ff
Michmethah Jos16ff
Middin Jos15
Midian Ex2, 4; Nu22; Jos13; KF11; Is9, 60; H3
Migdal-eder Gen35
  -el Jos19
  -gad Jos15
Migdol Ex14; Nu33; Je44, 46; E29ff
Migron SF14; Is10
Millo SS5
Minni Je51
Minnith Ju11; E27
Misgab Je48
Mishal Jos19, 21
Misrephoth Jos11, 13
Mizar, Hill of Ps42f
Mizpah Jos11, 18; Ju10, 21; SF4, 7; KF15; CS16; Ne3; Je40ff; Ho5
  Vale of Jos11
Mizpeh Jos15; Ju11; SF22
Moab Nu21ff, 33; De1ff, 34; Jos24; Ju11; SF12, 22; SS8, 23; KS3; CF11, 18;
    Ne13; Ps60, 108; Is11, 15ff, 25; Je9, 25, 27, 40, 48; E25; D11;
    Am2; Mi6; Zp2
Moabite country CF1, 8; Ru1
Moithcah Nu33
Moladah Jos15, 19; CF4; Ne11
Moreh Gen12, 22

559

APPENDIX B PLACE NAMES

Moreh, Hill of   Ju7
Moresheth   Je26; Mi1
  -gath   Mi1
Moriah, Mount   CS3
Moseroth   Nu33; De10
Mount of Olives   (Mount Olivet) SS15; KS23
Mozah   Jos18
Naamah   Jos15; Job2
Naaran   CF7
Naarath   Jos16
Nahalal Jos19, 21; Nu21
Naphtali De34; Jos20; Ju4; KF4,15; KS15;CS16, 34; Ps68; Is9; E48
Nahalol   Ju1
Naioth   SF19
Neah   Jos19
Nebaioth   Is60
Neballat   Ne11
Nebo   Nu32ff; CF5; Ez2; Ne7; Is15; Je48
  Mount   De32, 34
Negeb   Gen12f, 20; Nu13, 33; De1, 34; Jos11, 15; Ju1; SF27ff; SS24; CS28; Je13, 17, 32ff; E20ff, 47f; Ob1; Z7
Neiel   Jos19
Nephish   CF5
Nephtoah River   Jos15
  springs of   Jos18
Netaim   CF4
Netophah   SS23; KS25; Ez2; Ne7; Je40
Nezib   Jos15
Nibshan   Jos15
Nile River   Ex1ff; Is18ff, 63; Je46; E29ff, 32; Am8ff; Na3; Z10
Nimrah   Nu32
Nimrim   Je48
  Waters of   Is15
Nineveh Gen10; KS19; Is37; Jon1, 3f; Na1ff; Zp2
No   Je46; E30; Na3
  -ammon   Na3
Nob   SF21ff; Ne11; Is10
Nobah   Nu32; Ju8
Nod   Gen4
Nodab   CF5
Nohah   Ju20
Noph   Is19; Je2, 44, 46; E30
Nubia   Job31; Ps68; Pro20; Is43
Oboth   Nu21, 33
Og, Kingdom of   Nu32; De1
Old Pool   Is22

560

APPENDIX B PLACE NAMES

Olives (Olivet) Mount of   SS15; Z14
On   E30
Ono   CF8; Ez2; Ne6ff,11
   Plain of   Ne6
Ophel   CS27, 33; Ne3, 11
   Wall of   Ne3
Ophir (Uphaz)   KF9, 22; CF29; CS8; Job28; Ps45; Is13; Je10; D10
Ophni   Jos18
Ophrah   Jos18; Ju8ff; SF13
   of the Abiezrites   Ju6
Oreb, Rock of   Ju7; Is10
Outbreak-on-Uzza   (Perez-uzza) SS6; CF13
Paddan-aram   Gen25, 28
Pai   CF1
Palestina (Palestine)   Is14; Joe3
Pannag   E27
Parah   Jos18
Paran   Gen21; De1; KF11
   Mount   De33; H3
   wilderness of   Nu10, 12; SF25
Parvaim   CS3
Pas-dammin   SS23; CF11
Pathros   Ps68; Is11; Je44; E29ff
Pau   Gen36
Pekod   Je50; E23
Peniel   Gen32
Penuel   Ju8; KF12
Peor   Jos15; Ps106
   Mount   Nu23
Perath   Je13
Perazim, Mount   Is28
Perez-uzzah (uzza)   Gen15
Perizzite land   Gen15
Persia (Pharas)   CS36; Ez1, 3ff; Ne12; Est1; E27; D8, 10
Pethah-tikvah (Gate of Hope)   Ho2
Pethor   Nu22; De23
Pharas (Persia)   E27, 38ff
Philistia   KF4; Ps60, 83, 108; Is14; Je47; Joe3
Philistine country   KS8, 18
Pi-beseth   E30
   -hahiroth   Ex14; Nu33
Pirathon   Ju12; SS23; CF11
Pisgah, Mount   Nu21ff; De34
   springs of   De3, 4
   watershed   De3, 4; Jos12ff
Pishon River   Gen2

APPENDIX B PLACE NAMES

Pithom Ex1
Plain, Sea of the KS14
Pool, Lower Is22
 Upper Is36
Punon Nu33
Put (Pul) Is66; Je46; E27, 30, 38f; Na3
Raamah E27
Rabbah (Rabbath) De3; Jos13, 15; SS11, 17; CF20; E21, 25; Am1
Rabbath Ammon Je49
Rabbith Jos19
Rachal SF30
Rakkah Jos19
Ramah Jos18ff; Ju4, 19; SF1, 7, 15ff, 25; KF15; CF27; CS16; Ez2; Ne7, 11;
    Is10; Je31, 40; Ho5
Ramathaim SF1
Ramath-lehi Ju15
 -negeb Jos19
Rameses Ex1, 13; Nu33
 land Gen47
Ramoth De4; Jos20ff; CF6
 -gilead KF4, 22; KS8ff;   CS18, 22
 -mizpeh Jos13
 -negeb SF30
Reba Jos13
Rechah CF4
Red Sea (Sea of Reeds) Nu33; De1; Jos2, 24; KF9; Ne9; Ps106, 136;
    Je49
Reheboth Gen26, 36
Rekem Jos13, 18
Remeth Jos19
Rephaim Gen15; SS5, 23
 Vale of Jos15, 18; CF11, 14; Is17
Rephidim Ex17; Nu33
Reuben, land of KS10; E48
Rezeph KS19; Is37
Rhodes E27
Riblah Nu34; KS24ff; Je39, 52; E6
Rimmon Jos15, 19, 21; CF4, 6; Is10; Z14
 -Parez Nu33
 Rock of Ju20
Rissah Nu33
Rithmah Nu33
Rogelim SS17, 19
Rosen Gen10
Rosh Is66; E38ff
Sahmir Jos15

APPENDIX B PLACE NAMES

Salcah De3; Jos12; CF5
Salem Ps76
Salt, Valley of CS25
Samaria KF13, 16, 20ff; KS1ff; CS18, 25, 28; Is7ff, 36ff; Je23, 31, 41; E16; Ho7f, 10, 13; Am3ff, 6, 8; Ob1; Mi1
  Hill of KF16
Sansannah Jos15
Saphir Mi1
Sarid Jos19
Sea, The (Dead Sea) E39
Seba Ps72; Is43
Sebam Nu32
Secacah Jos15
Secu SF19
Seir Gen14, 32f, 36; Nu24; De1, 33; Jos11, 24; CS20ff, 25; Is21; E25, 35
  hill country of CF4
  Mount Jos15
Seirah Ju3
Sela Ju1; KS14; Is16, 42
  -hammalekoth SF23
Senaah Ez2; Ne7
Seneh, Rock of SF14
Senir CF5; E27
  Mount De3; So4
Sephar Gen10
Sepharad Ob1
Sepharvaim KS17ff; Is36ff
Shaalabin Jos19
Shaalbim Ju1; KF4
Shaalbon SS23; CF11
Shaalim SF9
Shaaraim Jos15; CF4
Shaarim SF17
Shadud Jos19
Shahazumah Jos19
Shalisha SF9
Shamir Ju10
Shapher, Mount Nu33
Sharon CF5, 27; So2; Is33,35
Sharuhen Jos19
Shaveh Gen14
  -kiriathaim Gen14
Shear-jashub Is7
Sheba KF10; Jos19; Job6; Ps72; Is60; Je6; E27, 38
Shebarim Jos7
Shechem Gen12, 33; Jos17, 20, 24; Ju9, 21; KF12; CF6ff; CS10; Ps60, 108; Je41; Ho6

APPENDIX B PLACE NAMES

Shelah, Pool of   Ne3
Shema   Jos15
Shemaiah   CS11
Shepham   Nu34
Shephelah   De1; Jos9, 11f, 15; Ju1; KF10; CF27; CS1, 9, 26, 28;
      Je17, 32ff; Ob1; Z7
Shephem   CF27
Sheshak (Babylon)   Je25, 51
Shigionoth   H3
Shihor (Sihor)   Jos13; CF13; Is23; Je2
Shikkeron   Jos15
Shilhim   Jos15
Shiloah River   Is8
Shiloh   Jos18ff; Ju21; SF1ff; KF2, 11, 14; CS7, 10; Ps78; Je7, 26, 41
Shimron   Jos11, 19
  -meron   Jos12
Shinar   Gen10f; Jos7; Is11; D1; Z5
Shining Rock (Bozez)   SF14
Shion   Jos19
Shittim   Nu25; Jos2ff; Mi6
  Gorge of   Joe3
Shoa   E23
Shochoh   SF17
Shuah   Job2
Shual   SF13
Shunem   Jos19; SF28; KS4
Shur   Gen16, 25; Ex15; SF15, 27
Shushan (Susa)   Ez4; Ne1; Est1ff; D8
Sibmah   Nu32; Jos13; Is16; Je48
Sibraim   E47
Siddim   Gen14
Sidon (Zidon)   Ju1, 18; SS24; KF16ff; CF22; Is23; Je25, 27, 47; E27ff;
      Joe3; Z9
  Greater   Jos11, 19
Sihon   Ne9; Je48
  kingdom of   Nu32; Jos13
Sihor (Shihor)   Jos13; CF13; Is23; Je2
Silla   KS12
Simeon   CS15, 34; E48
Simmagir   Je39
Sin   Ex16; Ne9; Ps68
Sinai   Ex16, 19; De33
  Mount   Ex19; Ne9; Ps68
  wilderness of   N1ff, 9, 33
Sinim   Is49
Siphmoth   SF30

APPENDIX **B** PLACE NAMES

Sirah SS3
Sirion, Mount De3
Sitnah Gen26
So KS17
Soco CF4; CS4, 11, 28
Socoh Jos15; SF17; KF4
Sodom Gen13f, 18f; De29; Is1ff, 13; Je23, 49ff; La4; E16; Am4; Zp2
Sorek, Valley of Ju16
Sores Jos15
Succoth Gen33; Ex13; Nu33; Jos13; Ju8; KF7, 20
  Valley of Ps60, 108
Suhar E27
Suph De1
Suphah Nu21
Susa (Shushan) Ez4; Ne1; Est1ff; D8
Syene Is49; E29ff
Syria Job39; Is7, 17; Ho12; Am1
Syrtes Ho9
Taanach Jos12, 17, 21; Ju1; KF4; CF7
Taanath-shiloh Jos16
Tabbath Ju7
Taberah Nu11; De9
Tabor Jos19; SF10; CF6;   Ps89; Je46
  Mount Ju4; Ho5
Tadmor CS8
Tahath Nu33
Tahpanhes (Tahapanes) (Tehaphnehes) Je2, 43f, 46; E30
Tamar KF9; E47ff
Tappuah Jos12, 15, 17; KS15
Tarah Nu33
Taralah Jos18
Tarshish CS20; Ps48, 72; Is2, 23, 60, 66; Je10; E27, 38; Jon1, 4
Tatam Jos15
Tehaphnehes (Tahapanes) (Tahpanhes) Je2, 43f, 46; E30
Tekoa Jos15; SS23; CF2, 4, 27; CS11, 20; Ne3; Je6; Am1
Tekoah SS14
Tel-abib E3
Telaim SF15, 27
Telassar KS19; Is37
Telem Jos15
Tel-harsha Ez2; Ne7
  -melah Ez2; Ne7
Tema Job6; Is21; Je25
Teman Gen36; Jos12; CF1; Job2; Je49; E25; Am1; Ob1; H3
Tharshish KF22
Thebez Ju9

APPENDIX B PLACE NAMES

Tibhath CF18
Tigris, River Gen2; D10
Timnah Jos15, 19; CS28
Timnath Gen38; Ju14
 -serah Jos19, 24
Tiphsah KF4
Tirza KF16
Tirzah Jos12; KF14; KS15; So6
Tishbe KF17
Tob Ju11; SS10
Tochen CF4
Togarmah E27, 38
Tolad CF4
Tophel De1
Topheth (Tophet) KS23; Je7, 19
Torrent of Egypt Nu34; Jos15; KF8; KS24; Is27
Transjordan De1, 4
Tubal Is66; E27, 32, 38ff
Tyre (Tyrus) Jos19; SS5, 24; KF5, 7, 9; CF22; CS2ff; Ps45, 83; Is23; Je25, 27, 47; E26ff; Ho9; Joe3; Am1; Z9
Ulai, Stream of D8
Ummah Jos19
Uphaz (Ophir) Je10; D10
Upper Pool Is36
Ur Gen11; Ne9
Uz Job1; Je25; La4
Uzza KS21
Uzzah SS6
  Outbreak on SS6; CF13
Uzzen-sherah CF7
Vaheb, Waterhole of Nu21
Vale of Achor Jos7,15;Is65; Ho2
   Aijalon Jos10
   Aven Am1
   Elah SF17, 21
   Gibeon Is28
   Jezreel Jos17; Ju6; Ho1
   Jordan SF31
   Lebanon Jos11f
   Megiddo CS35; Z12
   Mizpah Jos11
   Palm Trees De34; Ju1, 3; CS28
   Rephaim Jos15,18; CF11, 14; Is17
   Trouble (Emek-chor) Ho2
Valley of Abarim E39
   Ben-hinnom Jos15, 18; KS23; CS28, 33; Je7, 19, 32

APPENDIX B PLACE NAMES

Valley of Berakah CS20
   Craftsmen (Ge-harashim) CF4
   Blessing (Berakah) CS20
   Ge-harashim CF4
   Gog's Horde (Hamon-gog) E39
   Hinnom Jos15; Ne11
   Jehoshaphat Joe3
   Jericho De34
   Jiphtah-el Jos19
   Salt SS8; KS14; CF18; CS25
   Sorek Ju16
Valley of Succoth Ps60, 108
   the King's Pool Gen14
   the Sons of Hinnom CS33
   Zeboim SF13
Watchers, Field of the Nu23
Waterhole of Beer Nu21
   of Vaheb Nu21
Western Sea De34; Ps139
Yaan SS24
Zaanaim Ju4
Zaanan Mi1
Zair KS8
Zalmon Ps68
   Mount Ju9
Zalmonah Nu33
Zamri Je25
Zanoah Jos15; CF4; Ne3, 11
Zaphon Jos13
Zared, Gorge of Nu21; De2
Zarephath KF17; Ob1
Zarethan KF4
Zartanah KF4
Zeboim Ne11
   Valley of SF13
Zeboyim Gen14; De29
Zebulon Jos19
Zebulun Jos19; CS30; Ps68; Is9; E48
   land of Ju12
Zedad Nu34; E47
Zela Jos18; SS21
Zelzah SF10
Zemaraim Jos18
Zenan Jos15
Zephath Ju1
Zephathah CS14

APPENDIX B PLACE NAMES

Zer Jos19
Zered, Brook of De2
Zeredah KF11; CS4
Zererah Ju7
Zereth-shahar Jos13
Ziddim Jos19
Zidon (Sidon) Ez3; Is23; Je25, 27, 47; E27ff; Joe3; Z9
Ziklag Jos15, 19; SF27ff;   SS1ff; CF4, 12; Ne11
Zin Nu13, 27, 33ff; Jos15
  wilderness of De32
Zion SS5; KF8; CF11; CS5; Ps2, 9, 14, 20, 50f,
Zion Ps53, 65, 69, 84, 87, 97, 99, 102, 110, 132ss, 137, 146f, 149; So3;
      Is1ff, 10, 12, 14, 16, 28, 30, 33, 35, 40, 46, 49, 51ff, 59ff, 64,
      Is66; Je3f, 6, 8ff, 14, 25, 30ff, 50ff; La1f, 4ff; Joe2ff; Am1, 6;
      Mi1, 3ff; Zp3; Z1ff, 8f
  Mount Ps48, 74, 76, 78, 125f, 128ff; Is8, 10, 18, 24, 29, 31, 37; La5;
      Ob1; Mi4
Zior Jos15
Ziph Jos15; CF2; CS11
  wilderness of SF23, 26
Ziphron Nu34
Ziz CS20
Zoan Nu13; Ps78; E30
Zoar Gen13f, 19; De34; Is15, 19, 30; Je48
Zobah SF14; SS8, 10, 23; KF11; CF11, 18
Zobath-hamath CF18
Zoheleth, Stone of KF1
Zorah Jos15, 19; Ju13, 18; CS11; Ne11
Zuph SF9
Zur Jos13

NEW TESTAMENT

Abilene L3
Achaia A18f; PR15f; PCF16; PCS1, 11; ThF1
Adramyttium A27
Adria, Sea of A27
Aenon J3
Akeldama (Blood Acre) (Potter's Field) Mw27; A1
Alexandria A18, 28
Amphipolis A17
Antioch A6, 11, 13f, 18, 23; PG2; PTS3
Apollonia A17
Appii Forum A28
Arabia PG1, 4

APPENDIX B PLACE NAMES

Arimathaea   Mw27; Mk15; L23; J19
Armageddon   Rev16
Asia, Province of   A2, 6, 16, 19ff, 24, 27; PR16; PCF16; PCS1; PTS1; LPF1
Assos   A20
Athens   A17f; ThF3, 5; ThS3
Attalia   A14
Azotus   A8
Babylon   Mw1; A7; LPF5;   Rev14, 16ff
Beroea (Berea)   A17, 20
Bethabara (Bethany)   J1
Bethany   Mw21, 26; Mk11, 14; L19, 24; J1, 11f
Bethesda   J5
Bethlehem   Mw2; L2; J7
Bethphage   Mw21; Mk11; L19
Bethsaida   Mw11; Mk6, 8; L9f; J1, 12
Bithynia   A16; LPF1
Blood Acre (Akeldema) (Potter's Field)   Mw27; A1
Caesarea   A8ff, 18, 21, 23, 25
   Philippi   Mw16; Mk8
Calvary   L23
Cana-in-Galilee   J2, 21
Canaan (Chanaan)   Mw15; A7, 13
Capernaum   Mw4, 8, 11, 17; Mk1f, 9; L4, 7, 10; J2, 4, 6
Cappadocia   A2; LPF1
Cauda (Clauda)   A27
Cedron (Kedron)   J18
Cenchreae (Cenchrea)   PR16
Chanaan (Canaan)   Mw15; A7, 13
Charran (Harran)   A7
Chios   A20
Chorazin   Mw11; L10
Cilicia   A6, 15, 21, 27; PG1
City of David (Bethlehem)   L2
Clauda (Cauda)   A27
Cnidus   A27
Colossae (Colesse)   PCo1
Corinth   A18f; PCF1, 4, 16; PCS1, 6, 9f; PTS4
Cos (Coos)   A21
Crete   A27; TF1
Cyprus   A4, 11, 13, 15, 21, 27
Cyrene   Mw27; Mk15; L23; A2, 11, 13
Dalmanutha   Mk8
Dalmatia   PTS4
Damascus   A9, 22, 26; PCS11; PG1
Decapolis (Ten Towns)   Mw4; Mk5, 7

APPENDIX B PLACE NAMES

Derbe A14, 16, 20
Egypt Mw2; A2, 7, 13; Rev11; LH3, 11; LJu1
Emmaus L24
Ephesus A18ff; PCF15f; PE1; PTF1; PTS1, 4; Rev1f
Ephraim J11
Ethiopia A8
Euphrates, River Rev9, 16
Fair Havens A27
Field of Blood A1
Gabbatha (The Pavement) J19
Gadarenes, country of Mw8
Galatia (Gallia) (Gaul) A16, 18; PCF16; PG1; PTS4; LPF1
Galilee Mw2ff, 17, 19, 21, 26ff; Mk1, 3, 6, 9, 14ff; L1ff, 8, 13, 17, 23ff;
    J1, 4, 6f, 12; A1, 9f, 13
Gallia (Galatia) (Gaul) A16, 18; PCF16; PG1; PTS4; LPF1
Gaza A8
Gennesaret Mw14; Mk6; L5
Gergesenes, country of Mw8
Gethsemane Mw26; Mk14
Golgotha (Place of the Skull) Mw27; Mk15; A23; J19
Gomorrah (Gomorrha) Mw10; Mk6; PR9; LPS2; LJu1
Greece A20
Harran (Charran) A7
Hierapolis PCo4
Iconium A13f, 16; PTS3
Idumaea Mk3
Illyrium PR15
Israel Mw2, 8ff, 15, 19; L1f, 4, 7, 22, 24; J1, 3; A1ff, 9, 13, 26, 28; PR9ff;
    PG6; PE2; PPs3; LH8; LPS2; Rev7, 21
Italy A18, 27
Ituraea L3
Jairus Mk5
Jericho Mw20; Mk10, 18f; LH11
Jerusalem Mw2ff, 15f, 20f, 23; Mk1, 3, 7, 10f, 15; L2, 4ff, 9f, 13, 17ff, 21,
    L23f; J1ff, 10ff;A1f, 4ff, 8ff, 15f, 18ff, 25f, 28; PR15; PG1f, 4;
    PCF16; LH12; Rev3, 21
Joppa A9f
Jordan Mw3, 19; Mk1; Ls7; J1, 3, 10
Judaea (Judea) (land of Judah) (Juda) Mw2ff, 19, 24; Mk1, 3, 10, 13;
    L1ff, 21, 23; J3f, 7, 11; A1f, 8f, 11f,15, 21, 26, 28; PR15; PCS1;
    PG1; ThF2; LH8
Kedron (Cedron), Ravine of J18
Laodicea PC02, 4; PTF6;   Rev1, 3
Lasea A27
Libya A2
Lycaonia A14

APPENDIX B PLACE NAMES

Lycia A27
Lydda A9
Lystra A14, 16; PTS3
Macedonia A16, 18ff; PR15; PCF16; PCS1f, 7ff, 11; PPs4; ThF1, 4; PTF1;
Madian (land of Midian) A7
Magadan (Magdala) (Magedan) Mw15, 27f; Mk8, 15; L8; J19f
Malta (Melita) A28
Mesopotamia A2, 7
Miletus (Miletum) A20; PTS4
Mitylene A20
Mount of Olives (Olivet) Mw21, 24, 26; Mk11, 13f; L19, 21f; J8; A1
Myra A21, 27
Mysia A16
Nain L7
Naphtali (Nephthalim) Mw4
Nazareth Mw2, 4, 21; Mk1, 10, 14, 16; L1f, 4, 18, 24; J1, 18f;
    A2ff, 6, 10, 22, 26
Neapolis A16
Nephthalim (Naphtali) Mw4
Nicopolis Tt3
Nineveh Mw12; L11
Olives (Olivet), Mount of   Mw21, 24, 26; Mk11, 13f; L19, 21f; J8; A1
Onesiphorus PTS4
Pamphylia A2, 13ff, 27
Paphos A13
Patara A21
Patmos Rev1
Pavement, The (Gabbatha) J19
Perga A13f
Pergamum (Pergamos) Rev1f
Phenice (Phoenicia) (Phoenix) A11, 15, 21, 27
Philadelphia Rev1, 3
Philippi A16, 20; PCS13;   PPs1; ThF2
Phoenicia (Phenice) (Phoenix) A11, 15, 21, 27
Phrygia A2, 16, 18; PTF6
Pisidia A13f
Place of the Skull (Golgotha) Mw27;Mk15; L23; J19
Pontus A2, 18; LPF1
Potter's Field (Blood Acre) (Alkeldama) Mw27;A1
Ptolemais A21
Puteoli A28
Rama Mw2
Red Sea A7; PCF10; LH11
Rhegium A28
Rhodes A21
Rome A2, 18f, 23, 28; PR1; PE6; PPs4; PTS1, 4

571

APPENDIX B PLACE NAMES

Salamis A13
Salem LH7
Salim J3
Salmone A27
Samaria A1, 8f, 15; L17; J4
Samos A20
Samothrace (Samothracia) A16
Sardis Rev, 3
Sarepta L4
Seleucia A13
Sharon A9
Shechem (Sychem) A7
Sheep-pool (Bethesda) J5
Sidon Mw11, 15; Mk3, 7; L4, 6, 10; A12, 27
Siloam L13; J9
Sinai (Sina), Mount A7; PG4; LH12
Sion (Zion), Mount PR9, 11; LH12; LPF2; Rev14
Skull, Place of the (Golgotha) Mw27;Mk15; L23; J19
Smyrna Rev1f
Sodom (Sodoma) Mw10f; Mk6; L10, 17; PR9; LPS2; LJu1; Rev11
Spain PR15
Sychar J4
Sychem (Shechem) A7
Syracuse A28
Syria Mw4; Mk7; L2; A15, 18, 20f; PG1
Syrtis A27
Tarsus A9, 11, 22
Ten Towns (Decapolis) Mw4; Mk5, 7
Thessalonica A17, 27; PPs4; ThF1ff; PTS4
Three Taverns (Tres Tabernae) A28
Thyatira A16; Rev1f
Tiberius, Sea of J6, 21
Trachonitis L3
Transjordan Mw4; Mk3, 10

APPENDIX C *Races and Tribes*

OLD TESTAMENT

Aaronite Ne10, 12; CF27; CS13, 26
Abiezrite Ju6
Adullamite Gen38
Agagite Est3
Ahohite SS23; CF27
Amalekite Ex17; Nu13; De25;
    Ju1, 3, 6ff, 10; SF14f, 27ff; SS1; CF4
Ammonite Nu21; De2, 23; Ju3, 10; SF11ff;   SS8ff, 17, 23; KF11; KS24;
    CF11, 18ff; CS20ff, 24, 26ff; Ez9; Ne2, 4, 13; Je25, 40ff, 49;
    E21, 25; D11; Am1
Amorite Gen10; Ex3; Nu13, 22; De1ff, 7, 20; Jos3, 5ff, 9, 12, 24; Ju1, 3, 6;
    SF7; SS21; KF4, 9, 21; KS21; CF1; CS8; Ez9; Ne9; Is17; E16;
    Am2
Anakim Jos11, 14ff
Anamite Gen10; CF1
Apharsathchite Ex4
Apharsite Ez4
Arab (Arabian) CS17, 21, 26; Ne2ff, 6; Is13, 21; Je3, 49; E30
Aramaean Ju18;SS8,10;KF20, 22; KS5ff, 24; CF7, 18; CS1, 18, 22, 24,28;
    Is7, 9; Je35; Am9
Aramite Ju10
Arbathite SS23
Arbite SS23
Archevite Ez4
Archite Jos16; SS15ff; CF27
Arkite Gen10; CF1
Arvadite Gen10; CF1
Ashdodite Ne4
Asherite Nu7; Jos19, 21;   SS2; CF6; CS30
Ashurite E27
Assyrian Is10, 14, 43, 52; E16, 23, 31; La5; Ho11;Mi5
Avvim 5-6-08e2; Jos13
Avite KS17; CF17
Babylonian Ez4; Je32; E23
Barhumite SS23
Bashanite Nu21
Beerothite SS4, 23
Benjamite Nu7; Jos18, 21; Ju3, 10, 19ff; SF9, 13, 22; SS2ff,16, 19ff
    KF2, 12, 15; CF6, 9, 12, 21, 27; CS11, 15, 17, 25; Ne11; Est2;
    Ps68, Je37

APPENDIX C RACES AND TRIBES

Buzite Job32
Calebite SF25, 30
Canaanite Gen12f; Ex3; Nu13, 21; De7, 20; Jos3, 5ff, 9, 12ff; Ju1, 3; SS24; Ez9; Ne9;   Ob1; Z14
Caphtorite Gen10; De2; CF1
Carite KS11
Carmelite SS23
Casluhite Gen10; CF1
Chaldean (Chaldee) Gen11; KS24ff; CS36; Ez5; Ne9; Job1; Is13, 23, 43, Is47ff; Je21f, 24, 32, 35, 37ff; 43, 50ff; E1,12,23; D1ff, 9; H1
Chemarim Zp1
Cherethite (Cherethim) (Kerethite) SF30; SS15; KF1; E25; Zp2
Cushite SS18; CS12, 14, 16, 21; Je38ff, 46; D11; Am9; Zp2
Cuthite KS17
Danite Nu7; Jos19, 21; Ju1, 13, 18; CF27; CS2
Dedanim Is21
Dehavite Ez4
Dinaite Ez4
Edomite De23; SF14, 21;   SS8; KF11; KS8, 14, 16; CF18; CS21, 25, 28; Is43
Egyptian Ex2; Ju10; SF4, 30; SS23; CF11; Ez9; Is10, 19ff; Je46; E16, 29; La5
Elamite Ez4
Elkoshite Na1
Ephraimite Nu7; Jos16f, 21; Ju8, 10ff; SF1; CF9, 27; CS28; Ps78; Is7;Ho13
Ephrathite SF17; KF11; Ru1
Esau, descendants of   De21
Eshtaulite CF
Ethiopian CS12; Ps72; Is20; Je13, 38ff, 46; E30; D11; Zp2
Ezrahite KF4
Gabalite KF5
Gadite Nu7; De4, 29; Jos1ff, 12ff, 21ff; SS23; CF5ff, 12, 26
Garmite CF4
Gebalite Jos13
Gederite CF27
Gentile (non-Israelite) Je46
Gershonite Nu7; Jos21;   CF26, 29
Geshurite Jos12ff; SF27
giants, race of   Gen6; Nu13; De3; Jos12; SS21; CF20; Ez2
Gibeathite CF12
Gibeonite SS21; CF12; Ne3
Gileadite Ju10, 12; SS17ff; KS15; Ne7
Gilonite SS15, 23
Girgashite Gen10; De7; Jos3; CF1; Ne9
Gittite SS6, 15ff; CF7

574

APPENDIX C RACES AND TRIBES

Gizonite SS23; CF11
Gizrite SF27
Grecian (Greek) D8; Joe3
Gushurite De3
Hachmonite SS23; CF11, 27
Hagarene Ps83
Hagarite CF5
Hagerite CF27
Hamathite Gen10; CF1
Hamite CF4
Hararite SS23; CF11
Haruphite CF12
Hermonite Ps43
Hittite Gen23; Ex3; Nu13; De7, 20; Jos3, 9, 12; Ju3; SF26; SS11,   23ff; KF9ff; CF1, 11; CS1, 8; Ez9; Ne9; E16
Hivite Gen10, 34; Ex3; De7, 20; Jos3, 9, 12; Ju3; SS24; KF9; CF1; CS8; Is17
Horite Gen14; De2
Horonite Ne2, 13
Hushathite CF27
Ishmael, descendants of   Gen25
Ishmaelite Ju8; SS17; CF2, 27; Ps83
Israelite Gen46; Ex1ff; Le1ff; Nu1ff; De1ff; Jos3ff; Ju1ff, 6f, 13, 19ff; SF2, 4, 7, 9ff, 17, 28f, 31; SS3, 10f, 16ff, 21, 24; KF6, 8f, 11f, 16, KF18, 20, 22; KS3, 7ff, 16ff, 21; CF9ff; CS5, 7f, 10f, 13, 24f, 28, CS31, 33;Ez2f, 6ff, 10; Ne2, 10f, 13; Ps103; Je16, 23; E2ff, 8, E11ff, 18, 22, 24, 28ff, 33, 35, 37ff, 48; D1, 9; Am3, 9; Ho1, 3
Issacharite CF6, 21, 27
Ithrite SS23; CF2, 11
Jacob, descendants of Gen 37
Jahite CS11
Jairite SS20
Japheth, descendants of   Gen10
Japhletite Jos16
Jebusite Gen10; Ex3; Nu13; De7, 20; Jos3, 9, 12, 15, 18; Ju3, 19; SS5, 24; KF9; CF1, 11, 21; CS3, 8; Ez9; Ne9; Z9
Jeconiah, descendants of SF6
Jerahmeelite SF27, 30
Jew (reference to Israelites as) Ez2ff; Ne1ff, 13; Est2ff; Je41; Z8
Jewry (reference to Israelites as) D5
Joseph, descendants of   Jos16; Ju1; Ps78
Judaean Je32, 34, 38, 40f, 43ff
Judah, descendants of Jos7, 15, 21; Ju10; KF1ff; SF27ff
Judahite Nu7; CF6, 9; CS15, 25; Ne4ff, 11; Ps78
Kedarite Is42
Kenite Ju1, 4; SF15, 27, 30; CF2

APPENDIX C RACES AND TRIBES

Kenizzite Jos14
Kerethite (Cherethim) (Cherethite) SF30; SS8, 15, 20; KF1; CF18;
    E25; Zp2
Kittian CF1
Kohathite Nu7; Jos21; CS6, 9; 20
Korahite Nu26; CF9, 12, 26; CS20
Lehabite Gen10; CF1
Leummin Is43
Levite Nu3ff; Ju17; SS15; KF8; CF6, 9, 13ff, 27; CS5, 8, 11ff, 17, 19, 23,
    CS29, 34ff; Ez1ff; Ne3, 7ff, 13; Is66; Je33; E40, 45, 48; Ma3
Libyan CS12, 16; Je46; E30; D11; Na3
Lydian Gen10; CF1; Je46
Lubim CS12, 16
Maacathite De3; Jos12; CF4; SS23; Je40
Machirite Jos13
Mahavite CF11
Manahethite CF2
Manasseh Ju6ff; CF5ff, 9, 26ff; CS30ff
Manassite Nu7; De4; Jos13, 21ff
Mede (Median) Est1ff; Is13,21; Je25, 51; D5ff, 9, 11
Merarite Nu7; Jos21; CF15, 26
Meronothite CF27; Ne3
Meunite CF4; CS20, 26
Midianite Nu21; Ju6ff, 10
Mishraite CF2
Mithrite CF11
Moabite Nu21ff; De2ff, 23; Ju10; Ruff; SF14; SS8; KF11; KS3, 13, 24;
    CF11, 18; CS20ff, 24; Ez9; Ne13; Ps83
Morasthite Je26; Mi1
Naamathite Job2, 11, 20, 42
Naphtali, descendants of   Jos19, 21; Ju6ff
Naphtalite Nu7; CF2, 6ff, 27
Naphtuhite Gen10; CF1
Nazarite (Nazirite) Nu6; Ju13; SF1; La4; Am2
Nephelamite Je29
Nephilim Gen6; Nu13
Nephisim (Nephusim) Ez2
Nethinim Ne3; Ez8
Netophathite SS23; CF2, 9, 27; Ne12; Je40
Nubian CS12; Ps87; Is45; Je13
Paltite SS23
Pathrusite Gen10; CF1
Pekethite KF1
Pelethite SS8, 15, 20; CF18
Persian CS36; Est1ff; D6
Perizzite Gen13; Ex3; De7, 20; Jos3, 9, 12, 17; Ju3; KF9; CS8; Ne9

APPENDIX C RACES AND TRIBES

Philistine Gen10; Ex13; Jos13; Ju3, 10; SF4, 12, 17, 27ff; SS3; KF15ff;
  KS8,18; CF1,10ff, 14, 18; CS9, 17, 21, 26, 28; Ps87; Is2, 9, 11,
  Is14; Je25, 47; E16, 25; Am1, 6, 9; Ob1; Zp2; Z9
Pirathonite Ju12; SS23; CF27
Puhite CF2
Rechabite CF2; Je35
Rehobite SS8
Rephaim De3; Jos12; SS21; CF20
Reuben, descendants of Ex6
Reubenite Nu7; De3ff, 29; Jos1ff, 12ff, 21ff; CF5ff, 11, 26ff
Rhodian E27
Sabaean Is45; E23; Joe3
Sepharvite KS17
Shaalbonite SS23
Shelanite CF9; Ne11
Shem, descendants of Gen10
Shilonite KF15; CS9
Shimeathite CF2
Shuhite Job2, 8, 18, 25, 42
Shulamite So6
Shumathite CF2
Shunammite KF1ff; KS4
Sidonian (Zidonian) De3;   Jos13; Ju3, 10, 18; KF5, 11; KS23; Ez3; E32
Simeon, descendants of Ex6
Simeonite Nu17; Jos19, 21; CF4, 6, 27
Simite Gen10
Sinite CF1
Sophrite CF2
Suchathite CF2
Sukkiim CS12
Sukkite CS12
Susanchite Ez4
Syrian (Aramaean) KS7, 9ff; Is9; Je35
Tachmonite SS23
Tarpelite Ez4
Tekoite SS23; Ne3
Temanite Job2, 4, 15, 22, 42
Timnite Ju15
Tirathite CF2
Tishbite KF17; KS1, 9
Tizite CF11
Tyrian CS2; Ez3; Ne13; Ps87
Zareathite CF2
Zeboyim (Zeboim) Ho11
Zebulunite Nu7; Jos19, 21; Ju12; CF6, 27; CS30
Zemarite Gen10ff; CF1

APPENDIX C RACES AND TRIBES

Zerahite CF27
Zidonian (Sidonian) Ju3, 10, 18; KF11, 16; KS23; E32
Ziphite SF23, 26
Zorathite CF4
Zorite CF2
Zuphite SF1

NEW TESTAMENT

Arab (Arabian) A2
Athenian A17
Alexandrian A6, 18, 27
Asherite L2
Asian A20
Benjamite A13; PR11; PPs3
Canaanite Mw10, 15; Mk3; A13
Chaldaean A7
Colossian PCo1
Corinthian A18; PCF1; PCS1, 6
Cretan (Cretian) A2; TF1
Cypriot A4
Cyrenian Mk15; L23; A6
Damascene PCS11
Derbaean A20
Doberian A20
Egyptian A7, 21; LH11
Elamite A2
Emmorite A7
Ephesian A19, 21; PE1
Ethiopian A8
Gadarene Mw8; Mk5; L8
Galatian A18; PG1, 3
Galilean Mk14; L13, 22f; J4, 7, 12
Gerasene Mk5; L8
Gergesene Mw8; L8
Grecian (Greek) Mk7; J12; A6, 9, 14, 16ff, 20; PR1f; PCF10; PG2f; PCo3
Israelite Mw27; L1; J1; A7, 10; PR9, 11; PCS3,11; PPs3; LH11; LJu1; Rev2, 7
Italian LH13
Hebrew A6; LH1
Judah (Juda), tribe of LH7; Rev5
Laodicean PCo2; Rev3
Levite L10; J1; A4
Lycaonian A14
Macedonian A16, 19, 27

578

APPENDIX C RACES AND TRIBES

Magdalene Mw27f; Mk15f; L8, 24; J19f
Mede (Median) A2
Mesopotamian A2
Midianite A7
Nazarene Mw2; A24
Nephthalim Mw4
Ninevite L11
Parthian A2
Philippian PPs1, 4
Phoenician Mk7
Roman Mw22, 27; J11; A16, 25; PR1
Samaritan Mw10, L9f, 17; J4, 8; A8
Scythian PCo3
Syrian L4
Syrophenician Mk7
Tarsian A21
Thessalonian A20; ThF1, 5; ThS1, 3

THE BIBLICAL MALE LINE OF DESCENT

FROM ADAM TO JESUS

Adam and Eve
Seth: Enosh: Kenan: Mahalalel: Jared: Enoch: Methuselah:
Lamech: Noah: Shem: Arphaxad: Shelah: Eber: Peleg: Reu: Serug:
Nahor: Terah: Abraham: Isaac: Jacob: Judah: Perez: Hezron: Ram:
Amminadab: Nahshon: Salma: Boaz: Obed: Jesse: David:
Solomon: Reheboam: Abia: Asa: Jehoshaphat: Joram: Ahaziah:
Joash: Amaziah: Azariah: Jotham: Hezekiah: Manasseh: Amon:
Josiah: Jehoiakim: Jeconiah: Shealtiel: Zerubbabel: Abiud:
Eliakim: Azor: Zadok: Achim: Eliud: Eleazar: Matthan: Jacob:
Joseph and Mary
Jesus

www.ingramcontent.com/pod-product-compliance
Lightning Source LLC
Chambersburg PA
CBHW070712160426
43192CB00009B/1168